SPEECH AND LANGUAGE
Advances in Basic Research and Practice

Volume 1

Contributors to This Volume

James H. Abbs
Steven B. Davis
Judy B. Elliott
Jesse G. Kennedy III
Patricia K. Kuhl
James F. Lubker
Carol A. Prutting
Kenneth O. St. Louis

SPEECH AND LANGUAGE
Advances in Basic Research and Practice

VOLUME 1

Edited by

NORMAN J. LASS

Department of Speech Pathology and Audiology
West Virginia University
Morgantown, West Virginia

ACADEMIC PRESS
New York   San Francisco   London   1979
A Subsidiary of Harcourt Brace Jovanovich, Publishers

ACADEMIC PRESS, INC.
111 Fifth Avenue, New York, New York 10003

United Kingdom Edition published by
ACADEMIC PRESS, INC. (LONDON) LTD.
24/28 Oval Road, London NW1 7DX

ISSN: 0193–3434

ISBN 0–12–608601–X

PRINTED IN THE UNITED STATES OF AMERICA

79 80 81 82   9 8 7 6 5 4 3 2 1

Contents

Subject Index

List of Contributors

Numbers in parentheses indicate the pages on which the authors' contributions begin.

James H. Abbs (211), Speech Motor Control Laboratories, Waisman Center, Department of Communicative Disorders, University of Wisconsin, Madison, Wisconsin 53706

Steven B. Davis (271), Signal Technology, Inc., Santa Barbara, California 93101

Judy B. Elliott (337), Department of Speech, University of California, Santa Barbara, California 93106

Jesse G. Kennedy III (211), Speech Motor Control Laboratories, Waisman Center, Department of Communicative Disorders, University of Wisconsin, Madison, Wisconsin 53706

Patricia K. Kuhl (1), Department of Speech and Hearing Sciences and Child Development and Mental Retardation Center, University of Washington, Seattle, Washington 98195

James F. Lubker (49), Institute of Linguistics, Department of Phonetics, University of Stockholm, S-106 91 Stockholm, Sweden

Carol A. Prutting (337), Department of Speech, University of California, Santa Barbara, California 93106

Kenneth O. St. Louis (89), Department of Speech Pathology and Audiology, West Virginia University, Morgantown, West Virginia 26506

Preface

Speech and Language: Advances in Basic Research and Practice is a serial publication concerned with contemporary research in speech and language processes and pathologies. It provides opportunities for authors to review literature, discuss unresolved issues, offer suggestions for future research directions, relate accumulated data to theoretical discussions, and, whenever appropriate, apply the evidence and theories to clinical issues in speech and language pathology. As a vehicle for the publication of manuscripts that are too large for journal articles and too small for monographs, it serves a distinct purpose and fills a genuine need.

The articles in this series present critical reviews, theoretical syntheses, new principles, and/or the integration of recent findings. Because of the nature of the topics included in this publication, contributions to any single volume are not restricted to a single theme. The contents should prove useful both to scientists and to clinicians involved in research or practice on clinical issues and/or normal processes. Moreover, the level of writing is professional, not didactic, in nature and should have wide appeal to professionals and graduate students in a number of different disciplines, including speech and language pathology, experimental phonetics, speech science, linguistics, clinical and experimental psychology, anatomy, and physiology.

Volume 1 contains six chapters on a wide variety of topics. The first chapter (Kuhl) is concerned with the perception of speech in early infancy and the implications of such perception to the acquisition of language. Also included are discussions of the nature and origins of early predispositions toward speech and language and the application of basic findings to the early diagnosis of speech and language disorders. In the second chapter (Lubker) are discussions of the challenge and problems faced by speech clinicians in the study and treatment of pathological speech, the relationships between acoustic phonetics and speech pathology, and acoustic–perceptual methods for the evaluation of defective speech. The third chapter (St. Louis) provides a thorough literature review on linguistic and motor aspects of stuttering and an assessment of the theoretical positions that have been advanced to explain and treat them. Anatomic studies of the perioral motor system in 11 cadavers are presented in the fourth chapter (Kennedy and Abbs). These studies were conducted because the authors found that, ''Unfortunately, despite current research interest in the physiological mechanisms that underlie speech movements, we do not have descriptions of peripheral anatomy which provide this fundamental information. There are no currently optimal materials to which a speech physiologist can refer concerning the structure of the component parts of the speech mechanism.'' The fifth chapter (Davis) describes acoustic voice characteristics and contemporary techniques for obtaining acoustic measures for screening and treatment purposes. The sixth and final chapter (Prutting and Elliott) contains a reexamination of evidence regarding language behavior within a synergistic framework, thus permitting a holistic, rather than atomistic, analysis of the language system.

In addition to the eight contributors to Volume 1, to whom I am indebted for their skillful writing and cooperative spirit, I am particularly grateful to the staff of Academic Press who have been most supportive and cooperative in initiating this serial publication. I would also like to express my gratitude to my former mentors, Professors J. Douglas Noll, Kenneth W. Burk, Ralph L. Shelton, and John F. Michel, who instilled within me an appreciation for the unresolved issues in speech and language and the application of an empirical approach for their ultimate resolution.

NORMAN J. LASS

SPEECH AND LANGUAGE
Advances in Basic Research and Practice

Volume 1

The Perception
of Speech in Early Infancy

PATRICIA K. KUHL

Department of Speech and Hearing Sciences and
Child Development and Mental Retardation Center
University of Washington
Seattle, Washington

The perception of speech sounds by young infants is interesting from a number of perspectives. It is one of the earliest indications that an infant is attending to linguistically relevant information and may reflect the

SPEECH AND LANGUAGE: Advances in Basic
Research and Practice, Vol. 1

infant's biological predispositions which destine him to acquire language. In fact, under 6 months of age, there is little else one can learn about the infant's responses to linguistically meaningful units in addition to the perception and production of the phonetic units of language. It is hoped that this chapter will convince the reader that it is wise to explore the infant's capabilities and proclivities in these early months of life. The human infant's behavior may provide clues to an understanding of the seemingly special kinds of behavior that infants of a species, both human and nonhuman, display when the signal is one that is part of the species' communicative repertoire.

I. THE SPEECH PERCEPTION PROCESS: THREE INSTRUCTIVE EXERCISES

There are three highly instructive exercises that are particularly helpful in attempting to understand the complexity of the speech perception process. The first is an exercise with which most students in Speech and Hearing Science are familiar (for example, in an Introduction to Speech Production class) and consists of watching cinefluorographic films, lateral X rays of the oral cavity, while a talker is engaged in normal conversation. The second exercise might also be familiar to some students in the field and consists of trying to read spectrograms, visual records of the continuous frequency and intensity changes over time that occur when a speaker is engaged in conversation. The third exercise, an auditory one, involves listening to a foreign language and attempting to phonetically transcribe sentence-length utterances when there are no other sources of information (no knowledge of the lexicon or of syntactic and semantic rules) in addition to the acoustic signal.

In each of these examples, one is impressed by the continuous nature of the display. The X-ray films show articulators that are constantly in motion, the tongue darting about with apparent starting and stopping points that do not seem to be related to specific linguistic junctures. Spectrograms display nearly continuous change; the breaks that do occur in the visual record do not indicate syllable or word boundaries (Fant, 1973). Speech by a foreign speaker seems altogether too fast, resembling a senseless babble in which word boundaries are not identifiable.

These exercises are even more instructive if, prior to each, one listens to a talker in one's own native language. We hear words and phrases and are aware of meaning. We notice occasional slips of the tongue, attending both to the phonetic content of words as well as to the meaning the words convey. In the aggregate, segmenting the speech stream offers little difficulty to a listener familiar with the language being spoken, but segmenting an acoustic display of the speech stream by eye—or even by ear—or even by ear when listening to a foreign language—is profoundly difficult.

The dynamics of articulatory motion are such that while a word must at some level be a preplanned sequence of discrete units, each having, perhaps, a unique articulatory target, the physiological level involves nearly continuous motions of the articulators moving from target to target. The result is a continuous time-varying acoustic waveform that is not easily segmented into words or syllables using physical criteria; that is, the signal does not display discrete temporal segments separated by pauses or other characteristics that serve as boundaries for word-length units or phonetic units.

II. MODELS OF THE PERCEPTUAL PROCESS

Language can be described at many different levels. It can be described as a set of meaningful ideas, as a set of ordered sequences of lexical units, as a set of phonetic units (which, by themselves, have no meaning), and as a continuous acoustic waveform. In linguistic terms we have described the semantic, syntactic, phonologic, and acoustic aspects of language. In order to understand the importance and interdependence of each of these representations of language, we must review the current models of the perceptual process, ones that integrate notions of phonetic perception and linguistic analysis.

Current theories of speech perception assume that there are many interactive processes that transform an acoustic signal into a perceived message. Most tend to be active rather than passive models, indicating that the listener is an active participant in the perceptual process. One such model has been termed "analysis by synthesis" (Stevens & Halle, 1967). The model argues that the listener brings a considerable amount of information to the task, information which is derived from many different sources. Some of the listener's knowledge can be termed specifically linguistic; that is, it consists of information concerning the lexicon and syntactic and semantic rules. Other kinds of knowledge that the listener can use are nonlinguistic and have to do with his knowledge of the world, both generally and specifically, as in relating what is being said to situational and thematic concerns. This information can be used as a set of guidelines or constraints on the message that aid the listener in narrowing his decision about what the talker actually said.

In addition, however, the model argues that the listener engages in direct analysis of the phonetic content of the message. As the listener gathers data from his analysis of the signal, he continuously uses his knowledge of the language, the world, and the specific circumstances to revise his hypothesis about the message. When the match between the phonetic data and the hypothesis is reasonable, the listener accepts the hypothesized version.

In other words, most current models of speech perception argue that the direct analysis of phonetic units and the other sources of knowledge interact to determine what a person hears. A simple example from the visual world may help clarify this point. Presume you are assigned the task of identifying a number of pictures presented randomly, one at a time. It should be an easy enough task except that the pictures are rather fuzzy and you are allowed only brief looks at them before making at least a preliminary guess at what the pictures represent. Assume that, at first, you are given no information about the picture, no hints that might suggest a person, place, or thing. Your first brief glance, however, leaves you with the impression of a face and a body. Immediately the choices begin to narrow: you are looking at a person, probably a famous one. A set of features which distinguish people come to mind, and you must search for them in your next brief glance: is X male or female, tall or short, thin or stout, young or old?

In other words, your first glance severely restricts the kinds of guesses you would consider making, ruling out whole classes of responses simply by providing you with some critical features that are compatible with one set of observations and incompatible with another. Your active participation in the viewing process greatly enhances the probability that your response will be correct.

Expectations, or sources of knowledge, can alter the identification of the same stimulus; a pattern identified as *13* when a subject is expecting numbers is identified as *B* when he expects letters (Bruner & Minturn, 1955). Instructions can change the perception of an ambiguous figure from a rat to a man (Bugelski & Alampay, 1961) or from an old woman to a young woman as in the familiar reversible-figure examples.

Examples from auditory/linguistic perception abound; experimental studies have shown that a listener's performance depends upon the size and diversity of the catalog of alternatives from which the item was taken. When words are presented in isolation, anything that restricts the list, such as a closed set of alternatives, improves perception (G. A. Miller, Heise, & Lichten, 1951). In the same vein, words presented in a sentence are more intelligible than those same words in isolation (Miller *et al.*, 1951) because the sentence context itself serves to restrict the kinds of alternatives that are appropriate.

G. A. Miller and Isard (1963) demonstrated the independent effects of syntactic and semantic constraints using three types of sentences: ones which were described as grammatical and meaningful; sentences that were grammatical, but not meaningful (e.g., *Black bread his brought Don*); and those which were ungrammatical. They found systematic differences in the intelligibility of these strings when they were presented in noise, which depended upon their syntactic and their semantic integrity. More recently, Cole and Jakimik (in press) demonstrated these interactive effects with a measure of phonetic perception rather than the more global measures of intelligibility. In an error-detection task, listeners monitoring connected discourse (stories read aloud) detected an incorrectly produced word more accurately, and faster, when the word was highly predictable by the semantic context than when the word was less semantically predictable.

Stevens and House (1972) suggest that the dependence on one or the other of these two components is a kind of trade-off governed by the degree to which the listener's sources of knowledge can be utilized in decoding the utterance and the degree to which the phonetic elements can be directly decoded. The direct decoding of phonetic elements, as we will soon discuss, has traditionally been thought to be quite difficult due to the fact that many of the acoustic cues to phonetic units change dramatically with the surrounding phonetic context, its position in the utterance, or the speaker who utters it.

These ideas are particularly relevant to an understanding of the development of speech perception. We can expect that the child gradually acquires knowledge of the language and of the world, and the degree to which the child is cognizant of the rules which constrain the language and relations in the world determines the extent to which the direct acoustic analysis of the input must govern the child's perception. It would be difficult to argue that the very young infant has knowledge of the language-bound constraints; thus he would depend, to a greater degree, on the direct analysis of the acoustic message. Consider the addition of a new lexical item to a young child's vocabulary. No contextual information can be applied; the token is completely novel and acoustic analysis must direct what the child hears. Let us consider, then, the perception of phonetic units.

A. The Problem of Invariance

The most pressing problem in relating the acoustic signal to a sequence of discrete phonetic units has been the apparent lack of invariant acoustic cues for each unit. This is not a new or unfamiliar problem for psychologists who study pattern recognition; one of the oldest puzzles in psychology is to attempt to identify the features in a stimulus that govern what a viewer says s/he[1] sees or what a listener says she hears. The task of identifying the cues that specify a particular speech sound is similar to the task of identifying the cues that specify an orthographic symbol—both involve the perception of similarity amidst what appear to be fairly complex transformations. But the perception of these visual and auditory categories comes so naturally to adult human listeners that it is sometimes difficult to accept its complexities.

Consider the case of letter recognition. How does one recognize an *A*? All *A*'s do not actually look alike. Neisser (1967) explains, "There are capital A's and small A's and elite A's, slanted A's and straight A's. There are configurations . . . which look like A in certain contexts and like H in others. Finally, there are hand-printed and hand-written A's, whose variety is truly astonishing" (p. 46). Yet all are recognizable.

The last 30 years of research on speech has provided a wealth of information on the nature of the acoustic cues for speech sounds (for reviews, see Fant, 1973; Liberman, Cooper, Shankweiler, & Studdert-Kennedy, 1967; Minifie, 1973; Shoup & Pfeifer, 1976), but the results of these experiments have raised questions about the processes that underlie a listener's recognition of the phonetic similarity among what have appeared to be very diverse acoustic events. An adult listener's ability to recognize the similarity among phonemes uttered by different speakers or occurring in different phonetic contexts is described as perceptual "constancy" (Shankweiler, Strange, & Verbrugge, 1977), a term borrowed from the visual perception literature, because the acoustic cues in these instances do not appear to be constant, or invariant, across context. Consider the case of vowel recognition. The locations of the first and second formants (frequency regions of high-energy concentration) have been demonstrated to be critical cues for vowel recognition (Delattre, Liberman, & Cooper, 1951), but when a male, a female, and a child produce the vowel /a/, the formant frequencies differ considerably (Peterson & Barney, 1952), and the differences cannot be described as simple ratio transforms (Fant, 1973), as in the transposition of melodies (Ward, 1970).

The perception of the voiced–voiceless distinction provides another example. A speaker of English hears the /p/ in *pat, rapid,* and *tap* as somehow similar, but the acoustic cues that signal /p/ rather than /b/ (*bat, rabid,* and *tab*) in these contexts are quite different. In the initial position (*pat* vs *bat*), the relative timing between the onset of voicing and the transient produced by the release of the articulatory constriction (Lisker & Abramson, 1964) and the presence or absence of a low-frequency

---

[1] Tom Wicker (*The New York Times*, April 18, 1978) advises authors to cite the rather clumsy "s/he" the first time and then to adopt their own gender. This author accepts the advice and recommends Wicker's discussion of the topic.

component at the onset of voicing (Liberman, Delattre, & Cooper, 1958; Lisker, 1975; Stevens & Klatt, 1974; Summerfield & Haggard, 1977) differentiate /p/ and /b/. In medial position (*rapid* vs *rabid*) the duration of the articulatory closure and the length of the preceding vowel are important (Liberman, Harris, Eimas, Lisker, & Bastian, 1961; Lisker, 1957; Slis & Cohen, 1969a, 1969b) and in final position (*tap* vs *tab*) the length of the preceding vowel (Chen, 1970; Denes, 1955) and its tendency to be released (Malecot, 1958) are determining factors.

The voiced plosives (/b, d, g/) provide a third example. Either the frequency location of the burst of noise created when the plosive is released (F. S. Cooper, Delattre, Liberman, Borst, & Gerstman, 1952; Halle, Hughes, & Radley, 1957) or the directions of the second and third formant transitions (F. S. Cooper *et al.*, 1952; Delattre, Liberman, & Cooper, 1955; Liberman *et al.*, 1967) are sufficient in isolation to differentiate the three voices stops. However, neither cue in isolation provides an invariant acoustic characteristic across vowel contexts. For example, a 15-msec burst of voice centered around 1400 Hz is perceived as /p/ in front of the steady-state vowel /i/, but as /k/ in front of the steady-state vowel /a/ (F. S. Cooper *et al.*, 1952; Schatz, 1954). Similarly, changing the direction of the F_2 transition in any one vowel context changes the percept from /b/ to /d/ to /g/ (Liberman, Harris, Hoffman, & Griffith, 1957), but the F_2 transition direction that produces /d/ across all vowel contexts is not constant (Liberman *et al.*, 1967).

More recently, demonstrations by Port (1976), Minifie, Kuhl, and Stecher (1977), and Miller and Liberman (1977) demonstrate that the remote context can have an effect on the perception of particular phonetic cues. Port (1976) demonstrated that when tokens of *rabid* and *rapid*, differentiated intervocalically by the duration of silence, were placed in carriers which varied the rate of articulation, listeners heard the change from *rabid* to *rapid* at different durations of silence for the two different rates of articulation. Similarly, Minifie *et al.* (1977) demonstrated that the phonetic boundary between /b/ and /w/ in the initial and medial position of words shifted systematically when the words were lodged in sentence carriers that were computer manipulated to simulate normal as opposed to fast rates of articulation. The distinguishing acoustic cue was the tempo of formant-transition change. In fast carrier sentences, the phonetic boundary between /b/ and /w/ occurred at steeper transition slopes than it did in normal carrier sentences.

Despite the apparent lack of invariance associated with particular phonetic units, the search has by no means been abandoned. In fact, recent work has been a bit more successful in elucidating the nature of the acoustic cues for speech-sound categories. For example, recent work on the acoustic cues for the place of articulation feature in stop consonants (Blumstein & Stevens, 1976, 1977; Stevens & Blumstein, 1978) demonstrates that the gross shape of the short-term spectrum, sampled at the release of the articulatory constriction, may provide an invariant configuration which depends upon the place of articulation regardless of the vowel context in which the stop occurs. This attempt to discover invariant cues takes a somewhat different approach to the problem, looking at more static and holistic properties of the acoustic signal, rather than particular formants and their trajectories (F_2 transitions etc.). This approach is not entirely unique since Fant's (1960, 1973) work and that of other authors (Halle, Hughes, & Radley, 1957) has suggested that the global-spectrum approach might be more fruitful than the tracking of individual formant frequencies; but the more recent work by Blumstein and Stevens (1976, 1977) has taken the process one step further by distilling a composite acoustic description for each place of articulation and representing it as a spectral template. The template is being tested with many naturally and synthetically produced stop consonants in which the vowel context, speaker, and syllabic position are systematically varied. To date, results demonstrate that the alveolar template, for example, correctly accepts about 85% of the tokens with an alveolar place of articulation that were naturally produced by six speakers (four male, two female), in five different vowel contexts (Blumstein & Stevens, 1977). The same alveolar variations produced in final position are correctly accepted about 75% of the time if the short-term spectrum is sampled during the release burst of the consonantal constriction.

These recent attempts to identify the critical acoustic cues for speech are significant because they represent an attempt to analyze speech from an auditory-psychophysical point of view. That the auditory system examines these exact kinds of short-term spectra is not known, but the general approach is consistent with current auditory theory. Other examples in which knowledge of auditory processing is being used to examine speech sounds can be found in the recent work on the acoustic cues to vowel perception. Carlson, Fant, and Granstrom (1975) used psychoacoustic methods to determine the effective auditory correlates of formant frequencies in synthetic vowel stimuli, and Fant (1973) has used these effective auditory correlates in his analyses of vowels produced by different speakers. Others are engaged in the application of models of peripheral auditory processing to the study of vowels (Karnickaya, Mushnikov, Stepokurova, & Zhukov, 1975; Miller, Engebretson, Spenner, & Cox, 1977). Finally, neurophysiologists are beginning to study the responses of auditory nerve fibers to vowel stimuli in animal listeners (Reale & Geisler, 1979; Sachs & Young, 1979) in an attempt to discover the auditory correlates of speech events. These auditory approaches to the study of the perception of phonetic elements are likely to provide a better understanding of both complex auditory processing and the perception of speech.

B. Proposed Solutions to Phonetic Recognition

Most current models of phonetic recognition (Pisoni, 1978; Stevens & House, 1972) include the notion that speech sounds are identified in terms of their attributes or their features (Jakobson, Fant, & Halle, 1969). Arguing that phonetic units are perceived in terms of their component features is an attractive theoretical approach from a variety of perspectives. It accounts for some of the perceptual data concerning how listeners behave when syllables are presented in noise or presented dichotically, or when listeners are asked to recall them; it accounts for certain errors which occur when people listen to a word over and over and begin to perceive distortions; and, finally, it accounts for errors which occur when people talk.

Errors that occur when people listen to nonsense syllables in the presence of noise are not random; they are patterned according to some form of distinctive feature system (G. A. Miller & Nicely, 1955). In other words, when a listener's response to a nonsense syllable is incorrect, the answer is systematically related to the target sound that was presented. This is also true when nonsense syllables are presented dichotically (Studdert-Kennedy & Shankweiler, 1970). The syllable /ga/ presented to the left ear and the syllable /pa/ presented to the right ear oftentimes produced the response /ka/, a syllable sharing the voicing features with one of the inputs and the place feature with the other. Short-term recall of nonsense syllables also demonstrates an error pattern that can be described by distinctive feature theory (Sales, Cole, & Haber, 1969; Wickelgren, 1965, 1966). In more recent studies, listeners are presented with the same nonsense syllable over and over and begin to report that they hear new syllables. This is called the verbal transformation effect (Warren, 1976), and the new words that listeners report usually involve changes in one or two distinctive features. And finally, Fromkin (1971) has shown that some errors of metathesis, more popularly known as spoonerisms, involve modifications at the distinctive feature level (e.g., *clear blue sky* pronounced as "glear plue sky").

The notion that phonetic perception is accomplished by feature detectors has a relatively short history. Neurophysiological evidence of feature detectors was first reported by Lettvin, Maturana, McCulloch, and Pitts (1959). They found receptive fields in the visual ganglion cells of the frog that responded to diagonal movement of a concave dark object on a light background, a kind of bug detector cell. Hubel and Wiesel (1962) discovered single cells in the visual cortex of cat that responded selectively to the orientation of lines or to edges. Complex auditory feature detectors in the cortex of cat, sensitive to the extent and direction of frequency change, were reported by Whitfield and Evans (1965). Evidence that the production and perception of communicatively relevant auditory signals are intimately linked has been uncovered for certain species. Frischkopf, Capranica, and Goldstein (1968) and Capranica (1965) reported single units in the auditory nerve of bullfrog responsive only to the male bullfrog's mating call. More recently, Wollberg and Newman (1972) have described single cells in the auditory cortex of squirrel monkey that fire only to that species' isolation peep.

The notion that phonetic perception might be accomplished by feature-detecting systems was suggested by Abbs and Sussman (1971), but it was not until Eimas and Corbit (1973) published an experimental approach to the question that serious attention was given to the suggestion. The technique they employed was a familiar one in vision involving prolonged exposure to an adapting stimulus followed by presentation of a number of test stimuli. Effects of an adapting stimulus on the test stimuli were interpreted in terms of specific receptors or feature-analyzing systems.

Eimas and Corbit (1973) assumed that there were two voicing detectors, each sensitive to VOT values that lie within its phonetic category but both sensitive to the VOT value at the phonetic boundary. The authors reasoned that adaptation to a single speech token from the extreme end of a synthetic voiced–voiceless continuum (Abramson & Lisker, 1970) should fatigue its detector throughout the range over which it was sensitive, therefore leaving its opponent detector to respond more vigorously toward boundary values on the continuum. This unequal response by the two detectors to what once were stimuli near the boundary would produce a shift in the location of the boundary to the new point of equilibrium located closer to the adapting stimulus. The predicted results were obtained. The identification functions collected in the unadapted and adapted state for each listener were compared, and the resulting shifts toward the adapting stimulus were significant. More importantly, voiced and voiceless stimuli with different places of articulation also caused a shift in the location of the boundary; that is, it was possible to produce shifts in a /ba–pa/ boundary by adapting with /da/, suggesting that the effect was operating at a feature rather than at a phoneme level. In a second study, Eimas, Cooper, and Corbit (1973) demonstrated that the effect was central rather than peripheral in origin in that it was obtained as strongly when the adapting and test stimuli were delivered to different ears.

More recently, however, the adaptation data lead to a more equivocal interpretation. Ades (1974) failed to find adaptation effects for phonetic units across position in a syllable; for example, no adaptation on a /ba–da/ series occurred with an adapting stimulus such as /ab/. In addition, adaptation effects have been shown to be contingent upon vowel context. That is, adaptation to a stimulus such as /da–ti/ produced a voiced-stimulus adaptation effect on the /ba–pa/ continuum **and** a voiceless-stimulus adaptation effect on the /di–ti/ continuum (W. E. Cooper, 1974). J. L. Miller and Eimas (1977) demonstrated similar vowel-contingent effects for the place of articulation feature.

Blumstein, Stevens, and Nigro (1977) demonstrated that greater adaptation effects on voiced stops are obtained when the adapting stimulus contains both bursts and transitions than when either is present alone or when the two acoustic cues are in conflict with regard to the phonetic features with which they are normally associated. These results tend to support the notion that property detectors are not tuned to simple formant-specific attributes of speech sounds but to more spectrally integrative properties which result when certain articulatory postures are assumed. When the independent acoustic features are present alone, they stimulate the integrated property detector, but not to the same degree as would have occurred if both of the acoustic cues were present at the same time. As Blumstein *et al.* (1977) remark, "Thus, greater adaptation effects occur when both the acoustic fine structure and the consequent property of the adapting and test stimuli are isomorphic than when the adapting and test stimuli share only the property resulting from a filtering of two somewhat different acoustic structures" (p. 1311).

While we have yet to understand fully the nature and level(s) at which property-detecting mechanisms might operate, it is tempting to apply the notion of innately determined property-detecting mechanisms to infant listeners. There is, however, a set of questions that logically precede complex questions of this kind.

III. THE PERCEPTION OF SPEECH SOUNDS BY INFANTS

The basic questions that are particularly important for understanding the perception of phonetic units by infants form a kind of hierarchy. We want to know, first, whether infants at birth are capable of detecting the acoustic energy in speech sounds; that is, whether they demonstrate sensitivity that is sufficient to make speech sounds audible. Second, we want to know whether or not the infant at birth possesses sufficient acuity to differentiate the sounds of human speech, or whether the infant has to learn to differentiate through some sort of selective linguistic exposure, and/or whether she has to mature in order to possess the capability to discriminate them. A third issue revolves around the notion of perceptual constraints of the kind demonstrated by adult listeners under precisely defined listening conditions. To the extent that infants demonstrate perceptual phenomena such as categorical perception, one can argue that infant listeners appear to be tuned to distinctions that are linguistically relevant. We can then begin to isolate the nature and origins of the predispositions demonstrated by infants and debate the mechanisms (perhaps feature detectors) that account for these predispositions. The fourth issue has to do with a more global aspect of the infant's response to speech–sound categories, and that is whether the infant demonstrates category formation, or perceptual constancy, for categories based on phonetic segments or features. Since adult listeners recognize the similarities among speech sounds in spite of their apparent acoustic diversity, it is important to understand whether these similarities are recognized at birth or whether they are somehow learned.

These four types of questions require different methodologies. The first requires audiometric assessment, and while a review of those techniques is not within the scope of this chapter (see Wilson, 1978, for a review of behavioral results), we can state that by 6 months of age infants display threshold sensitivity that closely approximates that of adult listeners (Wilson, Moore, & Thompson, 1976). The second and third areas of inquiry involve testing the infant's ability to discriminate two single speech tokens. The two tokens are either naturally produced or synthetically generated. For questions involving categorical perception, the tokens are synthetically generated and are drawn from a continuum. The perceptual constancy question requires a different experimental technique, one that assesses the extent to which the infant recognizes the similarity among phonetic units that occur in varying contexts or in various positions in a syllable, or that are spoken by different speakers. In other words, many tokens must be presented, and some measure of the infant's ability to categorize the sounds must be obtained.

A. Methods

Speech–sound discrimination by young infants has been investigated using a variety of techniques including both behavioral and electrophysiologic approaches. The commonly used electrophysiologic techniques, heart-rate deceleration and auditory-evoked response, have not been used as extensively as the behavioral techniques and have produced somewhat equivocal data (for review, see Morse, 1978). The behavioral techniques, on the other hand, are responsible for the large data base on infant speech perception that we now have, and the results produced have been remarkably consistent. We will describe these behavioral methods in detail and examine the data base that they have produced.

There are two behavioral techniques that are currently in use in most laboratories: the high-amplitude sucking technique (HAS) and the head-turn technique (HT). The HAS has been widely used since 1969 when Siqueland and Delucia (1969) described its use for experiments on visual perception with infants. The head-turn technique has only recently been developed for use in obtaining auditory thresholds from infants (Wilson et al., 1976) and even more recently applied to speech–sound discrimination (Eilers, Wilson, & Moore, 1977) where it was dubbed VRISD (Visually Reinforced Infant Speech Discrimination). This latter head-turn technique is continually being modified to improve its validity and to adapt the basic paradigm to study different kinds of questions (Kuhl, 1979b, 1980).

B. The High-Amplitude Sucking Technique

The HAS technique has been described in detail by a variety of authors (Eimas, 1974; Morse, 1972; Kuhl, 1976a). Briefly, a speech sound is presented to the infant each time she produces a sucking response whose amplitude exceeds a criterion. That particular speech sound is presented until the infant's sucking rate drops below some decrement criterion (habituation). Then, experimental infants are presented with a different speech sound while control infants continue to be presented with the first sound.

Figure 1 demonstrates the procedure. The infant sucks on a blind nipple attached to a pressure transducer. The infant's sucking responses produce pressure changes inside the nipple that are monitored with a standard pressure transducer. The resulting pressure waveforms are shown at the bottom of the figure; an amplitude criterion is set for each infant during a no-sound baseline condition. After the baseline level has been established, a speech sound (typically 500 msec in duration) is presented immediately after each response with a maximum repetition rate of one per second.

Typical data from experimental and control infants are shown in Fig. 2. The abscissa is labeled in minutes before and after the shift point (the point at which the sound is changed for experimental infants). During the first minute of contingent sound presentation, the response rate typically

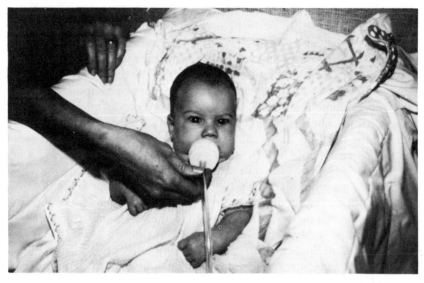

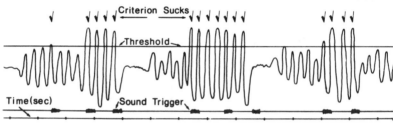

Figure 1. Eight-week-old infant sucking on a blind nipple to produce speech sounds. Pressure changes resulting from the infant's sucking responses are monitored and those sucking responses which exceed an amplitude criterion (labeled threshold) are defined as criterion responses; criterion responses trigger a speech–sound presentation with a maximum repetition rate of one per second. (Reprinted from Kuhl, 1976a.)

decreases. Most infants appear startled and stop sucking for a moment when the first sounds are presented, as suggested by the decrease in response rate between the baseline minute and the first minute of sound presentation. Eventually, however, the response rate increases and reaches a maximum. The same speech sound is presented until a 20% decrement in response rate occurs for 2 consecutive minutes. When this habituation criterion is met, infants in the experimental group are presented with a new sound while infants in the control group continue to hear the first sound. Both the experimental and the control infants are monitored for 4 minutes after the habituation criterion is met. The mean

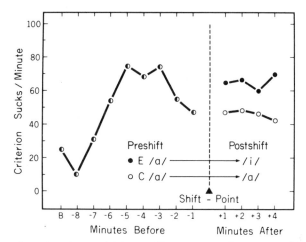

Figure 2. Minute-by-minute criterion sucking responses for one experimental and one control infant; responses are averaged for the preshift period. (Reprinted from Kuhl, 1976a.)

response rate for the 2 minutes immediately preceding the shift is subtracted from the mean response rate for the 2 minutes immediately following the shift to obtain a difference score for each infant. Experimental infants typically increase their response rates when the speech sound is changed (dishabituation) while control infants, who are presented with the same sound, either continue to decrease or do not change their response rates. Significant differences between the two groups of infants are taken as evidence that the infants can discriminate the two speech sounds.

There are minor differences in the procedure as it is used across the country that do not appear critical to the outcome of the experiment. However, there is one important difference between the way researchers employ the HAS technique that does appear to be critical; it pertains to the method of establishing a baseline level of responding. In the procedure described by Eimas (1974), the baseline was established by manipulating the sucking-amplitude threshold until approximately 20–30 criterion sucking responses were obtained from each infant. This means, of course, that the actual amplitude level varied for each child, and the percentage of the sucking responses that met criterion varied from infant to infant. Another technique used to establish a baseline level of sucking is to set the sucking-amplitude threshold at a level such that some consistent percentage of the infant's sucking responses (e.g., 50 or 80%) exceed the threshold.

Both procedures have been used widely and in many instances the data produced have been similar. In some cases, however, the second procedure produces results that cannot be interpreted. As a rule, the studies using the percentage criterion (e.g., Eilers & Minifie, 1975; Williams & Bush, 1978) have reported higher baseline scores than those using the absolute number criterion (e.g., Eimas, 1974, 1975b; Eimas, Siqueland, Jusczyk, & Vigorito, 1971; Kuhl & Miller, 1975b; Morse, 1972). It is common for baselines in the studies using the percentage criterion to be at least 40, and sometimes 50, criterion sucking responses per minute. This lenient criterion can deter the infant from learning the contingency between high-amplitude sucking responses and sound presentation in the experiment, since the absolute number of stimuli with which an infant can be presented during any 1 minute is restricted by the length of the stimuli (typically 500 msec). Consequently, in most studies, the maximum number of stimulus presentations is near 60 per minute. In other words, the infant will not be presented with over 60 presentations in a minute regardless of the number of sucking responses produced. When the infant is already producing between 40 and 50 sucking responses per minute during baseline, it is more likely that the contingency will not be learned because the infant reaches a ceiling at which increased sucking responses cannot result in increased sound presentation. This problem is difficult to deal with in studies in which a single group (experimental or, even worse, the control group) produces higher sucking responses during the baseline (no-sound) minute than during any other minute of the experiment, thus failing to demonstrate that they have learned the contingency, while the other group seems to have learned the contingency and demonstrates the normal increase in sucking responses from the baseline minute to the maximum minute. On the other hand, the absolute number criterion allows the infant to both increase and decrease sucking responses without reaching floor or ceiling effects, and these procedures tend to produce an increase in sucking responses from the baseline to the maximum minute, presumably demonstrating that the infant has learned the contingency. Since the infant produces only 20–30 criterion sucking responses during baseline, he has the opportunity to learn the contingency, once the experiment begins, by producing more criterion sucking responses per minute and thereby increasing the number of stimulus presentations.

Nearly 10 years have passed since Siqueland and Delucia (1969) described the HAS technique. Since that time, much debate has ensued over the typical pattern of results that is obtained. When many laboratories utilize the same or nearly the same technique, quite a few investigations are aimed at simply understanding why the technique works as it does. Kuhl and Miller (1975b) demonstrated that the typical increase in sucking responses both at the onset of the experiment and after habituation did not occur for a no-sound control group. Trehub and Chang (1977) demonstrated that the sound must be presented contingently on the high-amplitude sucking responses, rather than noncontingently, in order to demonstrate the dramatic increase between baseline and maximum. Williams and Golenski (1978) demonstrated a similar necessity for contingent sound presentation in order to obtain a reliable increase in sucking responses when the sound is changed. These results, along with the fact that many laboratories, each with small unavoidable modifications in the technique, have produced similar results, argue that the technique works on the principle of a conditioned-operant response.

The technique, however, has certain drawbacks. The fact that the speech sound serves as both the discriminative and the reinforcing stimulus makes it difficult to interpret negative results; it is impossible to separate the infant's inability to discriminate the two sounds from his lack of interest in them. In addition, only group data can be obtained. Sucking responses are under the control of many diverse factors and the pattern of responses is not shown by each and every infant. A third problem involves the high attrition rates (50–60%). Fourth, the technique works best for infants under 4 months of age. At older ages, infants become restless in infant seats and are not, in general, as interested in sucking continuously on a nipple.

C. The Head-Turn Technique

Many laboratories have attempted to develop a head-turn technique for use in speech–sound discrimination testing, but, until recently, no one had described a technique that had been extensively tested and found to work with a large number of infants. The technique was originally developed for assessing audiometric thresholds by a team of clinical audiologists at the University of Washington in Seattle (Wilson *et al.*, 1976). Later, it was adapted by Eilers *et al.* (1977) to study speech–sound discrimination. In the study by Eilers *et al.*, infants were trained to make a head turn whenever a speech sound, repeated once every second as a background stimulus, was changed to a comparison speech sound. A head turn which occurred during the presentation of the comparison stimulus was rewarded with the presentation of a visual stimulus, for example, a toy monkey that would clap cymbals when activated.

Two types of trials, change and control, are run. During a change trial, the stimulus is actually changed from one speech sound to another speech sound for the duration of the observation interval (typically 4–6 seconds). During control trials, the sound is not changed. For both types of trials, the Experimenter and the Assistant report whether or not a head turn has occurred during the specified observation interval. If both judges report that a head turn has occurred on a change trial, the trial is scored as correct; if one or neither reports a head turn, an error is scored. During a control trial, if either judge reports a head turn, the trial is scored as an error; if neither reports a head turn, the trial is scored as correct. Eilers *et al.* (1977) accepted a criterion of at least five out of six correct responses in six consecutive trials, half of which were change trials and half of which were control trials, as evidence that the infant discriminated the background stimulus from the comparison stimulus.

The experimental/control suite is shown in Fig. 3. The infant is held by a parent so that he faces an Assistant. The Assistant maintains the infant's attention at midline or directly in front of the Assistant by manipulating a variety of silent toys. A loudspeaker is located at a 90° azimuth to the Assistant and the visual reinforcer is placed directly in front of the loudspeaker. The toy animal is housed in a dark Plexiglas box so that the animal is not visible until the lights mounted inside the box are illuminated. The Experimenter is housed in an adjoining control room which contains a tape deck and a logic device. The two speech sounds being tested are stored on two separate channels of the tape; the onsets of the sounds are synchronized on the two channels and on each channel the sound repeats once every 1–2 seconds, depending on the specific experiment.

The basic technique has been improved in two ways since it was

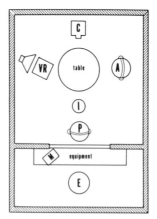

Figure 3. Experimental/control suite for the head-turn experiments. The reinforcer is located 90° to the left of the Assistant, approximately 5 feet from the infant. E, Experimenter; A, Assistant; P, parent; I, infant; VR, visual reinforcer; C, camera; M, video monitor.

originally described (Eilers *et al.*, 1977). First, the logic device controlling the experiment is more sophisticated. In the most recent modification of the technique, Kuhl (in press-b) describes a logic device which contains a probability generator; the state of the probability generator determines whether a change or a control trial will be run. The Experimenter begins a trial by depressing a start button and has no control over the type of trial that will be run; this ensures that the Experimenter cannot inadvertently (or otherwise) start change trials when the infant is restless or, conversely, start control trials when the infant is visually engaged by the toys. The logic device also times the trial interval, records both the Experimenter's and the Assistant's votes, scores the trial, activates the reinforcer when it is appropriate, records the latency of the infant's head-turn response, and prints all of the above data for each trial. This automatic recording system allows the agreement of the two judges to be assessed.

The second improvement in the technique consists of a number of added experimental controls, in addition to those necessitated by the change in the logic, which improve the validity of the technique. For example, Hillenbrand, Minifie, and Edwards (1979) and Kuhl (in press-b) report that both the mother and the Assistant wear headphones and listen to music (adjusted to mask the stimulus change) throughout the session. Neither can differentially change their behavior during change or control trials. Mothers do not know when trials occur, and the Assistant is informed that a trial is occurring by a small vibrating pin that is located on the vote button, which is held in the Assistant's hand. These added controls achieve a situation in which both the mother and the Assistant are blind and the Experimenter does not know ahead of time what type of trial, change or control, will be run.

The technique has been successfully employed with infants as young as 5.5 months (Wilson *et al.*, 1976) and as old as 18 months of age (Eilers *et al.*, 1977). It is ideally suited to infants in the 5.5- to 10-month age range. Beyond this age, infants tend to be increasingly restless and they become "object-permanence wise"; that is, the 10-month old appears to realize that the monkey is still in the box, even if the lights are out and it cannot be seen, causing the infant to want to peer in the box. For a 6-month old, "out of sight, out of mind" appears to hold.

Recently, Kuhl (in press-b,c) adapted the basic technique just described to test auditory category formation in infants. In this adaptation of the technique, Kuhl systematically increased the number of tokens in both the background and the comparison categories in a progressive experiment, requiring that the infant achieve 90% correct (9 out of 10 consecutive trials, half of which are change trials and half of which are control trials) at each stage in the experiment before advancing to the next stage.

To the extent that the infants learned responses to single tokens from a phonetic category generalized to novel tokens from the same phonetic categories, one could conclude that the infant recognized the similarity among speech tokens sharing a common phonetic feature, despite the many ways in which the tokens differ acoustically.

Table I describes the stimuli in the background category and in the comparison category for each of five stages in one of the category formation experiments (Kuhl, in press-b). In each category the number of vowels is increased until the two ensembles include six different tokens spoken by three different speakers (male, female, and child), each with two different pitch contours (rise and rise–fall). Figure 4 demonstrates the stimulus arrangements for change and control trials. During change trials, the stimulus category changes from /a/ vowels (the six vowels are randomly repeated) to /i/ vowels (again, the six vowels are randomly repeated) for the duration of the observation interval (6 seconds). During control trials, the /a/ vowels continue to be repeated randomly.

In the category-formation experiments, the data are reported in terms of the number of trials to criterion in each stage of the experiment. In the early experiments on category formation completed by Kuhl (1976c, 1977), generalization to novel tokens often occurred in the fewest number

Table I. The Stimulus Ensembles for the Background and Comparison Categories for All Five Stages of the Vowel Constancy Experiment[a]

	Experimental conditions	
	Background	Comparison
Initial training	/a/ (Male, fall)	/i/ (Male, fall)
Pitch variation	/a/ (Male, fall)	/i/ (Male, fall)
	/a/ (Male, rise)	/i/ (Male, rise)
Speaker variation	/a/ (Male, fall)	/i/ (Male, fall)
	/a/ (Female, fall)	/i/ (Female, fall)
Speaker × pitch variation	/a/ (Male, fall)	/i/ (Male, fall)
	/a/ (Male, rise)	/i/ (Male, rise)
	/a/ (Female, fall)	/i/ (Female, fall)
	/a/ (Female, rise)	/i/ (Female, rise)
Generalization	/a/ (Male, fall)	/i/ (Male, fall)
	/a/ (Male, rise)	/i/ (Male, rise)
	/a/ (Female, fall)	/i/ (Female, fall)
	/a/ (Female, rise)	/i/ (Female, rise)
	/a/ (Child, fall)	/i/ (Child, fall)
	/a/ (Child, rise)	/i/ (Child, rise)

[a] Adapted from Kuhl (in press-b).

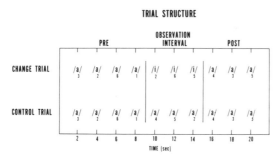

Figure 4. Stimulus presentation format for change and control trials demonstrating the stimuli presented prior to, during, and following each observation interval. During change trials, the stimulus changes from a random series of /a/s to a random series of /i/s. During control trials, a random series of /a/s is continuously repeated. The Experimenter and Assistant judge whether a head turn has occurred during the observation interval; if both agree that a head turn has occurred during the observation interval of a change trial, the trial is scored as correct. If only one or neither judges that a head turn has occurred, the trial is scored as incorrect. Conversely, if either one or both judges that a head turn has occurred during a control tiral, an error is scored. If neither judge that a head turn has occurred during the observation interval of a control trial, the trial is scored as correct. (Redrawn from Kuhl, in press-b).

of trials possible. However, as the category-formation task becomes more difficult (Holmberg, Morgan, & Kuhl, 1977), comparisons between the ease of learning for categories based on phonetic similarity versus the ease of learning for categories that do not share a phonetic dimension (i.e., random categories) will have to be made (see Kuhl, in press-c, for a discussion of this issue).

D. The Data Obtained from Behavioral Experiments on Infants

Table II lists all of the studies (to the author's knowledge) that have been published or that have been presented at conventions for which abstracts are available in English (Acoustical Society of America, American Speech and Hearing Association, Society for Research on Child Development) in the area of infant speech perception. The convention papers are indicated to remind the reader that the work has not as yet undergone a formal editorial review. The studies are divided into one of three groups: (1) those which are primarily directed at the issue of acuity for certain types of acoustic cues which underlie speech–sound distinctions; (2) those which are primarily directed at the infant's tendency to demonstrate categorical perception; and (3) those which are primarily directed at answering questions about perceptual constancy.

Table II. Studies of Infant Speech Perception

Reference	Age of subject (weeks)	Stimuli[a]	Type[b]	Procedure[c]	Results[d]
Acuity for phonetic contrasts					
Stop consonants: voicing					
Eimas, Siqueland, Jusczyk, & Vigorito (1971)	4, 16	pa(+20)pʰa(+40)	SYN	HAS	**
Trehub & Rabinovitch (1972)	4–16	pa(+20)/pʰa(+80); ba/pʰa; da/tʰa	SYN NAT	HAS	** **
Trehub (1973a)	4–16	aba/apʰa atʰaba/atʰapʰa mapʰa/pʰama	NAT	HAS	** ns ns
Eimas (1975b)	8–12	ta(+10)/tʰa(+60)	SYN	HAS	**
Eilers (1977a)	6–18	a:t/a:d at/a:d	NAT	HT	+ (5 out of 6 criterion) + (5 out of 6 criterion)
Stop consonants: place					
Morse (1972)	6	ba/ga	SYN	HAS	**
Eimas (1974)	8–12	dae/gae	SYN	HAS	**
Jusczyk (1977)	8	daeb/gaeb; baed/baeg aed/aeg; baeg/baem	SYN	HAS	** **
Jusczyk & Thompson (1978)	8	'daba/'daga da'ba/da'ga 'bada/'gada ba'da/ga'da	SYN	HAS	** ** ** **

Williams & Bush (1978)	6–12	da/ga (without burst)	SYN	HAS	**
		da/ga (with burst)			**

Fricatives

Eilers & Minifie (1975)	4–16	sa/va; sa/ʃa	NAT	HAS	**
		sa/za			ns
Eilers (1977a)[e]	5–19	sa/za	NAT	HT	− (5 out of 6 criterion)
		as/a:z			+ (5 out of 6 criterion)
		a:s/a:z			− (5 out of 6 criterion)
Eilers (1977b)	12	fa/θa	NAT	HAS	ns
		fi/θi			ns
Eilers, Wilson, & Moore (1977)	24–32	va/sa; sa/ʃa; sa/za	NAT	HT	+ (5 out of 6 criterion)
		as/a:z; a:s/a:z; at/a:d			+ (5 out of 6 criterion)
		a:t/a:d; a:t/at; fa/θa; fi/θi			− (5 out of 6 criterion)
	48–56	va/sa; sa/ʃa; sa/za	NAT	HT	+ (5 out of 6 criterion)
		as/a:z; a:s/a:z			+ (5 out of 6 criterion)
		at/a:d; fi/θi			+ (5 out of 6 criterion)
		a:t/a:d; a:t/at			+ (5 out of 6 criterion)
		fa/θa			− (5 out of 6 criterion)

Liquids and semivowels

Eimas (1975a)	8–12	ra/la	SYN	HAS	**

(continued)

23

Table II (*continued*)

Reference	Age of subject (weeks)	Stimuli[a]	Type[b]	Procedure[c]	Results[d]
Acuity for phonetic contrasts					
Jusczyk, Copan, & Thompson (1978)	8	'dawa/'daya da'wa/da'ya 'wada/'yada wa'da/ya'da	SYN	HAS	** ** ** **
Hillenbrand, Minifie, & Edwards (1979)	24–28	bɛ/wɛ; bɛ/uɛ; wɛ/uɛ bɛ/wɛ bɛ/uɛ wɛ/uɛ	NAT SYN	HT	** ** ns
Vowels					
Trehub (1973b)		a/i; i/u ta/ti; pa/pi	NAT	HAS	** **
Kuhl & Miller (1975b)[e]	4–16	a/i	SYN	HAS	**
Kuhl (in press-b)	22–26	a/i	SYN	HT	+ (9 out of 10 criterion)
Swoboda, Morse, & Leavitt (1976)	8	i/I	SYN	HAS	**
Kuhl (1977)[e]	22–26	a/ɔ	SYN	HT	+ (9 out of 10 criterion)
Stress					
Spring & Dale (1977)	4–16	ba'ba/'baba	SYN	HAS	**
Jusczyk & Thompson (1978)	8	'bada/ba'da	SYN	HAS	**
Pitch contour					
Morse (1972)	6	ba(rise)/ba(fall)	SYN	HAS	**
Kuhl & Miller (1975b)[e]	4–16	a(mon)/a(rise–fall)	SYN	HAS	**

24

Foreign language contrasts

				NAT	HAS	
Trehub (1976)	4–16	3a/ra pa/pã		SYN	HAS	** **

Categorical perception

Infants from English-speaking environments

Reference	Age	Stimuli		NAT	HAS	
Eimas, Siqueland, Jusczyk, & Vigorito (1971)	4–16	pa(+20)/p^ha(+40)		SYN	HAS	**
		ba(−20)/pa(0)				ns
		p^ha(+60)/p^ha(+80)				ns
Eimas (1974b)	8–12	dae/gae		SYN	HAS	**
		dae_1/dae_2				ns
Eimas (1975a)	8–12	ra/la		SYN	HAS	**
		ra_1/ra_2				ns
		la_1/la_2				ns
Eimas (1975b)	8–12	da(−70)/ta(+10)		SYN	HAS	**
		da(−40)/ta(+20)				ns
		da(−100)/da(−40)				ns
		da(−150)/da(−70)				ns
Eilers, Wilson, & Moore (1979)	24	pa(+10)/p^ha(+40)		SYN	HT	+ (5 out of 6 criterion)
		p^ha(+40)/p^ha(+70); ba(−20)/pa(+10)				− (5 out of 6 criterion)
		ba(−60)/pa(+10); ba(−30)/pa(0)				− (5 out of 6 criterion)
		ba(−50)/ba(−20); ba(−60)/ba(−20)				− (5 out of 6 criterion)
		ba(−60)/ba(−30)				− (5 out of 6 criterion)
Eilers, Gavin, & Wilson (in press)	24–32	pa(+10)/p^ha(+40)		SYN	HT	+ (5 out of 6 criterion)
		ba(−20)/pa(+10)				− (5 out of 6 criterion)

(continued)

25

020315

Table II (continued)

Reference	Age of subject (weeks)	Stimuli[a]	Type[b]	Procedure[c]	Results[d]
Infants from non-English-speaking environments					
Categorical perception					
Streeter (1976)	8 (Kikuyu infants)	ba(−30)/pa(0) pa(+10)/pʰa(+40) pʰa(+50)/pʰa(+80)	SYN	HAS	** ** ns
Eilers, Gavin, & Wilson (in press)	24–32 (Spanish infants)	pa(+10)/pʰa(+40) ba(−20)/pa(+10)	SYN	HT	+ (5 out of 6 criterion) + (5 of 6 criterion)
Perceptual constancy					
Fodor, Garrett, & Brill (1975)	14–18	Shared phone: pi, pa/ku pi, pu/ka pu, pa/ki No shared phone: pa, ka/pi pi, ka/pu pu, ki/pa	NAT	HT[f]	** ns
Kuhl & Miller (1975b)[e]	4–16	a(mon), a(rise–fall)/i(mon), i(rise–fall) a(mon), i(mon)/a(rise–fall), i(rise–fall) a(mon), i(rise–fall)/ a(rise–fall), i(mon)	SYN	HAS	** ns ns
Kuhl (in press-b)	22–26	a category/i category Three speakers (male, female, child) at each of two pitch contours (rise, fall)	SYN	HT	+ (9 out of 10 criterion)
Kuhl (1977)[e]	22–26	a category/ɔ category Three speakers (male, female, child) at each of two pitch contours (rise, fall)	SYN	HT	+ (9 out of 10 criterion)

Holmberg, Morgan, & Kuhl (1977)[e]	24	fV/θV category Four speakers (two male, two female) in each of three vowel contexts (/i, a, u/)	NAT	HT	+ (8 out of 10 criterion)
		sV/ʃV category Four speakers (two male, two female) in each of three vowel contexts (/i, a, u/)	NAT	HT	+ (8 out of 10 criterion)
		Vf/Vθ category Four speakers (two male, two female) in each of three vowel contexts (/i, a, u/)	NAT	HT	+ (8 out of 10 criterion)
		Vs/Vʃ category Four speakers (two male, two female) in each of three vowel contexts (/i, a, u/)	NAT	HT	+ (8 out of 10 criterion)

[a] VOT values are specified when this parameter is actually manipulated in synthetic stimuli. When the voicing contrast is being studied, the following notation is used: /b/ and /d/ indicate prevoiced stops, /p/ and /t/ indicate voiceless–unaspirated stops, and /pʰ/ and /tʰ/ indicate voiceless–aspirated stops. The following diacritics are used throughout the table: lengthening of the vowel (:); nasalization of the vowel (˜); primary stress (´); aspiration (ʰ).

[b] The speech stimuli were either computer synthesized (SYN) or naturally produced (NAT); in one study (Hillenbrand, Minifie, & Edwards, 1979), the natural stimuli were modified using a computer.

[c] Two behavioral techniques, the high-amplitude sucking technique (HAS) and the head-turn technique (HT), are specified; in one instance (Fodor, Garrett, & Brill, 1975), the head-turn technique was substantially different than the one used in other studies. See text for details of all procedures.

[d] If statistical tests were applied, statistically significant (p < .05) results are indicated by a double asterisk (**). If no statistical tests were employed, the arbitrary criterion employed by the authors is listed in parentheses. When infants met this criterion, a plus (+) is listed; when infants did not meet this criterion, a minus (−) is listed. ns, not significant.

[e] Convention paper.

[f] This procedure differs substantially from the one used in all other head-turn studies (see text for details). Statistical comparisons showed that infants learned a reinforcement contingency when the syllables in the reinforced category shared a phone (e.g., /pi/ and /pa/ vs /ku/), but not when the syllables in the reinforced category failed to share a phone (e.g., /pi/ and /ka/ vs /pu/).

Table II lists the following information concerning each study: the author(s) and date of publication or presentation, the age of the infants and the nature of their linguistic backgrounds (if other than American English), the stimuli that were presented and whether they were naturally produced or synthetically generated, the technique employed, and whether or not the infants provided evidence of discrimination or categorization of the tokens.

IV. COMMENTS ON ISSUES IN INFANT SPEECH PERCEPTION

In this section, a variety of questions will be discussed using the findings in Table II as a data base. The issues involve the data themselves as well as theoretical issues on the nature and origins of the infant's abilities.

A. Do Infants Demonstrate Sufficient Auditory Acuity to Differentiate the Segmental Units of Human Speech?

The extensive listings in Table II indicate that there are a large number of studies that have been designed to test the discrimination of two speech sounds that differ with respect to one phonetic feature. The attempt to manipulate a single acoustic feature and match all other acoustic features has been accomplished in three different ways: (1) in many studies the tokens are generated by computer, allowing one to carefully isolate and manipulate certain acoustic features of that stimulus; (2) in other studies, a single, naturally produced utterance is manipulated by computer to create two tokens that differ only with respect to the target dimension; and, (3) in some studies the experimental tokens are chosen from a large number of naturally produced exemplars such that the nontarget dimensions are matched as closely as possible.

Each of these techniques has its problems. Using natural speech can be problematic unless care is taken to really match the tokens. In addition, natural speech does not allow the investigator to manipulate the target dimension in small steps or to isolate the possible trade-off between different kinds of acoustic cues, each of which contributes to the perception of the phonetic unit being examined. On the other hand, synthetically generated tokens are sometimes of poor quality, making it difficult for untrained listeners to identify them accurately.

The measure of discrimination for the two procedures is quite different. The HAS studies employ a statistical comparison between the difference scores obtained by experimental and control groups. The HT studies employ an arbitrary criterion specified in terms of the total number of trials that are correct within a specified block of trials.

Table II lists studies which tested the discrimination of phonetic contrasts involving stop consonants, fricatives, liquids and semivowels, and vowels. In addition, two studies manipulating suprasegmental cues, such as pitch contour and stress, are listed, as well as contrasts that are not phonemic in English. While the early studies typically examined stop consonants in the initial position of syllables in an /a/ vowel context, recent studies have examined other sound categories, such as fricatives, medial- and final-position contrasts, and other vowel contexts. No studies involving nasal contrasts have been reported.

In the aggregate, the studies listed in Table II provide evidence that infants are capable of discriminating many speech–sound contrasts. Infants discriminate rather small acoustic changes in the frequency and temporal components of sounds when they are used to differentiate speech sounds. On the other hand, some of the early studies reported a failure to discriminate. Trehub (1973a), for example, reported that infants tested in the HAS technique did not demonstrate the ability to discriminate a voicing contrast in a multisyllabic utterance (/ataba/ vs /atapa/) or two syllables whose temporal order distinguished them (/mapa/ vs /pama/). These two failures have not been replicated and more recent studies have reported successful discrimination of phonetic contrasts in the medial position (Jusczyk & Thompson, 1978).

More recently, however, a variety of failures have been reported for single-syllable contrasts, particularly within the class of fricatives. Eilers and Minifie (1975) reported that infants failed to discriminate /sa/ from /za/ using the HAS technique. Eilers (1977a) reported that infants did not discriminate /fi/ from /θi/ or /fa/ from /θa/ at 3 months of age. Eilers et al. (1977) tested some of these same contrasts with older children using the HT (termed VRISD by the authors) technique and reported that 6- and 8-month old listeners failed to discriminate the two /f–θ/ contrasts and that the 12- and 14-month olds discriminated the /f–θ/ contrast in the /i/ vowel context but not in the /a/ vowel context.

The fact that an infant's behavior changes over time could mean a variety of things. A change in the infant's behavior over time could be due to either the need for specific linguistic experience, or the need for maturation, or a combination of the two. Studies on visual perception in human infants, supplemented by studies using infant monkeys, have attempted to demonstrate that certain kinds of visual experience are necessary for the development of normal visual perception. Some authors (Eimas, 1975b) have suggested a similar need for specific kinds of linguistic exposure to maintain the infant's innately demonstrated recognition of the differences between phonetic contrasts. On the other hand, maturational changes might also be responsible for changes in perception as the infant grows older. These maturational changes could relate directly to physiologic changes, such as increased myelinization of neural pathways (Hecox, 1975), or to more subtle changes in the ability to attend in an experimental setting and to remember the stimuli and the general task-related variables. It is also possible, of course, that both experience and maturation are important determiners of a change in perception. As infants are exposed to dimensions that are linguistically relevant in their own particular linguistic communities, they are increasingly likely to attend to, and remember, the acoustic details which represent these distinctions, even though linguistically relevant dimensions may not be acoustically prominent.

Unfortunately, we could attribute failure to discriminate fricatives to all three of these sources. The acoustic energy in both the /f/ and /θ/ is very low, and this presumably accounts for the difficulty in discriminating the sounds in noisy (i.e., most normal) environments. This difficulty in discriminating /f/ from /θ/ is well documented for children (Abbs & Minifie, 1969) and for adult listeners when speech is presented in noise (G. A. Miller & Nicely, 1955). One would expect, then, that infants would also demonstrate that these sounds are relatively difficult to discriminate. In this case it seems reasonable to suggest that specific linguistic experience will provide the infant with instances in which the /f–θ/ distinction is critical (*think* and *fink*), and this would increase the child's tendency to pay attention to the subtle distinction. It also seems reasonable to argue that as the infant matures, the ability to attend selectively to less prominent acoustic differences also increases. No one would argue that we have the infant's undivided attention in the behavioral techniques we now employ, but this is not exclusive to experiments in speech. Tasks that require auditory or visual monitoring on the part of the infant demonstrate that there are changes in the infant's ability to selectively attend to, and systematically explore, the features of the stimulus (see Gibson, 1969, for a review of this issue).

Support for the argument that the /f–θ/ contrast, though a difficult one, is not impossible for infants to discriminate comes from two recent studies completed in our laboratory (discussed in Holmberg *et al.*, 1977; Kuhl, 1980). Six-month-old infants were tested using the HT technique on the /f–θ/ contrast in the initial and the final positions of monosyllables. Instead of the five out of six criterion employed by Eilers *et al.* (1977) and

Eilers, Wilson, & Moore (1979), these authors required the infants to achieve eight out of ten consecutive trials correct and simply recorded the number of trials necessary to meet this criterion. An easier contrast (/s/–/ʃ/) was also tested. The data demonstrated that it was more difficult to discriminate /f/ from /θ/, in that it took more trials to reach criterion, but that infants could do so and could recognize the /f/ or /θ/, regardless of the speaker who produced the sound or the vowel context in which it appeared (see Section IV,D). No one has attempted to replicate the /sa-za/ finding with another pair of tokens. Since failure to discriminate any one pair of naturally produced syllables could be attributed to a number of factors, any further speculation about these results awaits their replication.

There is much work to be done on determining the effectiveness of acoustic cues that we consider to be primary cues to phonetic identity versus those that are known to play a role in adult perception but are considered to be secondary. The relative effectiveness of cues such as voice-onset time versus the presence/absence of low-frequency energy at voicing onset (Lisker, 1975; Summerfield & Haggard, 1977), both of which are known to influence voicing perception for adult listeners under certain circumstances, has not been investigated. Other cues to voicing that are known to be critical in medial and final positions, such as vowel duration, have not been well investigated. Eilers et al. (1977) demonstrate that infants are capable of discriminating the voicing contrast in the final position when syllables are naturally produced and have both the voicing cues and the vowel duration cues present. However, infants appeared to rely on the vowel duration cue, because when the vowels were of equal duration in the two stimuli chosen, the discrimination was not made. In general, adult listeners depend primarily on vowel lengthening to distinguish voiced and voiceless stimuli in the final position, but exactly how they perceived these same stimuli was not well documented.

In summary, then, the data attest to the fact that infants are capable of discriminating most, if not all, of the acoustic cues which distinguish the phonemes of English. Infants may get better at discriminating difficult contrasts, but this may be due to the increasing ability to attend to auditory monitoring tasks rather than to any specific linguistic exposure. This issue will resurface in the discussion on perceptual constraints and cross-language differences (Sections IV,B and C).

Very little is known about whether the ability to discriminate phonetic contrasts is hampered when the contrast is embedded in a sentence context. Preliminary data collected by Minifie and Hillenbrand (personal communication, 1977) suggest that 6-month olds discriminate a change from /b/ to /w/ in the middle of a sentence context. These kinds of studies should prove to be very interesting, given the changes in perception which occur for adult listeners when speaking rate is varied (Minifie et al., 1977).

Very little data exist on the perception of multisyllabic utterances in general and, more specifically, on the suprasegmental features that might be critical in differentiating larger units of speech. The perception of pitch contour, stress, and general features of rhythm and prosody will be important target areas of investigation in the near future.

B. Do Infants Demonstrate the Perceptual Constraints Typical of Categorical Perception in Adult Listeners?

Categorical perception for speech sounds has been verified in adult listeners for many phonetic features (Liberman *et al.*, 1967). The essential definition of categorical perception requires testing an adult listener's perceptual ability under two conditions: when stimuli from a computer-synthesized speech–sound continuum are presented singly for identification, and when they are presented in pairs for discrimination. The computer-synthesized continuum ranges from one speech sound to another (such as from /da/ to /ta/). The typical result demonstrates that the adult listener's perception is constrained in certain ways; that is, an adult listener's discrimination performance for two speech sounds that were given the same phonetic label is near chance levels, while discrimination performance for stimuli that were labeled differently is nearly perfect.

The early work on categorical perception demonstrated a distinct dichotomy between speech and nonspeech; speech was categorically perceived and nonspeech was not (Mattingly, Liberman, Syrdal, & Halwes, 1971). This phenomenon was thought to reflect the workings of a perceptual mechanism which responded only to the phonetic value of a speech sound, ignoring its precise acoustic details. More recently, however, clear demonstrations of categorical perception for acoustic continua that are not perceived as speech have been published (Cutting & Rosner, 1974; J. D. Miller, Wier, Pastore, Kelly, & Dooling, 1976; Pastore, 1976; Pisoni, 1977), and there can be no doubt that, given an appropriate continuum, these seemingly specific-to-speech results can be obtained with nonspeech stimuli. In addition, recent demonstrations show that changes in the discrimination of within-category speech–sound pairs can be manipulated either by training (Carney, Widen, & Viemeister, 1976) or by employing a discrimination procedure that reduces the degree to which the stimuli must be labeled and remembered (Pisoni, 1973; Pisoni & Lazarus, 1974).

The important role that categorical perception was thought to play in revealing the underlying operations of a speech–sound processor is evident from early writings on the subject (Studdert-Kennedy, Liberman,

Harris, & Cooper, 1970). It is not surprising, then, that the first work attempting to evaluate whether infant listeners demonstrated these same perceptual constraints was considered critical to the question of an infant's innate perception of speech sounds.

While infant listeners cannot label stimuli from a synthetic speech–sound continuum, results demonstrating that infants discriminated two stimuli from a synthetic-speech continuum that were labeled differently (by adult listeners) and did not discriminate between stimuli that were labeled similarly (by adult listeners) were taken as support for the notion that infants perceived the synthetic-speech stimuli in ways that resembled the categorical perception results in adult listeners. These findings were first shown for a voiced–voiceless (/ba–pa/) continuum by Eimas *et al.* (1971); subsequently the same results have been demonstrated for a place of articulation (/dae–gae/) continuum (Eimas, 1974) and a liquid (/ra–la/) continuum (Eimas, 1975a).

While our current descriptions of categorical perception must be tempered with all of the facts just reviewed, one cannot deny that it provides a vehicle for testing the degree to which an infant demonstrates differential sensitivity to certain kinds of acoustic stimuli, and how these differential sensitivities are modified by linguistic exposure. This brings us to another question which has been examined using the categorical perception approach.

C. Does Linguistic Exposure Modify the Way in Which Infants Perceive Speech Sounds?

Most of us are familiar with the difficulties adult listeners have in acquiring a second language. The problems a foreign speaker has in pronouncing speech sounds that are not phonemically distinct in his own language are acutely obvious to a native listener (a Japanese speaker interchanging /r/ and /l/, for example). Research demonstrates that Japanese adult listeners tested in an oddity discrimination task do not evidence the increased sensitivity at the boundary between the liquids /ra/ and /la/ that English-speaking adults do (Miyawaki, Strange, Verbrugge, Liberman, Jenkins, & Fujimura, 1975) indicating that at some stage of perceptual processing, a difference between English and Japanese adults exists. (It is possible, however, that with other testing procedures one could demonstrate that a Japanese adult listener is more sensitive to small changes in boundary stimuli than he is to small changes in nonboundary stimuli; the appropriate studies have not been done.) This has led to the hypothesis that infants discriminate all phonetic contrasts at birth regardless of their linguistic environments but that, due to the lack of exposure to certain phonetic units during development, the infant somehow loses the ability to distinguish them from contrasting phonetic units (Eimas, 1975b). The mechanism and time course of such desensitization is, of course, unknown.

Attempts to discover whether or not infants demonstrate differences in their tendencies toward categorical perception that can be attributed to linguistic exposure has received some attention, as Table II demonstrates, but we are still without a simple answer to the question. The evidence is fairly convincing that infants reared in non-English-speaking environments are capable of discriminating at least one phonetic contrast (voiceless unaspirated /pa/ from voiceless aspirated /pʰa/) that is phonemic in English but not in the infant's native language. Streeter (1976) demonstrated that 2-month-old African Kikuyu infants discriminated the English contrast in addition to a voicing contrast that is phonemic in the Kikuyu language but not in English (prevoiced /ba/ from voiceless unaspirated /pa/). Lasky, Syrdal-Lasky, and Klein (1975) demonstrated similar results for Spanish infants using a heart-rate technique.

On the other hand, the case for discrimination of the prevoiced /ba/ from the voiceless unaspirated /pa/ by American infants is not quite as clear. Recent studies (Eilers, Gavin, & Wilson, in press; Eimas, 1975b) have failed to provide evidence that American infants discriminate pairs of stimuli that are as close on the continuum as those discriminated by the Spanish and Kikuyu infants. As Kuhl and Miller (1978) note, however, there are a number of problems with these cross-language comparisons. First, the stimuli are synthesized to manipulate an acoustic cue that is acoustically fragile and is likely to be subject to variation due to the differences in acoustic calibration across laboratories. A recent set of studies claims to be immune to this criticism. Using the head-turn technique, Eilers, Wilson, and Moore (1979) and Eilers, Gavin, and Wilson (in press) tested 6-month-old American and Spanish infants in the same laboratory and demonstrated that while both groups perceived the English contrast, only the Spanish infants discriminated the Spanish contrast. As noted by the authors, however, it is still difficult to argue that linguistic exposure is the critical factor producing the observed differences. In neither case can we relate success or failure on the discrimination task to the presence or absence of the particular phonetic unit in the speech of the adult speakers of the language; that is, American infants are exposed to prevoiced stimuli (Lisker & Abramson, 1964; Smith & Westbury, 1975), while Spanish infants are not exposed to voiceless-aspirated stimuli (Lisker & Abramson, 1964). Thus, we are unable to specify the nature and time course of changes in phonetic perception that are attributable to linguistic exposure.

D. Do Infants Show Evidence of Perceptual Constancy for Speech-Sound Categories?

Only recently have researchers attempted to discover whether infants are capable of recognizing the similarity among sounds that have the same phonetic label when the sounds occur in different phonetic contexts, when they occur in different positions in a syllable, or when they are spoken by different speakers. Fodor, Garrett, and Brill (1975) examined the acquisition of a head-turn response for visual reinforcement in 14- to 18-week-old infants under two stimulus conditions. In both conditions, three syllables were randomly presented (/pi/, /ka/, /pu/), but only two of the three were reinforced. In one condition, the stimuli being reinforced were phonetically related (/pi/ and /pu/), and in the other condition, they were not (/pi/ and /ka/). If infants tend to hear the similarity between two syllables that begin with the same consonant, in spite of the differences in the acoustic cues for that consonant and in spite of the irrelevant differences between the two syllables that must be ignored (such as their vowels), then their tendencies to learn the association ought to differ in the two conditions. The proportion of head turns when phonetically similar sounds were reinforced was significantly greater than the proportion of head turns when phonetically dissimilar sounds were reinforced.

These data demonstrated that infants grouped the syllables beginning with /p/ more readily than they grouped syllables that did not share a phonetic feature, but that neither task was accomplished very accurately. Two factors may have made the task inordinately difficult. First, observations in our own laboratory on audiometric testing of infants demonstrate that, until 5.5 months of age, a large percentage of infants do not make volitional head-turn responses for a visual reinforcer with ease. At 5.5 months or older, infants make head-turn responses easily and 95–98% of the infants are conditionable. Second, the task was very difficult, involving a two-response differentiation. That is, a head turn either to the right or to the left, depending on the loudspeaker from which the reinforced stimulus was presented, was required. Head-turn responses to unreinforced stimuli were not recorded.

More convincing evidence on the degree to which infants recognize phonetic similarity has recently been obtained in our laboratory, using the head-turn technique described above (Kuhl, in press-b) with 6-month-old infants. In these tasks, infants were trained to respond when one speech token was changed to another speech token (e.g., from /a/ to /i/). The sounds were computer synthesized to simulate tokens produced by a male speaker. When infants met criterion (90% correct), the number of exemplars in each of the two vowel categories was systematically increased until each category included tokens produced by male, female, and child speakers.

The infant's performance was measured in terms of the number of trials until the criterion was met. The ease with which the transfer to new exemplars from the category occurred (where ease includes the number of trials to criterion as well as the response latency) indicated the degree to which the infant perceived the similarity among the tokens from a given category.

Results to date in these category-formation tasks strongly suggest that vowel categories are readily perceived by infant listeners. Tasks requiring the infant to recognize changes from the vowel category /a/ to the vowel category /i/ (Kuhl, in press-b) and from the vowel category /a/ to the vowel category /ɔ/ (Kuhl, 1977) result in near perfect transfer of learning to the new tokens from the category.

The investigation of consonant-based categories, such as the differentiation of voiced–stop categories across vowel context and across position in a syllable, should prove to be the most germane from a theoretical standpoint. These categories have been most problematic from the acoustic description point of view [although see recent descriptions by Blumstein & Stevens (1977)], and experiments on the adaptation effect (see Eimas and Miller, 1978, for a recent review) show vowel-contingent effects (W. E. Cooper, 1974; J. L. Miller & Eimas, 1977) and no adaptation effects when the adapting and test stimuli do not share the same position in the syllables (Ades, 1974).

Experiments on category formation for consonant-based categories have begun with the fricative categories listed in Table II. An easy contrast (/ʃ/ vs /s/) as well as a difficult one (/f/ vs /θ/) have been investigated in both the initial and final positions of syllables (Holmberg et al., 1977) in two recently completed studies. One might expect that consonant categories would be more difficult to recognize than the steady-state vowel categories because the infant must ignore prominent differences in the syllables, such as the differences between the vowels. These differences are acoustically prominent but irrelevant to the target distinction being examined.

In these experiments, relative difficulty was reflected in global measures, such as the average number of trials to meet criterion in the initial phase of the experiment when only two tokens were being discriminated, the total number of trials to complete the five stages of the experiment, and the total number of days that the infant was tested in the experiment. Using these metrics, the relative difficulty among the four contrasts tested in the category-formation experiments can be ranked as follows: /a/ vs /i/ is the easiest task, /f/ vs /θ/ is the most difficult task, and the /a/ vs /ɔ/ contrast as well as the /s/ vs /ʃ/ contrast are of intermediate difficulty.

These tasks should provide very interesting data on the infant's proclivity to recognize certain phonetic categories, and, more interestingly, on the nature and time course of the change in the formation of phonetic categories with increasing linguistic exposure.

V. BEYOND THE DATA: UNDERSTANDING THE NATURE AND ORIGINS OF EARLY PREDISPOSITIONS TOWARD SPEECH AND LANGUAGE

We have reviewed data which suggest that very young infants have sufficient auditory acuity to discriminate speech sounds, that they demonstrate certain perceptual constraints which make them appear adult like in their perceptual responses, and that they demonstrate the ability to perceive some speech–sound constancies. These data make it very tempting to borrow notions from the field of ethology and animal behavior to explain these predispositions.

There are many studies in the field of animal behavior that strongly suggest that infants of a species are specially predisposed toward the perception and the production of visual and auditory signals that are communicatively relevant to the species. The learning of vocal repertoires in certain song birds such as the canary or the white-crowned sparrow is the most relevant. The perceptual and neurological substrates that these birds demonstrate resemble those believed to be operating in human listeners. For example, song birds demonstrate a number of interesting constraints on learning. These constraints include the necessity of exposure to the appropriate conspecific auditory signal (Marler, 1970), a critical period during which this exposure must occur, and the predominance of the left hemisphere for the motor control of the production of the elements of song in the young bird; this control can be assumed by the right hemisphere if destruction of the left hemisphere occurs prior to the end of the critical period (Nottebohm, Stokes, & Leonard, 1976).

Marler (1973) attempts to explain these predispositions in the young bird using the notion of an auditory template. This template notion accounts for the bird's early selectivity to the conspecific song and prevents the bird from indiscriminately learning the song of another species. As Marler remarks, this mechanism ensures that learning is not left to chance, thus protecting the integrity of the species for reproduction and territorial cohesiveness. The template, however, is not perfectly specified. The bird requires exposure to fill in the details of the vocal repertoire and uses it, presumably, as a feedback device, relating the articulatory routines of the production system to the acoustic results which best fit the template, and the auditory results of the adult tutor-bird's songs.

However, we must realize the added complications of accounting for the behaviors of human infants. On the one hand, the infant probably would benefit from a perceptual predisposition that would cause the sounds of human speech to appear acoustically prominent. The infant might also benefit from a motor predisposition that would cause him to attempt to imitate the sounds of human speech. The infant does not tend to imitate birdsong, noises in the environment, or the music made by mobiles, even though he is exposed to them.

In the final analysis, we must account for both of these abilities: first, the ability to perceive the distinctions among speech sounds in ways that resemble the responses of adult listeners; and second, the child's eventual success at imitating speech sounds, thereby evidencing knowledge of the relationship between articulatory maneuvers and auditory results. These abilities encourage us to argue that the child is provided with some innate direction. On the other hand, the infant evidences flexibility; she learns to produce speech that is appropriate, both phonetically and rhythmically, to the language environment in which she is being raised. In other words, with whatever direction the infant enters the world, linguistic exposure is required to produce the observed changes in the production and perception of speech by adults of different linguistic backgrounds. In summary, then, there are two seemingly opposing selection pressures in operation. One pressure encourages innate predispositions which guide the infant toward species-specific courses of development, ensuring that ontogeny is not left purely to chance; the other pressure encourages flexibility so that the species adapts well to an ever-changing environment. Both direction and flexibility appear to be in operation during the acquisition of a vocal repertoire by human infants, but no currently existing model accounts for these facts.

The notion of ascribing auditory templates to human infants is probably premature, but whatever mechanisms we posit to account for the infant's proclivities, Marler (1976) argues that the infant may be recognizing relatively simple stimulus features. Marler (1976) cites Hailman's (1969) recent reanalysis of Tinbergen's (1951) classic example of the sign stimulus, which suggests that the infant of a species is predisposed toward recognizing simple stimulus features, and only with continued exposure to the stimulus does the infant develop a schema of the more global or configurational properties of the stimulus array. Human infants definitely demonstrate the appropriate sensitivities to phonetic boundaries, but we are still gathering data concerning how broadly tuned, or configurational, their recognition of speech–sound categories may be. The perceptual constancy data (Kuhl, in press-b) strongly suggest that some speech–sound categories are recognized.

Another approach to the issue of defining the nature and origins of the infant's perceptual predispositions is the recent work on the perception of speech–sound categories by nonhuman listeners (Kuhl, 1976b, 1978; Kuhl & Miller, 1975a, 1978; J. D. Miller, 1977; J. D. Miller & Kuhl, 1976). This comparative approach involves testing nonhuman listeners in two general tasks, one relating to categorical perception and the other to perceptual constancy, in an attempt to separate the effects of the general psychoacoustic predispositions of the mammalian auditory system from those which are specifically linguistic in nature.

The results to date (see Kuhl, 1978, in press-a, for a review) strongly suggest that nonhuman mammals are able to discriminate the sounds of human speech, that they demonstrate the ability to form categories based on a single phonetic dimension, such as voicing (Kuhl & Miller, 1975a), and that they seem to respond to a continuum of synthetically produced speech sounds as though they hear an abrupt qualitative change in the stimulus at the point (Kuhl & Miller, 1978) or in the general region (Morse & Snowden, 1975; Waters & Wilson, 1976) at which many of the world's languages divide the continuum into two phonetic categories. Kuhl and Miller (1978) and Kuhl (1978, in press-a) interpret these data as suggesting the possibility that certain phonetic contrasts evolved, as it were, precisely because they exploited the auditory system's natural perceptual categories.

These general notions need to be confirmed with further data suggesting that experiments testing other phonetic boundaries show similar results with nonhuman mammals. Until such time as we can fully compare the perceptual predispositions of nonhuman and human listeners, we must reserve judgment as to the exact nature and origin of the infant's predispositions.

VI. APPLYING BASIC SCIENCE FINDINGS TO EARLY DIAGNOSIS OF SPEECH AND LANGUAGE DISORDERS

Most clinical investigators argue that early diagnosis and intervention are needed in cases of disordered speech and language. While we have not as yet done systematic work on infants who are neurologically at risk (though see Morse, 1978; Swoboda, Morse, & Leavitt, 1976), it is likely that work on the perception of complex auditory signals with a variety of infant populations will be undertaken in the near future. In addition, longitudinal studies which examine the correlations between the performance of individual infants in the category-formation tasks and other early indicators of linguistic/cognitive functions would be meaningful. The category-formation tasks require not only the discrimination of two sounds but the recognition of the target dimension despite the potentially distracting acoustic dimensions; since auditory memory as well as memory for the rules of the game, and constant attention and monitoring of the auditory signal are required, it is highly likely that we will find differences among infants, ones that may correlate with later language delay. These tasks may eventually form part of a test battery for infants which may result in careful monitoring of particular infants.

VII. DIRECTIONS FOR THE FUTURE

The near future will probably bring increased reliance on an animal model to investigate the development of communicative repertoires that are critical to a species' survival. There will also be increased study of the relationship between speech production and speech perception in early infancy and, more specifically, early tendencies demonstrating that the infant has some notion of the relationship between articulatory postures and their resulting auditory events. A third area of increased investigation will probably involve the integration of work investigating the phonetic level of analysis within the context of larger linguistic units such as sentences and phrases. As the child acquires additional knowledge concerning specific linguistic rules as well as nonlinguistic information (about objects and relations in the world), we can begin to examine the interactions between perception at the phonetic level when it is aided by these various sources of information, as has been examined in adult listeners (Cole & Jakimik, in press).

Another area of concentration will be increased investigation of the recognition of temporal cues related to rhythm and stress perception by infants. Prosodic cues provide information about higher order linguistic units (Lea, Medress, & Skinner, 1975), but we know little about an infant's perception of these acoustic cues.

VIII. SUMMARY AND CONCLUSIONS

The data gathered during the first decade of research on the infant's perception of speech sounds indicate that the human infant makes discriminations that depend upon fine temporal and frequency changes in a complex auditory array. In addition, infants demonstrate perceptual constraints when listening to speech that can be characterized as adult like and appear to be predisposed to perceive certain speech–sound categories such as vowel and fricative categories. The mechanisms posited to account for these abilities are highly speculative. While the work on the neural and perceptual substrates of vocal communication in avian species is suggestive, it is premature to apply these notions directly to explain speech perception in early infancy. At this time, we cannot separate mechanisms in the human infant that are specifically linguistic from those that are more generally psychoacoustic in nature (Kuhl, 1978). A conservative approach, in which we hypothesize the absolute minimum in terms of special mechanisms, will probably be the most fruitful.

In the meantime, we know almost nothing about the time course of what may be a desensitization to speech–sound differences produced by specific linguistic exposure. Some transformation must be posited to explain the fact that speech–sound differences that were recognized in early infancy are no longer recognized (in certain testing formats) by an adult raised in a linguistic environment in which these perceptual differences are not phonemic. The precise nature/level of these perceptual changes in adult listeners is unknown, as well as their developmental time courses. These issues will direct our attentions in the near future.

References

Abbs, M. S., & Minifie, F. D. Effect of acoustic cues in fricatives on perceptual confusions in preschool children. *Journal of the Acoustical Society of America,* 1969, *46,* 1535–1542.

Abbs, J. H., & Sussman, H. M. Neurophysiological feature detectors and speech perception: A discussion of theoretical implications. *Journal of Speech and Hearing Research,* 1971, *14,* 23–36.

Abramson, A., & Lisker, L. Discrimination along the voicing continuum: Cross-language tests. *Proceedings of the Sixth International Congress of Phonetic Sciences, Prague, 1967,* 1970, pp. 569–573.

Ades, A. E. How phonetic is selective adaptation? Experiments on syllable position and vowel environment. *Perception & Psychophysics,* 1974, *16,* 61–67.

Blumstein, S. E., & Stevens, K. N. Perceptual invariance and onset spectra for stop consonants in different vowel environments. *Journal of the Acoustical Society of America,* 1976, *60*(Suppl. No. 1), S90(A).

Blumstein, S. E., & Stevens, K. N. Acoustic invariance for place of articulation in stops and nasals across syllabic contexts. *Journal of the Acoustical Society of America,* 1977, *62*(Suppl. No. 1), S26(A).

Blumstein, S., Stevens, K. N., & Nigro, G. N. Property detectors for bursts and transitions in speech perception. *Journal of the Acoustical Society of America,* 1977, *61,* 1301–1313.

Bruner, J. S., & Minturn, A. L. Perceptual identification and perceptual organization. *Journal of General Psychology,* 1955, *53,* 20–28.

Bugelski, B. R., & Alampay, D. A. The role of frequency in developing perceptual sets. *Canadian Journal of Psychology,* 1961, *15,* 205–211.

Capranica, R. R. *The evoked vocal response of the bullfrog: A study of communication by sound* (Res. Monogr. No. 33). Cambridge, Mass.: MIT Press, 1965.

Carlson, R., Fant, G., & Granstrom, B. Two-formant models, pitch, and vowel perception.

In G. Fant & M. A. A. Tatham (Eds.), *Auditory analysis and perception of speech.* New York: Academic Press, 1975. Pp. 55–82.

Carney, A. E., Widin, G. P., & Viemeister, N. F. Noncategorical perception of stop consonants differing in VOT. *Journal of the Acoustical Society of America,* 1977, *62,* 960–970.

Chen, M. Vowel length variation as a function of the voicing of the consonant environment. *Phonetica,* 1970, *22,* 129–159.

Cole, R. A., & Jakimik, J. Understanding speech: How words are heard. In G. Underwood (Ed.), *Strategies of information processing.* New York: Academic Press, in press.

Cooper, F. S., Delattre, P. C., Liberman, A. M., Borst, J. M., & Gerstman, L. J. Some experiments on the perception of synthetic speech sounds. *Journal of the Acoustical Society of America,* 1952, *24,* 597–606.

Cooper, W. E. Contingent feature analysis in speech perception. *Perception & Psychophysics,* 1974, *16,* 201–204.

Cutting, J. E., & Rosner, B. S. Categories and boundaries in speech and music. *Perception & Psychophysics,* 1974, *16,* 564–570.

Delattre, P. C., Liberman, A. M., & Cooper, F. S. Voyelles synthetiques a deux formantes et voyelles cardinales. *Maitre Phonetique,* 1951, *96,* 30–36.

Delattre, P. C., Liberman, A. M., & Cooper, F. S. Acoustic loci and transitional cues for consonants. *Journal of the Acoustical Society of America,* 1955, *27,* 769–773.

Denes, P. Effect of duration on the perception of voicing. *Journal of the Acoustical Society of America,* 1955, *27,* 761–764.

Eilers, R. E. *On tracing the development of speech perception in early infancy.* Paper presented at the meeting of the Society for Research in Child Development, New Orleans, March 1977. (a)

Eilers, R. E. Context sensitive perception of naturally produced stop and fricative consonants by infants. *Journal of the Acoustical Society of America,* 1977, *61,* 1321–1336. (b)

Eilers, R. E., Gavin, W. J., & Wilson, W. R. Linguistic experience and phonemic perception in infancy. *Child Development,* in press.

Eilers, R. E., & Minifie, F. D. Fricative discrimination in early infancy. *Journal of Speech and Hearing Research,* 1975, *18,* 158–167.

Eilers, R. E., Wilson, W. R., & Moore, J. M. Developmental changes in speech discrimination in infants. *Journal of Speech and Hearing Research,* 1977, *20,* 766–780.

Eilers, R. E., Wilson, W. R., & Moore, J. M. Speech discrimination in language-innocent and the language-wise: A study in the perception of voice-onset time. *Journal of Child Language,* 1979, *6,* 1–18.

Eimas, P. D. Auditory and linguistic processing of cues for place of articulation by infants. *Perception & Psychophysics,* 1974, *16,* 513–521.

Eimas, P. D. Auditory and phonetic coding of the cues for speech: Discrimination of the [r-l] distinction by young infants. *Perception & Psychophysics,* 1975, *18,* 341–347. (a)

Eimas, P. D. Speech perception in early infancy. In L. B. Cohen & P. Salapatek (Eds.), *Infant perception: From sensation to cognition* (Vol. 2). New York: Academic Press, 1975. Pp. 193–231. (b)

Eimas, P. D., Cooper, W. E., & Corbit, J. D. Some properties of linguistic feature detectors for speech. *Perception & Psychophysics,* 1973, *13,* 247–252.

Eimas, P. D., & Corbit, J. D. Selective adaptation of linguistic feature detectors. *Cognitive Psychology,* 1973, *4,* 99–109.

Eimas, P. D. & Miller, J. L. Effects of selective adaptation on the perception of speech and visual forms: Evidence for feature detectors. In R. D. Walk and H. L. Pick, Jr. (Eds.), *Perception and Experience.* New York: Plenum, 1978. Pp. 307–345.

Eimas, P. D., Siqueland, E. R., Jusczyk, P., & Vigorito, J. Speech perception in infants. *Science*, 1971, *171*, 303–306.

Fant, G. *Acoustic theory of speech production*. The Hague: Mouton, 1960.

Fant, G. *Speech sounds and features*. Cambridge, Mass.: MIT Press, 1973.

Fodor, J. A., Garrett, M. F., & Brill, S. L. Pi ka pu: The perception of speech sounds by pre-linguistic infants. *Perception & Psychophysics*, 1975, *18*, 74–78.

Frischkopf, L., Capranica, R., & Goldstein, M. Neural coding in the bullfrog's auditory system. *Proceedings of the IEEE*, 1968, *56*, 969–988.

Fromkin, V. A. The non-anomalous nature of anomalous utterances. *Language*, 1971, *47*, 27–52.

Gibson, E. *Principles of perceptual development*. New York: Appleton, 1969.

Hailman, J. P. How an instinct is learned. *Scientific American*, 1969, *221*, 98–106.

Halle, M., Hughes, G. W., & Radley, J. P. A. Acoustic properties of stop consonants. *Journal of the Acoustical Society of America*, 1957, *29*, 107–116.

Hecox, K. Electrophysiological correlates of human auditory development. In L. B. Cohen & P. Salapatek (Eds.), *Infant perception: From sensation to cognition* (Vol. 2). New York: Academic Press, 1975. Pp. 151–191.

Hillenbrand, J., Minifie, F. D., & Edwards, T. J. Tempo of frequency change as a cue in speech-sound discrimination by infants. *Journal of Speech and Hearing Research*, 1979, *22*, 147–165.

Holmberg, T. L., Morgan, K. A., & Kuhl, P. K. Speech perception in early infancy: Discrimination of fricative consonants. *Journal of the Acoustical Society of America*, 1977, *62*(Suppl. No. 1), S99(A).

Hubel, D. H., & Wiesel, T. N. Receptive fields, binocular interaction and functional architecture in the cat's visual cortex. *Journal of Physiology (London)*, 1962, *160*, 106–154.

Jakobson, R., Fant, C. G. M., & Halle, M. *Preliminaries to speech analysis: The distinctive features and their correlates*. Cambridge, Mass.: MIT Press, 1969.

Jusczyk, P. W. Perception of syllable-final stop consonants by 2-month-old infants. *Perception & Psychophysics*, 1977, *21*, 450–454.

Jusczyk, P. W., Copan, H., & Thompson, E. Perception by 2-month-old infants of glide contrasts in multisyllabic utterances. *Perception & Psychophysics*, 1978, *24*, 515–520.

Jusczyk, P., & Thompson, E. Perception of a phonetic contrast in multisyllabic utterances by two-month-old infants. *Perception & Psychophysics*, 1978, *23*, 105–109.

Karnickaya, E. G., Mushnikov, V. N., Stepokurova, N. A., & Zhukov, S. J. In G. Fant and M. A. A. Tatham (Eds.), *Auditory analysis and perception of speech*. New York: Academic Press, 1975. Pp. 37–54.

Kuhl, P. K. Speech perception in early infancy: The acquisition of speech-sound categories. In S. K. Hirsh, D. H. Eldredge, I. J. Hirsh, & S. R. Silverman (Eds.), *Hearing and Davis: Essays honoring Hallowell Davis*. St. Louis: Washington University Press, 1976. Pp. 265–280. (a)

Kuhl, P. K. Speech perception by the chinchilla: Categorical perception of synthetic alveolar plosive consonants. *Journal of the Acoustical Society of America*, 1976, *60*(Suppl. No. 1), S81(A). (b)

Kuhl, P. K. Speech perception in early infancy: Perceptual constancy for vowel categories. *Journal of the Acoustical Society of America*, 1976, 60(Suppl. No. 1), S90(A). (c)

Kuhl, P. K. Speech perception in early infancy: Perceptual constancy for the vowel categories /a/ and /ɔ/. *Journal of the Acoustical Society of America*, 1977, *61*(Suppl. No. 1), S39(A).

Kuhl, P. K. Predispositions for the perception of speech-sound categories: A species-specific phenomenon? In F. D. Minifie & L. L. Lloyd (Eds.), *Communicative and cognitive abilities—Early behavior assessment.* Baltimore: University Park Press, 1978. Pp. 229–255.

Kuhl, P. K. Models and mechanisms in speech perception: Species comparisons provide further contributions. *Brain, Behavior, and Evolution,* in press-a.

Kuhl, P. K. Speech perception in early infancy: Perceptual constancy for spectrally dissimilar vowel categories. *Journal of the Acoustical Society of America,* in press-a.

Kuhl, P. K. Perceptual constancy for speech-sound categories in early infancy. In G. Yeni-Komshian, J. Kavanaugh, & C. Ferguson (Eds.), *Child phonology: Data and theory.* New York: Academic Press, in press-c.

Kuhl, P. K., & Miller, J. D. Speech perception by the chinchilla: Voiced–voiceless distinction in alveolar plosive consonants. *Science,* 1975, *190,* 69–72. (a)

Kuhl, P. K., & Miller, J. D. Speech perception in early infancy: Discrimination of speech-sound categories. *Journal of the Acoustical Society of America,* 1975, *58*(Suppl. No. 1), S56(A). (b)

Kuhl, P. K., & Miller, J. D. Speech perception by the chinchilla: Identification functions for synthetic VOT stimuli. *Journal of the Acoustical Society of America,* 1978, *63,* 905–917.

Lasky, R. E., Syrdal-Lasky, A., & Klein, R. E. VOT discrimination by four- to six-and-a-half-month-old infants from Spanish environments. *Journal of Experimental Child Psychology,* 1975, *20,* 215–225.

Lea, W. A., Medress, M. E., & Skinner, T. E. A prosodically guided speech understanding strategy. *IEEE Transactions on Acoustics, Speech, and Signal Processing.* 1975, *23,* 1.

Lettvin, J. Y., Maturana, H. R., McCulloch, W. S., & Pitts, W. H. What the frog's eye tells the frog's brain. *Proceedings of the IRE* 1959, *47,* 1940–1951.

Liberman, A. M., Cooper, F. S., Shankweiler, D. P., & Studdert-Kennedy, M. Perception of the speech code. *Psychological Review,* 1967, *74,* 431–461.

Liberman, A. M., Delattre, P. C., & Cooper, F. S. Some cues for the distinction between voiced and voiceless stops in initial position. *Language and Speech,* 1958, *1,* 153–167.

Liberman, A. M., Harris, K. S., Eimas, P., Lisker, L., & Bastian, J. An effect of learning on speech perception: The discrimination of durations of silence with and without phonemic significance. *Language and Speech,* 1961, *4,* 175–195.

Liberman, A. M., Harris, K. S., Hoffman, H. S., & Griffith, B. C. The discrimination of speech sounds within and across phoneme boundaries. *Journal of Experimental Psychology,* 1957, *54,* 358–368.

Lisker, L. Closure duration and the intervocalic voiced–voiceless distinction in English. *Language,* 1957, *33,* 42–49.

Lisker, L. Is it VOT or a first-formant transition detector? *Journal of the Acoustical Society of America,* 1975, *57,* 1547–1551.

Lisker, L., & Abramson, A. A cross-language study of voicing in initial stops: Acoustical measurements. *Word,* 1964, *20,* 384–422.

Malecot, A. The role of releases in the identification of released final stops. *Language,* 1958, *34,* 370–380.

Marler, P. A comparative approach to vocal learning: Song development in white-crowned sparrows. *Journal of Comparative and Physiological Psychology Monograph,* 1970, *71*(2) 1–25.

Marler, P. Constraints on learning: Development of bird song. In W. F. Norman (Ed.), *The Clarence M. Hicks Memorial Lectures for 1970.* Toronto: University of Toronto Press, 1973. Pp. 69–85.

Marler, P. Sensory templates in species-specific behavior. In J. C. Fentress (Ed.), *Simpler networks and behavior.* Sunderland, Mass.: Sinauer Associates, 1976. Pp. 314–330.

Mattingly, I., Liberman, A., Syrdal, A., & Halwes, T. Discrimination in speech and nonspeech modes. *Cognitive Psychology*, 1971, *2*, 131–157.

Miller, G. A., Heise, G. A., & Lichten, W. The intelligibility of speech as a function of the context of the test materials. *Journal of Experimental Psychology*, 1951, *41*, 329–335.

Miller, G. A., & Isard, S. Some perceptual consequences of linguistic rules. *Journal of Verbal Learning and Verbal Behavior*, 1963, *2*, 217–228.

Miller, G. A., & Nicely, P. E. An analysis of perceptual confusions among some English consonants. *Journal of the Acoustical Society of America*, 1955, *27*, 338–352.

Miller, J. D. Perception of speech sounds by animals: Evidence for speech processing by mammalian auditory mechanisms. In T. H. Bullock (Ed.), *Recognition of complex auditory signals*. Berlin: Abakon Verlagsgesellschaft, 1977. Pp. 49–58.

Miller, J. D., Engebretson, A. M., Spenner, B. F., & Cox, J. R. Preliminary analyses of speech sounds with a digital model of the ear. *Journal of the Acoustical Society of America*, 1977, *62*(Suppl. No. 1), S13(A).

Miller, J. D., & Kuhl, P. K. Speech perception by the chinchilla: A progress report on syllable-initial voiced-plosive consonants. *Journal of the Acoustical Society of America*, 1976, *59*(Suppl. No. 1), S54(A).

Miller, J. D., Wier, C. C., Pastore, R. E., Kelly, W. J., & Dooling, R. J. Discrimination and labeling of noise-buzz sequences with varying noise-lead times: An example of categorical perception. *Journal of the Acoustical Society of America*, 1976, *60*, 410–417.

Miller, J. L., & Eimas, P. D. Studies on the selective tuning of feature detectors for speech. *Journal of Phonetics*, 1977, *4*, 119–127.

Miller, J. L., & Liberman, A. M. Some observations on how the perception of syllable-initial /b/ vs /w/ is affected by the remainder of the syllable. *Journal of the Acoustical Society of America*, 1978, *63* (Suppl. No. 1), S21(A).

Minifie, F. D. Speech acoustics. In F. D. Minifie, T. J. Hixon, & F. Williams (Eds.), *Normal aspects of speech, hearing and language*. Englewood Cliffs, N.J.: Prentice-Hall, 1973. Pp. 235–284.

Minifie, F. D., & Hillenbrand, J. Personal communication, 1977.

Minifie, F. D., Kuhl, P. K., & Stecher, E. M. Categorical perception of /b/ and /w/ during changes in rate of utterance. *Journal of the Acoustical Society of America*, 1977, *62*(Suppl. No. 1), S79(A).

Morse, P. A. The discrimination of speech and nonspeech stimuli in early infancy. *Journal of Experimental Child Psychology*, 1972, *14*, 477–492.

Morse, P. A. Infant speech perception: Origins, processes, and alpha centauri. In F. D. Minifie and L. L. Lloyd (Eds.), *Communicative and cognitive abilities—Early behavior assessment*. Baltimore: University Park Press, 1978. Pp. 195–227.

Morse, P. A., & Snowdon, C. T. An investigation of categorical speech discrimination by rhesus monkeys. *Perception & Psychophysics*, 1975, *17*, 9–16.

Miyawaki, K., Strange, W., Verbrugge, R., Liberman, A., Jenkins, J., & Fujimura, O. An effect of linguistic experience: The discrimination of [r] and [l] by native speakers of Japanese and English. *Perception and Psychophysics*, 1975, *18*, 331–340.

Neisser, U. *Cognitive psychology*. New York: Appleton, 1967.

Nottebohm, F., Stokes, T. M., & Leonard, C. M. Central control of song in the canary. *Journal of Comparative Neurology*, 1976, *165*, 457–486.

Pastore, R. E. Categorical perception: A critical re-evaluation. In S. K. Hirsh, D. H. Eldredge, I. J. Hirsh, & S. R. Silverman (Eds.), *Hearing and Davis: Essays honoring Hallowell Davis*. St. Louis: Washington University Press, 1976. Pp. 253–264.

Peterson, G. E., & Barney, H. L. Control methods used in a study of the vowels. *Journal of the Acoustical Society of America*, 1952, *24*, 175–184.

Pisoni, D. B. Auditory and phonetic memory codes in the discrimination of consonants and vowels. *Perception & Psychophysics*, 1973, *13*, 253–260.

Pisoni, D. B. Identification and discrimination of the relative onset time of two-component tones: Implications for voicing perception in stops. *Journal of the Acoustical Society of America*, 1977, *61*, 1352–1361.

Pisoni, D. B. Speech perception. In W. K. Estes (Ed.), *Handbook of learning and cognitive processes* (Vol. VI). Hillsdale, N.J.: Lawrence Erlbaum Associates, 1978.

Pisoni, D. B., & Lazarus, J. H. Categorical and noncategorical modes of speech perception along the voicing continuum. *Journal of the Acoustical Society of America*, 1974, *55*, 328–333.

Port, R. Effects of tempo of the preceding carrier on the perception of *rabid* and *rapid*. *Journal of the Acoustical Society of America*, 1976, *59*, S41(A).

Reale, R. A., & Geisler, C. D. *Auditory-nerve fiber encoding of two-tone approximations to steady-state vowels.* Paper presented at the second midwinter research meeting of the Association for Research in Otolaryngology, St. Petersburg Beach, January 1979.

Sachs, M. B., & Young, E. D. *Encoding of vowels in the population of auditory-nerve fibers: Place and periodicity mechanisms.* Paper presented at the second midwinter research meeting of the Association for Research in Otolaryngology, St. Petersburg Beach, January 1979.

Sales, B. D., Cole, R. A., & Haber, R. N. Mechanisms of aural encoding: V. Environmental effects of consonants on vowel coding. *Perception & Psychophysics*, 1969, *6*, 361–365.

Schatz, C. The role of context in the perception of stops. *Language*, 1954, *30*, 47–56.

Shankweiler, D., Strange, W., & Verbrugge, R. Speech and the problem of perceptual constancy. In R. Shaw & J. Bransford (Eds.), *Perceiving, acting, and knowing: Toward an ecological psychology.* New York: Lawrence Erlbaum, 1977. Pp. 315–346.

Shoup, J. E., & Pfeifer, L. L. Acoustic characteristics of speech sounds. In N. J. Lass (Ed.), *Contemporary issues in experimental phonetics.* New York: Academic Press, 1976. Pp. 171–224.

Siqueland, E. R., & Delucia, C. A. Visual reinforcement of nonnutritive sucking in human infants. *Science*, 1969, *165*, 1144–1146.

Slis, I. H., & Cohen, A. On the complex regulating the voiced–voiceless distinction I. *Language and Speech*, 1969, *12*, 80–102. (a)

Slis, I. H., & Cohen, A. On the complex regulating the voiced–voiceless distinction II. *Language and Speech*, 1969, *12*, 137–155. (b)

Smith, B. L. & Westbury, J. R. Temporal control of voicing during occlusion in plosives. *Journal of the Acoustical Society of America*, 1975, *57*, S71(A).

Spring, D. R., & Dale, P. S. Discrimination of linguistic stress in early infancy. *Journal of Speech and Hearing Research*, 1977, *20*, 224–232.

Stevens, K. N., & Blumstein, S. E. Invariant cues for place of articulation in stop consonants. *Journal of the Acoustical Society of America*, 1978, *64*, 1358–1368.

Stevens, K. N., & Halle, M. Remarks on analysis by synthesis and distinctive features. In W. Wathen-Dunn (Ed.), *Models for the perception of speech and visual form.* Cambridge, Mass.: MIT Press, 1967. Pp. 88–102.

Stevens, K. N., & House, A. S. Speech perception. In J. V. Tobias (Ed.), *Foundations of modern auditory theory* (Vol. II). New York: Academic Press, 1972. Pp. 3–26.

Stevens, K. N., & Klatt, D. H. Role of formant transitions in the voiced–voiceless distinction for stops. *Journal of the Acoustical Society of America*, 1974, *55*, 653–659.

Streeter, L. A. Language perception of 2-month-old infants shows effects of both innate mechanisms and experience. *Nature (London)*, 1976, *259*, 39–41.

Studdert-Kennedy, M., Liberman, A., Harris, K. S., & Cooper, F. S. Motor theory of speech perception. *Psychological Review,* 1970, *77,* 234–249.

Studdert-Kennedy, M., & Shankweiler, D. Hemispheric specialization for speech perception. *Journal of the Acoustical Society of America,* 1970, *48,* 579–594.

Summerfield, Q., & Haggard, M. On the dissociation of spectral and temporal cues to the voicing distinction in initial stop consonants. *Journal of the Acoustical Society of America,* 1977, *62,* 435–448.

Swoboda, P., Morse, P., & Leavitt, L. Continuous vowel discrimination in normal and at-risk infants. *Child Development,* 1976, *47,* 459–465.

Tinbergen, N. *The study of instinct.* London and New York: Oxford University Press (Clarendon), 1951.

Trehub, S. E. Infants' sensitivity to vowel and tonal contrasts. *Developmental Psychology,* 1973, *9,* 91–96.

Trehub, S. E. The discrimination of foreign speech contrasts by infants and adults. *Child Development,* 1976, *47,* 466–472.

Trehub, S. E., & Chang, H. W. Speech as reinforcing stimulation for infants. *Developmental Psychology,* 1977, *6,* 74–77.

Trehub, S. E., & Rabinovitch, S. Auditory-linguistic sensitivity in early infancy. *Developmental Psychology,* 1972, *6,* 74–77.

Ward, W. D. Musical perception. In J. V. Tobias (Ed.), *Foundations of modern auditory theory* (Vol. 1). New York: Academic Press, 1970. Pp. 405–443.

Warren, R. M. Auditory illusions and perceptual processes. In N. J. Lass (Ed.), *Contemporary issues in experimental phonetics.* New York: Academic Press, 1976. Pp. 389–417.

Waters, R. A., & Wilson, W. A., Jr. Speech perception by rhesus monkeys: The voicing distinction in synthesized labial and velar stop consonants. *Perception & Psychophysics,* 1976, *19,* 285–289.

Whitfield, I. C., & Evans, E. F. Responses of auditory cortical neurons to stimuli of changing frequency. *Journal of Neurophysiology,* 1965, *28,* 655–672.

Wickelgren, W. A. Distinctive features and errors in short-term memory for English vowels. *Journal of the Acoustical Society of America,* 1965, *38,* 583–588.

Wickelgren, W. A. Distinctive features and errors in short-term memory for English consonants. *Journal of the Acoustical Society of America,* 1966, *39,* 388–398.

Williams, L., & Bush, M. Discrimination by young infants of voiced stop consonants with and without release bursts. *Journal of the Acoustical Society of America,* 1978, *63,* 1223–1226.

Williams, L., & Golenski, J. Infant speech sound discrimination: The effects of contingent versus noncontingent stimulus presentation. *Child Development,* 1978, *49,* 213–217.

Wilson, W. R. Behavioral assessment of auditory function in infants. In F. D. Minifie & L. L. Lloyd (Eds.), *Communicative and cognitive abilities—Early behavioral assessment.* Baltimore: University Park Press, 1978. Pp. 37–59.

Wilson, W. R., Moore, J. M., & Thompson, G. *Sound-field auditory thresholds of infants utilizing Visual Reinforcement Audiometry (VRA).* Paper presented at the annual convention of the American Speech and Hearing Association, Houston, November 1976.

Wollberg, Z., & Newman, J. Auditory cortex of squirrel monkey: Response patterns of single cells to species-specific vocalizations. *Science,* 1972, *175,* 212–214.

Acoustic–Perceptual Methods for Evaluation of Defective Speech

JAMES F. LUBKER

Institute of Linguistics
Department of Phonetics
University of Stockholm
Stockholm, Sweden

Speech is a Complex which involves the production and the perception of an acoustic signal. These elements may, of course, be further subdivided and virtually any basic speech and hearing textbook will provide the reader with some sort of speech chain which attempts to describe the organization and the relationships of these subdivisions. Whatever the quality or clarity of such descriptions, they demonstrate that we are concerned with a **set** of processes and that the individual elements of the set cannot realistically be viewed in isolation. However simple any given description of a speech chain may be, very little reflection reveals that speech is a mind-bogglingly complex Complex. It involves at least the following areas of specialization: linguistics, phonology, physiological/ neurological phonetics, acoustics, acoustic phonetics, psychophysics, psychoacoustics, physiological acoustics, and the whole area of perception, not to mention knowledge of such paracommunication disciplines as psychology, physics, mathematics, medicine, physiology, computer science, and so on. It is not very likely that any single individual will be able to claim a deep and fundamental understanding of the **entire** Complex.

SPEECH AND LANGUAGE: Advances in Basic
Research and Practice, Vol. 1

That can be a very frustrating state of affairs since we have agreed that it is unrealistic to attempt to view any single element of the Complex in isolation. We seek an understanding of the **entire** process of just how human beings are able to communicate verbally with one another and we seek an understanding of Jakobson's often-quoted statement: "We speak in order to be heard in order to be understood" (Jakobson, Fant, & Halle, 1961, p. 13). *How* do we speak? *How* are we heard? *How* are we understood? These three questions must be viewed within the framework of the statement from which they were taken: that speaking, hearing, and understanding create an essentially indissoluble entity. The challenge of truly understanding how we produce an acoustic signal which listeners perceive as the intended message is exciting, demanding, and important. We are far from having met it.

Then there is an added complexity, an added challenge. A great number of human beings are not able to produce an acoustic speech wave which is perceived by listeners as being normal, if it is understood at all. Another large group of people are unable to perceive or understand a normal acoustic speech wave. These speech- and hearing-disabled individuals provide a dramatic illustration of the elemental importance contained in Jakobson's deceptively simple statement: being clearly understood and understanding clearly are the crucial end products toward which communication is directed, and, to the extent that these ends are not reached by an individual, he or she is said to have a speech and/or hearing disorder.

The problems faced by the speech clinician are thus very important and very difficult. They are also as intertwined as the strands of a rope with the problem areas listed above for normal speech communication. The clinician must provide diagnosis, prognosis, therapy planning, and evaluation of therapy. Certainly, these aspects of a clinician's work are highly dependent upon a thorough understanding of the elements and the relationships in the normal speech communication chain. Diagnosis and prognosis are most easily and accurately accomplished and expressed in relation to normal production, acoustic, and perception mechanisms. Evaluation of therapy can certainly be viewed as an expression of the patient's own self-progress, that is, her present status in relation to her initial status. The evaluation is rounded out and clarified by added descriptions of how far she is from producing a relatively normal speech sound wave.

This clearly implies the need for: (1) a continuing and improved elucidation of the normal system, and (2) methods and means for providing comparisons within and among speech defective individuals as well as between them and normal speaking individuals. Which is perhaps coming a long way to state the need for and the absolute importance of the triumvirate: description, prediction, and control within the study and treatment of pathological speech communication.

I have taken pains to stress the complexity and importance of all this because I believe that the agreement with which clinicians and phoneticians generally meet such statements as the preceding is often largely superficial. The clinician is often distrustful of attempts at objectivity, measurement, quantitative comparisons, and speech science laboratory efforts in general. The clinician often believes the phonetician to be largely insensitive to, if not totally unaware of, the real problems and needs of the clinic.

To a certain extent such beliefs and criticisms are valid. A not insignificant amount of phonetic research seems to be measurement simply for the sake of measurement, a fact which does not instill confidence in clinical viewers of such research (see Platt, 1964, for an excellent discussion of this problem as a general issue in scientific research). Further, many phoneticians are, in fact, **not** aware of, or particularly interested in, the practical needs of the clinic. Their goals are more or less exclusively involved with the elucidation of the normal speech communication processes. Such goals are warranted in and of themselves and require no justification beyond that of being an important part of man's attempt to understand himself. Nevertheless, such goals may not provide especially fertile ground for interaction between the clinic and the laboratory.

Thus we are faced with a situation in which, on the one hand, a good deal of research is being accomplished which may be potentially very useful but which is not being used or even tested clinically, largely because the possible users are either unaware of it or distrustful of it; and, on the other hand, the needs of the clinician are not being systematically attacked because the clinician has not been particularly effective in making those needs known, and because the phonetician has not been particularly eager to seek out those needs or to adapt his findings and make them more readily usable.

It is perhaps not so much that we are not speaking to the issues as it is that we are often not speaking very effectively to each other. It will be the purpose of this chapter to discuss certain relationships, or possible relationships, between acoustic phonetics and speech pathology. The basic theses will be the truth of Jakobson's statement that what we **perceive** is what we **hear** and what we **hear** is an acoustic wave produced by a speaker; that to the extent that perturbations in the acoustic wave are perceived as being somehow different or abnormal, a speech pathology can be said to exist; and that accurate description, prediction, and control are essential to an understanding of both normal and abnormal speech production.

Section I provides a general background and rationale for some more specific approaches to these issues.

I. A GENERAL BACKGROUND AND RATIONALE

Viewed in its simplest terms, speech production is that set of processes by which we encode a thought or linguistic concept into an açoustic wave. At the same simplistic level, speech perception is the decoding of an acoustic wave into a linguistically relevant message. This is the basis for a highly simplified speech chain (Fig. 1). The block diagram of Fig. 1 is of value in graphically demonstrating the interdependent character of the speech communication act and the central role of the acoustic wave. It shows the same encoded acoustic wave as the result, or output, of one set of processes and the raw material, or input, for another set of processes. Under such conditions, any error in the first set of processes can be assumed to result in a perturbation of the acoustic wave, relative to the acoustic output of a nonerror condition. If the second set of processes is tuned finely enough to detect the perturbation, the ultimate decoding of

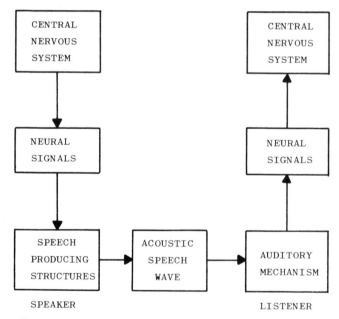

Figure 1.   Highly simplified block diagram of the speech chain.

the signal will result in a perceptual judgment ranging from a classification of the acoustic wave as mildly disordered to completely unintelligible.

Keeping in mind the dangers of relying too heavily on black boxes of any kind, let us increase the complexity of our speech chain somewhat, as shown in the diagram of Fig. 2. Here the Central Nervous System black box of Fig. 1 has been replaced by a complicated set of boxes which are intended to represent some sort of generative grammar (Chomsky & Halle, 1968). In addition, a Motor Control Component has been included to illustrate the need for a set of rules to act upon, and control, the output of a grammar (see also Allen, 1973; Kent, Carney, & Severeid, 1974). Rule boxes, such as the Motor Control Component or the more familiar Phonological Component (Chomsky & Halle, 1968), can, of course, be logically assumed to exist at many other locations in a chain such as that shown in Fig. 2, e.g., Fant's (1970) classical studies of relationships between vocal tract shapes and the acoustic wave. However, none of these rule boxes is going to be of much aid to our understanding until we have been able to specify the rules contained within them with sufficient accuracy to allow prediction of the output of the box. Phoneticians are attempting to accomplish just such rule specification and testing. These efforts are so numerous and varied that providing even a representative list would be beyond the scope of this chapter. Some examples, however, are: Abbs (1973), Allen (1973), Fant (1970), Hughes

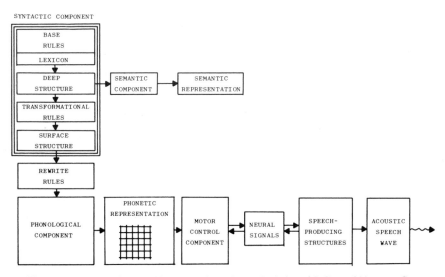

Figure 2. Block diagram of speaker side of speech chain, with Central Nervous System of Fig. 1 replaced by a set of black boxes representing a generative grammar with a Motor Control Component added.

and Abbs (1976), Kent *et al.* (1974), Klatt (1975), Lindblom, Lubker, and McAllister (1977a), Lindblom, Lubker, and Gay (in press), and MacNeilage (1970), to name only a very few. These and many other efforts are steadily increasing our ability to predict the functioning of the processes depicted in Fig. 2.

However, it will be noted that Fig. 2 is actually only half of Fig. 1. The entire listener process has been excluded from Fig. 2. Great complexity and a number of rule boxes are also inherent in the listener process; for example, there is some set of not yet fully specified neurophysiological rules to describe and predict the transduction of acoustic waves entering the external ear into some neural space–time pattern along the eighth cranial (vestibulocochlear) nerve. Appropriate rules must be applied to determine which patterns represent speech acoustic waves and which represent nonspeech acoustic waves. The speech patterns must then be directed through a set of grammatical processes similar to, if not actually identical to, those processes depicted in Fig. 2. More specifically, it must be assumed that some set of phonological rules is applied perceptually at an essentially prelinguistic level and that, finally, sets of linguistic rules are applied to allow the decoding or the establishment of a sound-to-meaning correspondence. We could postulate, then, a chain similar to that given in Fig. 3. It must be made clear that neither the absolute correctness nor the completeness of the model described in Fig. 3 is at issue in this discussion. Perhaps the arrows do not proceed in precisely this way during the production and perception of speech. Perhaps at least some aspects of perception involve a lower order link with the production channel. Perhaps additional rule boxes or decision points could be included. And perhaps such possibilities might even be probabilities. However, Fig. 3 is intended to emphasize only three points important to this discussion: (1) specification of the rules that control the various signal transductions is essential to an understanding and a prediction of the processes of production and perception; (2) structural damage, interference with neural transmission, or incomplete/in-error rule systems will result in either (a) an acoustic signal which is perturbed from the norm, or (b) the faulty perception of a normal acoustic wave; and (3) the acoustic wave is the central factor common to both production and perception.

Emphasis of these three points underscores once more the importance of measurement and prediction as well as the close relationship between knowledge of the normal processes and the understanding of deviations in those processes. Stated somewhat differently, disordered speech production is being defined within the framework of normal speech production, and such a definition stresses (a) the close relationship between the two, and (b) the fact that measurement and prediction of rules and systems are

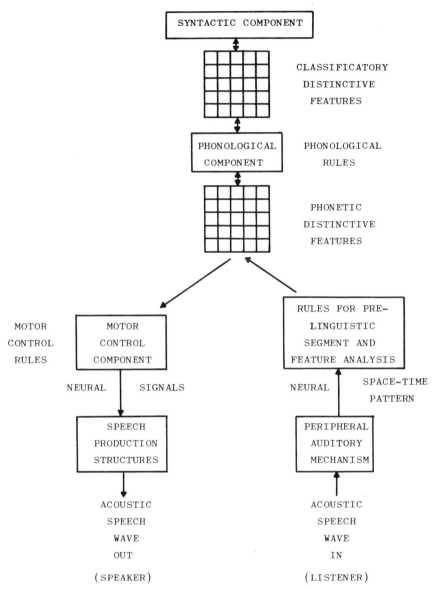

Figure 3. Block diagram of speech chain. See text for explanation.

essential to the successful exploitation of that relationship. These three points will now be discussed in somewhat more detail.

First, it is stated that specification of the rules that control the various signal transductions is essential to an understanding and to a successful prediction of the processes of speech production and perception. This is, in itself, very demanding. In addition to rule specification, we must also be able to specify the segment sizes upon which the rules act and the dimensions (or features) with which the rules operate. That is, two classical problems which have long existed in the study of phonological and motor control components are: (a) the specification of segment size (i.e., phoneme, syllable, syntagma, etc.) and (b) a selection of the appropriate feature (dimension) system or, perhaps more basically, a discovery of the proper features. Obviously, these problems are crucial to the development of the rule systems governing the signal transductions since a solution to them dictates the language with which the rules will operate. And just as obviously, the features or dimensions are of a complex, or multidimensional, nature and exist at each of the several levels in the system, i.e., at the phonological component, the motor control component, and so on. In addition, it is very likely that whatever the most appropriate feature or dimension system is, it will have different values or characteristics at the different levels in the system. That is, the rules may act upon different sized segments at different levels, they may be applied to different features (dimensions) at different levels, and any given feature may vary in description or specification or in relative weight from level to level.

Take as an example the feature, or dimension, of nasality. We might easily think of nasality as being of a binary character at the output of the phonological component in Fig. 3. That is, at some rather high level the speech production system specifies that a given segment is to be either nasal or nonnasal. We can speak, then, of (+)- or (−)nasal. We might further assume that this feature, along with others in the feature system, would be applied to phoneme-sized segments at this level. For example, at this level all three elements in the word *bat* would be assigned the feature (−)nasal, while in the word *man* we might assume the phonemes would be assigned (+) (−) (+) with regard to the feature nasal. However, as these commands moved through the motor control component of Fig. 3, we would expect that the motor control rules would have to be n-ary in nature in order to deal with the nasality feature. This expectation arises from the fact that the amount of velopharyngeal opening required to produce nasality (or the amount of closure required to insure (−)nasal) has been shown to be a variable, dependent upon such factors as tongue height, jaw opening, and nasal resistance (House & Stevens, 1956; Lubker & Moll, 1965; Warren, Duany, & Fischer, 1969; Warren & Ryon,

1967). Clearly, rules at the motor control level could not operate in a binary manner to accomplish the higher level requirement of nasality. Further, at the acoustic level the vowel /æ/ in *man* could no longer be (−)nasal; coarticulation rules would have made it (+)nasal. (Although such a conversion could have been made in the phonological component, it remains that at some point a conversion was made from (−)nasal to (+)nasal.) Indeed, listeners would regard that vowel as sounding unnatural in the environment /m_n/ if it were somehow to be produced as (−)nasal. This discussion could be extended considerably and is used here only as an example of the complexity of the rules, segments, and features (dimensions) and of their possible variability from level to level. Although only one feature was used in this example, it should be remembered that we are dealing with a multidimensional feature system.

As already indicated, it is precisely these complexities and variabilities that modern phoneticians are attempting to solve. Their goal is to model the total system with sufficient accuracy to permit a reasonable prediction of its behavior and output.

The second point made with regard to Fig. 3 was that any structural damage, interference with neural transmission, or incomplete/in-error rule systems will result in either (a) an acoustic signal which is perturbed from the norm, or (b) the faulty perception of a normal acoustic wave. Clearly, any fault in the transmission or transduction systems can potentially result in the disruption of the normal flow and operation of rules, and, if the severity of the disruption is sufficient, a speech or hearing disorder will result. Much of the preceding discussion has been devoted to describing the need for precise measurement, evaluation, and comparison in order to evaluate the severity of any such disruption.

The third major point of Fig. 3 is that the acoustic wave is central and common to both production and perception. It can be argued that insofar as speech and its disorders are concerned, any disruption on the production side of the chain that cannot be detected as a perturbation in the resultant acoustic wave form is really of little or no clinical concern. Taken further, this line of reasoning suggests that in order for any perturbation in the acoustic wave to be of concern, it must be great enough, or the perception system must be tuned finely enough, for listeners to detect it. The only clear exception to this would be in the very early stages of a progressive disorder, i.e., so that it is not yet perceptually detectable (an issue to which we will return in Section II,C).

With all this in mind, let me now return to the clinical situation and some of its basic constituent elements. Generally speaking, the first step in the clinic is diagnosis: a judgment of what it is that is wrong. Such a judgment requires more than a simple description of whatever physical or physiological anomalies might exist as causes of the disorder, e.g., an unrepaired cleft of the palate or an early stage of parkinsonism. It is well accepted that proper diagnosis should not pigeonhole patients but rather treat them as individual cases. As such, diagnosis requires a detailed and accurate description of what the speaker is doing when she speaks, what types of compensatory behavior she may have developed, and a description of the acoustic/perceptual results of her speaking behaviors. For such a broad view, a diagnosis must provide a statement of how this speaker's behavior results in something that is different from the normal speaker, and just **how** different that result actually is. This, in turn, results in a more effective prognosis. Prognosis amounts to an estimation of how difficult and lengthy a task it will be to modify the individual's speech behavior to the extent that listeners will judge her acoustic speech wave to be acceptable, if not normal. Such an estimation is facilitated by measurement and by a zero-point or bench-mark against which measurement is made. Central to both diagnosis and prognosis is a sufficiently detailed and accurate understanding of the normal system to allow prediction of the severity effect or severity criterion of any given system breakdown. With regard to the concept of severity criterion, consider that a normal bench-mark against which a pathological speaker is to be compared must exist in a multidimensional space, as implied by the discussion of rules, segments, and features. Any definition of normal must include a number of dimensions in order to be complete enough to be of any real value. Although, as discussed, segmentation is not a problem that has been completely solved at all levels of the system, normal speech is typically described in terms of specific phonemes. A description of any specific phoneme demands multidimensionality, as demonstrated by the many feature systems that have been proposed (e.g., Chomsky & Halle, 1968; Jakobson *et al.*, 1951). In addition, a number of prosodic features are essential to the description of speech, thus adding to the dimensionality. So, any specific normally produced speech segment could be described by locating it in a multidimensional (feature) space. In addition, any given disorder could be profitably viewed by describing how far away, in terms of such a space, the disordered utterances are from the normal ones. The greater the distance in the space, the greater the severity criterion, although, of course, some of the features (dimensions) would be expected to be of more importance to perception than would others, and therefore some type of weighting system would have to be applied. I will return to this discussion, but, for the moment, it should be clear that both diagnosis and prognosis would be facilitated by the type of precision that could be provided by statements regarding the severity of disorders within multidimensional frameworks.

Given accurate, complete diagnostic/prognostic statements, the next step is the planning of the actual program of therapy appropriate to the diagnosis. This carries with it the need for evaluation of results as the patient is taken through the planned therapy program. Again, this task seems most logically approached via evaluation in terms of a normal bench-mark: by imposing the requirement of being able to **define** or locate the normal speech condition, by being capable of **comparing** the pathological speech against it, by being able to **predict** the outcome of efforts to move the speaker toward the normal condition, and by being capable of **plotting** the actual movement as therapy progresses.

I have taken the view in this chapter that at any given level in the chain of events depicted in Fig. 3, description must be in terms of sets of rules acting upon certain temporal segments via certain sets of features. After such descriptions have been made, both explanation and prediction of output become possible. I have also taken the view that the rules, segments, and features are not likely to be precisely the same from level to level within the total system. Nevertheless, the goal of modern phonetics is the specification of these rules, segments, and features at the various levels in order to explain and predict the output. Finally, I have presented the view that diagnosis, prognosis, and evaluation of therapy would be most accurately and efficiently accomplished through the development of severity criteria statements comparing pathological to normal speech in terms of the multidimensional spaces of the features and segments.

Clearly, it is possible to develop such statements of severity criteria at a number of levels in the system. Just as clearly, it is important and necessary that we do so. And, indeed, muscle function, structural movement (including such parameters as acceleration and velocity), air flows and pressures, and the like are being investigated in both normal and pathological speech in a number of laboratories around the world. Such work is also being carried out in our own laboratory here in Stockholm, and I am thus firmly committed to its importance.

Such research, however, usually requires sophisticated and delicate equipment which can be rather expensive: electromyography techniques, movement transducing devices, cinefluorographic equipment, flow meters and pressure transducers, not to mention racks of signal-modifying devices such as amplifiers, filters, and the like. There is no doubt of the value of and the absolute **need** for the data which research involving such techniques and equipment can provide. But it must just as readily be admitted that bench-marks within frameworks of the type that would result from such research are, in fact, of little practical, immediate diagnostic, prognostic, or evaluative value to a **typical** speech clinic. It is an unfortunate fact that the vast majority of clinics simply do not have any direct or easy access to such large and well-equipped laboratories. They are therefore unable to obtain data on their patients which would allow them to develop the severity criteria relative to the normal bench-marks, regardless of how valuable or desirable such criteria might be. Most clinics are located in public schools, small hospitals, or universities not outfitted with modern phonetics laboratories, and thus just do not have electromyographic, cinefluorographic, aerodynamic, or movement-transducing equipment at hand. While the potential value of these data for the future and their immediate value for those clinical cases in the vicinity of such a laboratory cannot be questioned, their direct practical value to the vast majority of clinical settings is highly limited.

However, there remains the common factor of the output and input signal, which is readily available for easy sampling: the acoustic speech wave. And, there exists in virtually every speech clinic and speech room a tape recorder capable of faithfully sampling that acoustic wave.

It thus seems altogether reasonable to suggest that aspects of the acoustic wave might be developed to meet the demands of precise severity criteria for providing diagnosis, prognosis, and therapy evaluation. The remainder of this chapter will be devoted to a discussion of the potential for acoustic bases to clinical evaluations.

II. ACOUSTIC PHONETICS AND THE CLINIC: SOME SUGGESTIONS

Before beginning this section it is perhaps wise to summarize briefly the preceding pages. If it were possible to stop the flow of events from the central nervous system out to the acoustic speech wave at any point along the way, then the suddenly produced static condition would require multidimensional terms to describe it. For example, if one were to stop the flow at the output of the phonological component, a good description of the static event at that point might be obtained via a phonetic distinctive feature matrix as described by Chomsky and Halle (1968). Thus, we would have phonemic segments, with each segment described by a set of features.

Similar descriptions of the static result of stopped flow could be made at several points: e.g., at the syntactic surface structure, at the output of the motor control component, at the articulatory realization of the motor control, or at the acoustic wave itself. However, at any point at which one stopped the flow, it might be expected that the particular segments and the particular feature sets (and their weights) would be, at least to some extent, unique to that level.

Thus is implied a straightforward (although quite difficult) descriptive research need for the phonetician: answering the questions (a) what are the segments? and (b) what are the features? (and their weights) at any given level. However, although this research need is important, there is another which is even more important. The entire discussion has been based on the assumption that we are considering a flow process, one that changes from level to level. And so, there must be sets of rules (linguistic, neurophysiologic, acoustic, mathematical) which serve to govern that flow and execute those changes. The discovery of these control–rule systems is an essential research goal, since it is only through a knowledge of these rule systems that we will be able to explain and predict the function and behavior of the total language and speech generating system.

So, two research goals of phonetics are the development of the control–rule systems and the definition of the segments and features upon which the rules act. I have argued that, given at least a partial solution to such research problems, considered at any given level a particular segment could be efficiently and accurately described and related to other segments by locating it in some type of a multidimensional reference space.

It would be a logical consequence of this reasoning to argue further that a segment which was somehow in-error could also best be described by locating it in reference to the normal bench-marks of the nonerror segments. It is also logical to suggest that such an operation would have evident advantages with regard to diagnosis, prognosis, therapy planning, and therapy evaluation via the numerical specification of speech behaviors and alterations in them.

All of this is predicated on the assumption that such measures or severity criteria could, in fact, be realistically developed at the various levels in the speech chain. As pointed out, a great deal of research is being accomplished which is intended to (1) provide data and hypotheses relevant to the two phonetics research goals stated, and/or (2) either implicitly or explicitly attempt to describe how, and to what extent, the pathological speaker differs from the normal speaker at the several levels in the speech chain.

I have not dwelt upon the importance of such research because I feel that its value is self-evident. To know the motor control rules and to understand their operation, for example, is an essential requirement to understanding the entire production system and many of its disorders. Segments, features, rule systems, and departures from normal as investigated via electromyography, cinefluorography, movement transduction, aerodynamics, and so on are providing, and will continue to provide, avenues toward just the types of laboratory–clinic interaction I have described. That seems clear; but, I have argued, it is equally clear that such work is dependent upon very expensive and complex instrumentation which is limited to a very few well-equipped university laboratories. Thus, however important it is that such work continues, relatively very few speech-disordered individuals and their clinicians are able to derive an immediate, everyday clinical **use** from these efforts.

However, one level—the end product of the production system and the raw material of the perception system—is easily accessible. A tape recorder, available to any speech clinician, is all that is needed to sample the acoustic speech wave. Thus, an individual's speech behavior may be recorded and the recording sent to a laboratory where specifically requested analyses can be·made. It should be indicated that all of this is proposed as a tool for the clinician: an aid to improve the clinician's ability to describe objectively a speaker's behavior and the changes in that behavior during therapy.

And so, I have argued that from the point of view of everyday clinical work, acoustical analyses offer potentially rich sources of aid. I have stated this several times and in several ways and I feel that it is a clear and reasonable approach. Unfortunately, actually **making** the approach is more difficult than stating it or providing a rationale for it.

Although the normal acoustic speech wave has received intensive scrutiny for several decades, relatively little use has been made of acoustic analyses as clinical tools. Kent (1976, p. 442), in an excellent tutorial report on the use of acoustic studies in speech developmental disorders, states: "The existing data on the acoustic characteristics of children's speech are all too often sketchy in nature, but they hold the promise of sensitive methods for the study of speech maturation and developmental disorders." What I shall attempt to do now is suggest some potential means for fulfilling the promise suggested by Kent in the face of the sketchiness of existing clinically oriented acoustic data. I shall examine three areas: (1) the recent attempts at multidimensional analyses of speech and perception; (2) a measure of perceptual contrast; and (3) what amounts to feature comparison efforts. The discussion will not be exhaustive; hopefully it will be suggestive.

A. Multidimensional Analyses of Speech

Proponents of multidimensional scaling techniques for use in speech production and perception research contend that they offer a way to determine the psychological reality of perceptual dimensions. They contend, for example, that the techniques allow us to determine which aspects of the stimulus signal a listener actually uses to decide that a given vowel is that particular vowel and that it differs to a greater or lesser extent from other vowels. In a typical experiment on vowel perception, the following steps would occur: (1) listeners are asked to provide similarity or dissimilarity judgments of vowels (2) from which a confusion matrix of the type used by Miller and Nicely (1955) is developed. (3) The confusion data are then used as input to a multidimensional scaling program (4) which selects the dimensions the listeners used to make their similarity (or dissimilarity) judgments. Thus a psychologically real set of perceptual dimensions in a multidimensional space is developed. (5) An important fifth step remains, that of naming the dimensions.

It is easy enough to see that if such techniques do allow the experimenter to select the psychologically real dimensions of the stimulus, then they offer a powerful tool for both clinical and basic research in speech. It is also easy to see that many problems can be raised. This section will discuss some of these problems.

Johnson (1946) presented a lucid discussion of the concept of perception as an abstraction from reality. Indeed, a decision as to vowel quality, or consonant identity, or the wrongness of an utterance involves some central nervous system process: the development of a mental representation of that vowel or consonant or disordered utterance which must be an abstraction of the stimulus that generated it. To discuss the psychological reality of certain dimensions, one must first ask from what reality the dimensions are to be selected; one must ask what is being abstracted. There are several possibilities. One of these, the motor commands underlying the articulatory gestures, seems a highly unlikely choice since it has been well established that the same sounds can be produced by a rather wide variety of gestures (see, e.g., MacNeilage's, 1972, discussion). At least two other general possibilities remain: some aspect of the articulatory activity or some aspect of the acoustic wave. In the case of the former, it can be argued that there is a vocal tract area function target for vowels, which speakers strive to reach by whatever means possible, given variations in rate, stress, and so on. That target becomes the prime reality of any production/perception scheme. Alternately, it can be argued that it is important to produce specific characteristics in the acoustic wave form by whatever movements and vocal tract shapes are needed. Examples at the feature level of these two views are provided by the distinctive feature systems proposed by Jakobson *et al.* (1961) and by Chomsky and Halle (1968). As is well known, the features of Jakobson *et al.* are largely acoustic in nature, while those of Chomsky and Halle depend more upon articulatory characteristics. I do not intend to attempt to resolve the issue here, but it must be clear that whatever choice an experimenter makes will affect his labeling of the dimensions in step five. Arguments favoring the acoustic signal as the source of abstracting have been presented by Terbeek (1977), while Singh, Woods, and Becker (1972) have presented data attempting to select the best of four feature systems with regard to consonant perception. Unfortunately in the study of Singh *et al.* only articulatory-based systems were examined.

A second basic problem concerns the method to be used in obtaining the listener judgments of similarity or dissimilarity. From among a number of possible choices, three methods are most common: judgments on equal appearing interval scales, direct magnitude estimations, and some form of ABX or triadic comparisons. Although it seems clear from arguments presented by Terbeek (1977) and Singh *et al.* (1972) that the method selected can influence the end results of the experiment, which method is actually best under all conditions does not seem to be conspicuously clear.

Third, it must be decided which multidimensional scaling technique will be used. Torgerson (1958) and Kruskal (1964) described the more traditional methods. However, the great majority of work being published in speech production and perception makes use of more modern techniques developed independently at Bell Telephone Laboratories by Carroll and Chang (1970) and at UCLA by Harshman (1970). The Carroll and Chang method is generally referred to as INDSCAL and the Harshman method is called PARAFAC. The INDSCAL system is much more common in the literature, but Terbeek (1977) describes the two systems as being essentially identical. The INDSCAL and PARAFAC methods are intended to circumvent certain problems of the more traditional techniques, and the extent to which they have been used suggests that at least some experimenters believe that they have been successful. Carroll and Chang (1970, p. 285), for example, state: "If the model we postulate is true, then these uniquely determined coordinate axes will correspond to meaningful psychological dimensions in a very strong sense (as postulated they correspond to fundamental sensory, perceptual or judgmental processes that vary in salience, or strength of effect on perception, across individuals."

A fourth problem is to select the number of dimensions with which to make the analysis. Again, a number of techniques are available which allow the selection of an optimal number of dimensions to describe the data. Terbeek (1977) provides a good discussion of this problem. Although an unequivocal decision seems difficult to make, the decision methods appear to provide the means for a reasonably reliable and hopefully a valid choice.

Having made decisions on these problems, the experimenter is next faced with the output of the scaling program. This will amount to the particular vowels, consonants, or disordered utterances under examination arrayed as along a continuum on each of the several dimensions selected for analysis. The experimenter must then examine the array of samples along each dimension and attempt to obtain groupings that can be related to some aspect of the input stimuli (i.e., as discussed, some aspect of the articulatory behavior or some aspect of the acoustic wave). For example, if, in a study of American English vowels, a given dimension showed that the vowels /i, I, e, ɛ, æ/ were clustered at one end of the scale and the vowels /u, U, o, ɔ/ were clustered at the other end, and if one were working with the notion of abstracting from articulatory features, then that dimension might logically be referred to as a front–back dimension. It might further be assumed that the feature frontness–backness was an important aspect of vowel perception since listeners had used it in a definite way in making their similarity judgments. Assuming that the experimenter has analyzed his data to provide several additional dimensions, it would now be possible for him to locate the vowels of American English in a multidimensional space. The preceding discussions show, however, that the space and the locations of the items in it are, to at least some extent, shaped by the decisions and definitions made by the experimenter. If such definitions and decisions can be made in a reasonable, logical, and consistent manner, then it may be possible to make the valid claim that certain physical dimensions may be given psychological reality. The work by Carroll and Chang (1970) and the discussions by Terbeek (1977) seem quite convincing, but much more work is required to establish firmly the validity of the notion.

There has been a considerable amount of research published which has used multidimensional scaling techniques in the study of normal speech production/perception. For example, Hanson (1967) published an extensive study of perceptual distance in Swedish vowels using, for the most part, a three-dimensional vowel space. Pols, van der Kamp, and Plomp (1969) reported multidimensional analyses of Dutch vowels, also using a three-dimensional analysis. Singh and Woods (1971) reported data on American English vowels using, although somewhat arbitrarily, a three-dimensional space. Mohr and Wang (1968) studied American English vowels, but set out to test specifically the efficiency of five binary distinctive features selected a priori. Singh et al. (1972) have reported on 22 English consonants. This study is of additional interest because it examines several methods used to obtain similarity judgments and also evaluates four different feature systems in terms of the psychological reality of their constituent features. Wilson and Bond (1977) reported four salient dimensions in their study of American English vowels produced in varying contexts. And Terbeek (1977) provided an overview of the methods and problems before presenting his own quite detailed cross-language investigation of vowel perception in five languages (English, Thai, Turkish, German, and Swedish).

Thus, without going into detail, it would seem that a number of investigators have attempted to analyze the vowels and consonants of various languages in an attempt to determine the psychologically real dimensions which listeners use in perceiving them. Stated somewhat differently, they have attempted to locate vowels and consonants in multidimensional spaces. To the extent that these attempts have been successful, or valid, significant progress would seem to have been taken toward implementing the suggestions made in the preceding sections of this chapter.

To that end it would seem reasonable to attempt also to place pathological speech into similar multidimensional spaces. Far fewer attempts of this type have been made. Perhaps clinical researchers are waiting for more clear and definite results on normal speech. Perhaps the method itself needs more evaluation and testing. In any case, less work has been done with multidimensional scaling techniques on pathological speech. Only two will be mentioned here. One, by Danhauer and Singh (1975), studied the perceptual dimensions used by hard-of-hearing and deaf persons in their perception of vowels. The other, by Murry, Singh, and Sargent (1977), studied the perceptual features used by listeners in evaluating harsh voice quality. This later study found a total of five features which, taken together, explained 48% of the variance in the data. Even with this rather low value the authors were able to conclude that: "These strengths of the underlying dimensions of voice may indicate that multi-dimensional scaling will be a valuable tool in diagnosing voice abnormalities" (p. 1635).

Perhaps so. At least the technique offers the possibility of making precisely the types of diagnoses, prognoses, and therapy evaluations which were suggested earlier in this chapter. However, if the method is ultimately shown to be truly valid and applicable, a good deal more testing and refinement will be needed before it can actually be put to easy, everyday use. Such testing is surely warranted. More carefully done, large-scale, multilanguage research on normal populations is required (e.g., the work of Terbeek, 1977). Similar efforts, working with more speech sounds as well as with abnormal speech sounds, would seem appropriate. The potential value of the method, should it be successfully developed, would surely be worth the effort.

B. The Notion of Perceptual Contrast

This section is somewhat more theoretical, while remaining within the general concept of multidimensional articulatory and acoustic spaces. It is easy enough to conceive of such spaces if one simply thinks of the two-dimensional vowel spaces provided by plotting high–low vs front–back tongue position, or by plotting the first formant (F_1) against the second formant (F_2). Examples of such plots are shown in Figs. 4 and 5. If one adds a third dimension, for example, the third formant (F_3) to Fig. 5, then a multidimensional plot like that shown in Fig. 6 is generated. It can also be easily conceived that such spaces must have certain boundary conditions which are imposed by the physical limitations of the system (see Lindblom, 1972, for a more detailed discussion of this concept). For example, a high vowel can only be so high before it becomes a stop consonant, and a low vowel can only be so low before the tongue/jaw complex is simply unable to lower any further. Thus, there is a space, articulatory or acoustic (depending upon the viewpoint), which has a certain physical boundary, which is very probably a language universal. Movement and acoustic variability within such spaces are theoretically definable and probably are (or become during the language learning process) language specific.

Now, the notion of **perceptual contrast** is an old one in phonology. It has often been coupled with another notion, that of **least effort**, in the argu-

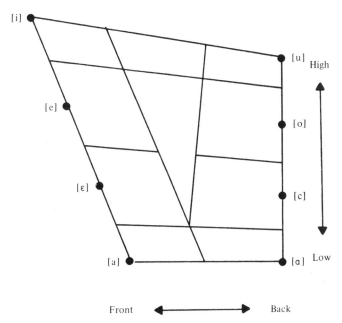

Figure 4. Vowel diagram produced with front–back vs high–low tongue positions as the controlling variables.

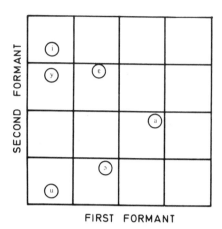

Figure 5. Vowel diagram produced with F_1 vs F_2 as the controlling variables.

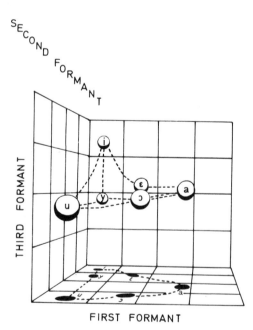

Figure 6. Three-dimensional vowel diagram produced by adding F_3 to the diagram of Fig. 5.

ment that speakers will exert only that amount of effort required to provide sufficient contrast for communication to be effective. That is, there is a conflict between the listener's need for as much perceptual contrast as possible and the speaker's need for maximal ease of articulation. As appealing as such notions might be, they have never had much predictive or explanatory value simply because they have never been quantified. [This issue has been discussed extensively and effectively by Lindblom (1972, 1975).]

If such quantification were available, it could then be argued that the speech output of individuals with speech disorders could profitably be viewed in terms of the principle of perceptual contrast. That is, either one or more of the sounds produced by such a speaker are so muddled that they cannot be contrasted accurately with other sounds in the speaker's space and are therefore confused with those other sounds; or one or more of the sounds are produced in such a bizarre and unusual manner that they will be completely inappropriate to normal space. This view is obviously similar to the view expressed in the discussion of multidimensional scaling. As will be seen, however, a somewhat different approach will be used.

It would seem that the first question which must be asked is whether a notion such as perceptual contrast can, in fact, be quantified. My colleague Lindblom has discussed this problem in detail (1972, 1975).

Lindblom approached this question by first using confusion data on Dutch vowels (Klein, Plomp, & Pols, 1970; Pols, Tromp, & Plomp, 1973) coupled with a spectrum-based acoustic distance measure proposed by Plomp (1976). Plomp has proposed a model of the peripheral auditory process which views that process as a filter bank consisting of one-third octave band filters. For each input stimulus an output spectrum, based on passage through such a filter bank, can be obtained. An output spectrum can simply be thought of as a table of output sound pressure levels (SPLs) in decibels, with a level specification for each stimulus i and a third-octave frequency band n, so that any such level measurement would be denoted as $L_{i,n}$.

Given such an output for any input stimulus to the auditory system, Plomp next devised a procedure to supply a single number to describe the difference between any two input stimulus spectra; that is, to generate a single number to describe the perceived difference between two such spectra as are exemplified in Fig. 7. There are at least two possible approaches to this problem. One is very similar to the multidimensional scaling methods which have been discussed. In that approach, the m different frequency bands for a particular stimulus are seen as the coordinates of a single point in a multidimensional space with m dimensions.

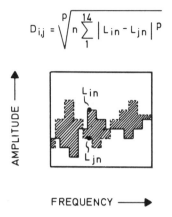

Figure 7. Comparison of two acoustic spectra after having been passed through the one-third-octave band filter. See text for discussion.

Thus different stimuli are represented as different points in that space. Under these conditions a listener's dissimilarity judgment might be modeled by considering the linear (Euclidean) distance between the two points for the stimuli in question. A second approach can also be considered. It is derived from the work of Zwicker and Scharf (1965) demonstrating that the loudness of a complex tone can be quite accurately predicted as the sum of the contributions of the different frequency bands in the analysis. Plomp therefore hypothesized that the perceptual distance between any two stimuli might be considered as the sum of the differences between the stimuli for each band of the one-third-octave filter analysis. That is, the dissimilarity would be determined by the areas **between** the two spectral curves, shown graphically as the shaded area in the output curves of Fig. 7. A mathematical statement can describe both of these approaches:

$$D_{i,j} = \sqrt[p]{\sum_{n=1}^{m} |L_{i,n} - L_{j,n}|^p} \tag{1}$$

where:

$D_{i,j}$ = the acoustic distance between two stimuli i and j
$L_{i,n}$ = the SPL of the stimulus i in the nth frequency band
$L_{j,n}$ = the SPL of the stimulus j in the nth frequency band
m = the total number of frequency bands

If p is set to equal 2, we will have the formula for a Euclidean distance, as in the first approach. If p is equal to 1, we would have the second model in which the summed areas between the two spectra are the determinants of the perceived distance. Plomp calculated correlation coefficients between listeners' dissimilarity estimates and the spectrum-based distance computations based upon a variety of values for p. While none of the correlations was lower than .80, the coefficient of 2 showed a somewhat better relationship between dissimilarity judgments and the spectrum-based distances, thus suggesting rather strongly that vowel quality is a multidimensional attribute of sound, and perceived differences in quality are related to the differences in auditory spectral representations.

Lindblom tested this spectrum-based acoustic distance measure by using it in conjunction with the data referred to on confusions in the perception of Dutch vowels. This test is shown in Fig. 8, which demonstrates a lawful relationship between the number of confusions and the spectrum-based acoustic distance measure. It would thus appear that Lindblom has, at the very least, supplied a testable numerical definition of the notion of perceptual contrast. [Work by Shepard (1972) is very relevant here but discussion of it will be deferred to Section II,C.]

The next question would be, can a clinical application be made of such a definition of perceptual contrast. We have recently made an attempt to do so (Lindblom, Lubker, & Pauli, 1977b) and the results are, I think, provocative. In this research we considered the problem of hypernasality and sought a formal procedure whose input would consist of speech samples from a given speaker and whose output would be related to the com-

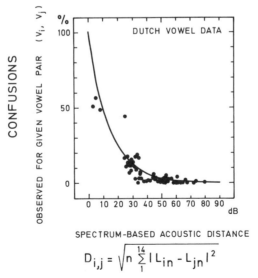

$$D_{i,j} = \sqrt{n \sum_{1}^{14} |L_{in} - L_{jn}|^2}$$

Figure 8. Percentage confusions observed for a given vowel pair plotted as a function of spectrum-based acoustic distance.

municative efficiency of the samples under analysis. No attempt was made to predict how nasal a sample sounds to a listener; i.e., we did not attempt to determine the acoustic correlates of the perceptual judgments of nasality. Instead, the measure sought was intended to describe certain functional aspects of speech utterances by giving an indication of how easily speech segments will be kept apart by a listener. Such a measure would in no way be limited to the evaluation of hypernasality but could be used with any class of speech segments whose spectral characteristics serve as perceptual cues for phonemic distinctions within that class.

Given this procedure to provide a single number related to the probability that a listener will confuse any two vowels (i.e., any pair of spectral representations) and given that this procedure was to be used in the evaluation of hypernasality, two points must be made about nasality in general and nasalized vowels in particular.

First, it can be shown that in any vowel system containing both nasal and oral vowels, there will be fewer nasal than oral vowels. Linguists have interpreted this to indicate that nasal vowels are less perceptually distinct than oral ones and are therefore less favored in vowel systems.

Second, studies showing the effect of nasal coupling on vowel spectra (Fant, 1970; Fujimura & Lindquist, 1971; House & Stevens, 1956) have demonstrated characteristically complicated interactions of resonances and antiresonances. One of these characteristics is that the first formant bandwidth tends to be increased and its center of gravity tends to be shifted upward in frequency. A result of this characteristic is that if one views the spectral envelopes of a set of nonnasalized vowels and also a set of their nasalized counterparts, the vowels in the nasalized set bear a very considerable visual similarity to one another, while the members of the nonnasal set are quite distinct.

These two observations lead quite naturally to the idea of testing hypernasality via the procedure available for determining spectrum-based acoustic distance. We did so under two different conditions. Figure 9 shows the results of applying Eq. (1) to the spectral envelopes of vowels produced with and without nasal coupling. The data for this figure are from House and Stevens (1956), and the amount of nasal coupling is 3.72 cm^2. The acoustic distance, computed with Eq. (1), for nasalized vowel pairs is given on the y axis and for nonnasal pairs on the x axis. As can be seen, all but one of the vowel pairs falls below the line of identity, meaning that in all but one pair the x (nonnasal) value was larger than the y (nasal) value. This, in turn, can be interpreted to mean that, with only one exception, the acoustic distance between any two vowels is greater when the vowels are produced without nasal coupling. Thus, at least for the

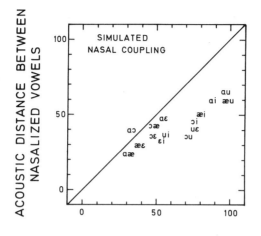

Figure 9. Result of applying Eq. (1) to simulated vowels with and without nasal coupling (3.72 cm² coupling). Nasalized vowel pairs are on the y axis and nonnasalized pairs on the x axis.

data of House and Stevens, nasal vowels are less distinct than oral vowels.

Figure 10 shows a second application of Eq. (1). In this we used recorded samples of a young adult male speaker with a cleft palate producing the words *see, yet, bath, awe, full,* and *tooth,* both with and without a palatal obturator in position. Spectral analysis was done at the midpoint of the vowels and Eq. (1) was applied to the two sets (with and without obturator) of vowel spectra. The spectrum-based acoustic distance for the condition without obturator is plotted along the ordinate and the productions with obturator along the abscissa. Again, all but one of the vowel pairs fall below the line of identity, thus leading to the conclusion that vowels produced without the obturator were less distinct than those produced with the obturator. It should be noted that a series of informal listening tests corroborated these observations.

Thus, the notion of *perceptual contrast* would appear to have both theoretical and experimental implications for the speech clinic. Certainly, the experimental aspect is incomplete, and larger scale studies with clinical populations as well as the development of a procedure based not only upon vowels but also upon the spectral analysis of sentence length segments would be necessary. Nevertheless, it is clearly quite possible, as

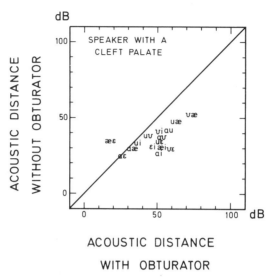

Figure 10. Results of applying Eq. (1) to American English vowels spoken by a patient with a cleft palate without (*y* axis) and with (*x* axis) his palatal obturator.

has been discussed (Lindblom *et al.*, 1977b), to program a computer to answer questions such as: (1) What is the functional adequacy of an individual's speech relative to that of normal speakers? and (2) What is the status of the individual relative to his immediate previous performance before management or at the outset of therapy? It would be premature at this point to suggest a single approach to answering these questions. First, the method needs more thorough investigation. One natural way of defining an individual's distinctiveness index, the functional adequacy of his speech, would be to express his score as a percentage of a reference score (normal speech or the speaker's own behavior at the initiation of therapy) and to specify changes in his performance along a scale of distinctiveness from 0 to 100 (the reference). Such an evaluation could be applied to all of the phonetic segments tested or broken down into judgments of groups of segments (vowels, fricatives), or both. It seems clear that a quantified notion of the perceptual contrast concept, when implemented on a computer, would be a reasonable, inexpensive, fast, automatic, reliable, and quantitative approach to the problems of diagnosis, prognosis, and therapy evaluation as outlined in the introductory pages of this chapter. Further, from the clinician's point of view, the method would require no equipment more esoteric than a tape recorder and a standardized speech sample. Tape recorded samples could be mailed to a laboratory with an appropriately programmed computer. A clinician would thus be able to obtain quick, reliable aid or corroboration in diagnosis and prognosis as well as be able to obtain accurate, numerical evaluations of management and therapy. It is the thesis of this chapter that these should be strong clinical recommendations for any procedure.

However, as with the methods of multidimensional scaling, it is quite clear that much has to be done before the method can be assumed valid for clinical use. It does, however, represent a second broad area in which principles of phonetics can be demonstrated to be potentially of very considerable clinical value.

C. Feature Comparisons

A rather large and diverse potential source of cooperative interaction between acoustic phonetics and the speech clinic remains to be considered. In this group of applications no particular attempt is made to establish any type of psychological reality for sets of features, to determine the number of dimensions underlying a segment, or to attempt to develop a numerical definition for the use of notions such as contrast or confusion. Nevertheless, it will be seen that this group of applications is firmly based on the concept of features and, further, that there is, at least implicitly, a clear tendency to view normal and disordered speech together, with normal features being used as bench-marks to allow some type of severity criterion statements to be made.

Specifically, this section will be concerned with the kinds of acoustic phonetics applications referred to by Kent (1976) in his tutorial on speech development and maturation. Kent suggests that acoustic data relevant to the study of speech development and its disorders in children have been developed in three general areas: (1) voice fundamental frequency (F_0), (2) formant patterns in vowel productions, and (3) the temporal properties of speech (including such properties as voice onset time, rates of formant movement, and segment durations). A similar approach will be used in the present discussion of applications of acoustic phonetics relative to: (1) voice disorders, or the voicing feature, and (2) problems of timing and coordination of the movements and shapes of the vocal tract.

It is thus clear that what is to be considered now is the difference between normal and pathological speakers in terms of features (F_0, VOT, etc.) selected more or less a priori. While Sections II,A and II,B emphasized the evaluation of whole sets of groups of features or concepts of perceptual contrast, this section will emphasize the evaluation of the role of individual features. This distinction, which may at times be somewhat vague or even artificial, will be maintained for the sake of organization [see the discussion of Shepard (1972) in Section II,C,1].

Before taking up some of the specific issues, two general comments or assumptions should be made. First, it has been explicitly assumed throughout this chapter that the clinician need not have direct access to anything more than an ordinary tape recorder. However, it has also been assumed that the clinician is able to send or somehow deliver recordings made on that tape recorder to a laboratory where acoustic analyses can be made. Second, it is hoped that all readers recognize that the sound spectrograph is not the only instrument available for acoustic analysis. Modern computers and a number of specialized instruments offer rapid and accurate measurement of virtually any speech acoustic characteristic of interest for a very wide variety of types of voices and speakers. Discussions of the limitations of spectrographic analysis in, for example, female and children's voices will not be emphasized, except perhaps in certain instances where such limitations may be critical.

1. Voice Disorders: The Voicing Feature

Many aspects of the voicing feature are of clinical importance. Most germane to the present discussion is the fact that these aspects can be easily and accurately measured. Take, for example, the discussion of voice evaluation provided by Boone (1977). Boone discusses the need for clinical evaluations of vocal pitch (F_0), loudness, quality (breathiness, hoarseness, harshness, etc.), and related observations (pitch breaks, phonation breaks, glottal fry, hard glottal attack, etc.). Means are available to provide quantitative evaluation of virtually all of these aspects of voicing. A variety of pitch extraction computer programs demonstrated to be effective on children's and adults' voices exist (Rabiner, Cheng, Rosenberg, & McGonegal, 1976). In addition, a number of electronic or hardware types of pitch extractors are available (see, e.g., Fant, 1958, 1968; Fourcin & Abberton, 1971). Such devices provide accurate and reliable measures of variables such as mean F_0, intonation, range and variability of F_0, instantaneous F_0 at any point, and so on. It should also be mentioned that the sound spectrograph allows quantification of F_0 but, as has often been pointed out, this technique presents certain difficulties with children's voices. With regard to the measurements of intensity, virtually the same conditions exist. Fant (1958, 1968) has discussed hardware techniques for the measurement of intensity; in addition, computers can be applied with ease to this measurement task. It should also be pointed out, particularly with regard to voice fundamental frequency and intensity, that not only are there many measurement methodologies available, but the use of these methodologies in the measurement of F_0

and intensity usually provides the bases for laboratory exercise for beginning students in phonetics. These are extremely straightforward techniques. The remaining two areas listed by Boone, quality and related observations, are also amenable to measurement, although perhaps not always in such a straightforward way as F_0 and intensity. Combinations of the various hardware techniques and specialized computer programs (e.g., Pfeifer's, 1976, SCRL Interactive Laboratory System) would be able to handle the measurement of pitch breaks, phonation breaks, glottal fry, and so on. Quality disorders such as breathiness, hoarseness, or harshness might be somewhat more difficult, although the descriptions of these disorders as given by Boone certainly suggest methods of measurement. Breathiness, for example, is described as being an audible escape of air, while harshness is said to be "probably related to aperiodicity of laryngeal vibration" (Boone, 1977, p. 94). These terms are acoustically quantifiable. Recall also the multidimensional scaling approach to hoarseness of Murry *et al.* (1977).

Thus, it seems clear that clinically important aspects of the voicing feature are quite measurable. Furthermore, there has been a good deal of normative data gathered concerning them, at least in regard to fundamental frequency and its variation. [See Kent's (1976) discussion.] In other words, these would seem to be specific cases in which normal bench-marks either exist or could easily be developed and in which voice disorder severity criteria could easily be established relative to those bench-marks. Unfortunately, this approach seems to be remarkably rare. In speech pathology textbooks the clinical evaluation of voice is largely a subjective judgment, to the extent that, for example, a given voice may be simply judged as too high in pitch for that individual's age and sex. Therapy would then be initiated to lower the speaker's habitual pitch level during speech. There is no doubt that such approaches work and speaking behavior is altered, usually for the better, via the use of such subjective techniques. I do not argue the fact that a clinician can establish, simply by listening, whether or not a speaker is using an appropriate pitch or loudness level, or whether or not there are abnormal pitch breaks or quality deviations. Assuming that any physical causes of the disorders have been removed, there can also be no argument that a capable clinician is able to work effectively toward the elimination of the undesired behavior without ever having measured it.

However, there is a world outside of the clinic room and the clinician should be prepared to tell family and friends of the patient **how serious** the voice disorder was, **how much** improvement has taken place, or **how far** from normal the patient is. Quantification would greatly facilitate the ability to do so. Further, the clinician should feel obligated to describe for professional colleagues any unique aspects of especially successful clinical techniques, and description simply demands objectivity and quantification.

Thus it is that the primary message regarding the relationship between acoustic phonetics and the speech clinic in terms of voice disorders and the voicing feature is a simple message, indeed. The techniques are there, the path toward using them is wide open, and their use is clinically highly justifiable. This would seem to be a case in point in which the phonetician and the clinician have not been communicating very effectively with each other in terms of available techniques, problems, and knowledge.

Shepard (1972) has considered in detail many of the issues discussed in the preceding pages. Although his work is not directly concerned with voice or with voice disorders, it is included at this point simply because, both as theory and technique, it seems to fit best here. Shepard's views are very similar to those of Lindblom (1972, 1975), discussed earlier. Shepard views the psychological representation of speech sounds in terms of their locations in Euclidean spaces, their distances from one another in those spaces, and their perceptual confusability. He points out that there are sophisticated computer algorithms which are capable of converting complex patterns such as the acoustic speech wave into "graphical form much more readily interpreted by the human investigator" (p. 107). He further points out (along with Lindblom) that speech sounds can be located in a Euclidean space so that the frequency with which any two sounds will be confused is closely related to the distance between them. He goes on to suggest that if "the psychological data are allowed to speak for themselves" (p. 108), it will be possible for the computer to provide information regarding the dimensions or features underlying phonemes.

Shepard tests his views on data such as the classical work of Peterson and Barney (1952) on vowels and of Miller and Nicely (1955) on consonants. It would seem that concepts such as Shepard's could be profitably extended to the pathological speech populations. Indeed, this is a main thesis of this chapter. His notions tend to incorporate several of the ideas proposed here and thus contribute to the vagueness referred to above, of the lines between the three areas which are being discussed. It has been included at this point because similar concepts have already been discussed and because a good place to begin application of such notions might be with a feature-type of breakdown and a perceptual distance type of study on voice disorders.

Work just beginning at the Speech Transmission Laboratory in Stockholm is promising in this regard. In this project factor analyses of the perception of voice disorders is being tested (Fritzell, Hammarberg, & Wedin, 1977) and coupled with various acoustical analysis techniques (Gauffin & Sundberg, 1977). These efforts are in a preliminary stage, but their goals are exactly what is being called for in this chapter. Fritzell *et al.* pose the question: "Could we measure the change brought about by our voice therapy?" (p. 31) and then state: "The present study, reported in this paper and the following one, is an attempt to use acoustic voice analysis for clinical purposes, to supplement our clinical observations by acoustic data. The ultimate goal is a handy little electronic box, into which we plug the voice of our patient, and out come valid and reliable figures of relevant acoustic parameters" (p. 31). In the preliminary work five factors were isolated that accounted for 85% of the total variance: steady–unstable, breathy–overtight, hypo–hyperkinetic, light–coarse, and chest–head register. In the companion report, Gauffin and Sundberg (1977) consider the acoustic correlates of these factors and the results are, indeed, promising.

Acoustic characteristics of voice have also received attention in regard to another immediate clinical application, although not in the speech clinic, per se: the acoustic analyses of baby-cry in an effort to provide early diagnosis of a variety of disorders. Michelsson and Sirviö (1976) and Sirviö and Michelsson (1976) have presented data or references suggesting that specific acoustic aspects of baby-cry can provide early diagnosis for a number of disorders, for example, congenital hypothyroidism, Down's syndrome, meningitis, hydrocephalus, jaundice, oxygen deprivation, and various specific brain damages. Rosenhouse (1977) has used baby-cry analysis to differentiate among hunger, pain, alarm, and illness. Prescott (1975) has suggested the use of baby-cry to detect developmental and hearing disorders. These and similar reports (see Kent's, 1976, tutorial) are provocative and deserve careful attention, for if they are correct they will offer extremely valuable early and therefore preventative diagnostic information.

2. Timing and Control of Articulatory Movements and Shaping of the Vocal Tract

Much of the preceding discussion on voice disorders and the voicing feature is applicable here as well, although perhaps on a broader scale. Two facts can be stated at the outset: (1) there are many speech disorders which are due to problems of timing, control, and coordination of articulatory movements and the shaping of the vocal tract; and (2) there are also a great many research techniques available and a considerable amount of data relevant to the acoustic manifestations of vocal tract shapes and articulatory timing and coordination. For example, the long series of Haskins Laboratories research specifying acoustic characteristics of consonants (e.g., F. S. Cooper, Delattre, Liberman, Borst, & Gerstman, 1952; Delattre, Liberman, & Cooper, 1955; Liberman, Delattre, & Cooper, 1958; Liberman, Delattre, Cooper, & Gerstman, 1954; Lisker, 1957; Lisker & Abramson, 1967); the classic studies of Fant and his co-workers on the acoustic theory of vowel production (Fant, 1970); and the steady stream of excellent research on normal speech in the current literature (W. E. Cooper, 1974; Klatt, 1975; Stevens & Klatt, 1974; Strange, Verbrugge, Shankweiler, & Edman, 1976; Verbrugge, Strange, Shankweiler, & Edman, 1976; Wang & Bilger, 1973; Zlatin & Koenigsknecht, 1976). The question arises as to whether or not these two facts have been coordinated. As with voice disorders, the answer is not a positive one. The **clinically** oriented acoustic data are sketchy, indeed.

Rather than describe the limited research concerning attempts to apply acoustic phonetics to articulatory disorders, I will devote the remainder of this section to a discussion of a proposal which exemplifies the possibilities of the use of acoustic phonetics in developing severity criteria relevant to bench-marks in articulatory timing and coordination and in vocal tract shaping. I have selected the dysarthrias as an example since they offer such a wide variety of difficulties with articulatory timing and coordination.

Darley, Aronson, and Brown (1969a, 1969b, 1975) have described a diagnostic/evaluative technique for use in the dysarthrias. The technique provides the promise of a very early differential diagnosis of dysarthria as well as an evaluation of management and therapy. The technique is based entirely on listener judgments of certain perceptual features.

Darley *et al.* used a subject population of 212 dysarthric speakers, each diagnosed as representing one of seven different kinds of dysarthria. Tape recorded samples of the speech of these individuals were ranked on a seven-point scale for each of the 38 perceptual items listed in Table I. It was found that the perceptual items differed both in degree and order of importance among the dysarthric groups. The experiments of Darley *et al.* thus demonstrate quite clearly that, using the set of perceptual criteria which they propose, trained listeners are able to provide early and accurate differential diagnosis of dysarthria and, in addition, are able to accomplish precise and accurate evaluation of therapy.

There are, however, some difficulties. First, the task is not a simple one. Providing rank scores on seven-point scales for 38 items for only one speaker is an exacting and time-consuming task, even for a trained and highly experienced listener. This brings up the second point, that most

Table I. Perceptual Items Used by Darley, Aronson, and Brown (1969a) for the Differential Diagnosis of Dysarthria

1. Pitch level	20. Audible inspiration
2. Pitch breaks	21. Grunt at end of expiration
3. Monopitch	22. Rate
4. Voice tremor	23. Phrases short
5. Monoloudness	24. Increases of rate segments
6. Excess loudness variation	25. Increase of rate overall
7. Loudness decay	26. Reduced stress
8. Alternating loudness	27. Variable rate
9. Loudness (overall)	28. Intervals prolonged
10. Harsh voice	29. Inappropriate silence
11. Hoarse (wet) voice	30. Short rushes of speech
12. Breathy voice (continuous)	31. Excess and equal stress
13. Breathy voice (transient)	32. Imprecise consonants
14. Strained–strangled voice	33. Phonemes prolonged
15. Voice stoppages	34. Phonemes repeated
16. Hypernasality	35. Irregular articulatory breakdown
17. Hyponasality	36. Vowels distorted
18. Nasal emission	37. Intelligibility (overall)
19. Forced inspiration–expiration	38. Bizarreness (overall)

speech clinicians simply are not all that well trained or experienced with regard to the several dysarthrias.

However, it is entirely possible that the careful application of the knowledge and techniques of acoustic phonetics could overcome these problems and allow the very promising concepts of Darley *et al.* to be automatically, reliably, and quickly applied. From an examination of the 38 items in Table I, it is immediately evident that, for many of them, techniques are already available which could provide a numerical specification of the items, while for others it would require only very little imagination to think of ways to provide such numerical specification. In fact, some acoustic studies of the dysarthrias have already been reported: Lehiste (1965) published spectrographic data on the dysarthrias, and Lindblom, Lubker, and Fritzell (1974) have presented data specifically designed as acoustic verification of the perceptual features of Darley *et al.* It seems quite clear from such preliminary efforts that tape recordings of dysarthric speech can be subjected to acoustic analyses of the perceptual items described by Darley and his co-workers, or, in some cases, to modifications of those items. Assuming that such analyses were carefully calibrated against the judgments of trained listeners to assure that they were both reliable and valid, then the variable of listener experience would have been eliminated. It would then be a matter of a clinician supplying a laboratory with a tape recording of dysarthric speech and the laboratory, after doing the required analyses, supplying the clinician with scores (perhaps severity criteria?) on the various perceptual items, which the clinician could then use as an aid in diagnosis, planning of therapy, or evaluation of therapy. If, however, the acoustic analyses were of the types used by both Lehiste (1965) and Lindbolm et al. (1974) (i.e., sound spectrographs or other hardware types of analysis), then the time spent per subject for analysis might actually be increased over that spent in the original perception task. Thus, in order for such automated analyses to be realistic, they would have to be truly automated: computer programs would have to be written to handle the analyses. This should not prove prohibitively difficult since many program systems already exist which provide quite sophisticated analyses (see Pfeifer's, 1976, description of the ILS system). I do not for a moment discount the difficulties that would be involved in tailoring these programs or developing new ones, but it does not seem at all unreasonable to suggest that we aim for a situation in which a tape recording of dysarthric speech (or any speech, for that matter) is played into a computer which is programmed to print out severity criterion scores on each of a series of items similar to those presented by Darley et al. These printouts would provide precisely the same information as the judgment scores in the original publications of Darley et al., but much more rapidly and without having to use highly trained or experienced listeners.

Since the point of the preceding paragraphs was to present a proposal of how acoustic phonetics might be used to aid the clinician working with disorders of articulatory timing and coordination, much of what was said may seem more what if? than substance based. There is, however, some substance to the proposal: the method of Darley et al. seems to work; the perceptual items which they propose have, for the most part, quite clear acoustic bases which are, in turn, measurable, and specific techniques for the measurement either exist or could be developed.

Nevertheless, for the present it must remain largely a what-if?, simply because of the lack of large-scale, well-controlled efforts to coordinate the two facts noted at the beginning of this section. The remark by Kent (1976, p. 442), quoted in Section II, is especially relevant here: "The existing data on the acoustic characteristics of children's speech are all too often sketchy in nature, but they hold the promise of sensitive methods for the study of speech maturation and developmental disorders." Indeed, the clinical acoustic data **are** sketchy, but the promise **is** there.

III. SUMMARY AND SOME CONCLUDING STATEMENTS

There is an area of reality in which the interests and goals of the phonetician and the speech pathologist coincide. That reality centers around a statement made in the opening paragraphs of this chapter: being clearly understood and understanding clearly are the crucial end products toward which communication is directed. There can be little argument with the general contention that breakdowns in the normal process of speech production will be more clearly understood and the treatment of those breakdowns will be facilitated by cooperative efforts of phoneticians and speech pathologists. This chapter has approached that general contention from a somewhat more specific point of view: the relationships between **acoustic** phonetics and the speech clinic. It has been strongly suggested that phonetics can provide knowledge, and techniques for obtaining that knowledge, about the features, segments, and rules of normal speech production, and that phonetics can thereby provide bench-marks which may range from simple descriptive statements to complicated predictive rules of normal function. It has further been suggested that speech pathology can combine its knowledge and experience concerning disordered speech with the bench-marks of phonetics to locate and describe disordered speech behavior relative to normal speech behavior effectively. Given the techniques, the knowledge, and the experience of these two disciplines, it should be possible to develop severity criteria which objectively state how far from normal an individual speaker is and how difficult a task it will be to effect a reasonable reduction of that distance. The idea is, I believe, a good one. However, the terms are unfortunately vague and the vagueness is not at all easy to eliminate. There are plenty of good bench-marks, but they have seldom been developed with specific clinical needs in mind. Also, there are certainly plenty of clinical needs but they are rarely viewed in the quantified or measured terms required for application to bench-marks and severity criteria.

I have discussed three general areas in which attempts are being, or could be, made. Since this discussion was not intended to be a review of the literature, I have doubtlessly excluded specific research. Nevertheless, there have not been many attempts at close cooperation between acoustic phonetics and speech pathology, even though the argument that they would benefit from such interaction is a valid one. Thus, the three areas of possible interaction have been **suggestions** rather than compilations or lists of hard data. They have certainly not been cookbook explanations.

Thus, this chapter is a statement of need and a call for research and cooperation. I most sincerely hope that within a very few years this will be achieved.

References

Abbs, J. H. The influence of the gamma motor system on jaw movements during speech: A theoretical framework and some preliminary observations. *Journal of Speech and Hearing Research,* 1973, *16,* 175–200.

Allen, G. D. Segmental timing control in speech production. *Journal of Phonetics,* 1973, *1,* 219–237.

Boone, D. R. *The voice and voice therapy* (2nd ed.). Englewood Cliffs, N.J.: Prentice-Hall, 1977.

Carroll, J. D., & Chang, J.-J. Analysis of individual differences in multidimensional scaling via an *n*-way generalization of "Eckart–Young" decomposition. *Psychometrika,* 1970, *35,* 283–319.

Chomsky, N., & Halle, M. *The sound pattern of English.* New York: Harper, 1968.

Cooper, F. S., Delattre, P. C., Liberman, A. M., Borst, J. M., & Gerstman, L. J. Some experiments on the perception of synthetic speech sounds. *Journal of the Acoustical Society of America,* 1952, *24,* 597–606.

Cooper, W. E. Adaptation of phonetic feature analyzers for place of articulation. *Journal of the Acoustical Society of America,* 1974, *56,* 617–627.

Danhauer, J. L., & Singh, S. A. A multidimensional scaling analysis of phonemic responses from hard of hearing and deaf subjects of three languages. *Language and Speech,* 1975, *18,* 42–64.

Darley, F. L., Aronson, A. E., & Brown, J. R. Differential diagnostic patterns of dysarthria. *Journal of Speech and Hearing Research,* 1969, *12,* 246–269. (a)

Darley, F. L., Aronson, A. E., & Brown, J. R. Clusters of deviant speech dimensions in the dysarthrias. *Journal of Speech and Hearing Research,* 1969, *12,* 462–496. (b)

Darley, F. L., Aronson, A. E., & Brown, J. E. *Motor speech disorders.* Philadelphia: Saunders, 1975.

Delattre, P. C., Liberman, A. M., & Cooper, F. S. Acoustic loci and transitional cues for consonants. *Journal of the Acoustical Society of America,* 1955, *27,* 769–773.

Fant, G. Modern instrumentation and methods for acoustic studies of speech. *Acta Polytechnica Scandinavica,* 1958, No. 246.

Fant, G. Analysis and synthesis of speech processes. In B. Malmberg (Ed.), *Manual of phonetics.* Amsterdam: North-Holland Publ., 1968. Pp. 173–277.

Fant, G. *Acoustic theory of speech production* (2nd ed.). The Hague: Mouton, 1970.

Fourcin, A. J., & Abberton, E. First applications of a new laryngograph. *Medical Biology Illustrated,* 1971, *21,* 172–182.

Fritzell, B., Hammarberg, B., & Wedin, L. Clinical applications of acoustic voice analysis: Part I, Background and perceptual factors. *Speech Transmission Laboratory Quarterly Progress and Status Report,* 1977, *2/3,* 31–38.

Fujimura, O., & Lindquist, J. Sweep-tone measurement of vocal tract characteristics. *Journal of the Acoustical Society of America,* 1971, *49,* 541–558.

Gauffin, J., & Sundberg, J. Clinical applications of acoustic voice analysis: Part II, Acoustical analysis, results, and discussion. *Speech Transmission Laboratory Quarterly Progress and Status Report,* 1977, *2/3,* 39–43.

Hanson, G. Dimensions in speech sound perception. *Ericsson Technics,* 1967, *23,* 175 pp.

Harshman, R. Foundations of the PARAFAC procedure: Models and conditions for an "explanatory" multimodal factor analysis. *UCLA Working Papers in Phonetics*, 1970, *16*, 84 pp.

House, A. S., & Stevens, K. N. Analog studies of the nasalization of vowels. *Journal of Speech and Hearing Disorders*, 1956, *21*, 218–232.

Hughes, O. M., & Abbs, J. H. Labial–mandibular coordination in the production of speech: Implications for the operation of motor equivalence. *Phonetica*, 1976, *33*, 199–221.

Jakobson, R., Fant, C. G. M., & Halle, M. *Preliminaries to speech analysis: The distinctive features and their correlates* (2nd ed.). Cambridge, Mass.: MIT Press, 1961.

Johnson, W. *People in quandaries*. New York: Harper, 1946.

Kent, R. D. Anatomical and neuromuscular maturation of the speech mechanism: Evidence from acoustic studies. *Journal of Speech and Hearing Research*, 1976, *19*, 421–447.

Kent, R. D., Carney, P. J., & Severeid, L. R. Velar movement and timing: Evaluation of a model for binary control. *Journal of Speech and Hearing Research*, 1974, *17*, 470–488.

Klatt, D. H. Voice onset time, friction, and aspiration in word-initial consonant clusters. *Journal of Speech and Hearing Research*, 1975, *18*, 686–706.

Klein, W., Plomp, R., & Pols, L. C. W. Vowel spectra, vowel spaces and vowel identification. *Journal of the Acoustical Society of America*, 1970, *48*, 999–1009.

Kruskal, J. B. Multidimensional scaling by optimizing goodness of fit to a non-metric hypothesis. *Psychometrika*, 1964, *29*, 1–27.

Lehiste, I. Some acoustic characteristics of dysarthric speech. *Bibliotheca Phonetica*, 1965, Pt. 2.

Liberman, A. M., Delattre, P., & Cooper, F. S. Some cues for the distinction between voiced and voiceless stops in initial position. *Language and Speech*, 1958, *1*, 153–167.

Liberman, A. M., Delattre, P., Cooper, F. S., & Gerstman, L. J. The role of consonant–vowel transitions in the perception of the stop and nasal consonants. *Psychological Monographs*, 1954, *68*(8, Whole No. 379).

Lindblom, B. Phonetics and the description of language. *Proceedings of the 7th International Congress of Phonetic Sciences*, 1972, pp. 63–97.

Lindblom, B. Experiments in sound structure. Paper presented at the 8th International Congress of Phonetic Sciences, Leeds, England, August 1975.

Lindblom, B., Lubker, J., & Fritzell, B. Experimentalfonetiska studier av dysartri. *Papers from the Institute of Linguistics, University of Stockholm (PILUS)*, 1974, *27*, 1–102.

Lindblom, B., Lubker, J., & Gay, T. Formant frequencies of some fixed-mandible vowels and a model of speech motor programming by predictive simulation. *Journal of Phonetics*, in press.

Lindblom, B., Lubker, J., & McAllister, R. Compensatory articulation and the modeling of normal speech production behavior. *Proceedings of the Symposium on Articulatory Modelling*, Grenoble, 1977, pp. 147–161. (a)

Lindblom, B., Lubker, J., & Pauli, S. An acoustic-perceptual method for the quantitative evaluation of hypernasality. *Journal of Speech and Hearing Research*, 1977, *20*, 485–496. (b)

Lisker, L. Closure duration and the intervocalic voiced–voiceless distinction in English. *Language*, 1957, *33*, 42–49.

Lisker, L., & Abramson, A. S. Some effects of context on voice onset time in English stops. *Language and Speech*, 1967, *10*, 1–28.

Lubker, J. F., & Moll, K. L. Simultaneous oral–nasal air flow measurements and cinefluorographic observations during speech production. *Cleft Palate Journal*, 1965, *2*, 257–272.

MacNeilage, P. F. Motor control and the serial ordering of speech. *Psychological Review*, 1970, *77*, 182–196.

MacNeilage, P. F. Speech physiology. In J. H. Gilbert (Ed.), *Speech and cortical functioning*. New York: Academic Press, 1972. Pp. 1–72.

Michelsson, K., & Sirviö, P. Cry analysis in congenital hypothyroidism. *Folia Phoniatrica*, 1976, *28*, 40–47.

Miller, G. A., & Nicely, P. E. An analysis of perceptual confusions among some English consonants. *Journal of the Acoustical Society of America*, 1955, *27*, 338–346.

Mohr, B., & Wang, W. Perceptual distances and the specification of phonological features. *Phonetica*, 1968, *18*, 31–45.

Murry, T., Singh, S., & Sargent, M. Multidimensional classification of abnormal voice qualities. *Journal of the Acoustical Society of America*, 1977, *61*, 1630–1635.

Peterson, G. E., & Barney, P. E. Control methods used in a study of the vowels. *Journal of the Acoustical Society of America*, 1952, *24*, 175–184.

Pfeifer, L. L. *User's guide: SCRL Interactive Laboratory System*. Santa Barbara, Calif.: Speech Communications Research Laboratory, 1976.

Platt, J. R. Strong inference. *Science*, 1964, *146*, 347–353.

Plomp, R. *Aspects of tone sensation*. New York: Academic Press, 1976.

Pols, L. C. W., Tromp, H. R. C., & Plomp, R. Frequency analysis of Dutch vowels from 50 male speakers. *Journal of the Acoustical Society of America*, 1973, *53*, 1093–1101.

Pols, L. C. W., van der Kamp, L. J., & Plomp, R. Perceptual and physical space of vowel sounds. *Journal of the Acoustical Society of America*, 1969, *46*, 458–467.

Prescott, R. Infant cry sound: Developmental features. *Journal of the Acoustical Society of America*, 1975, *57*, 1186–1191.

Rabiner, L. R., Cheng, M. J., Rosenberg, A. E., & McGonegal, C. A. A comparative performance study of several pitch detection algorithms. *IEEE Transactions on Acoustics, Speech, and Signal Processing*, 1976, *24*, 399–418.

Rosenhouse, J. A preliminary report: An analysis of some types of a baby's cries. *Journal of Phonetics*, 1977, *5*, 299–312.

Shepard, R. N. Psychological representation of speech sounds. In E. E. David & P. B. Denes (Eds.), *Human communication: A unified review*. New York: McGraw-Hill, 1972.

Singh, S., & Woods, D. R. Perceptual structure of 12 American English vowels. *Journal of the Acoustical Society of America*, 1971, *49*, 1861–1866.

Singh, S., Woods, D. R., & Becker, G. N. Perceptual structure of twenty-two pre-vocalic English consonants. *Journal of the Acoustical Society of America*, 1972, *52*, 1698–1713.

Sirviö, P., & Michelsson, K. Sound-spectrographic cry analysis of normal and abnormal newborn infants. A review and a recommendation for standardization of the cry characteristics. *Folia Phoniatrica*, 1976, *28*, 161–173.

Stevens, K. N., & Klatt, D. H. Role of formant transitions in the voiced-voiceless distinction for stops. *Journal of the Acoustical Society of America*, 1974, *55*, 653–659.

Strange, W., Verbrugge, R., Shankweiler, D., & Edman, T. Consonant environment specifies vowel identity. *Journal of the Acoustical Society of America*, 1976, *60*, 213–224.

Terbeek, D. A cross-language multidimensional scaling study of vowel perception. *UCLA Working Papers in Phonetics*, 1977, *37*, 271 pp.

Torgerson, W. *Theory and methods of scaling*. New York: Wiley, 1958.

Verbrugge, R., Strange, W., Shankweiler, D., & Edman, T. What information enables a listener to map a talker's vowel space? *Journal of the Acoustical Society of America*, 1976, *60*, 198–212.

Wang, M. D., & Bilger, R. C. Consonant confusions in noise: A study of perceptual features. *Journal of the Acoustical Society of America,* 1973, *54,* 1248–1266.

Warren, D. W., Duany, L. F., & Fischer, N. D. Nasal pathway resistance in normal and cleft lip and palate subjects. *Cleft Palate Journal,* 1969, *6,* 134–140.

Warren, D. W., & Ryon, W. E. Oral port constriction, nasal resistance, and respiratory aspects of cleft palate speech: An analog study. *Cleft Palate Journal,* 1967, *4,* 38–46.

Wilson, H. F., & Bond, Z. S. An INDSCAL analysis of vowels excerpted from four phonetic contexts. *Journal of Phonetics,* 1977, *5,* 361–367.

Zlatin, M. A., & Koenigsknecht, R. A. Development of the voicing contrast: A comparison of voice onset time in stop perception and production. *Journal of Speech and Hearing Research,* 1976, *19,* 93–111.

Zwicker, E., & Scharf, B. A model of loudness summation. *Psychological Review,* 1965, *72,* 3–26.

Linguistic and Motor Aspects of Stuttering

KENNETH O. ST. LOUIS

Department of Speech Pathology and Audiology
West Virginia University
Morgantown, West Virginia

SPEECH AND LANGUAGE: Advances in Basic
Research and Practice, Vol. 1

I. INTRODUCTION

The challenge faced in attempting to integrate the numerous theoretical positions relating to stuttering with the practically countless number of experimental findings in this area is powerful indeed. Yet, as knowledge accumulates, the need arises—and re-arises—to take stock of that knowledge and to organize it into the most coherent and parsimonious packages possible. My primary purpose in this chapter is to summarize the available research on linguistic and motor aspects of stuttering and to assess the theoretical positions which have been advanced to explain them. Entertaining no illusions of how well the laboratory findings in stuttering will fit the available theoretical explanations, I shall attempt to indicate which motor and linguistic findings have been partially explained, or fully explained, and which ones have not.

The urgency of providing this kind of state of the art assessment is readily apparent to the clinical speech pathologist. In recent years, as the promises of behavioral and other explanations of stuttering have become less attractive (e.g., Martin & Ingham, 1973), a number of new approaches to treating stuttering have reawakened interest in motor and linguistic phenomena. It is also apparent that such new approaches to treatment, as well as some older ones, should be considered in light of the facts regarding linguistic and motor aspects of stuttering.

II. LINGUISTIC DETERMINANTS OF STUTTERING

Systematic research into linguistic aspects of stuttering began at the University of Iowa in the 1930s following a pilot study conducted on 13 stutterers in 1926 (Bryngelson, 1955). This research was conducted primarily by Spencer Brown and included investigations designed to identify those speech and language characteristics which could account for the locus of stuttering within the speech sequence. Brown concluded that most stutterings were associated with linguistic variables which were "conspicuous, prominent, or meaningful" to the speaker (Brown, 1945, p. 192).

Brown's contribution to research and thought in stuttering cannot be underestimated. His conclusions have been accepted as important facts to be known about stuttering (e.g., Bloodstein, 1975a). More important, most of the subsequent linguistic research related to stuttering has its roots in Brown's work.

A systematic review and an analysis of the research bearing on linguistic determinants of stuttering are presented. The data will be considered under the broad linguistic categories of phonological, syllabic, morphological, and syntactic variables. It should be noted that most linguistic research has been conducted with adult stutterers, but a growing body of data has dealt with stuttering in children. Therefore the research will be evaluated separately for adults and children.

A. Phonological Variables in Stuttering

1. Initial Sound: Adults

Many stutterers report having difficulty saying words beginning with certain sounds. One hypothesis to account for this is that some sounds are inherently more difficult to say than others. The possibility of selective phonetic difficulty generated studies of a number of potential phonological determinants of stuttering.

Probably the most consistent and undisputed phonological fact arising from the research is that nearly all stuttering occurs on the initial sound of words. Johnson and Brown (1935) reported that 92% of the stutterings of 32 adult stutterers engaged in oral reading occurred on initial sounds. Only 14 of these 32 stutterers experienced stuttering on any point **other** than the initial sound. Moreover, 13 of these 14 subjects stuttered on no more than 2% of later-occurring sounds. The remaining subject stuttered on 15% of these sounds.

In a similar study, Hahn (1942b) recorded 98% of all stutterings on initial sounds. In 1946, Sheehan recorded 25 consecutive stutterings from each of 20 adult stutterers. Ninety-six percent of the stutterings occurred on initial sounds (Sheehan, 1974). Hejna (1955) found that nearly all the stutterings of 18 adult stutterers speaking spontaneously occurred on the initial sounds of words. Taylor (1966a) recorded 97% of the stutterings of 12 teenage and adult stutterers on word initial sounds in oral reading. The initial sound factor also appears in single words read one at a time

(Wingate, 1967) and in nonsense words (St. Louis & Martin, 1976). Since this factor is so consistent and so powerful, it has received little recent attention.

2. Initial Sound: Children

In 1938, Egland recorded the spontaneous speech of three stutterers from 3 to 4 years of age in a variety of puppet interactions (Egland, 1955). Ninety-one percent of total stutterings were in word-initial positions, and all of the remaining 9% were in medial positions. None were in final positions.

Little additional data have been generated on initial sound loci of stuttering in children. Bloodstein (1974) accepts as a foregone conclusion that nearly all stutterings occur on the first sound or syllable of words.

3. Consonant versus Vowel: Adults

The phonological variable which has received the most attention is the distribution of stuttering on consonants and vowels. Johnson and Brown (1935) rank-ordered initial sounds in the oral reading of their 32 stutterers according to the median and mean percentage of stuttering. All phonemes associated with more than the mean stuttering frequency were consonants, and 80% of those associated with less stuttering were vowels. Hence, they concluded that consonants were more often associated with stuttering than vowels. The same was true of adult stutterers reading noncontextual material (Brown, 1938a). Hahn (1942b) found the same general result but pointed out that individual variation did occur. For example, one of his stutterers emitted 40% of his total stutterings on vowels sounds.

Brown (1945) reanalyzed Johnson and Brown's (1935) data by assigning plus values to all words associated with greater than the mean frequency of stuttering, 9.7%. For this "phonetic factor" he included as plus words all words beginning with consonants **except** /ð, h, w, m, t/. Minus words began with these five consonants and all vowels and diphthongs. Plus values were also given for three other factors to be discussed (Sections II,C,D): a grammatical factor, a word position factor, and a word length factor. In this analysis, each word received a word weight of 0, 1, 2, 3, or 4 according to the number of plus values it received. The mean values for 31 stutterers for each word weight were as follows: $0 = 1.74\%$, $1 = 4.44\%$, $2 = 9.03\%$, $3 = 15.29\%$, and $4 = 18.53\%$. It is clear that the probability of stuttering increases as more of the four factors that characterize a word occur. What cannot be determined from these results is the relative importance of each of the four factors. Thus, the predictive power of the consonant–vowel factor in these data, although important, cannot be assessed in comparison with the other three factors.

In 1946, Oxtoby replicated Brown's findings using essentially the same word weights to analyze the oral reading of 24 stutterers who were instructed to try to modify their stuttering in various ways (Oxtoby, 1955). The word weights accounted for 78 out of 80 mean stuttering frequencies in the expected direction. In 1946, Sheehan found that 82% of stutterings in oral reading and spontaneous speech occurred on consonants as compared to 18% on vowels. This 5:1 ratio characterized all subjects (Sheehan, 1974). Hejna (1955) found greater than chance occurrence of stuttering on consonants and less than chance occurrence on vowels in the spontaneous speech of stutterers.

Trotter (1956) used stuttering severity judgments, as opposed to frequency counts, in an oral reading task and confirmed Brown's (1945) findings. Again, however, we cannot determine the specific contribution of the consonant–vowel factor in accounting for his results.

Silverman and Williams (1967) analyzed the oral reading of adult stutterers according to Brown's (1945) four factors. Of their 15 stutterers, 13 encountered more stuttering on words beginning with consonants other than /t, w, h, ð/ compared to those consonants and vowels.

Taylor (1966a) found that initial consonants were associated with stuttering 14.5% of the time in oral reading compared to 2.7% for vowels, or in a ratio of 5.37:1. Using a factor analysis of a number of variables, the consonant–vowel factor was twice as strong as that for word position and about seven times as strong as the word length factor. Taylor also considered the effects of the grammatical function of words on the loci of stuttering. She found, however, that consonants were usually the first sound of content words (nouns, verbs, adjectives, and adverbs) and vowels were usually the first sound of function words (pronouns, conjunctions, prepositions, and articles). She concluded that the grammatical factor was therefore an artifact of the distribution of consonants and vowels.

Soderberg (1962) was the only investigator **not** to find significantly more stuttering on consonants than vowels. Stutterers read lists of words beginning exclusively with vowels, voiced consonants, and voiceless consonants. Both frequency and duration of stuttering were recorded, but neither measure resulted in significant differences in stuttering among means of the three groups. However, there were trends for longer stuttering durations on words beginning with voiced and unvoiced consonants than on those beginning with vowels. Taylor (1966b) suggested that the reason Soderberg failed to find the consonant–vowel effect was that his reading lists were not representative of the usual distribution of consonants and vowels in prose or spontaneous speech.

Recently, Wingate (1976, 1977) reported that the consonant–vowel effect is an artifact of the frequency of occurrence of consonants and vowels as word-initial sounds. In an unpublished study (Wingate, 1973) in which four lists of the 1000 most frequently spoken words of English were analyzed, he found that 81% of all words began with consonants.

4. Consonant versus Vowel: Children

In 1937, Mann compared the stutterings on words beginning with 32 speech sounds in word lists and essays in the oral reading of 29 stutterers with a mean age of 10 years in the third to ninth grades (Mann, 1955). Using a definition of stuttering which included normal disfluency, she found that, in general, consonants were stuttered more than vowels in word lists and essays, although there were exceptions.

D. E. Williams, Silverman, and Kools (1969) applied Brown's (1945) four factors to the speech of 76 kindergarten through sixth-grade children. Kindergarteners and first graders imitated sentences; the remaining subjects read orally. Fifty-nine percent of the stutterers had more "disfluent" words on words beginning with vowels and /t, w, h, θ/ (minus values) compared to 41% not showing this effect. In spite of the trend favoring Brown's consonant–vowel factor, this difference was not statistically significant.

5. Relative Difficulty of Various Phonemes: Adults

Considerable effort has been directed at determining which consonants are most likely—or least likely—to be stuttered. Johnson and Brown (1935) rank-ordered phonemes according to median and mean percentages of stuttering. Using mean percentages, most consonants ranked above the mean value, and all vowels ranked below. Beyond this consonant–vowel difference, individual subject differences were much greater than group similarities with regard to those consonants which were most often associated with stuttering. Nonetheless, a general group ranking was discernible, especially in light of similar findings by Brown (1938a) in noncontextual reading and Hahn (1942b) in oral reading. To illustrate, the ranks according to frequency of stuttering for the 14 subjects who exhibited stuttering in Brown's (1938a) study using random word lists was correlated with the ranks of the same subjects in Johnson and Brown's (1935) study of contextual oral reading. The rank-order correlation coefficient between the mean rankings was .91, whereas the **highest** coefficient for any of the 14 subjects was .68.

Quarrington, Conway, and Siegel (1962) selected four consonants associated with high stuttering frequency (/g, d, l, p/) in Johnson and Brown's (1935) study and four associated with low frequency (/w, s, f, h/). Using words equated for syllable stress, length, and frequency of occurrence, and counterbalanced for sentence position and grammatical class, they found that the "high stuttering frequency" consonants were not associated with stuttering significantly more than the "low stuttering frequency" consonants. These results are difficult to interpret because the authors' criteria for selection of sounds are not clear. For example /p/, a high stuttering sound, and /s/, a low stuttering sound, both had the same median percentage of stuttering values in Johnson and Brown's study. The results on relative difficulty of sounds from Quarrington *et al.* (1962) must therefore be accepted with caution.

In a study using nonsense words, St. Louis and Martin (1976) found that the duration of stuttering could best be accounted for by initial consonants. However, wide intersubject variability occurred; certain stutterers stuttered predominantly on certain sounds, but these were different across subjects.

6. Relative Difficulty of Individual Phonemes: Children

Mann (1955) had 29 10-year-old stutterers read word lists and essays aloud and found that the rank-order correlation coeffcents between the two speech tasks in relation to which sounds occasioned the greatest to least stuttering was .81. Five sounds, /ʃ, v, ʌ, tʃ, θ/, received the highest mean ranks in both groups. The rank-order correlation coefficient between the difficulty of the 32 sounds in Mann's children and Johnson and Brown's (1935) adults was .64. Two sounds, /tʃ/ and /v/ were reported to rank among the five (*sic*: six) most stuttered sounds in both groups.

7. Phoneme Frequency: Adults

Fairbanks (1937) analyzed Johnson and Brown's (1935) results according to the frequency of occurrence of various phonemes in English. He found no significant correlation between the occurrence of stuttering and phoneme frequency. Hahn (1942b) concurred after he found that the percentage of occurrence of various sounds within his reading passages had no appreciable effect on the ranking of sound difficulty. Soderberg and MacKay (1972) replicated these findings with carefully controlled nonsense words.

8. Phonetic Context: Adults

MacKay and Soderberg (1970a) investigated the effects of phonetic context on the occurrence of stuttering. Based on the theoretical formulations of MacKay (1970a, 1970b) drawn from normal speech errors, they hypothesized that stuttering on the same earlier speech segments would be differentially affected by later phonetic characteristics, programmed, but yet to be uttered. Fifteen stutterers and two groups of 15 nonstutterers repeated pairs of syllables five times at their maximum rate. The stimuli were characterized as follows:

Completely same	*ska–ska*
Allophonically same	*ska–ski*
Allophonically different	*ska–sti*
Completely different	*ska–pri*

In each case, repetitions, prolongations, and blocks were counted on the same first consonant (e.g., *s*) or consonant blend (e.g., *sk*). Both stutterers and nonstutterers experienced repetition errors; however, only the stutterers prolonged or blocked on any sounds. Since the stutterers' prolongations and blocks paralleled their repetition errors very closely, only the repetitions of the two groups are considered here. Figure 1 shows the number of repetition errors for the three groups: stutterers, controls matched for age, sex, handedness, educational achievement, and motor skills (years of typing and piano playing), and randomly selected, unmatched nonstutterers. The stutterers had many times more errors than the two groups of nonstutterers, who behaved similarly. Both stutterers and nonstutterers had the fewest errors on the first syllable when initial consonants were identical. They had slightly more repetitions when the initial consonants were allophonically the same, and slightly more yet when the initial segments were completely different. As hypothesized, however, when consonants were allophonically different (e.g., *ska–sti*), a large increase in stuttering frequency was observed. The hypothesized explanation for this increase was that when syllables in close temporal proximity contain repeated units which require different allophonic shapes (e.g., *s* in *ska–sti*), greater difficulty is encountered in programming the unit than when the syllables contain units which are identical or have no repeated units.

In another study, Soderberg (1972) used the same general procedure to determine the effect of varying the number of distinctive feature differences between consonants in the first and second syllable pairs which were otherwise identical. Using features of voicing, manner, and place of articulation, experimental stimuli differed in zero (e.g., *gla–gla*), one (e.g., *gla–kla*), two (e.g., *gla–pla*), and three (e.g., *gla–sla*) distinctive features. Each of 20 stutterers uttered the syllable pairs five consecutive times at maximum rate. Significantly more stuttering occurred on the first consonant when the second differed by one distinctive feature than when it differed by zero, two, or three features. It was concluded that an

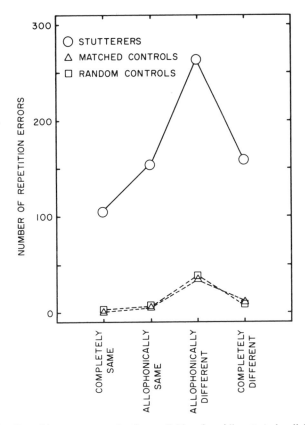

Figure 1. Repetition errors on the first syllable of rapidly uttered syllable pairs as a function of allophonic similarity or difference of the second syllable from stutterers, matched controls, and random controls. (Adapted from MacKay & Soderberg, 1970a.)

adequate account of stuttering must explain such phonetic interactions at the distinctive feature level.

In a study mentioned previously, St. Louis and Martin (1976) had eight stutterers produce 64 C_1VC_2V bisyllabic nonsense words (e.g., *bapi*) twice at their normal rate. The words contained eight consonants (/b, p, d, t, v, f, z, s/) in all combinations in the first and second consonant positions. Half the subjects stressed the first syllable (e.g., *bápi, bápi*) and half stressed the second syllable (e.g., *bapí, bapí*). Cumulative relative duration of stuttering on the first syllable for the two utterances of each word was the dependent variable.

As noted earlier, the first consonant (C_1, as in *bapi*) accounted for the

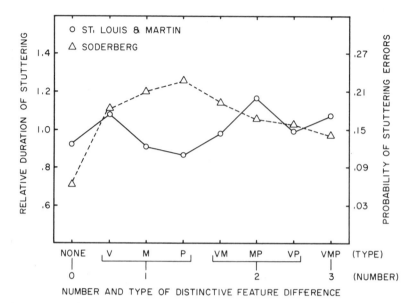

Figure 2. Comparative profiles of stuttering on bisyllabic nonsense words from two studies as a function of the number and type of distinctive feature differences between the two consonants. The solid line represents the mean relative duration of stuttering of eight stutterers (St. Louis & Martin, 1976); the dotted line represents the probability of stuttering errors of 20 stutterers (Soderberg, 1972).

greatest amount of variance in stuttering.[1] The second consonant (C_2, as in *bapi*) had some effect on stuttering on the first syllable, but the effects were much less pronounced—and different—than those exerted by the first consonant. Grouping initial consonants (C_1) or second consonants (C_2) according to three distinctive features was less explanatory than considering isolated consonants. The results were analyzed, as those just discussed by Soderberg (1972), according to the number of distinctive feature contrasts. Figure 2 compares the data from the two experiments.

It is clear that the type of distinctive feature difference interacts with the number of distinctive feature differences, even in Soderberg's results. For example, in his study the mean for differences in one feature are greater than differences in two features, but differences in voicing alone have a slightly lower probability of stuttering than differences in manner and place combined. It is obvious that the results of St. Louis and

---

[1] This and the previous discussion involve only the control condition. The experimental condition will be discussed in Section V,C.

Martin's study do not replicate those of Soderberg. However, many differences exist between the two studies relative to experimental stimuli, speech tasks, and dependent variables.

Contextual effects at the distinctive feature level were present to some degree in St. Louis and Martin's study. A tendency was observed that longer durations of stuttering were associated with C_1 when the distinctive feature component of C_2 was different from that in C_1. In fact, significantly more stuttering occurred on the same initial syllables when C_1 and C_2 contained contrasting feature components for manner and place (e.g., C_1 a stop and C_2 a fricative) than when components were noncontrastive (e.g., C_1 and C_2 both stops). For voicing, differences were not significant.

Except for these contrastive component differences, distinctive features provided no more parsimonious explanation of stuttered speech than individual phoneme differences, since individual differences were often disguised in group data.

B. Syllabic Variables in Stuttering

1. Syllabic Stress: Adults

Brown (1938b) analyzed the results of his earlier study (Johnson & Brown, 1935) in part to determine the effect of syllable accent or stress on the occurrence of stuttering. All 32 stutterers had more stuttering on accented than on unaccented syllables. Since most stuttering occurred on beginning syllables, and since most beginning syllables were accented, it was possible that the increased stuttering on accented syllables was due to their occurrence at the beginning of words.[2] Therefore, stutterings on second or subsequent syllables of polysyllabic words were analyzed. Twenty-four, or 75%, of his subjects had significantly more stuttering on accented than on unaccented syllables, and another four subjects showed the same effect but did not reach statistical significance. Hahn (1942b) was intrigued that stuttering often occurred on other than initial sounds of words such as *important, expensive,* and *before.* He commented that in such words stuttering almost invariably was associated with stressed syllables. In spontaneous speech, Hejna (1955) found more stuttering on stressed than on unstressed syllables in spontaneous speech, both in initial positions and later syllabic positions of polysyllabic words.

Perhaps because of the confounding of word accent and word position,

[2] This is what Wingate (1976) reported from an analysis of three word lists of English. He concluded that less than 20% of English words have primary stress on any syllable other than the first syllable.

Brown (1945) did not include the former as one of his four factors to account for the occurrence of stuttering. This was unfortunate, because many of the later investigations of the loci of stuttering left the syllabic stress variable uncontrolled, as noted by Soderberg and MacKay (1972) and Wingate (1976, 1977).

St. Louis and Martin (1976) found that four stutterers who stressed the first syllable of bisyllabic nonsense words experienced longer stuttering durations than four subjects who stressed the second syllable of the same words. This finding must be interpreted with caution, however, because the two most severe stutterers with the longest stuttering durations were placed, by random assignment, into the group required to stress the first syllable. Also, the overall sample size was small, four stutterers in each group.

2. Syllable Position: Adults

MacKay and Soderberg (1970e) constructed nonsense word pairs which used identical phonemes but which were arranged in syllables in three ways: CVC (e.g., sap), CCV (e.g., spa), and VCC (e.g., asp). Thirty stutterers and 48 nonstutterers were asked to repeat syllable pairs at maximum rate. Preliminary data analysis indicated that no repetition errors occurred for either group on syllable final consonants (e.g., VCC). Repetition of vowels, or segments including vowels, was about equal for both groups with all three kinds of syllables. However, stutterers had many times more repetition errors of initial consonant(s) in CCV or CVC syllables than nonstutterers.

The same researchers conducted another study designed to assess the effect of syllabic position on contextual influences (MacKay & Soderberg, 1970d). Stutterers rapidly repeated nonsense syllable pairs which were of the following form:

Syllabic structure	Sample stimuli
CV–CCV	ta–tro
CVC–CV	tat–ro
CCV–CCV	pra–plo
CCVC–CV	prap–lo

Preliminary analysis indicated that significantly more stuttering errors occurred on the first of interacting segments when they occupied the same syllabic position (e.g., ta–tro and pra–plo) than when they occurred in a different syllabic position (e.g., tat–ro and prap–lo).

C. Morphological Variables in Stuttering

1. Word Length: Adults

Based on the commonly observed phenomenon that stuttering is often associated with long and difficult words, Brown and Moren (1942) partially reanalyzed the results of the data collected by Johnson and Brown (1935) to assess the influence of word length on stuttering. They analyzed stuttering on adjectives and prepositions only because adjectives were found to have the greatest frequency of stuttering and prepositions next to the least frequency in a prior analysis (Brown, 1937). Brown and Moren found that stuttering increased as word length within each category increased. This was true when length was determined either by the number of syllables or the number of printed letters per word. Hejna (1955) found that greater than expected stuttering in spontaneous speech occurred on words whose printed length was greater than six letters. Less than expected values occurred on words of two or three letters.

In studies combining factors of word length with other factors, Brown (1945), Oxtoby (1955), and Trotter (1956) concluded that words of greater than five letters in printed length are important in determining the frequency and severity of stuttering. Silverman and Williams (1967) concurred and reported that 93% of their stutterers were more disfluent on long than on short words. It must be remembered, however, that word length in these studies was only one of four factors considered additively.

Most recent studies have attempted to separate the influence of word length from other interacting linguistic variables. Quarrington et al. (1962) attempted to control for word length in an investigation of the relative influence of grammatical class, word position, and initial sound in determining stuttering. For both initial and final words in six-word sentences, adverbs were stuttered most, but these words were also longer than three other grammatical classes by approximately one to one and a half letters in printed length. Thus, word length may have been an important confounding variable in their study.

Schlesinger, Forte, Fried, and Melkman (1965) suggested that longer words were stuttered more than shorter words in a passage from a third-grade Hebrew textbook. These authors did not independently vary word length; instead, they found that low-frequency words were stuttered more than high-frequency words. Citing Zipf's (1949) finding that long words are less frequent than short words (in English), they offered the alternative explanation of their word frequency results that long words are stuttered more than short words for "purely phonetic reasons" (p. 36).

In another study, however, Schlesinger, Melkman, and Levy (1966) did investigate the effect of word length. They had 31 young stutterers read lists of words which varied as a function of three degrees of word length and three levels of word frequency. Words were controlled for initial sound. Word length was a more powerful predictor of stuttering than word frequency, although both variables were important. Of the total experimental words stuttered, 55% were three-syllable words, 31% were two-syllable words, and 14% were one-syllable words. Taylor (1966a) found words of six or more letters in a sixth-grade reading passage to be associated with significantly more stuttering than shorter words. However, the word length factor was not as potent as either the consonant–vowel factor or word position in a sentence.

Soderberg (1966) categorized word lists into three lengths according to the number of syllables in the word. Short words were one syllable, medium words were two syllables, and long words were three, four, or five syllables. The word lists were systematically varied as a function of high, medium, and low word frequency and were controlled for word stress, initial sound, and grammatical function. Twenty stutterers read each list, one word at a time. Word length and, to a lesser extent, word frequency were found to be independent, statistically significant factors in accounting for the frequency of stuttering. Moreover, stuttering frequency increased from a mean of 2.85 stutterings on short words, to 4.00 for medium words, and 4.87 for long words.

Wingate (1967) had 14 stutterers read two lists of words exposed by a special window apparatus. The first list consisted of one-syllable word pairs (e.g., *fan* and *see*) while the second list was composed of phonetically identical two-syllable words (e.g., *fancy*). In spite of only half the number of words shown in the second condition, more stutterings occurred on the longer words (22.1%) than on the shorter words (8.7%).

One of the most controversial linguistic interactions is that between word length and information load. The latter term, to be discussed in detail under syntactic variables (Section II,D), refers to the predictability of a word from context. Highly predictable words have low-information loading and unpredictable words have high-information loading.

Lanyon (1969) attempted to separate the overlapping effects on stuttering of word length and information load in both oral reading and spontaneous speech. In the case of oral reading performance, he partially reanalyzed Quarrington's (1965) data of 24 adult stutterers reading a 95-word passage. Word length was significantly correlated with stuttering frequency even when the information value of the words was held constant. The converse was **not** true; that is, whereas information value was significantly related to stuttering when all words were considered, it was not significantly related to stuttering when word length was held constant.

Lanyon concluded that word length was a more potent factor than information load.

Lanyon (1969) also reported a study of eight adult stutterers engaged in spontaneous speech. He found that word information was significantly related to word length but not to stuttering when information was the dependent variable. On the contrary, word length was found to be significantly related to stuttering (measured in binary fashion of whether a word was stuttered or not), again supporting the superior predictive power of word length over information load.

Soderberg (1971) considered the total number of stutterings of 19 adult stutterers during oral reading of a 141-word passage. In two independent analyses, he found that both word length and word information were significant variables in accounting for stuttering. In the independent analyses, word length and word information were considered on **separate** words from the passage, controlled carefully for initial sound, grammatical class, frequency, and sentence position. However, when the **same** words representing high and low levels of word length and information were selected, the two factors were found to interact, as Lanyon (1969) had found. Soderberg had classified stutterings according to type as either prolongations or repetitions. Stuttering type was found to be important in the above interaction. Short words had lower information values and fewer stutterings than long words and were either repeated or prolonged to about the same degree. However, long words were associated with significantly more repetitions than prolongations when they contained low information values and significantly more prolongations when they reflected high information.

Danzger and Halpern (1973) counterbalanced 72 words according to three levels of abstraction, three grammatical classes, two levels of frequency, and two levels of length. Long words contained at least two syllables and at least six letters; short words were of one syllable and had no more than four letters. In an analysis of variance, word length was the only statistically significant factor beyond the usual significance level of $p < .05$. Word frequency ($p < .10$) accounted for some of the variance, but neither abstraction nor grammatical class was apparently important. The authors speculated that the stutterer's "image" of a longer word may contain more possibilities of phonemic error than the "image" of a shorter word, thereby accounting for the word length factor.

2. Word Length: Children

D. E. Williams *et al.* (1969) analyzed the verbal imitations or oral reading performance of 76 elementary school-aged stutterers according to Brown's (1945) four factors. Long words occasioned more stutterings than short words in 66% of their group, a significant difference from chance.

3. Word Frequency: Adults

As noted previously, Zipf (1949) found that longer words occur less frequently in English than shorter words. Since word length is clearly an important determinant of stuttering, the need to assess the independence of word frequency and word length is apparent.

Hejna (1963) reported that low-frequency words were stuttered more than high-frequency words. Schlesinger *et al.* (1965) classified 153 words from a third-grade Hebrew text as either high or low frequency in Hebrew according to published word counts. The words were controlled for a predominance of stuttering on certain sounds by some stutterers by eliminating those sounds from consideration for all stutterers, and the words were systematically varied as a function of high or low information load. The variables of frequency and information load were interrelated. More stuttering occurred on high information than on low information words, and, within the high information category, low-frequency words were stuttered more than high-frequency words (13.0 versus 10.6%). However, within the low information group, frequency had little apparent effect (6.6 versus 7.9% for low and high frequencies, respectively). In another study investigating the interaction of word frequency and word length, Schlesinger *et al.* (1966) found that word frequency, as well as length, had an effect on stuttering. Of the total experimental words stuttered, 47% were low frequency, 29% were medium frequency, and 24% were high frequency.

In a study referred to earlier, Soderberg (1966) investigated the influence of word frequency and word length on stuttering during the reading of word lists. The lists were varied as a function of three levels each of word frequency (according to Thorndike–Lorge word lists) and word length. The reader will recall that both factors were statistically significant in a two-way analysis of variance, but word length was a stronger factor than word frequency in determining stuttering. As was the case with word length, mean stuttering frequencies for the word frequency values showed a progressive increase from high to low frequencies, or from common to uncommon words.

In another study of word length described in the previous section, Wingate (1967) found that stuttering was significantly more likely on low-frequency than on high-frequency one-syllable words. He found no difference between high- and low-frequency words for two-syllable words.

Danzger and Halpern (1973) considered the effects of word frequency on stuttering in the reading of word lists further counterbalanced according to word abstraction, grammatical class, and word length. After the highly significant effect of word length, word frequency was weakly instrumental in accounting for the observed stutterings. Neither abstraction nor grammatical class was significant.

Recently, Ronson (1976) studied the interaction of word frequency and grammatical complexity in the oral reading of 16 stutterers. He found that stuttering significantly increased from higher to lower frequency levels of key words in simple active declarative sentences and negative sentences. Nearly the same effect was present for passive sentences, but this was not statistically significant. Ronson analyzed the three levels of frequency and three sentence types with subjects grouped according to mild, moderate, and severe stutterers. This yielded 27 different means which, but for four minor exceptions, were distributed in the expected order. Nevertheless, word frequency was found to make a significant difference in the declarative and negative sentences only for severe stutterers. It is likely that the small number of degrees of freedom in the error term (8) prevented other statistically significant differences in the analysis of variance of Ronson's very consistent data.

4. Word Frequency: Children

In a different kind of experiment, Boysen and Cullinan (1971) investigated the effects of word frequency on the object naming latencies of stuttering and nonstuttering children of elementary school age. Overall, their stutterers had **shorter** latencies than controls, and latencies were shorter for high-frequency than for low-frequency words. While the authors recognize the potentially confounding effect of other factors (such as word length), they suggest that perhaps the low-frequency words involve more complex motor planning.

D. Syntactic Variables in Stuttering

1. Word Position: Adults

The position of a word within a sentence, phrase, or utterance has been found to be important in determining the probability of stuttering. Brown (1938b) analyzed Johnson and Brown's (1935) data to assess the effect of word position. Of the approximately 10,000 words read by each of 32 stutterers, the first, second, and third words of 698 sentences, 178 paragraphs, and 60 sections (topical categories) were compared to the remaining words. The results for initial sentences, paragraphs, and sections were quite similar. Approximately three-fourths of the subjects experienced more stuttering on the first words (72–81%) as compared to other word positions. Percentages declined for the second and third positions, 47–72% and 38–50%, respectively. Brown (1945) therefore considered the first three word positions of a sentence as predictive of stuttering and assigned plus value weights for them. Subsequent positions were assigned minus value. Increasing word weights were associated with more stuttering, a finding replicated by Oxtoby (1955) and Trotter (1956). Silverman and Williams (1967) found that 80% of their stutterers were more disfluent on the first three words of a sentence compared to the later words.

Hejna (1955) analyzed the spontaneous speech of stutterers and reported greater than chance stuttering frequencies on the second, third, fourth, sixth, and seventh word positions. No group trends were apparent for the **first**, fifth, and eighth through the fifteenth word positions.

Quarrington et al. (1962) suggested that Hejna's failure to find the position effect in the first word in spontaneous speech was perhaps due to the prevalence of stereotypic "starter" words used by some stutterers. They constructed 64 six-word sentences with experimental words varied as a function of word position (first and last), grammatical class, and initial sounds, and controlled for syllabic stress, word length, and word frequency. Word position was the most powerful factor in a four-way analysis of variance, significant at the $p < .005$ level of significance. Mean percentage of stuttering was 45.3% on the first words and 24.1% on the last words.

Conway and Quarrington (1963) assessed three positions in seven-word sentences which varied along three levels of contextual constraint: (1) meaningful sentences, (2) partially meaningful sentences (each third word being determined by only two other words), and (3) random word sequences. Experimental words were controlled for initial phoneme, grammatical class, syllabic stress, word length, and word frequency. Word position and contextual constraint were both significantly predictive of stuttering. Mean stuttering values showed a declining gradient from initial to final position for all three levels of contextual constraint.

Quarrington (1965) extended the above findings by jointly analyzing word position and information load in a short passage of "banal prose" read once by each of 24 adult stutterers. The number of stutterings per word was significantly correlated with word position ($r = -.49$), even when word information held constant ($r = -.45$).[3] The same was true for

---

[3] The reader will recall that when the variable of word length was controlled in a reanalysis of these data, the word position correlation was rendered insignificant (Lanyon, 1969).

word information but to a lesser extent, indicating that word position and word information are independent factors affecting stuttering.

Taylor (1966a) subjected the prose reading of nine stutterers to a factorial analysis and found that initial, medial, and terminal word position was a statistically significant factor falling between the consonant–vowel factor and word length factor in predictive strength. Positions were considered both within sentences and within phrases bounded by commas. Taylor (1966a, 1966b) considered the probability that a word in any position would be stuttered if no prior word in the phrase were stuttered. She ran separate analyses for her six mild and three severe stutterers. For both mild and severe groups, position gradients were roughly parallel and declined as a function of increasing numbers of words spoken fluently before stuttering. An important finding, too, was that there was an alternating pattern between even- and odd-numbered positions. Taylor and Taylor (1967) then analyzed the results of four of the nine stutterers in terms of the number of fluent words between adjacent instances of stuttering. Again, an alternating pattern emerged up to the ninth word between stutterings.

Soderberg (1967, p. 803) investigated the effects on stuttering of word position within "phonologically marked macrosegments," each containing just one primary stress and ending in a terminal juncture. Words in a 141-word passage were categorized according to grammatical class and rated for information load. Ten stutterers read the passage, and their stutterings were divided into repetitions and prolongations. Clauses up to six words in length showed the usual declining position gradient, but clauses of greater than six words did not. Soderberg found that stuttering occurred in "vollies" of decreasing frequency with greater than expected levels on the first, third, and seventh words in the clause. He suggested that this alternating pattern, as well as that observed by Taylor (1966a), could be explained by variations, in the opposite direction, in word information. Word position and word length were highly correlated ($r = .88$). Soderberg explained the predominance of stuttering on the first word in clauses in terms of grammatical uncertainty which is independent of grammatical class. In medial clause positions, stuttering is observed predominantly on content words of high-information rather than low-information function words because, once the clause is begun, difficult word choice is the primary problem presented to the speaker. In final clause position, lexical uncertainty and word information are minimal; therefore, stuttering is unlikely, regardless of the grammatical class of words.

Hannah and Gardner (1968) analyzed the spontaneous speech performance of eight stutterers who were instructed to paraphrase a story they had read silently. As in Soderberg's study, trained linguists segmented the speech material into clauses or "macrosegments." These clauses were then further divided into preverbal, verbal, and postverbal segments as well as into syntactic classes. The greatest percentage of stuttering occurred in postverbal segments (48%) with about equal frequencies in the preverbal (27%) and verbal (25%) segments. This finding is at odds with previous research which has shown the greatest frequency of stuttering early in clauses and sentences.

Lanyon (1969) **indirectly** showed that word position was not an important variable in predicting stuttering, again in the spontaneous speech of stutterers. In one analysis, word position and fluency were unrelated to word information. In another analysis, fluency and initial sound were related to word length, but word position was not.

Tornick and Bloodstein (1976) had 14 stutterers read 20 short sentences such as *She learned to swim* and 20 long sentences such as *She learned to swim in the clear water of the lake.* Stuttering was compared only on the identical parts of each sentence. Surprisingly, the majority of stutterings did not occur in the beginning segments of the long sentences. Only 35% of the total stutterings on the long sentences occurred on the initial clause; 65% occurred on the second clause.

2. Word Position: Children

D. E. Williams *et al.* (1969) found that 66% of 76 elementary aged stutterers had more stuttering on words of five or more letters in printed length compared to shorter words.

Bloodstein and Gantwerk (1967) sampled the spontaneous speech of 13 preschool children, ages 3 to 6 years, in free-play sessions. The data were analyzed for the comparative incidence of stuttering on various grammatical classes. Conjunctions and pronouns were associated with greater than chance occurrences of stuttering. The authors, however, attributed these findings to a positional factor. They hypothesized that words such as *he, I, it, but, so* are prominent at the beginning of young children's sentences and that their position is more important in determining stuttering than their grammatical class.

From a single-subject analysis of protocols from six other preschool stutterers, Bloodstein (1974) again explained the loci of stuttering primarily in terms of word position. He hypothesized that the earliest stutterings occur at the beginnings of sentences and major syntactic subdivisions. As the stutterers grow older, stutterings are found at the beginning of smaller syntactic units such as phrases and, finally, at the beginning of words within syntactic units.

3. Grammatical Class: Adults

Brown (1937) reanalyzed the data of Johnson and Brown (1935) to determine whether stuttering was observed more frequently on some grammatical classes than others. The words in the oral reading passages of his 32 stutterers were first analyzed according to 23 grammatical categories. Only 18 of the categories occurred sufficiently often in the reading passages for statistical treatment, so the analyses were made on these 18 categories as shown in Table I. These categories were found to be quite consistent within subjects and among subjects. The median "consistency coefficient" between rank-orders of the grammatical categories for one-half of the data of each subject compared to the other half was .91 (range = −.41 to +.99). The median rank-order correlation coefficient between individual ranks and overall group ranking was .85 (range = .36 to .97). Brown reported that, since none of the differences among subdivisions within each category (i.e., adjectives) were statistically significant, the data were regrouped according to the eight traditional parts of speech as shown in Table II. The first four grammatical classes (adjectives, nouns, adverbs, and verbs) were given plus values in predicting stuttering in Brown's (1945) multifactor reanalysis. The remaining four classes (pro-

Table I. Median Percentage of Stuttering on 18 Grammatical Categories Arranged from Most to Least Stuttering[a]

Rank	Grammatical class	Median percentage stuttering
1	Participial adjectives	14.1
2	Proper nouns	9.6
3	Gerunds	8.1
4	Adjectives	8.0
5	Adverbs	7.0
6	Nouns	6.6
7	Root verbs (in verb phrase)	5.3
8	Simple verbs	4.7
9	Subordinating conjunctions	3.8
10	Relative pronouns	3.2
11	Personal pronouns	2.6
12	Infinitives	2.1
13	Coordinating conjunctions	2.0
14	Prepositions	1.9
15	Auxiliary verbs	1.6
16	Possessive pronouns	1.2
17	Articles	.6
18	Prepositions linked to verbs	.0

[a] Adapted from Brown (1937, p. 208).

Kenneth O. St. Louis

Table II.   Median Percentage of Stuttering on Eight Grammatical Categories Arranged from Most to Least Stuttering[a]

Rank	Grammatical class	Median percentage stuttering
1	Adjectives	8.2
2	Nouns	7.7
3	Adverbs	6.5
4	Verbs	3.8
5	Pronouns	2.5
6	Conjunctions	2.0
7	Prepositions	1.8
8	Articles	.6

[a] Adapted from Brown (1937, p. 209).

nouns, conjunctions, prepositions, and articles) were accorded minus values, or not indicative of stuttering. In the current literature, these two groups are referred to as content and function words, respectively.

Brown's criterion for statistical significance was obviously very strict. For example, participial adverbs, with a median percentage of stuttering of 14.1, were not significantly different from adjectives, with a median percentage of 8.0 (Table I). Moreover, none of the differences in the reranking shown in Table II were statistically different either. In a later study (Brown, 1938b), several examples of nonsignificance are provided. In one case, Brown stated that 31 cases had significantly more stutterings on the first, or accented, syllable than on later unaccented syllables. "The remaining case had a difference in the same direction which was 2.3 times its standard error, **with 99 chances in 100 of being a true difference**" (emphasis added, Brown, 1938b, p. 113). Returning to the 1937 study on grammatical class, if Brown had used the current $p < .05$ significance level, it is likely that his grammatical categories would have been quite different.

Hahn (1942a) replicated Brown's (1937) findings in the oral reading of 43 stutterers. With minor variations in rank, the four highest grammatical categories were the same: adjectives, nouns, verbs, and adverbs. These were followed by prepositions, pronouns, articles, conjunctions, and interjections, also very similar to Brown's results.

The grammatical factor was found to be one of four important but interrelated factors in predicting stuttering frequency and severity during reading (Oxtoby, 1955; Trotter, 1956). In the spontaneous speech of high school stutterers, Hejna (1955) observed greater than expected levels of stuttering on nouns and adjectives and less than expected levels on prepositions, articles, expletives, and interjections. No significant trends were observed for pronouns, verbs, adverbs, and conjunctions. Silverman and Williams (1967) found that 93% of their stutterers had more stuttering on nouns, verbs, adjectives, and adverbs than other grammatical categories.

Quarrington *et al.* (1962) had 27 adult stutterers read six-word sentences varied along dimensions of grammatical class (nouns, verbs, adjectives, and adverbs), word position, and initial sound. Grammatical class was found to follow word position in strength as a predictor of stuttering. The rank-order of difficulty, from most to least frequent stuttering was: adverbs, verbs, adjectives, and nouns. This ranking was different than that of Brown (1937) or Hahn (1942a). As pointed out in the discussion of word length, this effect may be confounded with word length as adverbs had the greatest number of letters in printed length. However, nouns which were lowest in the ranking of Quarrington *et al.* (1962) were next to adverbs in length.

Taylor (1966a) divided experimental words from oral reading into content and function categories. Too few entries were present to include the content–function dichotomy in the factorial analysis of initial sound, word position, and word length. Nevertheless, content words were associated with more stuttering than function words. The point–biserial correlation coefficient between this dichotomy and stuttering frequency was .12 ($p <$ .05). Similar correlations were then run separately for words beginning with consonants and vowels. In the latter cases, correlations were near zero, indicating that there were no differences in stuttering between content and function words starting with vowels and between those starting with consonants. Therefore, Taylor (1966b) postulated that the apparent effect of grammatical class was due to the consonant–vowel factor. She concluded that when separated from the factors of initial sound, word position, and word length, the grammatical factor has not been demonstrated.

Soderberg (1967) observed that 10 stutterers stuttered more often on content "lexical" words (nouns, verbs, adjectives, and adverbs) than function words (articles, personal pronouns, possessive pronouns, conjunctions, prepositions, auxiliaries, interrogatives, and noun determiners). In Soderberg's 141-word passage, it was found that function words were most prevalent in initial clause positions while content words were most prevalent in final positions. In neither initial nor final positions were greater than expected values of stuttering observed on content or function words. However, content words in medial positions were associated with significantly more stuttering and function words with significantly less stuttering than would be expected by chance. Since most of the stuttering in clause-initial positions occurred on function words, Soderberg joins

Taylor (1966a, 1966b) in questioning Brown's (1945) notion that content words are stuttered more than function words.

Soderberg also analyzed his data according to type of stuttering symptom. He observed a general pattern, but not without some variability, that content words were often associated with stuttering prolongations, and function words were usually associated with stuttering repetitions. This was true particularly in medial clause positions.

Wingate (1967) found that stutterers had relatively more stuttering on both short and long content words than on function words. In his investigation, however, grammatical classes were not represented equally.

Hannah and Gardner (1968) analyzed spontaneous speech samples of eight stutterers according to syntactic units within clauses: subject, verb, and object/complement/optional adverb. As mentioned earlier, they also considered preverbal, verbal, and postverbal segments which roughly corresponded to the three syntactic units. Forty-four percent of the stutterings occurred within the object/complement/optional adverb category (usually in the postverbal position), 30% occurred in the subject category (usually preverbal position), and 26% occurred in the verb category (verbal position). These differences were not statistically significant, however. Objects, complements, and optional adverbs were analyzed separately, yielding 20, 16, and 8%, respectively, to total the 44% within that category. In addition, the authors divided the words within preverbal, verbal, and postverbal segments into content and function words. In all three positions, there were more content than function words, but Spearman rank-order correlations between the frequency of these words and the percentage of stuttering were higher for function words (.32, .25, and −.43) than for content words (.04, .17, and .28). Taken together, these findings do not support the notion that content words are stuttered more than function words.

Danzger and Halpern (1973) had 16 stutterers read nouns, verbs, and adjectives varied systematically according to level of abstraction, length, and word frequency. Mean percentage of stuttering on the three grammatical classes was as follows: nouns, 19.8%; adjectives, 16.8%; and verbs, 16.5%. In a four-way analysis of variance, these differences were not statistically significant.

4. Grammatical Class: Children

Bloodstein and Gantwerk (1967) found that the spontaneous speech of preschool stutterers differed considerably from the results obtained with adults. Significantly greater than chance occurrences of stuttering were present for conjunctions and pronouns, and significantly less than chance occurrences were observed for interjections and nouns. No significant differences were obtained for adjectives, adverbs, articles, prepositions, and verbs. The reader will recall that the greater than expected stutterings on conjunctions and pronouns were attributed to a position effect.

D. E. Williams *et al.* (1969) found that 65% of their 76 elementary school stutterers had more stuttering on nouns, verbs, adjectives, and adverbs than on other grammatical classes. These results were obtained from verbal imitation and oral reading of sentences. Helmreich and Bloodstein (1973) commented on the fact that D. E. Williams *et al.* (1969) found the traditional grammatical factor and that Bloodstein and Gantwerk (1967) had not. They hypothesized that a change in the grammatical distribution of a child's stutterings occurs sometime around the preschool to elementary school years.

Harvey-Fisher and Brutten (1977) analyzed part-word repetitions in the spontaneous utterances of five 4- to 6-year-old stutterers in terms of grammatical class. Considering the categories of nouns, verbs, pronouns, and conjunctions, progressively more stuttering occurred on categories in the order listed. The inordinately high percentages of stuttering on conjunctions and pronouns are in agreement with Bloodstein and Gantwerk (1967).

5. Information Load: Adults

Many researchers investigating the linguistic determinants of stuttering have attempted to determine the probability that any given word will be stuttered. With the procedures developed in information theory, it became possible to assign a probability value to every word in the speech sequence. Thus, any word could be given a probability of stuttering and a probability of occurrence (or information load) and the relationship between the two could be determined.

Information load is expressed in several terms: predictability from context, grammatical uncertainty, transition probability, contextual constraint, or word information. The various procedures for determining information load are quite similar; words are assigned values reflecting the degree to which they can be guessed from previously (or later) occurring words within a written or spoken sequence. For example, if listeners were presented with the sequence *John will take* ____ and asked to predict the next word, the article *a* would have a high probability of being guessed. Being quite predictable from context, *a* can be said to contain low information load. On the other hand, if listeners were asked to guess the next word of *I am going to* ____, the verb *find* would have a lower probability of guesses. Being relatively unpredictable from context, it would have high information load.

Conway and Quarrington (1963) had 23 stutterers read 72 seven-word sentences with three levels of contextual constraint. Critical words varied as a function of position and were controlled for initial sound, grammatical class, word stress, and word length. Information load (contextual constraint) and word position were statistically significant factors with the most stuttering occurring on normal "text-order" sentences such as *Heroes gain considerable praise in our culture.* Less stuttering occurred on "three-order" sentences such as *Heroes in the continual noise is communication,* and least stuttering occurred on "zero-order" sentences such as *Heroes station majority part manner glass consume.*

Quarrington (1965) found that stutterings on words of a short reading passage were significantly correlated with information load of the words and word position. Information load was determined by the mean guesses of 46 normal speakers.

Schlesinger *et al.* (1965) determined information loads of words in a passage from a third-grade Hebrew text by averaging the guesses of 60 college students for each word. Experimental words were varied according to word frequency and controlled for excessively stuttered sounds for any of their 10 stutterers. Their data indicated that word information interacts with word frequency. High information words (words of "**low** transition probability" in this study) were stuttered significantly more (11.7%) than low information words (7.2%). Word frequency was relatively unimportant within the low information class (6.6 and 7.9% for high and low frequencies, respectively), but frequency appeared to make a difference among high information words (10.6% for high frequency and 13.0% for low frequency).

In a similar task for nine stutterers, Taylor (1966a) parceled out the effects of initial sound, word position, word length, and grammatical class (indirectly) on stuttering. While she did not directly assess the effects of information loadings in her study, she argued in this paper and in another (Taylor, 1966b) that information load "uncertainty" was one of the strongest explanatory mechanisms underlying all of the variables affecting the loci of stuttering.

As mentioned earlier, Soderberg (1967) found that information load was highly correlated with stuttering ($r = .88$). He found, not surprisingly, that high information words occurred predominantly on the initial word of clauses and that the majority of low information words were distributed quite evenly between medial and final positions. Similar to the results for content versus function words, differences in stuttering between high and low information words were not significantly different from chance at clause-initial and -final positions. However, information load differences were significant in medial positions. Soderberg speculated that high uncertainty at the beginning of clauses would elicit stuttering regardless of the word class. In medial positions the search for high information content words would evoke more stuttering than the more automatic low information function words. Overall low uncertainty in final positions again would render word class an insignificant variable and stuttering less likely to occur.

Type of stuttering tended to follow word information as well as word class. Prolongations occurred more frequently than chance on high information and content words and repetitions more frequently on low information and function words.

Lanyon (1968, 1969) compared the effects of information loading of words in oral reading and spontaneous speech of stutterers. The 1968 study of three stutterers was treated as a pilot study for the 1969 investigation. Lanyon (1969) reanalyzed Quarrington's (1965) data on the oral reading of 24 stutterers but recalculated Quarrington's correlations between word information and stuttering after controlling for word length. In this way, Quarrington's significant correlation of .32 was reduced to a nonsignificant .16. Therefore, Lanyon asserted that word information was **not** an important predictor of stuttering.

Lanyon also analyzed the spontaneous speech of eight stutterers. This analysis is considerably different from the results already reviewed. Instead of using stuttering as a continuous dependent variable, fluent words were randomly paired with stuttered words to yield one of four two- or three-level **independent** variables (fluency, sentence position, word length, and initial sound). In two parallel three-way analyses of variance using word information as the **dependent** variable, word length was the only significant contributing factor in either analysis. Fluency was not a significant factor. Lanyon used these rather unorthodox results to reject the notion that stuttering is related to word information load in either the oral reading or spontaneous speech of stutterers.

Soderberg (1971) suggested that Lanyon's lack of confirmation of the factor of information load might have been due to his definition of stuttering, a definition which included the disfluencies of normal speakers. Using at least 70% agreement of seven speech pathologists to identify prolongations and repetitions, he analyzed the oral reading of 19 stutterers. [Nine additional stutterers were added to the 10 in his earlier study (Soderberg, 1967) and subjects read the same 141-word passage.] All of the data were analyzed first for high and low word information by selecting words controlled for initial sound, grammatical class, frequency, length, and position. Significantly more stuttering occurred on the high information words. In a similar but separate analysis, word length was found to be a significant factor. Since these results were not in agreement with Lanyon (1969), Soderberg chose 40 words representing two levels each of word information and length so that the two variables could be assessed in the same analysis. He noted that the words could not be as carefully controlled as in the two independent analyses. In the simultaneous analysis, word information was found not to be a significant variable, in support of Lanyon's finding. However, when stuttering types were considered, it was found that significantly greater than chance occurrences of repetition were on low information words and prolongations on high information words. This replicated Soderberg's (1967) result. However, further analysis showed that this effect was true only for long words.

Soderberg postulated that since long words were always associated with more stuttering than short words, stuttering increased with word length for "phonetic" reasons (i.e., increased articulatory complexity). However, the degree of uncertainty or information load of the longer words may determine the type of stuttering disfluency which will occur.

Kroll and Hood (1976) had 14 adult stutterers and matched controls read two 150-word passages, one of high information loading and the other of low information loading. Although the passages were "calibrated" for information load, they were not controlled for initial sound, word length, or word position (Miller & Coleman, 1967). Subjects read each passage repeatedly under two sets of instructions, the results of which are not pertinent to this discussion. Pooled results for information load indicated significantly less adaptation for the high information than for the low information passage. Inspection of the adaptation curves revealed that, while subjects adapted on both passages, the slope was less steep for the high information passage than for the low information passage.

6. Grammatical Complexity: Adults

Hannah and Gardner (1968) found that grammatical complexity was an important factor in accounting for the stuttering of eight subjects in spontaneous speech. They found, for example, that stuttering which occurred in postverbal segments of clauses varied as a function of how the postverbal segment was expanded. When the postverbal segment was either one word or a clause, significant positive correlations between the frequency of occurrence of the structure and the frequency of stuttering were observed. This was partly, but not significantly, so when a postverbal segment was expanded into a longer unit, such as noun plus modifier, adjective plus intensifier, or adverb plus adjective. However, when the postverbal unit was expanded into a phrase (e.g., adverbial, adjectival, prepositional), stuttering was negatively correlated with frequency of occurrence of the structure. The authors concluded that when a postverbal segment is expanded, the mere addition of words, as in phrases, is not sufficient to occasion more stuttering. However, when a more complex structure, such as an embedded clause, is added, the increased complexity causes more stuttering. The authors commented that "it is possible that a number of linguistic factors may be operating at any one point to make certain language units more difficult for the stutterer than others" (Hannah & Gardner, 1968, p. 859).

Tornick and Bloodstein (1976) investigated the effects of sentence length on stuttering. Fourteen stutterers read 20 short sentences and 20 long sentences, the long sentences being identical to the short sentences except that they contained an added clause. Significantly greater mean stuttering frequencies occurred on the first portions of the long sentences (15.9) than on the entire identical, short sentences (13.9). The authors postulated that this difference was due to the greater demands on motor planning at the beginning of long sentences than of short sentences.

Ronson (1976) found that 16 stutterers had progressively more stutterings on the same selected words in (1) simple active declarative sentences (e.g., *The kind gentle teacher helped the seven new children.*), (2) negative sentences (e.g., *The kind gentle teacher didn't help the seven new children.*), and (3) passive sentences (e.g., *The seven new children were helped by the kind gentle teacher.*). The mean frequency of stuttering for these sentence types, respectively, averaged across three-word frequency levels, were: 1.96, 2.18, and 2.27. Ronson did not test the significance of these differences, and they likely would have been nonsignificant with his procedure. Nonetheless, there is a consistent trend for increased grammatical complexity of sentences to result in more stuttering on otherwise similar words.

Other studies have investigated the language abilities of stutterers instead of linguistic analyses of their stutterings. Knabe, Nelson, and Williams (1966) recorded the responses of 16 stutterers and 16 nonstutterers to personal questions (e.g., *How do you feel when someone laughs at the way you are talking?*) and impersonal questions (e.g., *Describe a Wisconsin winter.*). Stutterers were not significantly different from controls on nine linguistic measures, but differed only on degree of disfluency. The type of question showed different responses within both groups. On the average, personal questions were associated with significantly longer responses (time and total words), greater use of different words, and differences in content and function word output as well as personal and nonpersonal pronoun output.

Onufrak (1973) found stutterers made significantly more errors than controls in estimating the location of 20-msec "clicks" placed in selected vowels within sentences. However, both groups showed similar patterns. The author concluded that stutterers have basically intact linguistic systems but have greater than normal variance on tasks involving restructuring verbal information.

7. Grammatical Complexity: Children

Very little data are available on the effects of grammatical complexity on the occurrence of stuttering in children; yet the interaction between these two factors is suspected by a number of workers. Bloodstein (1974) hypothesized that early stuttering is related to syntactic structures. That is, stuttering first occurs at the beginning of syntactic units, particularly those the child perceives as complex.

On the other hand, a number of studies have investigated the language abilities of stuttering children. A. M. Williams and Marks (1972) found 28 elementary school aged stutterers to differ from norms on the Illinois Test of Psycholinguistic Abilities (ITPA) (Kirk & McCarthy, 1961). Stutterers were significantly lower than expected levels on the Auditory Vocal Sequencing subtest and significantly higher on the Auditory Vocal Association and Vocal Encoding subtests.

Westby (1975) tested three groups of kindergarten children: stutterers, highly disfluent (but not stuttering) children, and "typically" fluent children. The groups were not significantly different on Developmental Sentence Scoring scores (L. L. Lee, 1974), but the stuttering and highly disfluent nonstuttering children made significantly more grammatical errors than the typical nonstuttering children. On other receptive and expressive measures the stutterers were similar to the highly disfluent nonstutterers and both of these groups were somewhat inferior to the typical nonstutterers.

H. L. Murray and Reed (1977) found seven preschool stutterers to be lower than a matched control group on the Preschool Language Scale (Zimmerman, Steiner, & Evatt, 1969), Expressive and Receptive subtests of the Northwestern Syntax Screening Test (L. L. Lee, 1971), and the Peabody Picture Vocabulary Test (Dunn, 1965).

Brookshire and White (1977) reported a language-based carryover program for two 4-year-old stutterers. Both children were deficient in expressive language skills after traditional stuttering therapy. After 6 months of maintenance therapy involving practice using pronouns, progressive verb endings, and other grammatical structures, fluency was maintained and gains were noted on both an imitative and spontaneous test of expressive language.

Stocker and Parker (1977) compared 22 pairs of matched preschool and school-aged children on the Auditory Sequential Memory subtest of the ITPA (Kirk, McCarthy, & Kirk, 1969) and the Auditory Attention Span for Related Syllables subtest of the Detroit Test of Learning Aptitude

(DTLA) (Baker & Leland, 1967). On the ITPA subtest, a test involving memory for digits, the stutterers and nonstutterers were roughly equivalent. However, on the DTLA, which requires memory of meaningful linguistic information, stutterers scored an average of 35 months below their controls. After 6 months of therapy for the experimental group using the Stocker Probe Technique (Stocker, 1977), 11 pairs of stutterers and controls were retested. The stutterers showed marked gains on the DTLA subtest, but the nonstutterers showed an unexplained decrease on this test. The authors offered the interpretation that the therapy-induced fluency in eight of the eleven retested stutterers allowed them to retrieve previously suppressed linguistic skills. However, this conclusion must be interpreted with caution because the authors attributed memory for digits to **right**-hemisphere function, apparently from an incorrect interpretation of Kimura's (1961) research using digits in dichotic listening.

E. Linguistic Determinants: Summary

Can anything meaningful be extracted from this confusing array of data? Do we know linguistically what accounts for the locus of stuttering? The answers are yes and no, depending on our level of analysis.

For the most part, Brown's (1945) four factors (content words, early words in a sentence, long words, and words beginning with consonants) are sufficient to account for most stutterings at least in the oral reading of adults. Nevertheless, this kind of analysis tells us nothing relative to the importance of individual factors. More significantly, it does not identify all of the important factors. Additionally, stutterings are influenced by the position of sounds within words, phonetic context of words, syllabic stress, syllabic position, word frequency, information loading of words, and grammatical complexity of the sentences in which they appear.[4] While recent studies have attempted to control for these factors, none has succeeded in ruling out the confounding and overlapping effects of all of them. Perhaps such a study would be impossible either to design or to analyze meaningfully.

However, it is possible at this point to speculate about the relative potency of each of the linguistic determinants reviewed in this chapter. What follows is an attempt to interpret factors in terms of their overall predictive influence on stuttering.

---

[4] Stuttering is obviously influenced by semantic and communicative factors not considered within the loci of stuttering research, such as propositionality, semantic satiation, emotional loading of words, communicative stress, and general anxiety level. Since these factors include strong cognitive, attitudinal, and emotional components, linguistic components are extremely difficult to isolate.

1. Most Powerful Factors

Position is probably the most powerful factor predicting the loci of stuttering. Initial sound is unquestionably and consistently associated with stuttering; nearly all stutterings occur in relation to the first sound of a word. This is closely related to word position. The first words in a conversation, reading, paragraph, sentence, clause, or utterance are associated with more stuttering than later words. Additively, the initial sound and initial word position factors probably account for the nearly universal phenomenon that stutterers exhibit the greatest amount of stuttering when they first begin to talk. This factor, so well established in oral reading of adults, also holds solidly in the early stutterings of children and in the spontaneous speech* of adults.

Word length is probably the next most powerful factor. Longer words quite consistently are stuttered more often than shorter words in oral reading when other confounding factors are held constant. However, the reason for this fact is not clear because length usually interacts with some of the phonological determinants and all of the other morphological and syntactic determinants of stuttering. Yet, the effect of word length is probably not so powerful in the spontaneous speech of young and older stutterers as it is in oral reading with adults.

Another powerful factor in predicting stuttering is syllable stress. While often overlooked, the evidence is clear that most instances of stuttering occur on stressed syllables as well as words in a sentence which receive heavier than average vocal intensity. Quite likely, syllabic stress will be one linguistic factor relating directly to the motor factors to be reviewed in the next section.

2. Less Powerful Factors

The consonant–vowel effect is an important factor in predicting the loci of stuttering, but its independence is somewhat questionable. For example, more words begin with consonants than vowels, and words which begin with consonants are usually longer than words beginning with vowels. Nevertheless, when other factors are held constant, consonant production is typically associated with substantially more stuttering than vowel production.[5]

Stuttering in the spontaneous speech of children does not appear to occur on consonants as frequently as it does in adults. Whether this is a positional effect remains to be determined by further research.

---

[5] Wingate (1976, 1977) does not agree. He concludes that stuttering is a problem of producing stressed vowels.

3. Least Powerful Factors

The following factors do not exert strong predictive influence on the loci of stuttering, although their existence has been clearly demonstrated. Moreover, designation as least powerful factors is not intended to connote either unimportant or irrelevant. It is quite likely that an understanding of the subtle influences on stuttering will clarify many of the misunderstood phenomena of the disorder.

Information load, or predictability from context, has been used to explain practically all of the linguistic factors of stuttering (Taylor, 1966b). Nonetheless, recent research has not accorded it such a high degree of importance. Perhaps one reason for recent disinterest in information load is that the theoretical framework from which it derives has been so severely criticized. Sequential probability models of grammar do not have the explanatory power of generative transformational models (Bever, Fodor, & Weksel, 1965; Chomsky, 1957, 1965; MacKay, 1970b).

As with many other factors, confounding between information load and other linguistic variables is inevitable. High information words tend to occur early in the speech sequence, begin with consonants, and carry heavy English stress. They also tend to be content words and low-frequency words. While information load may seem to be a parsimonious explanation of most of the linguistic factors affecting stuttering, its basis solely on sequential probability does not allow explanatory hypotheses of why certain high- or low-probability words occasion different amounts of stuttering than others.

If other factors are carefully controlled in the oral reading of adults, more stuttering occurs on low-frequency words than on high-frequency words, on content words (nouns, verbs, adjectives, and adverbs) than on function words (pronouns, conjunctions, prepositions, and articles), and on words in complex grammatical structures than on words in simple grammatical structures. Perhaps the most questionable of these is the grammatical factor, as several researchers have been able to account for the content–function word effect by other means. Furthermore, it has not as yet been demonstrated in the spontaneous speech of preschool-aged stuttering children.

Limited research on the effects of phonetic and syllabic context on stuttering has shown fruitful avenues for further investigation. However, the outcome of that research is yet unclear. Although these least powerful factors are demonstrable in the oral reading of adult stutterers, they have not been sufficiently demonstrated in the spontaneous speech of either younger or older stutterers.

III. MOTOR DETERMINANTS OF STUTTERING

One must conclude from the review of linguistic determinants of stuttering that some sounds, syllables, words, or sentences are inherently more difficult for the stutterer to say than others. Isolating linguistic factors provides only a partial account of this fact. In addition, motor abilities of stutterers must also be considered, particularly with regard to phonetic, syllabic, and word length factors. A full account must determine the extent to which deficiencies in motor abilities of stutterers are responsible for differences in the degree of stuttering on some speech units compared to others. It is obvious that the motor ability of the speaker interacts with linguistic material to be uttered. For this reason, motor abilities of stutterers must be considered before the interaction of linguistic and motor variables can be satisfactorily evaluated.

A. Fine Motor Abilities of Stutterers

Systematic research into the fine motor abilities of stutterers began more than 50 years ago in the United States. It was assumed that if stuttering is the result of a breakdown in the fine motor coordination essential for speech, then a similar breakdown should be evident in other complex skills requiring precise control of small muscle groups.

1. Finger-Tapping Abilities

The search for fine motor analogs of motor speech has centered primarily on the ability of stutterers to tap their fingers in rapid and patterned sequences. Such performances are typically compared to those of nonstutterers in order to determine the presence or absence of subtle motor deficits. If stutterers are shown to be inferior to controls on finger tapping, a skill which eliminates much of the confounding of emotional variables associated with speaking, then the presence of a generalized motor problem in stutterers is indicated.

Studies of finger tapping in stutterers have tested both speed of tapping (rate) and accuracy of maintaining a regular pattern (rhythm). We will first consider studies investigating rate of tapping.

West and Nusbaum (1929) found adult stuttering males to be significantly slower than nonstuttering males in maximum rate of finger tapping. However, female stutterers were nonsignificantly faster than female controls. H. M. Cross (1936) found that stutterers were inferior to nonstuttering controls on rate of finger tapping, but not significantly so. The same general results were found by Rotter in 1938; stutterers were inferior to controls, but differences were not statistically significant (Rotter, 1955). In a more carefully controlled study, however, Strother and Kriegman (1943) found no significant differences between stutterers and nonstutterers, with stutterers scoring slightly **higher** than controls. Their subjects were matched for age, sex, handedness, and rhythm discrimination.

Snyder (1958) compared 75 mild, moderate, and severe stutterers with 25 nonstuttering speech-defective adults controlled for age, sex, education, socioeconomic status, and anxiety. On a speed of tapping test, progressively higher scores were observed for severe stutterers, moderate stutterers, mild stutterers, and nonstutterers.

In an unpublished study, MacKay and Soderberg (1970c) investigated the finger-tapping abilities of stutterers and controls when various arbitrary patterns were required. The experimental variables in the study were derived from a model of speech production errors (MacKay, 1970a, 1970b).

Subjects were 14 right-handed stutterers and 48 nonstutterers. Twelve members of each group were matched for age, sex, handedness, and years of experience typing and playing a musical instrument. The experimental task consisted of tapping four telegraph keys with the four fingers of the left hand at maximum rate. Prior to the experimental task, all subjects were asked to tap one key 20 times with each finger individually at maximum speed. There were no finger differences for either group, but stutterers as a group were slower than nonstutterers.

The experiment was designed to measure errors in finger patterns involving stressed elements (tapping harder than usual), repeated elements (tapping with the same finger twice in a sequence), and both stressed and repeated elements. With fingers numbered from 1 to 4, samples were as follows:

Stressed elements 1 (3) 2 4
Repeated elements 3 1 3 2 4
Stressed and repeated elements 3 1 (3) 2 4

The patterns were designed primarily to look at the main effects on element 3 in the above patterns and errors were scored as "omission" (omitted taps) and "stutters" (repeated taps).

For the 12 stutterers and matched controls, the following results were observed. In terms of error types, stutterers had more stutters than nonstutterers, while the reverse was true for omissions. For both groups, there were greater than expected occurrences of stutters on stressed elements, significantly so for the stutterers. The converse was true for omissions; they occurred more frequently on unstressed elements, and the difference was significant for nonstutterers. For both groups, stutters occurred more on initial elements than later elements. Conversely, omissions occurred less on initial than later elements. Both stutters and omissions occurred more frequently on repeated than on nonrepeated elements.

The data for all 62 subjects were then combined to assess the general effects of stress and repeated elements. Stutters on the first and second repeated elements were more likely if the first were stressed than if it were unstressed. Again, omissions showed the opposite effect. They were more likely on the first repeated element if it were unstressed as compared to stressed.

Caution must be exercised in overemphasizing the results of one study. Nevertheless, the results of MacKay and Soderberg's (1970c) study suggest strongly that stutterers are different from nonstutterers in executing patterns of finger movement. They suggest that:

> the stutterer's problem must lie mainly in integrating a sequence of movements rather than in producing the individual movements by themselves, a finding in accord with the view that stuttering reflects a problem in the serial order of behavior. (p. 14)

Blackburn (1931) conducted the first of a series of studies investigating the ability of stutterers to tap rhythmically. Using Pearson coefficients of variation [(standard deviation × 100)/mean tapping rate] to assess subjects' "regularity" of tapping, he found no significant differences between stutterers and nonstutterers. Wulff (1935; also cited in Strother & Kriegman, 1943, p. 323) found that stutterers were not inferior to nonstutterers in the ability to tap rhythmic patterns. In the rhythm subtest of a standardized battery of motor tests, H. M. Cross (1936) found no significant differences between stutterers and right-handed controls, but differences were close to significance between stutterers and left-handed controls.

Strother and Kriegman (1944), using the same matched pairs of stuttering and nonstuttering subjects reported earlier (Strother & Kriegman, 1943), again found no significant differences between stutterers and nonstutterers on tapping patterns in three-quarter time (tap–tap—tap—tap, etc.). Stutterers again were slightly superior to nonstutterers. Seth (1958) tested stuttering and control youths on a test of motor rhythm. With the arm unsupported, subjects were instructed to tap "fairly rapidly" in as rhythmic a pattern as possible. Test trials alternated between right and left index fingers. Stutterers were significantly inferior to normals with both hands. Differentially, their left-handed performance was significantly inferior to that of their right.

Snyder (1958) found that both moderate and severe stutterers were significantly inferior on rhythmic tapping than nonstuttering speech defectives. Mild stutterers demonstrated significantly more accurate rhythmic tapping than severe stutterers.

Zaleski (1965) investigated the ability of 100 7- to 14-year-old children to continue tapping a metronomic rhythm for 20 repetitions after the metronome was turned off. The group consisted of 50 stutterers and 50 nonstutterers. Stutterers deviated significantly more than nonstutterers from the predicted time to complete the task if the metronome had been left on, 1.62 and .96 seconds, respectively.

2. Other Fine Motor Abilities

Many other fine motor skills, besides finger tapping, have been assessed in stutterers. Anderson (1923) found that stutterers and controls were not significantly different in (1) rate of foot tapping or (2) accuracy of consecutively tapping within three circles with one hand, except for one group of younger stutterers in the latter task. West and Nusbaum (1929) assessed the combined maximum rate of eyebrow wrinkling and jaw opening and found both male and female stutterers to be inferior to their respective control groups. Spriesterbach (1940) tuilized the same procedure and found stutterers to be insignificantly superior to controls.

Kasanin (1932) reported a Russian study showing a positive relation between intelligence and motor development, as measured by the Oseretsky Tests of Motor Proficiency (Oseretsky, 1923, translated to Portuguese by da Costa, 1943) in 50 stuttering children. Westphal (1933) tested 26 pairs of stuttering and nonstuttering school-aged boys on a number of motor skills, including the accuracy of beanbag tossing and the rate of fitting pieces into a form board. Although a trend was observed in favor of the nonstutterers, differences were not statistically significant.

Bills (1934) found stutterers to be slightly slower than controls in identifying the names of colors by pressing the appropriate button for each color shown. Stutterers had about twice as many "blocking" errors (hesitations during the task) as normals, and their "blocks" were significantly longer.

H. M. Cross (1936) found stutterers to be nonsignificantly different from controls on a one-handed pursuit task, but significantly inferior on a two-handed spool-stacking test. In 1938, Rotter found that stutterers were slower than controls in sorting cards (dropping them into appropriate slots), but significantly so only with the left hand and both hands separately (Rotter, 1955). Similarly in 1947, Ross recorded the speed with which subjects could turn a deck of playing cards, one at a time, placing them in another stack (Ross, 1955). Stutterers were significantly slower at this task than nonstutterers.[6]

Kopp (1946) administered the Oseretsky tests to 50 stuttering children and all but four were found to be "retarded" in motor development according to the test norms. Finkelstein and Weisberger (1954) sought to replicate these results. Not only did they fail to replicate Kopp's findings, but found that 15 stuttering children were slightly superior to matched normal controls. They concluded that the test norms which had been standardized in Russia, then translated to Portuguese before English, must have been inaccurate.

Snyder (1958) found that nonstuttering speech-defective subjects performed superiorly to stutterers on a wide range of coordination tasks involving aiming, speed of movement, matching symbols to digits, steadiness, and finger dexterity. Mild stutterers demonstrated better coordination on most tasks than moderate stutterers. Likewise, moderate stutterers were better coordinated than severe stutterers.

Schilling and Krüger (1960) tested 100 stuttering, 100 articulatory defective, and 100 normal speaking children on the Oseretsky tests. Stutterers scored lower than normals but higher than articulatory defective children.

Recently M. H. Cooper and Allen (1977) found that seven nonstutterers were significantly less variable in a rhythmic finger-tapping task for 4 minutes than eight stutterers. Half of the stutterers had been released from therapy while half were currently in therapy. These two subgroups did not differ, however, on the variability in the finger-tapping task. It was found in this investigation that subjects' finger-tapping scores moderately correlated with timing variability in 80 repetitions of a single sentence, .67 for stutterers and .32 for nonstutterers.

B. Speech Motor Abilities of Stutterers

1. Respiratory Abilities

a. *Rate and Rhythm of Voluntary Respiratory Movements.* Emanating from the same basic rationale as most of the early finger-tapping studies, researchers looked at the abilities of stutterers to breathe rapidly and/or rhythmically to determine if voluntary motor control in stutterers was inferior to that of nonstutterers. Blackburn (1931) and Seth (1934) re-

---

[6] The editors reported that "the stutterers were superior" (p. 366) on this test. Their statement is apparently an error. Ross (1955) measured "the time, in seconds, needed to perform this task [of turning the deck of cards]" (p. 362). The stutterers averaged 26.96 seconds, compared to 24.38 seconds for the controls.

quired subjects to pant rhythmically while they measured costal breathing movements. Both concluded that stutterers were inferior to controls in the volitional rhythmic contraction of the diaphragm.

Hunsley's (1937) procedure was similar, except that it required subjects to pant to a three-quarter pattern at various speeds. Stutterers made significantly more errors than nonstutterers, and the performance of both groups declined as the speed of the required pattern increased.

b. Breathing Irregularities Associated with Stuttering. Much of the early research on stutterers focused on respiration because abnormalities in breathing were often observed clinically and breathing irregularities were quite easy to measure. Beginning early in this century in Europe, studies by Halle (1900), Ten Cate (1902), and Gutzmann (1912) reported a variety of abnormalities in the breathing movements of stutterers. In the United States, the first detailed investigation of breathing in stutterers was conducted by Fletcher (1914). Fletcher placed pneumographs around the thorax and abdomen of nine subjects aged 12 to 24 years. The resulting pneumograms showed simultaneous tracings at both levels during inhalation and exhalation. Fletcher confirmed that stuttered speech was characterized by numerous breathing abnormalities and variability when compared to nonstuttered speech. Typical abnormalities were: attempts to speak on residual air; breaks in the usual rhythm observed between inhalation and exhalation; exhalations interrupted by inhalations, or vice versa; and simultaneous, opposing movements of the thorax and abdomen. Fletcher observed that typical abnormal breathing patterns emerged for individual stutterers but were present only during stuttering.

Robbins (1919) recorded from a thoracic pneumograph placed under the armpits to compare the breathing of stutterers with nonstutterers. Both groups read the same passage. He concluded that all stutterers breathe abnormally while stuttering and agreed with Fletcher (1914) that the characteristic form of breathing varies with each stutterer.

Travis (1927a) analyzed thoracic and abdominal pneumograms of six severe adult stutterers and "several" nonstuttering controls. Subjects were asked to speak spontaneously. Qualitative analysis of the tracings indicated that during stuttering, movements of the thorax and abdomen were often in opposition, whereas normal speech was characterized by "fairly close correspondence" (p. 674) between thoracic and abdominal movements. Other abnormalities observed were marked prolongation of inhalation, clonic and tonic spasms of the breathing musculature, and fine tremors in the abdominal musculature. It should be noted that Hill (1944, p. 297) believed that the prolonged inhalations reported by Travis (1927a) were in fact tonic contractions of the respiratory musculature.

Trumper (1928) studied 82 adult stutterers and found that half of them had lowered vital capacities. These individuals compensated for their reduced air volumes by periodic deep breaths, rapid shallow breathing, or a definite increase in air volume per breath. Depth of breathing was inversely related to the degree to which vital capacity was below normal.

One of the most carefully performed studies of breathing movements was conducted by Fossler (1932). He recorded pneumograms from the thorax, abdomen, and midthorax (tip of the sternum) of 13 adult stutterers and 13 controls as they spoke spontaneously. Amplitude and duration of inhalation and exhalation were analyzed. Coefficients of variation for the duration of inhalation and exhalation during speech were larger for stutterers than for nonstutterers, with severe stutterers showing more variability than mild stutterers. Variability was only one-third as great for both groups during rest breathing than during speech. Stutterers had from two to five times more anomalous breathing curves than normal speakers, although the rank-order of frequency of the normal curves was similar for both groups. Stutterers had approximately double the number of exhalations interrupted by inhalations as controls. Moreover, stuttering was sometimes—but not consistently—characterized by tonic or clonic breathing spasms, antagonistic movements at different levels, attempts to speak on inhalation, greatly prolonged exhalations, and breaks in the normal rhythm of speech. As noted in previous research (Fletcher, 1914; Robbins, 1919), individual subject patterns were highly variable.

E. Murray (1932) wondered if stutterers had abnormal breathing movements even when they were not speaking. Thus, he analyzed midthoracic pneumograms from 18 matched pairs of child and adult stutterers and nonstutterers during rest breathing, silent reading, and reasoning. Stutterers were much more variable than nonstutterers in amplitude and duration of both inhalations and exhalations in all conditions. They also had larger and longer inspirations and longer expirations—but slightly smaller in amplitude—during silent reading than controls. Both groups had shallower and faster breathing in silent reading and reasoning as compared to rest breathing, but the differences for stutterers were more pronounced. Comparing his results to those of Fossler (1932) who used propositional speech, Murray found less variability of amplitude and duration of inhalation and exhalation in silent reading and reasoning compared to overt speech. The stutterers and nonstutterers were, respectively, approximately one-third and two-thirds less variable in silence than during speech.

Most of Murray's stutterers showed a variety of irregular breathing patterns compared to about one-third of the normals who showed a few irregularities. Finally, Murray found no direct relationship between the degree of abnormalities manifested by a stutterer and the severity of his stuttering.

Fagan (1932) reported a variety of breathing abnormalities in a female adult stutterer who also had stutter-like symptoms in her writing. Abdominal and thoracic pneumographic tracings showed antagonistic movements, tonic and clonic spasms, and other irregularities during vocal and "graphic" stuttering episodes.

Preliminary to the study discussed in the previous section on rhythmic breathing abilities, Seth (1934) discussed abdominal and thoracic pneumographic traces obtained from his stutterers and normal speakers. Breathing records during stuttering were characterized by arhythmic movements, by breaks, interruptions, and reversals in the usual processes of inhalation and exhalation, and by discoordination between abdominal and thoracic movements.

Morley (1937) recorded from thoracic and abdominal pneumographs of adult stutterers and nonstutterers as they were engaged in a variety of speaking situations. Stutterers were found to exhibit larger means and standard deviations in the amplitudes of inhalation and exhalation than controls. When durations were considered, stutterers had longer and more variable inhalations than controls. Exhalation durations were somewhat different. Normals showed considerable variability across speaking conditions, while stutterers evidenced consistently long exhalations in all situations.

Individual breathing patterns for stutterers were analyzed according to number and type of abnormalities. Fifty-nine percent of the stutterers' breathing curves contained abnormalities compared to 32% for the controls. Of these abnormalities, tonic interruptions, or "plateaus" in normal exhalation curves, were the most common abnormality and most often related to overt stuttering (85%).

Strother (1937) analyzed "vertical" breathing movements from thoracic and midthoracic pneumograms. "Horizontal" movements were determined by pneumographs placed on either side of the lower thorax at the level of the floating ribs to detect asymmetrical respiratory activity.

A total of 31 records were analyzed from 26 subjects. The following vertical symptoms were considered to be abnormal: antagonistic movements between thoracic levels, prolonged inhalation, inhalation interrupted by exhalation, and vice versa, and clonic or tonic interruptions. Vertical abnormalities were present in the traces of all but one subject. Two subjects showed horizontal abnormalities, or asymmetry in the activity of the lateral sides of the abdomen. All of these abnormalities were observed only during stuttering "spasms," with none occurring in fluent utterances.

All of these published reports found breathing irregularities in adult stutterers. Steer (1935, 1937) wondered if the same were true of young stutterers. He first reported a preliminary investigation of 12 stuttering children, 5 and 6 years of age. Pneumograms were recorded from the thorax and abdomen of the subjects during silence and self-formulated speech. During silence, the thorax and abdomen functioned in synchrony, but during stuttering a wide range of abnormal breathing movements was observed. Two years later, he published a report on 67 stutterers from 3 to 13 years of age and 20 3- to 5-year-old controls. Thirty subjects in the experimental group were comparable in age to the control group. When these age-equivalent subjects were compared, a greater percentage of stutterers manifested breathing abnormalities than controls. Notable examples were asynchronous abdominal and thoracic movements, speaking during inhalation, general inequality in successive wave forms, and obvious lack of movement in either the thorax or abdomen. In contrast, a larger proportion of nonstutterers evidenced unusually long durations of inhalation or exhalation, interruption of exhalation by inhalation, and opposition in breathing between the thorax and abdomen. Considering only the **number** of breathing irregularities observed, the two groups of subjects were not significantly different. Nonetheless, Steer tentatively concluded that the child stutterer presents a malfunctioning respiratory system.

Van Riper (1936) investigated breathing movements of stutterers prior to stuttering when they did—or did not—expect to stutter. He recorded midthoracic pneumographic traces from 37 adult stutterers who uttered single words. The experimental sequence proceeded as follows. First, a word was exposed in a display box; second, the subject was instructed to signal with a key if he expected to stutter on the word; third, a light was switched on to signal the subject to say the word; and fourth, the subject spoke the word. In this carefully analyzed study, a number of interesting and provocative findings were reported. Breathing movements prior to speech indicated that subjects were likely to prolong inhalation if stuttering was expected but slightly prolong exhalation if expectancy was not signaled. Variability of movements was greater during expectancy than during nonexpectancy. Forty-three percent of the subjects manifested rehearsal movements prior to the speech attempt, which showed striking resemblances to the movements during stuttering which followed.

Overall, Van Riper observed that breathing abnormalities were unrelated to any group of sounds, a finding reported previously by Fossler (1932). Nevertheless, 14 stutterers (38%) seemed to show characteristic and consistent breathing patterns on words beginning with the same sound or syllable. To test this impression, pneumographic traces of three instances of the word *be* were individually traced on separate cards for 10 of the 14 stutterers. Fifteen judges were then asked to match the two additional traces to one trace representing each stutterer. The results overwhelmingly supported the impression that characteristic patterns existed. All 10 sets were correctly matched by nine judges, and seven sets were correctly matched by all 15 judges.

Breathing movements of stutterers have also been investigated during unusual activities. For example, Hill (1942) found that respiratory movements of stutterers were more variable than those of controls when subjects were interrupted during a well-learned, nonvocal perseveration task. Also, Mosier (1944) presented stuttering and nonstuttering adults with flashcards showing words that were difficult to pronounce. A wide range of breathing irregularities was observed during the smooth and interrupted speech of both groups of subjects, although to a greater extent in the stutterers.

After a superb review of the literature, Hill (1944) concluded that one of the most common physiological characteristics of adult stutterers is a sharp inspiratory gasp prior to, or during, stuttered words. Other relatively common breathing irregularities mentioned were thoracic–abdominal oppositions, differences in movement patterns, lack of precise temporal synchrony between the thorax and abdomen, and shallow breathing. Hill explained these and other physiological abnormalities observed in stutterers as the result of generalized organismic reactions to shock, startle, or surprise. Citing similar findings for normal subjects under conditions of shock, he argued, quite convincingly, that stutterers are not physiologically different from normal speakers.

Perhaps due to Hill's (1944) *coup de grâce* on the notion of physiological abnormalities of stutterers, little research was conducted on stutterers' breathing movements for many years. In recent years, however, new theoretical perspectives and technology have been responsible for renewed interest in this area.

Schilling (1960) used a technique of recording movements in diaphragms of stutterers which he called "roentgen kymography." Essentially this procedure transposed serial X rays to a continuous graphic record of movement changes. Forty-six percent of his stutterers had abnormal features of movement during quiet breathing. Short, clonic contractions were interspersed in the normal breathing rhythm.

Metz, Conture, and Colton (1976) measured thoracic movements of two adult stutterers and one nonstutterer by anteriorly and posteriorly placed sensors at the level of the thorax and abdomen connected to magnetometers. Laryngeal activity was also measured by electromyographic (EMG) traces from the lateral cricoarytenoid muscle, a glottal adductor. Prior to uttering **fluently** spoken words, chest wall diminution (exhalation) typically began **after** preparatory laryngeal muscle activity in all three subjects. Conversely, prior to 70% of the stuttered words in the two stuttering subjects, chest wall movements began **before** laryngeal activity.

Myers (1977) found that while imitating single words, 17 adult stutterers showed greater increases in breathing rate and deeper breathing just prior to stuttered words than before nonstuttered words. However, when the task involved answering questions, some interesting differences were observed. Stuttered words again were preceded by faster breathing rates than fluent words, but stuttering occasioned shallower inhalations and exhalations than fluency. It should be noted that these differences were not statistically significant and that considerable individual subject variability occurred.

c. Aerodynamic Irregularities Associated with Stuttering. As part of a previously mentioned study, Travis (1927a) recorded the pressure of the breath stream in adult stutterers. Surprisingly, he made little mention of the results of breath pressure except to note that the normal speech of stutterers showed "fairly fixed relations between movements of the abdomen, thorax, larynx, and breath stream" (p. 674). No mention was made of pressure abnormalities during stuttering, but irregularities were visibly evident in plates showing thoracic–abdominal antagonistic movements, asynchrony between movements of the larynx and breathing apparatus, and tonic spasms of the breathing musculature.

Little research interest was directed at aerodynamic aspects of stuttered speech until the last decade, undoubtedly for technological reasons. Recent developments in aerodynamic instrumentation are primarily responsible for renewed interest in breathing and stuttering.

After a series of studies on coarticulation and stuttering (to be discussed in Section III,B,3), Agnello and his associates began using intraoral air pressure and spectrographic analysis to study the speech of stutterers. In determining the voice onset characteristics of voiced and unvoiced stops, Agnello and McGlone (1970) discovered that a sudden drop in intraoral air pressure occurred at the time of consonant release and corresponded to the voice onset time described by Lisker and Abramson (1964). In two studies of voice onset (Agnello & Wingate, 1971, 1972), it was reported that stuttering was associated with very high intraoral air pressures. Furthermore, even the fluent productions of CV syllables by stutterers were characterized by higher than normal intraoral air pressure values.

Hutchinson (1973) studied aerodynamic properties of the speech of six adult stutterers during a brief reading task under three conditions: oral sensory deprivation (trigeminal nerve anesthesia), placebo injections, and control. He measured intraoral air pressure with a nasal catheter positioned in the oropharynx and airflow with a face mask. Both sensors were coupled to a pneumotachograph and displayed on an optical oscillograph. Results for oral sensory deprivation were qualitatively similar to those for normal sensory feedback, although stuttering was more frequent and more severe after nerve block. Hutchinson identified seven aerodynamically defined stuttering patterns in the speech of the stutterers. These patterns were also observed in eight additional adult stutterers subjected to similar procedures under normal feedback conditions (Hutchinson, 1975). The seven aerodynamic patterns are listed in Table III in conjunction with auditory perceptual correlates (i.e., the type of stuttering typically heard), identifying characteristics, and potential physiological mechanisms.

Hutchinson (1975) found that each of the eight stutterers exhibited unique profiles with regard to the frequency of occurrence of each aerodynamic pattern in his speech. In fact every stutterer exhibited one or two types more frequently than the others.

Hutchinson and Navarre (1977) analyzed the speech of five adult stutterers and five controls while reading a standard passage under normal and rhythmic metronome pacing. Twelve target phonemes /p, t, k, b, d, g, f, θ, s, v, ð, z/ were embedded within the passage. Comparing aerodynamic measures on **fluent** words, rhythmic stimulation produced consistently lower peak intraoral air pressures and longer onset and offset pressure durations than the normal condition in both groups. Airflow rate values increased during metronomic pacing for nonstutterers but decreased for stutterers. During stuttering, the onset slopes were steeper for the onset of intraoral air pressure than during the stutterers' fluent speech. In addition, pressures, flow rates, and durations were inordinately high.

Adams, Runyan, and Mallard (1975) matched six adult stutterers with six normal speakers in an aerodynamic study. Each subject read 12 familiar CVC words aloud and in a whisper into a tight-fitting face mask coupled to a pneumotachograph. Analyses involved only fluent productions. For both groups, whispered speech was characterized by higher airflow rates for initial consonants than normal speech, but the reverse was true for the airflow rates for final consonants. Also, whispering was associated with a greater volume of air expended between the two consonant airflow peaks but slightly shorter durations. The stutterers generated higher values than the controls for all the variables measured, significantly so for initial and final airflow rates during whispering, as well as for duration and volume of airflow in both conditions. The authors

TABLE III. Summary of the Seven Aerodynamic Patterns of Dysfluent Speech[a]

Dysfluency type	Frequency	Auditory perceptual correlate	Identifying characteristics	Potential physiological mechanisms
I	37	Syllable repetition	Repeated elevations in intraoral air pressure with successful release and appropriate transitions into subsequent phonetic elements	Normal posturing of articulators but initial productions reflected slightly elevated physiological tension and prolonged articulatory contact
II	34	Brief prolongation	Gradual elevation in intraoral air pressure (prolonged rise time)	Prolongation of the occluded articulatory contact with progressive contraction of the expiratory muscles
III	44	Prolonged silent block	(1) Relaxation: multiple intraoral air pressure peaks separated by relatively wide, deep valleys; no concomitant air flow and voicing	Brief relaxations and reactivations of the muscles required to build up intraoral air pressure while prolonging the articulatory contact
			(2) Tremor: multiple intraoral air pressure peaks separated by relatively narrow, shallow valleys; no concomitant air flow and voicing	Mandibular, lingual, laryngeal, respiratory tremor
IV	28	Breathy, aspirated prolongation	(1) Prolonged air flow rate during onset of a phoneme	Appropriate posturing of articulators in an unoccluded position with progressive contraction of the expiratory muscles
			(2) Excessive peak air flow rate during moment of stuttering or contingent upon its release	Rapid effortful contraction of the muscles of forced exhalation
V	4	Abbreviated	Simultaneous cessation of intraoral air pressure, air flow rate, and voicing	Abrupt laryngeal occlusion
VI	8	Prolonged	Rapid build-up of intraoral air pressure with subsequent sustaining of pressure at a constant level. No concomitant air flow and voicing	Prolongation of the occluded articulatory contact with fixation of the expiratory muscles
VII	7	Prolonged pause between two syllables	Continuous intraoral air pressure fluctuations in an intersyllabic space bounded by normal syllable productions	Prolonged articulatory contact with lingual, mandibular, or respiratory tremor

[a] From Hutchinson (1975, pp. 108–109).

suggested that stutterers bring a "greater pumping force to bear on their supply of pulmonic air" (p. 9). They reasoned that the greater pumping force would generate larger volumes of air through the vocal tract.

Ford and Luper (1975) measured intraoral air pressure and subglottic air pressure (via a hypodermic needle inserted in the trachea) of three adult stutterers who spoke a list of words beginning with /p, b, m, h, i, a/. Each stuttered word was repeated until fluent. Voicing and electromyographic traces of lip muscles were also recorded. Comparisons were made on the above sound between stuttered and fluent productions of the same words.

While it is somewhat inappropriate to separate the aerodynamic measures from the others, a number of interesting results were observed. In some stutterings, subglottic and intraoral air pressures were roughly equivalent to fluent productions. In others, they were markedly reduced, and in still others, they appeared excessive. In several cases, the simultaneous recording of both air pressure measures provided important information about the status of the glottis. For one stutterer, breaks in voicing were accompanied by a failure of subglottic and intraoral pressures to equalize, thus indicating that the glottis was closed rather than open. In general, the traces indicated consistent patterns which were different for each stutterer.

2. Phonatory Abilities

In the past few years, a surge of research interest in stuttering has centered on the larynx. At a recent conference on "Vocal Tract Dynamics and Disfluency," Freeman (1975) declared that the old notion that stuttering was primarily concerned with vocalization (e.g., Hunt, 1861/1967; Kenyon, 1943) was "an idea whose time had come" (p. 229). In a similar vein, Perkins, Rudas, Johnson, and Bell (1976) observed that:

> Rational analysis, clinical investigation, and systematic research are lending support to an old suspicion: many of the abnormal disfluencies judged as stuttering involve problems of smooth coordination of phonation with articulation and respiration. (p. 509)

Research on phonatory characteristics of stuttering seems to have reawakened for two main reasons. First, recent advances in electrophysiological and acoustic measurements coupled with computer-assisted methods of data analysis have rendered the larynx more accessible to scientific scrutiny. Second, theoretical positions have been advanced (Wingate, 1969a, 1970) stating that stuttering is usually characterized by phonatory problems and that altered vocalization is responsible for most conditions in which stuttering is reduced or absent.

a. Voice Onset and Offset. Bar, Singer, and Feldman (1969) recorded electromyograms (EMG) from the cricothyroid muscle of one severe adult stutterer and one nonstutterer as 300 words were exposed individually on a screen. The subject was instructed to rehearse each word subvocally for 10 seconds, signal whether or not he expected to have difficulty, then say the word. The stutterer and the nonstutterer had earlier onset of cricothyroid muscle activity when they expected difficulty than when they did not. For the stutterer, earlier subvocal EMG activity characterized expectancy followed by actual stutterings compared to unconfirmed expectations of difficulty. Finally, the subvocal activity for the stutterer was more intense than that for the nonstutterer.

Since 1971, Adams and his associates have conducted a series of experiments designed to test Wingate's (1969a, 1970) theoretical position that vocalization is a cruicial element in stuttering and that most fluency enhancing techniques involved altered vocalization. In two identical experiments, Adams and Reis (1971, 1974) had 14 adult stutterers read two short passages five times each, one passage containing a combination of voiced and voiceless sounds and the other containing all voiced sounds. The passages were similar in percentage of continuant and stop consonants, number of sentences, content, and word familiarity. As expected, significantly greater adaptation occurred with the all-voiced passages compared to the voiced–voiceless passages. The voiced–voiceless passage produced significantly more stuttering in the 1971 study but not in the 1974 replication. In both studies, however, stutterings in this passage tended to occur at points which required the initiation of phonation.

Adams, Riemenschneider, Metz, and Conture (1974) constructed three passages: one with all types of sounds, voiced and voiceless, stops and continuants (I); another with all voiced sounds, stops and continuants (II); and a third with all voiced sounds, all continuants (III). Fourteen adult stutterers read each passage five times in succession, but the data of only seven subjects who exhibited sufficient stuttering and the adaptation effect were treated statistically. Significant differences in degree of adaptation among the three passages were reported, with the greatest difference between passages I and III (all types of sounds versus voiced continuants) and the least difference between passages II and III (voiced stops and continuants versus voiced continuants). The authors hypothesized that passages I, II, and III were progressively more complex motorically, suggesting that the requirement of phonation had the greatest facilitating effect on adaptation. This conclusion may be premature, however, due to differences in stuttering frequency among the passages. For example, the median stuttering frequency at the first reading of passage I was 5, but was 9 for passage III. Both passages reduced to two stutterings by the fifth reading. Even if passage I had adapted to 0, the adaptation would be less $(5 - 0 = 5)$ than that of passage III $(9 - 2 = 7)$ because less stuttering occurred at the outset.

Manning and Coufal (1976) identified disfluencies of 11 adult stutterers and 11 controls in standard reading passages. Stuttering and normal disfluencies were classified according to the type of phoneme-to-phoneme transition involved: voiced–voiced, voiced–voiceless, voiceless–voiced, or voiceless–voiceless. The results for the stutterers supported previous findings, namely, that maintaining voicing results in the least stuttering. While the voiced–voiced transitions accounted for 61% of the total number of transitions, only 8% of the stutterings occurred on them. Voiced–voiceless and voiceless–voiced transitions each accounted for 17% of the transitions but were stuttered 10% and 11%, respectively. Voiceless–voiceless transitions occurred least frequently (5%), but 11% of them were stuttered. Interestingly, the distribution of disfluent transitions for the nonstutterers was very similar to that of stutterers, although the absolute frequencies of normal disfluency were many times less. Since nonstutterers, too, had greater than expected difficulty with voiceless–voiceless transitions, the hypothesis that voiceless-to-voiced transitions are responsible for stuttering was called into question.

Considerable research has been directed at the temporal aspects of voice onset and offset in stutterers. From spectrographic analysis of CV and VC syllables, Agnello and Wingate (1971, 1972) reported that stutterers were slower than normal in initiating voicing at the beginning of syllables and terminating it at the end, even during fluent utterances. Recently, Agnello (1975) reported on 23 stutterers and 23 nonstutterers who fluently uttered /pa, ba, ap, ab/ three times each. He measured voice onset time (VOT) (the time between the articulatory release and vocal onset in CV syllables) and voice termination time (VTT) (the time between the vocal offset and the consonant onset in VC syllables) from a simultaneous printout of intraoral air pressure and spectrographic traces. Stutterers were significantly slower than nonstutterers in VOT and VTT. Data from one additional stutterer who stuttered during the task were also discussed. For example, during the production of /pa/, he attempted to initiate voice prior to the pressure release of /p/, and, in effect, produced the vocal timing for /ba/.

To determine whether the voicing lag observed in adult stutterers was perhaps due to long-established learned coping patterns, Wendell (1973) investigated the same phenomenon in 11 6- and 7-year-old stuttering children and controls. VOTs and VTTs were slower for children than for adults, and stuttering children were slower than nonstuttering children (except in VTT for /ab/ in which stutterers were faster than controls). In general, too, the children were more variable than adults, perhaps explaining the reversal for /ab/.

Adams and Hayden (1976) tested 10 adult stutterers and 10 matched controls in the ability to initiate and terminate phonation of /a/ immediately after the onset and offset of a 1000-Hz tone. No stuttered productions were analyzed. Both groups became more proficient in rapidly initiating and terminating phonation with practice, but the stutterers were significantly slower than nonstuttering controls.

These results are reinforced by a similar study which assessed the ability of 11 stutterers and matched controls to initiate vocalization immediately following a visual stimulus (Starkweather, Hirschman, & Tannenbaum, 1976). In this study, subjects uttered 26 syllables representing a wide variety of voice, manner, and place features as well as several syllable types. As in Adams and Hayden's (1976) study, both groups improved over three trials, but stutterers were significantly slower than controls. Within both the stuttering and nonstuttering groups, the outstanding finding was that the latency of vocalization was practically identical for all types of phonatory sequences and syllables.

When stutterers and nonstutterers were compared on CV and VC syllables, some very interesting results emerged. As expected, on CV syllables in which the consonant was voiced, stutterers were significantly slower than controls. Contrary to expected results, however, when the consonant in a CV syllable was unvoiced, no significant differences were observed. Considering that the average normal delay in voice onset is 100 msec in unvoiced CV consonants (Fujimura, 1972), and that the stutterers averaged a 65-msec delay over the controls, the authors argued that the built-in delay in unvoiced sounds allowed the stutterers time to compensate for their inability to match the controls on CV syllables with voiced consonants. They hastened to add, however, that this conclusion does not mean that unvoiced consonants are easier than voiced sounds for stutterers in connected speech. The task in question here simply involved the utterance of one syllable which the stutterer was highly prepared to say on signal.

To assess sound-shifting ability, Kerr and Cooper (1976) instructed 15 adult stutterers and 15 controls to prolong the first of a pair of phonemes and then produce the second immediately after a visual signal. Stutterers were significantly slower than controls in shifting to the second phoneme regardless of whether the shift was voiced–voiceless, voiced–voiced, or voiceless–voiced. This order of shifts, from slower to longer delays, characterized the results for both groups of subjects, although the differences did not reach statistical significance.

In a slightly different design, Reardon (1977) had five adult stutterers and five controls produce V, CV, and VC syllables immediately after a cue and then terminate them after a second cue. Stutterers were significantly slower than normal speakers in initiating vocalization and slower, though nonsignificantly so, in terminating voice. Significantly shorter voice initiation and termination times were observed for stutterers for vowels than either CV or VC syllables.

In a study of two stutterers and one nonstutterer previously discussed, Metz *et al.* (1976) recorded electromyographic (EMG) activity from the lateral cricoarytenoid muscle (LCA), the primary adductor of the vocal folds. Chest displacement (respiratory activity) was simultaneously recorded. Data were analyzed by comparing the onset of exhalation with the onset of vocal fold adduction as the subjects began to utter isolated words on signal. In the fluent words produced by all three subjects, 94% were characterized by LCA adductory activity **preceding** chest wall diminution. The median difference for fluent words was 290 milliseconds. By contrast, 70%[7] of the stuttered words of the two stutterers were characterized by LCA activity which **followed** respiratory movements by 125 milliseconds.

b. Voice Irregularities Associated with Stuttering. Two early studies investigated vocal disturbances in stutterers by looking at amplified oscillographic traces of the voices of stutterers (Bryngelson, 1932; Travis, 1927b). Both studies documented a wide variety of voicing irregularities associated with stuttering, such as marked variations in waveform, intensity, and duration. However, the instrumentation used in these studies was so crude that the fine timing measurements reported are undoubtedly suspect. Probably for this reason additional descriptive studies of voice were not conducted for nearly 40 years.

Chevrie-Müller (1963) used a procedure called glottography, which electrically records the opening and closing patterns of the vocal folds, to study the phonation patterns of 27 stutterers. She found a number of phonatory abnormalities in some, but not all, of her stutterers, such as: arhythmic vocal fold vibrations, unpredictable glottal opening, clonic flutterings of the folds, and partial or complete absence of voicing during rapid glottal activity.

Recently, Gautheron, Liorzou, Even, and Vallancien (1973) used glottographic and acoustic printouts to study the speech of four adult stutterers during conversation. The stutterers consistently demonstrated greater periods of silence between a consonant and a vowel than normal speakers. The soft vocal attacks of normal speakers, characterized by gentle undulating movements of the folds, were replaced by hard irregular glottal

---

[7] The authors noted that the exact number of "temporal perturbations" referred to here may be altered slightly in a current reanalysis and extension of this study.

attacks in stutterers. Transitions from voiceless consonants to vowels were typically delayed in stutterers, and delays greater than 180 milliseconds were often followed by repetitions.

Stromsta (1965) analyzed spectrographically speech samples from 63 young stutterers. Stutterings were often characterized by lack of formant transitions and abnormal terminations of phonation. Follow-up questionnaires 10 years later were returned for 38 of the subjects. Of 27 subjects who had originally showed voicing irregularities, 24 were reported to be still stuttering. Ten of the eleven subjects who originally showed normal formant transitions and voice terminations were reported to have stopped stuttering.

Several investigations utilizing direct and indirect observations of the larynx have reported voicing irregularities in stutterers. From anterior–posterior X rays of one stutterer's larynx, Fujita (1966) observed asymmetric tight glottal closures which also involved closure of the pharynx during "blocking-type" symptoms. Also, irregular and inconsistent abductions and adductions of the larynx and pharyngeal cavity were observed during stuttering. Similarly, a Japanese film of the larynx documented phonatory attempts of a stutterer which where characterized by closure of the larynx at three levels: the true vocal folds, the ventricular folds, and the epiglottis (tuberculum of epiglottis constricting with the arytenoids) (Kamiyama, Hirose, Ushijima, & Niimi, 1965; also cited in Freeman & Ushijima, 1975b). McCall (1975) also observed sphincteric laryngeal closures in stutterers during stuttering; EMG traces and a fiberoptic laryngoscope were utilized in this study.

Different types of laryngeal activity have been found to characterize various stuttering symptoms. Conture, McCall, and Brewer (1977) videotaped laryngeal activity of 10 severe stutterers from a fiberoptic laryngoscope. The larynx was visible (not obscured by the epiglottis) in 64% of the total recorded stutterings. Fluent speech was associated with smooth laryngeal activity but stutterings were characterized by abnormal movement patterns. During the majority (60%) of part-word repetitions, the larynx was relatively fixed and partly abducted. Most prolongations (72%) were characterized by tight glottal adduction and, although infrequent, all instances of broken words were associated with glottal abduction. It must be noted that some repetitions and prolongations did not fit the above patterns; however, the differences noted were statistically significant.

Freeman and Ushijima (1974) reported on an EMG and fiberoptic film study of the larynges of two stutterers. Although the glottis was often obscured by the epiglottis, EMG traces indicated that the normal reciprocity between abductor–adductor forces was often disrupted during stuttering. Moreover, stuttering was typically characterized by excessive activity of the lateral cricoarytenoid muscle, a laryngeal adductor. In subsequent reports of EMG results from laryngeal and articulatory muscles (Freeman, 1975; Freeman & Ushijima, 1975a, 1975b), the same antagonistic abductor–adductor activity was observed during stuttering. For example, one stutterer was described saying the word *ancient* three times, twice stuttered and once fluently. During stuttering, the posterior cricoarytenoid which, during fluency, was active only in abducting the folds for nonvoiced phonemes /tʃ/ and /t/, contracted throughout the word. Two adductors, the vocalis and lateral cricoarytenoid, also were associated with excessive activity during stuttering.

In addition, stuttering was characterized by disruptions in the usual synchrony of the laryngeal adductor muscles. Other findings included excessive tension during stuttering with greater increments in the laryngeal than the articulatory musculature. Both antagonistic abductor–adductor activity and the overall level of laryngeal muscle activity markedly decreased when previously stuttered sentences were read fluently under the influence of white noise masking, rhythm, and choral reading (Freeman & Ushijima, 1975b).

Allen, Peters, and Williams (1975) analyzed spectrographically three stutterers' fluent and stuttered utterances in identical contexts. Stuttered utterances were variable but often were characterized by long silent gaps, longer than normal segment durations, higher than normal fundamental frequency, and glottal arrests.

Ford and Luper (1975) obtained simultaneous information on aerodynamic, phonatory, and labial EMG patterns of three adult stutterers. Problems in voicing were idiosyncratic and usually related to problems at other levels in the vocal tract. Lack of coordination in motor activity were found to precede, accompany, or follow the onset of phonation.

Hoekstra (1975) reported that stutterers vocalized within a more limited frequency range than nonstutterers. To determine voice frequency characteristics in children, Schmitt and Cooper (1976) matched 12 male stutterers, aged 7 to 12 years, with 12 nonstuttering controls according to age, height, weight, and race. The highest, lowest, and mean fundamental frequency of each subject's voice was determined. The two groups did not differ on any of these voice frequency measures. The authors speculated that their lack of positive findings might be due to testing stuttering children of mild to moderate symptomatology, whereas most phonatory studies of stuttering were conducted on adults with moderate to severe symptoms.

3. Articulatory Abilities

a. Rate and Rhythm of Voluntary Articulatory Movements. A number of early studies investigated stutterers' abilities to produce rapid speech or speech muscle movements (diadochokinesis) or rhythmic speech movements (rhythmokinesis). Spriestersbach (1940) found no statistically significant differences between stuttering and nonstuttering subjects in maximum rate of jaw opening, tongue protrusion, and lip closure. Experimental subjects were slightly superior in jaw and tongue movements but slightly inferior in lip movements. Strother and Kriegman (1943) also found stutterers' diadochokinetic rates slightly (but insignificantly) higher for jaw openings, repeated /t/ productions (tongue tip to alveolar ridge), and lip closures. By contrast, Rickenberg (1956) found that stutterers were significantly slower than controls in repeatedly uttering consonant–vowel (CV) syllables (/pa, ba, ma, ta, da, na, ka, ga, ŋa/).

Rhythmic execution of jaw, tongue, and lip movements was investigated by Blackburn (1931), Hunsley (1937), and Seth (1934) (except tongue movements). These three investigations showed significant differences favoring nonstutterers. Studies by Wulff (1935) and Strother and Kriegman (1944), however, found no significant differences between stutterers and nonstutterers on these tasks. Uttering repetitive /pataka/ sequences, Zaleski (1965) found stuttering children deviated significantly more from a prior metronomic stimulus than nonstuttering children.

b. Temporal Characteristics of Speech. A great many stuttering treatments indirectly involve the stutterer adopting a slower than usual rate of speaking. A number of these will be reviewed later (Section V). Also, "slowing down" is one of the most common reported techniques utilized by recovered stutterers to maintain fluent speech (Shearer & Williams, 1965).

Bloodstein (1944) and Johnson (1961) reported slower than normal reading rates in adult stutterers, an unsurprising result considering the fact that it takes time to stutter. A number of studies have approached the relationship between rate and stuttering by determining the effect on stuttering of varying speaking rates. Johnson and Rosen (1937) found that instructing stutterers to read faster than normal resulted in more stuttering, and slower than usual in less stuttering. Fransella (1965) also found that stuttering was reduced when subjects were asked to reduce their reading rates. Adams, Lewis, and Besozzi (1973) found that 18 adult stutterers manifested half as much stuttering on a 120-word passage when words were presented one at a time, about one per second, than when they were instructed to read the passage aloud in the usual way. The median speech rates in these two conditions were 27.6 and 134.5 words per minute, respectively. Ingham, Martin, and Kuhl (1974) assessed the effects on stuttering in spontaneous speech of speaking slower and faster than normal in three adult stutterers. By means of a series of lights, subjects were given feedback every minute regarding how successful they were in either speaking more slowly or more rapidly than baseline rates. The procedures were effective in reducing speech rate in all three subjects and in increasing rate in two of them. The effects on stuttering, however, were complex. Absolute stuttering frequencies always decreased, but percentage of stuttering increased in one subject because word rate decreased proportionally more than stuttering. This carefully designed study suggests that the effect of speaking rate on stuttering varies from one stutterer to another.

Obviously, speech rate is affected by pauses. Whereas pauses and hesitation phenomena have been investigated at length in normal speech (Goldman-Eisler, 1968; Maclay & Osgood, 1959; Mahl, 1961), relatively little attention has been directed to pauses per se in stuttered speech. Love (1965) reported that, speaking fluently, 10 stutterers had more short pauses in their speech than 10 normal speakers. However, due to a possible measurement error in the final pause count, Love and Jeffress (1971) reran the study with 25 matched pairs of stutterers and controls. Both groups believed themselves able to read aloud fluently. Subjects read two passages, each twice in succession. Tape recorded samples were analyzed in two ways, each yielding comparable results. Significantly more 150- to 250-msec pauses were observed in the speech of the stutterers than in the speech of the nonstuttering controls.

Temporal aspects of the speech of stutterers was addressed by M. H. Cooper and Allen (1977) in a different way. These researchers investigated the abilities of subjects to repeat various speech segments over and over "in the same way." They compared 10 stutterers, five in therapy and five no longer in therapy, with five nonstutterers. In a carefully counterbalanced design, subjects repeated "easy" and "hard" sentences (similar except for frequency of occurrence of selected words), "easy" and "hard" paragraphs (containing the "easy" and "hard" sentences in context), a nursery rhyme ("Pease Porridge Hot"), and a finger-tapping task (discussed in Section III,A,1). Tape recorded speech signals were modified by electronic means such that durations between designated units could be reliably identified and counted. The dependent variable was "relative variance" (RV), a measure "smoothed" by statistical procedures to minimize atypical variations. No significant differences were observed between RVs for "easy" and "hard" sentences or between "easy" and "hard" paragraphs. The time from beginning to end of 80 repetitions of a single sentence typically constituted subjects' least variability, or best timing. This same sentence within a paragraph was more variable than when repeated alone. The most variable measure was the total time in each repetition of the paragraph. The most accurately timed intervals within the nursery rhyme (i.e., the time to say *Pease porridge* or *9 days old*) were about as accurate as those for single-sentence repetitions.

Group comparisons were made by averaging the mean rank of RVs for each subgroup. Significantly higher ranks were obtained for normal speakers over stutterers for all tasks except the 80-sentence repetition task and paragraph duration, for which rank differences were nonsignificant. Within the stutterers, significant ranks favoring the stutterers no longer in therapy over those still in therapy were present for these same two measures, single-sentence repetition and paragraph duration. Finally, it is important to note that a wide range of timing abilities was observed among both stuttering and normal subjects, with considerable overlap between the two. Cooper and Allen concluded that normal speakers were more accurate timers than stutterers on most experimental tasks. Second, stutterers released from therapy were more accurate timers than their counterparts still in therapy, when these subgroups did differ.

   c. Articulatory Irregularities Associated with Stuttering. The first detailed study of the articulatory apparatus of stutterers from a neuromotor standpoint was generated by the theory that stutterers lack a sufficient margin of cerebral dominance in the conscious control of the bilaterally paired speech musculature (Travis, 1934). Twenty-four adult stutterers and 24 nonstutterers spoke spontaneously while electromyographic (EMG) "action currents" were recorded from surface electrodes placed over the right and left masseter muscles. In all but two of the normal speakers and in all of the stutterers' fluent speech, the left and right traces were roughly symmetrical with respect to amplitude, frequency, and bilateral onset. However, for 18 of the stutterers, stuttering was associated with striking asymmetries in amplitude, frequency, timing (i.e., appearance of activity first in one masseter, then the other), and pattern. For six of the stutterers, described as "extremely mild cases" (Travis, 1934, p. 133), action currents during stuttering were considered normal. One of the two normal speakers with abnormal traces was described as a "noticeably uncertain, hesitant speaker" (p. 133).

   In a replication of this study, D. E. Williams (1955) recorded EMGs bilaterally from electrodes on the masseter muscles of the jaw during the reading of single words. No differences in bilateral amplitude of potentials were evident in the data for his 15 adult stutterers and an equal number of nonstutterers. Similarly, no differences were noted for the instant of appearance of action potentials (nerve impulses reaching the muscles) between groups. "Faked" stuttering in the nonstuttering group produced as many anomalies in EMGs as the "real" stuttering of stutterers. This was not the case in Travis' (1934) study. Williams concluded that there was no evidence that stutterers were "basically" different from normal speakers neurophysiologically.[8]

Shaffer (1940) compared 10 adolescent and adult stutterers with 10 adult nonstutterers on various temporal measurements of jaw opening and voicing during the production of voiced and voiceless stops. Subjects uttered 46 CVC words beginning and ending with the six English stops. Stutterers manifested significantly longer intervals between initiation of jaw movement and initiation of phonation and durations of the jaw excursion during opening than nonstutterers. The same differences were true of the stutterers' fluent speech compared to their stuttered speech.

Sheehan and Voas (1954) recorded EMG activity from the right masseter muscle of 12 stutterers as they uttered multisyllabic words. The six subjects who stuttered during the experiment (Group 1) were matched with those who did not (Group 2), although this comparison was not originally planned. Group 1 had significantly longer durations between the onset of voice and the maximum masseter activity than Group 2. Similarly, when the words which individuals in Group 1 either stuttered or uttered fluently were compared with the same words for the matched Group 2 subjects, "masseter delays" were still greater for Group 1. Differences between the two subgroups were not significant between the peak masseter activity and the end of the voice records. This result was interpreted to suggest that the point of maximum EMG activity was located near the end of the stuttering block, not near its beginning. While this conclusion may be warranted, it is open to question. First, the words were not of the same length, ranging from two to four syllables, which undoubtedly influenced the second duration. Second, the words were not sufficiently similar phonetically to require masseter activity at precisely the same point after the onset of voicing, obviously a potential source of error for the first variable.

Shrum (1967) recorded EMGs of young stutterers and nonstutterers in a reading and choral reading condition. Multiple leads from many parts of the body were analyzed: the jaw, neck, chest, forearm, abdomen, and leg. The groups showed no significant differences on beginning areas, patterns, or spread of tension before and during speech. Stutterers differed

---

[8] Van Riper (1971) raised questions about D. E. Williams' (1955) conclusion based on the fact that only a few of the "action currents" arrived simultaneously to the right and left masseters in any of his subjects.

from nonstutterers only in that tension began significantly earlier before speaking and tended to persist after words. Stutterers had been asked after each word whether they had expected to stutter, and the investigators pointed out that the early anticipatory tension was greater on "expected" and "stuttered" words than on nonstuttered words.

Massengill, Luper, Bryson, and Gertner (1967) employed standard photographic and cinefluorographic films of the speech mechanisms in a study of severity of stuttering. Films were made of 15 adolescent subjects during single-sound phonation and prose reading. The judged severity of stuttering on two occasions from audio tapes was positively correlated with the cine film measures. On the contrary, judged severity from regular films was negatively correlated with both audio tapes and cine films. Severe stutterers tended to have fewer palatal–pharyngeal wall contacts than less severe subjects.

Zinkin (1968) studied cinefluorographic films of the pharynx taken during stuttering and reported considerable lack of coordination between pharyngeal and other articulatory movements. Instances were observed in which pharyngeal movements were relatively fixed while other articulators moved. The converse was also observed; that is, examples of static articulator gestures were observed during periods of pharyngeal movement.

In a study of three adult stutterers referred to in the two previous sections, Ford and Luper (1975) recorded EMG data from two lip muscles: orbicularis oris and depressor labii inferior. During stuttering, tremor activity, simultaneous contraction in the two antagonistic muscles, delayed contraction, and other abnormalities were observed in these muscles. Myers (1977), also referred to earlier, recorded EMGs from several supraglottal throat muscles of 17 stutterers during word and question tasks. Significantly greater EMG activity was recorded in the 5 seconds prior to stuttered words being repeated than before imitation of fluent words. However, the reverse finding was true of the question task. These results indicate that perhaps many of the physiological findings reported for stutterers may be task specific. Clearly, more research on this question is warranted.

A number of studies have focused on coarticulatory characteristics of stuttered speech. Coarticulation refers to the normal phenomena during speech whereby the production of a given sound is influenced by other sounds which occur before and after the sound in an utterance.

One of the first investigators to report that stuttered speech has abnormal transitional movements was Stromsta (1965). He reported that stutterers often fail to show the typical rising or falling formant transitions of normal speech seen on spectrograms.

Agnello and his associates conducted a series of investigations on coarticulatory differences in stuttering. Like Stromsta, Agnello inspected spectrograms of stuttered and fluent speech. A number of acoustic irregularities were observed in stutterers, some of which were not even perceptible to listeners. Even in nonstuttered speech, stutterers often failed to assimilate adjacent phonetic segments, particularly in the normal transition of the second formant (Agnello, 1966; Agnello & Buxton, 1966). Spectrograms of stuttered speech were markedly abnormal, characterized by limited variance in formant structures, compressed frequency at the lower end of the speech spectrum, shorter phonation durations, lack of coordinations between voicing and specific articulatory movements, and numerous instances of coarticulatory failure. For example, repetitive stutterings often involved repetitions characterized by second formant patterns which did not show usual transition patterns. Only when the appropriate transition pattern toward the next sound was achieved did the stuttering terminate. In addition, there was a positive relationship between the severity of stuttering and the likelihood of first and second formant patterns which were parallel and lower in frequency than normal.

Because of these articulation deficiencies, the accessory behaviors developed by stutterers were viewed as coping behaviors to approximate correct coarticulation patterns. For example, many transitional movements were interpreted as "hanging on" attempts to approximate the next required articulatory target (Agnello, 1975; Agnello & Goehl, 1965; Agnello, Wingate, & Moulin, 1970).

The coarticulatory feature which has occupied the bulk of Agnello's attention in recent years is the timing of voice onset and offset. This research was discussed in Section III,B,2,a on phonatory abilities.

Van Riper, who is one of the leading proponents of the view that stuttering reflects abnormal coarticulation timing, hypothesized that coarticulation difficulty may reflect difficulty in the appropriate activation of agonist–antagonist sets of muscles (Van Riper, 1971). Electromyographic data from one stutterer were shown which illustrates simultaneous, presumably antagonistic, EMG activity in the orbicularis oris (lip constrictor) and anterior belly of the digastric (jaw depressor) during a long repetitive stuttering. An extreme mandibular jerk preceded final utterance of the word. Van Riper (1971) also suggested that the lack of coarticulatory timing is reflected in the stutterer's insertion of the neutral, or 'schwa,' vowel in syllabic repetitions. For example, in attempting to say *key*, the stutterer is likely to say /kə–kə–kə–ki/.

In spite of the theoretical simplicity and appeal of the notion that stuttering reflects a lack of coarticulation, it has received little recent empirical support. One investigator who demonstrated a number of coarticulatory influences during stuttering was Tatham (1973), who carefully analyzed temporal relationships between EMG traces from the upper lip (orbicularis oris) and the acoustic signal of one adult stutterer. The subject repeatedly read five sentences 17 times, but Tatham analyzed 16 repetitions of only one sentence, *Maybe he should pay very poor people more.* (Sounds requiring upper labial constriction are in bold print.) Stuttering occurred on the initial /m/ in *maybe* six times. Comparing fluent versus stuttered productions of *maybe*, significantly longer durations in EMG activity were observed between the onset of the lip closure for /m/ and (1) complete closure for /m/ and (2) release of /b/ when *maybe* was stuttered. In a more definitive test, observations of EMG activity were compared on later segments, all nonstuttered, as a function of whether the initial /m/ was stuttered or not. Durations of EMG activity during labial constriction for /b/ (in *Maybe* . . .) were significantly greater for stuttered than for fluent sentences. They were larger, but insignificantly so, for the combined duration necessary for labial constriction of /ʃ/ and /p/ in (*Maybe he should pay* . . .). Peak amplitude of EMG activity during the production of /b/, /ʃ/, and /p/ was considered similarly. Sentences stuttered on /m/ had larger peak values for /b/ and /ʃ/ but **smaller** for /p/ than nonstuttered sentences, although these amplitude differences were not statistically significant.

Pearson coefficients of variation were computed for amplitude and duration of EMGs for /m, b, ʃ, p/ in *Maybe he should pay.* . . . Duration variability coefficients for stuttered utterances reduced from 49.1 on /m/ to 16.6 for /b/ and then to 13.9 for /ʃ/ and /p/ combined. Fluent utterances were characterized by 15.8, 16.5, and 26.1 for these segments, respectively. The reduction to normal variability from /m/ to /b/ for stuttered utterances suggests a "settling down" effect in EMG activity as the stutterer emerged from stuttering on /m/ into fluency on /b/. It appeared, however, that this effect inhibited normal variability observed in later phonemes, /ʃ/ and /p/, in fluent utterances. This progressive reduction in variability after stuttering occurred across approximately six phonological segments and at about the same time when the normal utterance was permitting itself more variability.

Amplitude variability showed a somewhat different pattern. Stuttered segments became more variable from /m/ to /b/. This was true even though peak amplitudes decreased.

Freeman and Ushijima (1975b) displayed EMG traces from the superior longitudinal[9] muscle of the tongue and the interarytenoid and lateral

---

[9] The text refers to the inferior longitudinal muscle but the figure indicates the superior longitudinal muscle. Clearly, one is in error.

cricoarytenoid muscles of the larynx in stuttered and fluent utterances of the word *causes*. In the stuttered utterance, /kə–kɔżiż/, the traces showed activity in the tongue directed at elevating the tip to the alveolar ridge for the "devoiced *z*" during the initial repetition /kə/. This finding also contradicts the notion that coarticulatory movements do **not** occur during stuttering.

In a study cited by Guitar (1975), Knox found that stutterers demonstrated inappropriate phonetic transitions and a slower than normal rate of articulation in the fluent syllables prior to stuttering. On the contrary, Hutchinson and Watkin (1974) reported that only 12% of the stutterings they studied were characterized by abnormal phonetic transitions characteristic of a lack of coarticulation. Guitar (1975) reported that one of his four stutterers typically displayed excessive EMG activity in the orbicularis oris prior to stuttering, but the stutterings which followed were **not** characterized by excessive lip tension.

Montgomery and Cooke (1976) studied part-word repetitions of 16 adult stutterers spectrographically and perceptually. All stuttered samples were preselected to be free of tension and struggle. The authors found that consonant durations of stuttered CVs were approximately 40 milliseconds longer than nonstuttered samples from identical contexts. Surprisingly, however, the durations of vowel segments were practically identical in stuttered and fluent segments. When formant transitions were inspected in sample pairs, 62% showed differences. Unlike Agnello's (1966) report that stutterers tended not to show second formant transitions, 69% of the stuttered segments had formant transitions, although in many cases different from those in fluent segments. The authors suggested that different transitions could be due to moving to appropriate vowels from abnormal consonant postures. When five trained listeners judged the vowels of the samples, only 23% were identified correctly, but this was significantly greater than chance. There was no evidence that the stuttered segments contained an inordinate percentage of schwa vowel occurrences, a prediction made by Van Riper (1971) and others.

Hutchinson and Watkin (1976) studied jaw movements in four adult stutterers and two nonstutterers. They used strain gauge transducers to measure both amplitude and velocity of jaw movement. Jaw openings and closings were significantly faster during stuttering preceding or during production of the vowel /æ/ for the four stutterers than for the two nonstutterers. The authors suggested that this was due to a "catching up" movement in the stutterers, possibly mediated by the gamma loop system.

Temporal irregularities were also noted between phonation and jaw movements. In some cases, maximum jaw excursion preceded voice onset; in other cases it was substantially delayed.

A substantial number of stutterers, particularly those who are severe, manifest tremors or rapid oscillating movements in the articulators (Van Riper, 1971). Welsh (1970) attached a movement sensor to the lower jaw of three adult stutterers to record tremor frequencies. Frequencies ranged from 7.0 to 13.5 Hz with a mean of 9.3 Hz. Platt and Basili (1973) utilized EMG traces from the masseter and suprahyoid muscles under the chin to record muscle activity in three adult stutterers selected for evidence of mandibular tremors during stuttering. Subjects uttered two series of CV(C)C words beginning with /b/ or /p/. In addition, they isometrically contracted their jaws five times. Tremor frequencies were not significantly different between stuttering and isometric contraction; mean frequencies were 8.5 and 9.2 Hz, respectively. Amplitude differences were not statistically significant either, although significantly higher levels of EMG activity were recorded for the suprahyoid group than for the masseter muscle. From these results, the authors suggested that the stuttering tremor is the same as the isometric tremor.

Fibiger (1971) recorded bilateral EMG activity from five facial muscles controlling the lips in four adult stutterers. The subjects read single words and connected text as well as spoke spontaneously. Stuttering was often associated with a tremor of about 8 Hz, the low end of the usual range (8–12 Hz) for the normal "physiological tremor." Fluent speech was free of such tremors. It should be noted that the subjects in this study were not selected because of obvious tremor activity.

Tremors were typically synchronous bilaterally although they often began on one side one burst prior to starting in the contralateral muscle. An interesting relation between tremors and phonation was also noted. Typically, the stuttering tremor was most pronounced prior to phonation, but generally needed to cease for approximately 100 msec prior to the onset of voicing. If a tremor began during phonation, (1) it was typically masked (i.e., every second burst would have a lowered intensity) and, (2) depending on the intensity of the voice, it could impede the continuation of phonation. In the latter case, weak voicing usually stopped 50–100 msec after the onset of a tremor. On the other hand, strong vocal production usually ended a tremor. To illustrate, Fibiger reported that one of his subjects was able to modify his stuttering by using a smooth syllable transition while maintaining voicing. During these "slides," tremor activity was markedly diminished. From this investigation Fibiger concluded that stuttering is the manifestation of a normal physiological tremor with exaggerated amplitude induced by psychological stress.

McCall (1975) observed tremor activity in a study of temporal summation of electrical stimulation of the tongue of stuttering and nonstuttering subjects. Stutterers tended to manifest physiological tremors in their tongues when required to protrude them for a sustained period. In addition, similar levels of current produced markedly longer muscle contractions in the stutterers' tongues compared to those observed in the control subjects.

C. Motor Determinants: Summary

Again, a staggering array of data has been presented. And again, it seems that each investigator is one more blind man trying to describe the elephant of stuttering. Unquestionably, fine motor coordination, respiration, phonation, and articulation interact in such complex ways that any attempt to separate them seems to defy common sense and reason. Yet, researchers have been forced to focus their attention on isolated factors, for to attempt to control all possible confounding variables would be impossible. The same logic has guided the organization of motor determinants of stuttering in this section.

Fully cognizant of the fact that any summary of motor determinants will be dangerously oversimplified, I offer the following list of factors arranged from most to least powerful. Categorization of factors is determined by (1) the degree of agreement among different researchers, and (2) the breadth of potential to explain the myriad problems of stuttering.

1. Most Powerful Factors

Of all the foci of disabilities in stutterers reviewed, it seems that the greatest convergence of recent findings has been on laryngeal function. While certainly it is too soon to ascribe the cause of stuttering to a malfunctioning larynx, the research pointing to phonatory problems has been impressive. One of the most powerful motor factors explaining stuttering disabilities is delayed voice onset and offset. Stutterers have difficulty initiating and terminating voice in the precise time constraints of normal speech. This finding has been replicated in nearly every experiment in which it has been measured.

Voicing irregularities observed during stuttering, such as antagonistic abductor–adductor contractions, vocal fry, and excessive laryngeal tension, seem to precede and co-occur with stuttering. The fact that they often precede observable stuttering symptoms strongly suggests that they may somehow determine the form and severity of the symptoms which follow. For this reason, phonatory problems may be viewed as a common underlying condition of many, or most, stutterers.

Aerodynamic irregularities can also be considered among powerful explanatory factors of stuttering symptoms. In fact, most of the observable abnormalities of stuttering can be described in terms of imprecise control of air pressure and airflow during speech. When aerodynamic influences of the glottis are considered, a more comprehensive and understandable picture of laryngeal function emerges than the traditional view of vocal dysfunction resulting solely from faulty neurological commands. Several researchers have proposed that stuttering should be understood in terms of deficits in the precise timing of respiration and phonation which, in turn, generate the complex supraglottal articulatory symptoms (Adams, 1974, 1975b; Agnello, 1975; Wingate, 1969a).

2. Less Powerful Factors

Somewhat less powerful in motoric explanations of stuttering behavior are articulatory irregularities. Viewing stuttering as a lack of appropriate coarticulation has theoretical appeal and some empirical support. However, recent research has suggested that coarticulation does occur during stuttering, although in abnormal forms. Most recent work in this area has shifted to the study of voice onset timing discussed previously.

Articulatory irregularities have been reported among stutterers in virtually all of the studies reviewed. In spite of this fact, they cannot be accorded the same explanatory potential as phonatory problems because the findings are, as yet, scattered and piecemeal. Perhaps we must wait until the research will allow meaningful separation of roles of the pharynx, palate, tongue, jaw, and lips, before articulatory irregularities contribute significantly to an understanding of stuttering.

Breathing irregularities have long been recognized as being intimately associated with stuttering. Nevertheless, stuttering cannot be explained in terms of known breathing abnormalities alone. In the first place, most of the research in this area is at least 40 years old and was conducted with crude instrumentation. More importantly, most of the irregularities in breathing observed during stuttering are also observed in nonstutterers during stress or startle reactions (Hill, 1944). It is likely, however, that breathing movements will soon be accorded more importance in the understanding of stuttering as respiratory irregularities are carefully correlated with aerodynamic measures.

Temporal characteristics of the speech of stutterers cannot explain stuttering. Nevertheless, the reports that reduced speaking rates are associated with less stuttering certainly are in accord with the impression that stutterers are better able to modify their stuttering when they slow down. It must be pointed out that the effects of speaking rate on stuttering are far from clear. Reported speech timing deficits in stutterers have theoretical appeal and, if replicated, could provide important links between the linguistic and motor determinants of stuttering.

Pause irregularities, although generally ignored, have the potential for generating important explanatory hypotheses regarding stuttering. It is quite likely, for instance, that the finding that stutterers' fluent speech contains an abnormal number of short pauses is related to voice onset problems and coarticulation deficiencies.

3. Least Powerful Factors

Studies which have investigated rate and rhythm of voluntary articulatory movements are important in a comprehensive review of the research bearing on the motor abilities of stutterers. The weight of the evidence does suggest that stutterers are somewhat inferior to nonstutterers in these tasks. However, this generalization cannot account for stuttering symptoms we typically observe. In the first place, a few of the most carefully designed studies did not demonstrate differences between stutterers and controls. A much more important reason for their inability to explain stuttering is that there is little reason to assume that stuttering reflects a disorder of speed or rhythm of movement. Rate and rhythm tasks are chosen to reflect generalized motor deficits but, as a consequence, are not theoretically related to the population being studied, in this case stuttering. It has been shown that abnormal populations besides stutterers are inferior on diadochokinetic, rhythmokinetic, and timing tasks. As a result, their explanatory potential for stuttering is reduced considerably.

The same reasoning can be applied to finger-tapping abilities of stutterers. Rate or rhythm deficiencies in tapping abilities may differentiate stutterers from normals, but quite likely also differentiate many other groups from normals.

However, the study showing contextual effects in finger tapping (MacKay & Soderberg, 1970c) has much greater explanatory potential. This study indicated deficiencies among stutterers in the tapping of arbitrary temporal patterns. While unlikely to become diagnostic of stuttering, this kind of deficiency has much greater potential for understanding specific motor problems of stutterers than simple rate and rhythm deficiencies.

Rate or rhythm of respiratory movements, such as panting, has practically no explanatory power for motor deficits in stuttering. Except for normal breathing and speaking, we have far too little voluntary control over our breathing movements to generate sensible measures of speed or rhythmic skills.

General tests of fine motor skills or coordination cannot explain much about stuttering either. In general, the skills they measure are too far removed from the motor symptoms of stuttering and hence suffer from even less face validity than speed and rhythm tests involving the speech musculature. At best, demonstrated deficiencies in fine motor coordination generate nothing more than a correlational pattern for stutterers compared to controls. It is important to recall, however, that many controlled studies of fine motor abilities other than finger tapping have not demonstrated deficits in stutterers.

IV. LINGUISTIC AND MOTOR MODELS OF STUTTERING

Numerous conceptual models have been put forth which explain stuttering on the basis of linguistic and motor determinants. Following is a brief description of several such models which reflect either recent theoretical advances or currently popular explanations. The list is not exhaustive nor is it meant to be. Perhaps it should be viewed as a sampling of current thought.

Each model will be described and evaluated in light of the data presented earlier. Particular attention will be given to the data each model purports to explain as well as the data it seems to ignore.

A. Stuttering as a Defect in Phonetic and Syllabic Contextual Programming (MacKay)

The first model to be discussed was derived from normal speech errors and only later applied to stuttering. It views stuttering as a defect in phonetic and syllabic contextual programming. In a series of investigations, MacKay (1969, 1970a, 1970b, 1972) analyzed various published collections of normal speech errors. The four major types of errors and examples of each are as follows: (1) Spoonerisms (e.g., *waste the term* is mistakenly produced as *taste the worm* and *overinflated state* becomes *overinstated flate*), (2) synonymic intrusions (e.g., *Don't shell!* is spoken instead of the two competing responses *Don't shout!* and *Don't yell!* or *symblem* is uttered instead of *symbol* or *emblem*), (3) masked—or omitted—phonemes (e.g., *repress* becomes *repess*), and (4) "stutters" or repeated phonemes (e.g., *lily* becomes *l–lily*). MacKay generated a number of hypotheses to explain the form of the speech errors he analyzed. For example, he postulated explanations of why *shout* and *yell* combine to form *shell* instead of such variants as *yeout, yshout,* or *shet*. He then tested each hypothesis by comparing the observed data with chance occurrences. Following is a summary of the main findings derived from MacKay's analysis of normal speech errors.

Errors tended to occur in conjunction with identical, "inducing," phonemes located either before or after the erred phoneme. "Stutters," or normal repetitions, were most likely when the inducing phoneme followed the "stuttered" phoneme, but still occurred at a greater than chance level when the inducing phoneme preceded the "stuttered" phoneme. Error phonemes ("stutters," phoneme reversals in Spoonerisms, and masked phonemes) were most likely when the inducing phoneme (or the other reversed phoneme for Spoonerism errors) was in the next adjacent syllable, and error probability decreased as the inducing phoneme occupied less proximal positions. Importantly, the inducing and erred phonemes were never in the same syllable but tended to occupy the same syllabic position, either both in the initial position or both in the final position. Errors were more likely in initial syllabic positions and even more likely in the first syllable of a word than in later positions. Consonants were more likely to be in error than vowels, and consonants were never transposed with, or induced by, vowels. Also, erred phonemes in Spoonerisms tended to be similar to the reversed phoneme in distinctive features, with the exception of place of articulation. Otherwise, the two phonemes were almost always similar or identical with regard to features of openness, voicing, and nasality. "Stuttered" phonemes tended to be allophonically similar (i.e., differing in one or two distinctive features) to adjacent phonemes but neither exactly the same nor completely different (zero or three distinctive feature differences).

"Stutters" were most often associated with stressed syllables. Masked (omitted) phonemes usually occurred in unstressed syllables. Synonymic intrusions were also greatly influenced by syllabic structure. Obviously, when two words are combined, the first must be broken at some point. A significant majority (60%) of breaks in multisyllabic words occurred between syllables (e.g., at points represented by the lines in the word *de/port/ment*). Breaks which occurred within syllables rarely occurred within a consonant cluster. Furthermore, breaks usually preceded the vowel rather than followed it. Considering the kinds of words combined in synonymic intrusions, the syllabic structures of both words before their breaks were more often similar than the portions following the breaks. This was true when breaks occurred either between or within syllables.

From these and other findings, MacKay derived a "syllabic structure hypothesis" which states that the syllable is composed of two basic units, an initial consonant group and a vowel group. The vowel group contains both a vowel nucleus and a final consonant group. This explains why breaks in synonymic intrusions tended to occur between the two major groups.

MacKay proposed a model of normal speech production at the phonetic level. Diagrammed in Fig. 3, the model is composed of a "buffer system" which displays phonetic units in abstract form but in correct serial order.

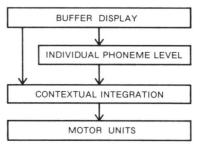

Figure 3.   An oversimplified model of speech production at the phonetic level. (From MacKay, 1970a.)

The buffer feeds into an individual phoneme level partially activating—or "priming"—a set of singly represented phonemic units which are unordered. The buffer also generates a set of programs for modifying the phonemes according to contextual constraints. These levels then feed into a motor unit level where the contextual variants are coded. The model in Fig. 3 does not show one of the most important elements, a "scanner," which sweeps over the motor variants in the motor unit level in a unidirectional manner at a voluntarily determined rate. When a partially primed unit is passed by the scanner, it receives an added boost of excitation, bringing it to threshold for a series of motor commands to be sent to the speech musculature.

It is within the priming and scanning process that the errors previously summarized are assumed to occur. Figure 4 presents a schematic view of the motor unit level with preprimed units and the scanner which sweeps over them. Speech programming in which no error occurs is shown on the left of the figure. It can be noted that stressed units receive greater priming by the buffer system prior to scanning and, consequently, are nearer to the motor unit threshold, the necessary level for final activation. The right side of the figure diagrams what is hypothesized to occur in "stutters," or repetitions, induced by a later occurring phoneme. To account for the error, an additional assumption is made. When two contradictory aspects of similar programs, such as the two similar allophones of /k/ in the figure, are present in the same program, they react in a mutually inhibitory fashion. In other words, when the first unit is activated by the scanner, the other **simultaneously** becomes inhibited, as shown by the opposite directions of the curved lines. Inhibition is followed by hyperexcitation of the second unit and inhibition of the first. This mutual cyclic activity continues for a period determined by damping properties within the units. In this figure, two peaks of the first /k/ reached threshold, thus a "stutter" occurred.

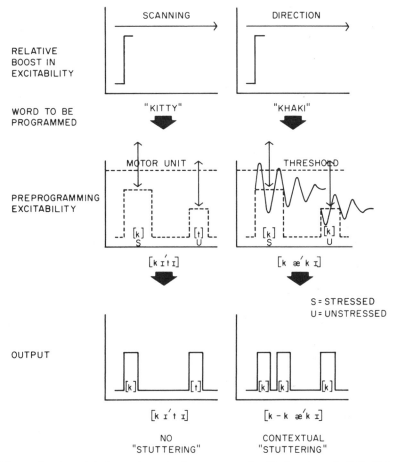

Figure 4. A model of speech production programming for fluent words (left side) and contextual "stuttering" (right side). (Adapted from MacKay, 1970a.)

MacKay (1970a) and MacKay and Soderberg (1970c) suggest that the contextual programming model can also account for pathological stuttering in three ways as shown in Fig. 5. For the nonstutterer, hyperexcitability of motor units following their activation is not sufficient to exceed the motor unit threshold for stuttering. Yet, stressed units come closer to threshold than unstressed units. Model 1 for stutterers postulates the same preprimed levels for stressed and unstressed units as normal, but a lowered motor unit threshold. Model 2 hypothesizes greater levels of hyperexcitability than normal. Model 3 postulates greater prepriming for stressed units, but normal thresholds and excitability boosts. According

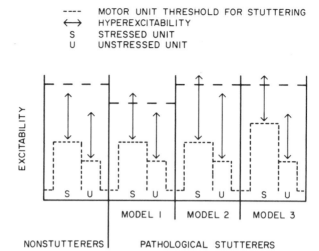

Figure 5. Three models of pathological stuttering. (Adapted from MacKay & Soderberg, 1970c.)

to MacKay and Soderberg (1970c), all of these models explain part of the data obtained on stutterers and nonstutterers, but none explains them alone.

MacKay (1970a) suggests that the model for "stutters" (Fig. 4) can be extended to explain pathological prolongations in two ways. First he proposes that individual features may interact in a mutually inhibitory way. For example, the lip movements for /p/ may be stuttered silently with neither airflow nor phonation, as if the motor units for phonation were inhibited, while those for lip movement were in a state of oscillation. Perhaps it was no coincidence, then, that Ford and Luper (1975) described one stutterer in whom just this phenomenon seemed to occur. MacKay's second alternative for prolongation is that if oscillations between contradictory elements were rapid enough, fusion might appear, thus lengthening the speech sound.

Normally masked or omitted phonemes are explained in terms of the time required for a unit to reach threshold and the rate of scanning. To illustrate, let us assume that two units, the first unstressed and the second stressed, are passed over by the scanner. The first will be omitted if the time required for it to reach threshold is greater than the time required for the scanner to activate the second unit and for it to reach threshold. It must be remembered that the sweeping rate of the scanner is voluntary and determines speaking rate. If it sweeps rapidly, an omission is likely to occur; however, if scanning occurs at a slow rate, the first unit will reach threshold before the second and no omission will occur. MacKay (1970a) suggests that this model can be used to explain pathological blocking, or involuntary speech stoppages, in stutterers. He speculates that the reason the stutterer blocks while the normal speaker omits a phoneme is that the former, who is closely monitoring his speech, simply stops when a planned phoneme does not materialize.

MacKay (1970a) admits that the context-dependent model of stuttering was not derived from stuttered speech and, therefore, has serious limitations. Yet, he feels confident that it is a significant beginning in understanding the causal factors producing stuttering.

The greatest strength of the phonetic and syllabic context-dependent model of stuttering is its predictive potential. Derived from the speech errors of normal adults, it generated a series of experiments with stutterers which, for the most part, were supportive of the model both for speech and for finger tapping (MacKay & Soderberg, 1970a, 1970b, 1970c, 1970d, 1970e; Soderberg, 1972; Soderberg & MacKay, 1972). The model provides explanations for the fact that stuttering tends to occur on stressed syllables and that certain words, such as *statistics,* are inherently more difficult to say than others. It is not unreasonable to assume that this kind of model may eventually permit mathematical determination of the relative production difficulty of various speech sequences. Certainly, a context-dependent model has helped generate more meaningful analogs of stuttering behavior, such as stressed and repeated patterns of finger tapping instead of rate or rhythm of taps.

The syllabic structure hypothesis, which assumes that the initial consonant cluster is distinct from the vowel and final consonant cluster, appears to have some explanatory potential for stuttering. It predicts more stuttering on initial than final consonants in a syllable since final consonants are associated with the vowel.

The concept of the buffer system is useful in explaining the coarticulation problems observed in stuttering. Perhaps the number of units displayed in the buffer is the maximum limit of adjacent sound influences.

A voluntarily determined scanning rate may help account for the data indicating that stutterers have less difficulty when speaking slowly. Finally, the model suggests different processes underlying repetitions, prolongations, and blocks.

A phonetic and syllabic context-dependent model does not seriously address the research on speech motor abilities of stutterers. The data on respiration, phonation, and articulation do not contradict the model; they simply are not considered.

B. Stuttering as Tension and Fragmentation (Bloodstein)

Bloodstein (1975a) advanced the following hypothesis about the etiology of stuttering:

> Stuttering is an anticipatory struggle reaction. In its clinical form, it represents a relatively severe degree of tensions and fragmentations that are a common occurrence in the speech of normal young children. It develops readily in circumstances in which speech pressures are unusually heavy, the child's vulnerability to them unusually high, or the provocations in the form of communicative difficulties or failures unusually frequent, severe, or chronic.[10] (p. 301)

For at least two decades, Bloodstein has explained stuttering in terms of an anticipatory struggle reaction (Bloodstein, 1958). However, in recent years he has increasingly considered the two additional notions of tension and fragmentation (Bloodstein, 1969, 1974, 1975a, 1975b). These two concepts allegedly relate to the "underlying structure" of stuttering rather than to its overt manifestation. Therefore, neither tension nor fragmentation can typically be observed in the stutterer. We observe, instead, their sequelae: repetitions, prolongations, hard attacks, and silent stoppages. This relationship can be seen in Fig. 6 which diagrams the tension and fragmentation model of stuttering. From this model, stuttering can be seen to derive from any combination of pressures which result in a child believing that speaking is difficult and requires excessive compensatory efforts (anticipatory struggle). In more advanced stuttering, anticipatory struggle reactions become learned responses to situations, words, or listeners in which a history of past difficulty is present. In either case, however, the anticipatory struggle reaction manifests itself in stuttering symptoms by virtue of tension in the vocal tract or in fragmentation of the utterance.

Tension typically produces prolongations of continuant sounds or hard attacks of stop consonants. In the latter case, the stop phase of the consonant is prolonged, presumably with a high degree of intraoral air pressure, followed by a greater than normal explosion of air and onset of voicing. This combination of factors results in a notably hard glottal attack. Tension can also result in complete stoppage of the airstream from an excessively tense and prolonged stop phase of a consonant or from an attempt to vocalize with a tightly closed glottis. Such stoppages are probably typical only of severe stutterers (Van Riper, 1971).

---

[10] Bloodstein believes that there is a strong continuity between the normal disfluencies of young nonstutterers and the early disfluencies of young stutterers (Bloodstein, 1970, 1975a). Since this chapter does not deal with normal disfluency, the "continuity hypothesis" will not be discussed.

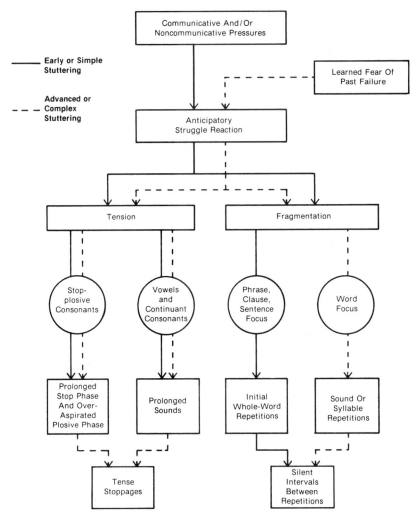

Figure 6. A tension and fragmentation model of stuttering. (Adapted from Bloodstein, 1974, 1975a, 1975b.)

The result of fragmentation depends on the speaker's conception of the locus of difficulty in speech. Early or mild stutterers probably are only vaguely aware of where their difficulties lie; therefore, they tend to fragment natural syntactic units such as phrases, clauses, or sentences. The result is repetition of the first word of the syntactic unit. Rarely do these repetitions occur in the middle or at the end of a syntactic unit. One of Bloodstein's proposed reasons for difficulty at the beginning of an utterance unit is that the speaker evaluates the "motor plan" of the utterance on which he anticipates difficulty, in this case a syntactic unit. The motor plan is assumed to be most complex at the beginning of the unit or in "getting started" (Bloodstein, 1972). Sometimes silent hesitations are associated with repetitions as in *I'm—I'm a big girl.*

Advanced stutterers view the locus of their difficulty as the word, or perhaps certain groups of words, such as all words beginning with *p*. Therefore, they fragment words, and these fragmentations result in sound or syllable repetitions. Again, because the motor plan is presumably more difficult at the beginning, they tend to repeat the initial sound or syllable or, occasionally, a later occurring stressed syllable.

The model of stuttering as tension and fragmentation elucidates a number of research findings rather well, particularly those with child stutterers. It predicts that the "word bound" factors influencing the loci of stuttering, such as consonant–vowel, word frequency, word length, information load, and grammatical class, will not be present in the stuttering of preschoolers. Linguistic data on preschool stutterers are extremely limited. Nonetheless, there is some empirical support for this hypothesis. For example, preschool stutterers seem to have more stuttering on conjunctions and pronouns than content words, presumably because the former typically begin syntactic units (Bloodstein, 1974; Bloodstein & Gantwerk, 1967; Harvey-Fisher & Brutten, 1977). There is some evidence, however, that preschool stutterers have more difficulty on long, unfamiliar words than on short, familiar words (Egland, 1955).

The shift of focus from syntactic units to words which takes place somewhere around the early elementary years may explain why Brown's four factors held up for elementary school children (D. E. Williams *et al.,* 1969). Finally, although not directly predicted by the model, the difference in focus may help explain why most of the studies conducted with adults speaking spontaneously (Hannah & Gardner, 1968; Lanyon, 1969) have yielded different results than the vast majority which sampled oral reading.

The tension aspect of the model appears consistent with much of the research using electromyography. The data consistently indicate higher levels of muscle activity during stuttering than during fluency.

Bloodstein's hypothesis regarding different stuttering symptoms being generated by different mechanisms has widespread support (e.g., Hutchinson, 1975; MacKay, 1970b; Soderberg, 1967). There is little agreement, however, on the nature of these mechanisms.

Other than excessive tension, motor deficiencies observed in stutterers are not dealt with in the tension and fragmentation model. It provides no hints, for example, as to whether or not stutterers suffer from a generalized motor deficit, a phonatory problem, or some other motor impairment.

Probably the major weakness of the tension and fragmentation model is that it does not satisfactorily explain why speech becomes fragmented. The only support given for the hypothesis that "getting started" in speech involves a more complex motor plan than continuing or finishing an utterance is the observation that people seem to have the greatest difficulty getting started in several fine motor skills. While Bloodstein is probably correct in this supposition, an explanation of why getting started is difficult is **not** provided. To take a specific example: Why are stressed syllables within some words perceived to be more difficult than the initial syllable of those words? The model does not suggest an answer.

C. Stuttering as a Defect in Prosodic Transition to Stressed Syllables (Wingate)

Wingate (1969b) described stuttering as a "phonetic transition defect," or a problem not of producing one sound but of generating the appropriate transitions from one sound to the next. Since then, the phonetic transition hypothesis has undergone considerable refinement (Wingate, 1969a, 1970, 1976, 1977). Recently, he described stuttering as a "prosodic defect" manifested as "an intermittent disorder of actualizing stress increase" (Wingate, 1976, p. 260). Combining terms in his early and later formulations, Wingate's view of stuttering might be termed a defect in prosodic transition to stressed syllables. This reformulation captures most of the necessary elements of Wingate's most recently published view. "Prosodic" refers to the various suprasegmental features such as juncture, intonation patterns, and stress (or accent) changes which cut across the typical phonetic segments. "Transition" defect still implies that stuttering is a problem of movement between sounds rather than stuttering "on" a sound. "To" means that the problem in stuttering occurs in transitions toward—not away from—the next sound. "Stressed syllable" captures the essence of Wingate's most recent refinement. He is convinced that stuttering is almost inevitably associated with syllable production, notably in production of the vowel in each syllable. Vowels carry considerably more acoustic energy than consonants, and the primary source of that increased energy is phonation. Furthermore, the effort required for vowel production is magnified in **stressed** syllables, and these syllables are most likely to be stuttered.

These relationships are shown in Fig. 7. As can be seen in the figure, stuttering results from linguistic and motor difficulties, both of which interact to produce the stutterer's intermittent inability to "actualize" the

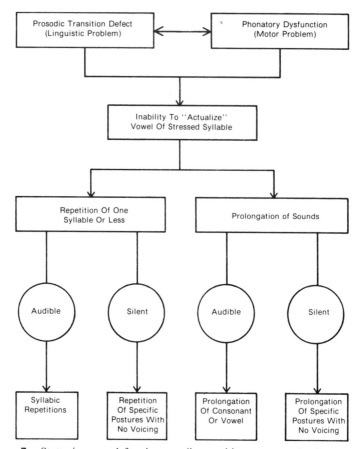

Figure 7. Stuttering as a defect in prosodic transition to stressed syllables. (Adapted from Wingate, 1976, 1977.)

vowels of stressed syllables. Observable stuttering symptoms are audible or silent repetitions and prolongations of segments one syllable or less in length.

Wingate is convinced that the primary locus of stuttering is on stressed syllables. He states:

> I do not know of anything else in the vast literature on stuttering that approaches the explanatory power of this single dimension [linguistic stress as a phonatory event]. (Wingate, 1977, p. 49)

The unequivocal fact that most stuttering occurs on the initial syllable of words is seen as an artifact of the distribution of syllabic stress in words. Wingate (1976) cited evidence that about 80% of the most frequently used English words are monosyllabic or have primary stress on the first syllable. The predominance of stuttering on consonants versus vowels is also viewed as an artifact of the frequency of sounds in the language. In an unpublished analysis of four lists of the 1000 most frequently spoken words of English, Wingate (1973) found that an average of 81% of the words began with consonants.

Since stuttering tends to occur on long words, content words, unfamiliar words, and words of high information load, Wingate (1977) assumes that the "overlapping" among them indicates a common quality. He proposes that the common dimension may reflect the inherent difficulty involved in saying such words. He further hypothesizes that word length and familiarity are basic aspects of the content–function word distinction, and that content words regularly carry the stress peaks in spontaneous speech.

By looking at general patterns, and disregarding selected contradictory findings, Wingate has generated a potentially powerful model of stuttering. His model comes closest of any yet advanced to explaining the linguistic findings of stuttering. Furthermore, it is not inconsistent with most of the data regarding the motor abilities of stutterers. Nonetheless, a few of his generalizations are not quite consistent with research results.

Wingate states that the factors of initial word position and the consonant–vowel effect are artifacts (1) of the frequency of occurrence of stressed syllables in the initial word position, and (2) of the frequency with which English words begin with consonants. Assuming that his figures of approximately 80% are accurate for both cases, then about 80% of stutterings should occur on initial word syllables and about 80% of those should be on consonants. The evidence suggests higher percentages in both cases. Hahn (1942b), Johnson and Brown (1935), and Taylor (1966a) reported that 98, 92, and 97%, respectively, of the total stutterings occurred on initial sounds of words in oral readings of adults; Egland (1955) reported 91% for children. With respect to consonant and vowel distributions, Hahn's (1942b) analysis was made from 78% initial **and medial** consonants and 22% initial vowels. Of these, only 3% of the stutterings occurred on initial vowels. Taylor (1966a) considered 79% initial consonants versus 21% initial vowels, but stuttering occurred on only 4% of the vowels. From these data, it seems that the initial word and consonant–vowel effects may not be artifacts entirely. Clearly, as Wingate (1977) points out, there is "overlapping" among the major linguistic features of stuttering. Nevertheless, as he so aptly points out with respect to Johnson's (1961) interpretation of overlapping of the distributions of disfluency types between stutterers and nonstutterers, overlap per se is not sufficient to suggest that the variables in question are not, in fact, distributed differently (Wingate, 1976, p. 57).

These arguments are not meant to suggest that Wingate is wrong; rather they are made to indicate that Wingate's stressed syllable locus hypothesis is overstated. For example, a great many stutterers have difficulty answering the telephone with the word *hello,* a word typically stuttered on the first syllable and stressed on the second syllable.

Wingate's prosodic transition model of stuttering is not inconsistent with most of the data on voice onset and voicing irregularities of stutterers. In fact, a great deal of the research on phonatory abilities of stutterers was motivated by his theoretical position which holds that modified vocalization is responsible for the fluency enhancing properties of a wide variety of stuttering "treatments" (e.g., singing, choral speaking, whispering, shadowing, rhythm, delayed auditory feedback, auditory masking, and others) (Wingate, 1969a, 1970).[11]

One finding in the coarticulation literature is not entirely consistent with the model's prediction of stuttering on vowels. Montgomery and Cooke (1976) found that stuttered CV syllables appear to be abnormal during the consonant segment but normal in the following vowel. Otherwise, the model of stuttering as a defect in prosodic transition to stressed syllables is quite consistent with the articulatory data on stutterers. Fine motor abilities, temporal speech characteristics, and respiratory abilities are not considered within the model.

D. Stuttering as a Defect in Coarticulatory Timing (Van Riper)

Van Riper (1971) defined a stuttering behavior as a "word improperly patterned in time and the speaker's reaction thereto" (p. 15). The concept of improper temporal patterning is too broad and requires some limitations for inclusion in this chapter. One central theme in Van Riper's view particularly germane to linguistic and motor models is a breakdown in timing of coarticulatory events in the production of syllables. His view is thus represented, in part, by a model of stuttering as a defect in coarticulatory timing. The model is shown graphically in Fig. 8.

Like Wingate, Van Riper holds that stuttering reflects a breakdown primarily at the level of the syllable. He hypothesizes that the stability of

---

[11] The research which specifically tests the modified vocalization hypothesis is not reviewed in this chapter because it does not bear **directly** on motor and linguistic determinants of stuttering. Instead it seeks to explain why various treatments are effective.

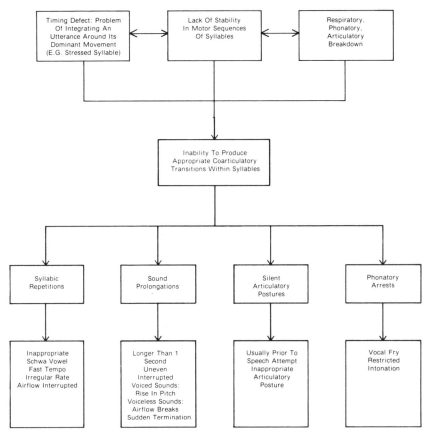

Figure 8. Stuttering as a defect in coarticulatory timing. (Adapted from Van Riper, 1971.)

motor patterns which maintain the integrity of syllables is somehow lacking in stutterers, due in part to overreliance on auditory feedback for speech control instead of appropriate monitoring via tactile–kinesthetic–proprioceptive feedback. In addition, stutterers are thought to be deficient in their ability to "time," or integrate, long motor sequences. Such "timing" is said to involve the imposition of higher order integration to achieve the proper serial order of a large number of discrete motor sequences, similar to that described by Lashley (1951). A dominant movement, such as a stressed syllable, is what typically "times" a speech sequence up to a phrase in length. Stutterers are intermittently unable to achieve such "timing," thereby producing sequences with inappropriate coarticulation.

While Van Riper has not specifically stated that stutterers have underlying physiological difficulties which affect breathing, voicing, and articulating, he conspicuously does not reject the notion either. Therefore, it is probably accurate to say that he does not rule out the possibility of organic deficiencies in these speech-related functions.

In essence, then, stuttering is the result of deficiencies in (1) the stability of motor patterns for syllables, (2) the ability to integrate a large number of discrete events in correct temporal order, and (3) speech-related respiration, phonation, and articulation. The combined result of these shortcomings is fractured syllables characterized by improper coarticulatory transitions between sounds.[12] The core stuttering behaviors which result are syllabic repetitions, sound prolongations, silent articulatory postures, and phonatory arrests.

The alleged core behaviors of stuttering contain ample evidence of coarticulatory abnormalities. For example, early stuttered repetitions of CV syllables often contain the schwa vowel instead of the target vowel (e.g., /sə–sə–sə–sup/). In such repetitions, it appears that the stutterer is searching for the appropriate coarticulatory features for the sound(s) he is attempting to say. When the correct features are achieved, the stuttering is terminated. In other stuttering moments, precise timing of transitional events between sounds is often lost due to breaks in airflow, excessive tension, and inappropriate postures.

Agnello, who has conducted considerable research in the area of coarticulation and stuttering basically concurs with Van Riper's view. He hypothesized that "the primary feature of . . . stuttering is essentially within the articulatory transition from phone to phone (inter or intra syllable)" (Agnello, 1975, p. 40). Like Van Riper, he believes that the control of the larynx is not independent of supraglottal articulation. For example, he attributes the lack of proper formant transitions in stop consonant–vowel syllables in stuttered speech to excessive supraglottal air pressure values resulting from articulatory constrictions higher in the vocal tract. In turn, the excessive air pressure causes phonatory difficulties.

Van Riper's model of stuttering as a defect in coarticulatory timing is not concerned with most of the linguistic determinants reviewed earlier. However, like Wingate's model, it singles out the syllable as the important locus of stuttering. Moreover, it suggests that syllabic stress is important in that stressed syllables are central in the programming of

---

[12] Van Riper believes that these breakdowns are exacerbated by psychological stress. Since emotions are not discussed in this chapter, that aspect of Van Riper's model was purposely omitted.

normal speech. Van Riper attributes increased stuttering on most of the other linguistic factors, such as word length, word position, information load, and initial sound, to the stutterer's past history of failure.

Evaluated in light of the research on the motor abilities of stuttering, Van Riper's model fares well. A defect in timing may explain some of the problems stutterers have in maintaining rhythmic repetitions of various speech and nonspeech tasks. It is consistent with virtually all of the research on respiratory, phonatory, and articulatory abilities of stutterers, perhaps because of its generality. As noted earlier, however, recent research on coarticulation suggests that coarticulation is not lacking during stuttering but is **different** from normal patterns. While such evidence is not clearly supportive of Van Riper's model, neither is it contradictory. Coarticulatory timing is a concept broad enough to embrace a variety of abnormal patterns.

E. Stuttering as a Defect in Airflow and Vocalization (Adams)

Adams (1974, 1975b) described stuttering as a defect in airflow and vocalization. In this model, irregularities in respiration and phonation are viewed as primary stuttering events while articulatory irregularities are seen as secondary coping strategies. A graphic representation of Adams' model is shown in Fig. 9. Stuttering is seen as a breakdown in timing, smooth initiation, and maintenance of exhalation and voicing. When such breakdowns occur, the speaker either repeats the same articulatory gesture or prolongs the articulatory posture being attempted.

Since speech typically occurs on exhalation, Adams' model explains stuttering in terms of the combined effects of insufficient transglottal air pressure and glottal resistance. Transglottal air pressure is the difference between supraglottal air pressure and subglottal air pressure. Obviously, then, transglottal air pressure is influenced by virtually all the structures in the entire vocal tract. In order for voicing to occur, subglottal air pressure must exceed supraglottal air pressure and be able to overcome the resistance imposed by the glottis itself. The breakdowns observed in stuttering can result from a wide variety of behaviors contributing to any combination of insufficient subglottal air pressure, excessive supraglottal air pressure, and excessive glottal resistance. Adams states that insufficient subglottal air pressure in stutterers is caused by any, or all, of the following respiratory irregularities documented in the literature: (1) fixations, or passive and active forces of inhalation and exhalation occurring simultaneously; (2) mistiming, or exhalations interrupted by short inspiratory gasps; (3) shallow breathing, or insufficient inhalations and/or

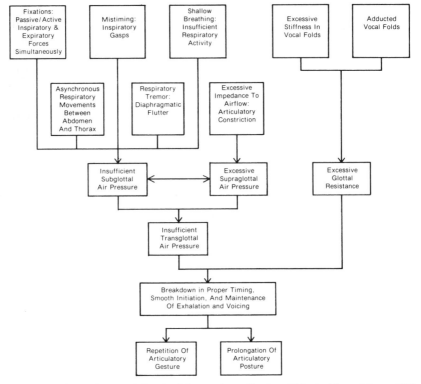

Figure 9. Stuttering as a defect in airflow and vocalization. (Adapted from Adams, 1974, 1975b.)

exhalations; (4) asynchronous respiratory movements, or antagonistic movements between the thorax and abdomen; and (5) respiratory tremors, or diaphragmatic flutter.

Excessive supraglottal air pressure in stutterers is usually caused by the secondary coping strategies in the upper articulators. Without compensatory adjustments of the expiratory musculature, constrictions or blockages of the airflow by the tongue or lips raise the supraglottal air pressure above the level of subglottal air pressure and cause a cessation of phonation. Excessive glottal resistance is attributed either to excessive stiffness within the vocal folds or to completely adducted folds prior to phonation.

Viewing stuttering as a defect in air flow and vocalization predicts that the stutterer will attempt to compensate for aerodynamic deficiencies in one area by changes in other areas. Adams accounts for difficulties in the respiratory and laryngeal mechanisms by classical conditioning but does not rule out the possibility of "some kind of subtle organic influences" (Adams, 1975b, p. 30). He accounts for supraglottal articulatory irregularities by operant conditioning. By implication, then, the respiratory irregularities contributing to insufficient subglottal air pressure can be viewed as either organic deficiencies or classically conditioned responses to stress. In either case, the logical thing for the stutterer to do when subglottal air pressure is insufficient would be to relax his larynx and oral musculature, thereby reducing both glottal resistance and supraglottal air pressure. However, there is no evidence that the stutterer responds to reduced subglottal air pressure in this way. Instead, he typically tenses muscles in the larynx, the upper articulators, or both, making phonation less likely. Therefore, much of the struggle associated with stuttering involves abnormal respiratory movements aimed at generating sufficient subglottal air pressure to overcome the combined effects of glottal resistance and supraglottal air pressure. Classically conditioned adduction of the glottis prior to, or during, phonation would probably have much the same effect.

The model of stuttering as a defect in airflow and vocalization is the only one discussed in this paper which accounts for the wide variety of breathing abnormalities observed in stutterers in anything more than a superficial way. Second, it is the only one which adequately explains the inseparable relationship between phonation and respiration as noted by Ford and Luper (1975).

It is interesting to note that Wingate (1969a) nearly predicted a model of stuttering based on aerodynamic and voice interrelationships. He wrote:

> At this point one is compelled to recall the early stuttering research on breathing irregularities and voice which has long been ignored or dismissed in one way or another. It seems evident that renewed and more careful exploration in this area is indicated. Modern instrumentation and improved techniques of analysis should reveal important data and relationships which have remained obscure. (p. 685)

It is ironic that Wingate himself did not specify more clearly the relationship between breathing and voice.

Adams' model accounts for the fact that supraglottal air pressure is excessive during the stuttering (Hutchinson, 1975; Hutchinson & Navarre, 1977) and fluent speech of stutterers (Agnello & Wingate, 1971). In addition, while the model does not predict the seven aerodynamic patterns of stuttering described by Hutchinson (1975) (Table III, Section II,B,1), they provide meaningful additions to it.

The defective airflow and vocalization model is not inconsistent with the data on phonatory abilities of stutterers. It seems reasonable to speculate that delayed voice onset and difficulty in shifting from voiceless to voiced sounds in stutterers is due to excessive glottal stiffness. Indeed,

Adams intended that the model would account for such vocal problems since he has been a principal investigator of phonatory difficulties in stutterers.

Adams believes that his model also accounts for most articulatory abnormalities observed in stutterers. He cites the studies of Shaffer (1940) and Stromsta (1965) which suggest that stutterers manifest excessive glottal resistance, and reports by Fibiger (1971) and Van Riper (1971) that phonatory and articulatory abnormalities are related. In general, the model is not inconsistent with articulatory data; however, there is no definitive evidence yet to conclude that articulatory disturbances are secondary to respiratory and phonatory breakdowns.

The airflow and vocalization model does not account directly for any of the linguistic determinants of stuttering. Indirectly, the initial sound effect could be explained by more complex respiratory and phonatory requirements involved with beginning to talk than continuing speech once it has begun. The consonant–vowel effect might be explained by the fact that consonants as a group require greater intraoral air pressure than vowels.

The fact that stuttering occurs primarily on stressed syllables is not quite consistent with Adams' interpretation of increased vocal effort. In one study he ascribed the fluency enhancing effect of increased vocal intensity associated with auditory masking to increased subglottal air pressure (Adams & Moore, 1972). If syllabic stress were achieved by the same mechanism, then Adams' model would predict less—not more—stuttering on stressed syllables.

F. Stuttering as a Learned Extricatory Response to a Laryngeal Abductor Reflex (Schwartz)

In a recent book entitled *Stuttering Solved,* M. F. Schwartz (1976) described, in lay terms, his new approach to the theory and treatment of stuttering. He stated that "it was my discovery of the physical cause of the stuttering block that enabled me to develop a relatively simple treatment" (p. 12). Earlier, M. F. Schwartz (1974, 1975a, 1975b) described a theoretical model of the core of the stuttering block. Specifically, he stated that the core of the stuttering block is the "tendency, under conditions of psychological stress, for the loss of supramedullar, inhibition controls upon the PCA (posterior cricoarytenoid muscle) in the presence of subglottal air pressure associated with speech" (M. F. Schwartz, 1975b, p. 137). His model of stuttering as a learned extricatory response to a laryngeal abductor reflex is shown in Fig. 10.

Central to the model is an "airway dilation reflex" (ADR) which flares the nostrils, moves the body of the tongue forward, dilates the pharynx,

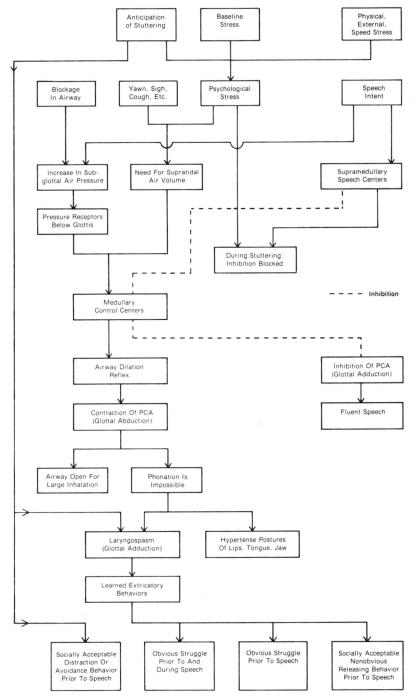

Figure 10. Stuttering as a learned extricatory response to a laryngeal abductor reflex. (Adapted from M. F. Schwartz, 1974, 1975a, 1975b, 1976.)

and abducts the glottis (the only response shown in Fig. 10). The ADR is normally active when there is a blockage of the airway or a need for greater than normal (supratidal) air volumes, as for yawning, sighing, or coughing. According to Schwartz, the ADR is mediated in the medulla and can be elicited by increased subglottic pressure receptors in the trachea. During normal speech subglottic pressure is elevated, but the ADR is not elicited because higher central nervous system (supramedullary) speech centers **inhibit** the medullary center which mediates the reflex. This supramedullary inhibition breaks down, however, under periods of psychological stress. As a result, the ADR is elicited and causes the PCA to contract and the glottis to abduct. Phonation is thus rendered impossible. The response to this reflexive glottal abduction is what comprises stuttering. The speaker who finds himself unable to phonate typically overcomes the abduction by a vigorous adductory effort, or a "laryngospasm." He may also attempt to "do battle supraglottally" (M. F. Schwartz, 1974, p. 174) by tensing the lips, tongue or jaw. Overt stuttering, then, consists of learned extricatory behaviors to escape from the laryngospasm or to avoid its occurrence altogether.

M. F. Schwartz (1976) lists several kinds of stress which contribute to stuttering. Baseline stress consists of the speaker's amount of psychological and muscle tension present at any given time. In addition, physical stress (e.g., fatigue), external stress (e.g., bad news), and speed stress (e.g., need to talk in a hurry) may add to the stutterer's psychological stress. Finally, other factors, such as situations of communicative stress, sound and word fears, and verbal uncertainty, trigger anticipation of stuttering which adds to psychological stress. As the stutterer acquires a large repertoire of struggle and coping behaviors, anticipation of stuttering alone becomes sufficient to evoke a laryngospasm or a set of distracting or avoidance behaviors to prevent its occurrence.

Not reflected in Fig. 10 are the kinds of strategies utilized by stutterers to release themselves from stuttering. One strategy is an inspiratory gasp which would drop subglottic air pressure, release the ADR and laryngospasm, and allow continuation of speech.

Schwartz's model of stuttering and his approach to therapy (to be discussed in Section V,E) have been controversial. Part of this controversy centers around the way in which the approach was originally publicized, via the popular press and television, instead of the usual scientific journals. It has also been criticized on its scientific accuracy, logic, and explanatory power. Reviewing the same literature on respiratory and laryngeal physiology which M. F. Schwartz (1974) used to support his model, Freeman, Ushijima, and Hirose (1975) raised a number of issues. They questioned whether or not the PCA is the strongest intrinsic muscle of the larynx (such that its uninhibited action would abduct the glottis) to which M. F. Schwartz (1975a) conceded that it was at least one of the strongest laryngeal muscles. In addition, Freeman *et al.* (1975) raised the serious question as to whether the PCA is reflexively active in controlling glottal width during exhalation. M. F. Schwartz (1975a) did not really refute this criticism except to state that he had arrived at his interpretation of the data in question "within the context of a larger model" (p. 14). Zimmermann and Allen (1975) wondered how the model could account for stuttering on voiceless sounds (when the PCA should be active). M. F. Schwartz (1975b) explained that an increase in subglottal air pressure associated with such sounds was responsible for conditioned laryngospasms.

The model of stuttering as a learned extricatory response to a laryngeal abductor reflex does not account for the linguistic findings of stuttering and it was probably not meant to do so. Like Van Riper, M. F. Schwartz (1976) believes that specific sounds and words associated with stuttering are determined by an individual stutterer's history of failure.

Schwartz' model does not predict any general motor coordination deficits in stutterers. Most respiratory and articulatory irregularities are seen as learned extricatory behaviors. The commonly observed stuttering symptoms of exhalations interrupted by inhalations and speaking on residual air do make sense within the ADR explanation. Both are associated with lower subglottic air pressure and, hence, the likelihood of an ADR-produced laryngospasm is reduced.

Since the PCA is hypothesized to contract prior to many stutterings, the research on laryngeal behavior of stutterers should document this fact. To date, abduction of the larynx has not been reported as any consistent pattern prior to stutterings. Freeman and Ushijima (1974), who recorded EMGs from a number of laryngeal and supraglottal muscles in a severe stutterer, did not observe activity in either the PCA or genioglossus (a muscle which pulls the tongue forward) prior to stutterings. In other words, they found no evidence of the ADR. Other researchers using glottography or fiberoptic viewing of the glottis have not reported consistent abduction of the larynx prior to stuttering. On the contrary, Conture *et al.* (1977) reported glottal abduction as the primary laryngeal symptom **during**—not prior to—part-word repetitions. In this case, it is difficult to imagine that the stutterers were struggling to free themselves from **adductory** laryngospasms. It is possible, however, that part-word repetitions reflect a supraglottal response to the ADR instead of the usual laryngospasm as proposed by M. F. Schwartz (1974). If so, it seems reasonable to assume that laryngeal abduction during stuttering should occur only infrequently, not in 72% of all part-word repetitions analyzed from nine out of ten subjects in the study of Conture *et al.* (1977).

M. F. Schwartz (1974) proposed that Agnello and Wingate's (1972) finding that stutterers had longer than normal voice onset times in stop consonant–vowel syllables was due to problems in neural inhibition of the PCA. When reminded that the speech samples were fluent utterances (Zimmermann & Allen, 1975), M. F. Schwartz (1975b) modified his hypothesis. Instead, he suggested that in the fluent speech of stutterers, Agnello and Wingate were observing a "low-stress, low level expression" (M. F. Schwartz, 1975b, p. 137) of the ADR. The modified interpretation, while possible, is nonetheless a *post hoc* explanation with little predictive potential.

In summary, whereas any kind of laryngeal irregularities **during** stuttering could be explained by Schwartz's model, direct evidence of the reflexive contraction of the PCA prior to speech is lacking. Since his model hinges on that presumption, unqualified acceptance of the model must await further empirical verification.

G. Preliminary Linguistic and Motor Models of Stuttering

Several additional investigators have developed models to explain various linguistic and motor facts about stuttering. In spite of their theoretical importance, none of these models has been articulated in sufficient detail to be included as a fully developed account. Alternatively, a number of preliminary models will be presented and followed by comments regarding their explanatory usefulness.

1. Stuttering as a Disorder in Language Systems and Processing (Hamre)

Hamre (1976) proposed "a language systems and processing model" of stuttering. The model, shown in Fig. 11, indicates that stuttering is a problem at two levels, a linguistic level termed "language systems" and a psychophysiological level termed "language processing." As can be seen in the vertical dimension of the diagram, stuttering is primarily a phonological problem involving segments (phonemes and allophones) and prosody. Furthermore, it is a problem chiefly in speech formulation and execution.

The horizontal dimension indicates that stuttering is a context-sensitive disorder at both levels primarily in linguistic rules. Here, "context-sensitive" is intended to indicate that the rules contain interdependencies

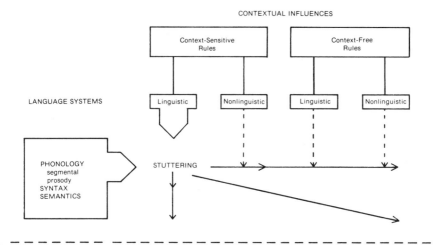

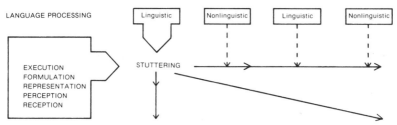

Figure 11. A language systems and processing model of stuttering. (From Hamre, 1976.)

among the variables, as in the case of later occurring sounds influencing the production of earlier sounds. Context-sensitive situational rules are also operative, such as in the combined effects on the frequency of stuttering to authority figures on a "good day" as opposed to a "bad day." However, the model predicts that situational rules will reveal very little about the nature of stuttering per se.

Context-free linguistic and situational rules also apply. For example, a stutterer may stutter primarily on words beginning with /n/, but, by itself, this is rather useless information.

Finally, the model predicts a "spread of effect" proceeding from simple to complex stuttering. As stuttering increases in severity, it begins to influence, or be influenced by, variables at other levels. For example, an unusually severe instance of stuttering may affect the speaker's ability to generate appropriate syntax and/or his ability to perceive sensory stimuli.

Hamre's language systems and processing model is an interesting way of conceptualizing the problems observed in stuttering. For example, it predicts that the most significant linguistic problems in stuttering will be found in the area of phonology rather than morphology or syntax. Moreover, it predicts that research into the psychophysiological aspects of stuttering which focus on motor programming and speech production will come closer to understanding the basic defects involved than research into perceptual processes.

The major weakness of Hamre's model is its lack of specificity. For example, it suggests that stuttering is a problem of speech programming and production but does not adequately define these terms. Obviously, a great many other disorders, such as articulation disorders, also would fit into the same category.

2. Stuttering as a Defect in Laryngeal Function

To date, a carefully articulated theory of vocal fold dysfunction in stuttering which is derived from recent research on the phonatory abilities of stutterers has not been advanced. Schwartz' model (Section IV,F) centers on the stutterers larynx but, for the most part, was not derived from research on the vocal abilities of stutterers.

The views of two groups of researchers will be presented to represent two different—but complementary—preliminary models of stuttering. The spokesman for the first group of investigators is Freeman, who has collaborated primarily with Ushijima and Hirose. The second group includes Conture, McCall, and Brewer.

According to Freeman and her associates, stuttering can be viewed primarily as a problem of laryngeal abductor–adductor imbalance. During fluent speech, reciprocity is observed between the activity of the posterior cricoarytenoid (PCA), the vocal fold abductor, and the various adductors, interarytenoids (INT), thyroarytenoid or vocalis (VOC), and lateral cricoarytenoid (LCA). However, during stuttering, this reciprocal balance breaks down and the muscles contract antagonistically. One of the most common stuttering patterns is a vigorous contraction of the muscles of the "laryngeal sphincter," the INT, VOC, and LCA. This typically results in complete adduction of the vocal folds and, often, adduction of the ventricular folds as well. When the ventricular folds are adducted, "vocal fry" is the typical acoustic result.

The LCA is normally involved in strong medial compression of the vocal folds in activities such as swallowing and producing hard glottal attacks (i.e., glottal stops). This muscle undergoes the greatest increase in activity during stuttering. In fact, the limited evidence suggests that the degree of LCA activity is directly related to the severity of stuttering.

The second group of researchers who have advanced a preliminary model for stuttering as a laryngeal problem is Conture et al. (1977). While being careful not to overinterpret their data, these investigators suggest that part-word repetitions and sound prolongations may result from different laryngeal mechanisms. They suggest that typical repetitions are associated with high levels of antagonistic abductor and adductor muscle activity which leaves the posterior vocal folds partly abducted. As a result, they predict that most repetitions should be associated with a breathy vocal quality. In contrast, most prolongations are associated with quite complete and tense adduction and probably a vocal fry quality.

These two preliminary models, taken together, explain most of the vocal irregularities observed in stuttering. Since the research of these groups was very limited in scope, the models do not address the other motor and linguistic determinants of stuttering reviewed in this chapter.

3. Stuttering as a Defect in Initial Tonus

In Prague, Czechoslavakia, Morávek and Langová (1967) proposed that the central deficit in stuttering is "initial tonus" (IT) which occurs prior to the initiation of phonation. In their view, IT occurs in the laryngeal musculature and involves more muscles than are normally required for phonation as well as greater than usual tension. Normal phonation is impossible, and, as a result, the stutterer increases his muscular effort even more. This compensatory effort results in stuttering.

The cause of IT is seen as a problem in motor speech commands which involves voicing. Morávek and Langová assume that the cortical commands are intact but are "deformed" by the addition of commands for muscle tension in the basal ganglia, specifically the region of the connections between thalamic and striopallidal nuclei. This deformation results from psychological stress. In any case, an "accessory sound" is generated by the attempts to break up the IT, and this serves as an "acoustic prosthesis" to end the blocking of the cortical program. Thus, the stutterer is allowed to continue speaking.

Morávek and Langová's (1967) model is primarily speculative and is not based on neurophysiological evidence. The alleged areas of weakness, i.e., the basal ganglia, are practically impossible to investigate during speech. Therefore, the model is essentially impossible to test. Nonetheless, it could account for much of the laryngeal tension observed in stutterers even in their fluent speech. It does not predict stutterings on voiceless consonants and would have difficulty explaining them.

H. Linguistic and Motor Models: Summary

The striking impression one is left with after reviewing these linguistic and motor models of stuttering is the inability of any of them to provide a satisfactory account of all the data. Nevertheless, they have focused attention on many fruitful areas of inquiry which otherwise may have gone unnoticed. Let us review the models and point out such areas.

MacKay's model of stuttering as a defect in phonetic and syllabic contextual programming highlights the importance of linguistic programming in stuttering. It suggests that certain phonetic sequences are inherently more difficult to say than others and proposes that phonetic or syllabic contexts are important determinants of such difficulty. The model also suggests that speech production units involved in stuttering vary in size, from distinctive features to phrases. Finally the model proposes that different stuttering symptoms (repetitions, prolongations, and blocks) are determined by selective programming differences.

The latter hypothesis, that repetitions and prolongations reflect different linguistic processes, is also suggested by Bloodstein's model of stuttering as tension and fragmentation. His model also directs our attention to important differences in the early stuttering of children as opposed to more advanced forms in adults.

Wingate's view of stuttering as a defect in prosodic transition to stressed syllables highlights the importance of the moment-to-moment changes in voicing necessary to generate appropriate stress and intonation patterns in fluent speech. It suggests that stuttering involves difficulty in producing the syllable, particularly the stressed syllable. Finally, it emphasizes the importance of transition: the stutterer has difficulty not in producing single sounds but in moving from one sound to the next.

Van Riper's notion of stuttering as a defect in coarticulatory timing, like MacKay's model, stresses the importance of contextual programming in stuttering. And, like Wingate's formulation, it also singles out the syllable as the primary candidate of difficulty for the stutterer. Lest the reader be left with the impression that consideration of the syllable is new, we quote from Fletcher (1914) who, more than 60 years ago, wrote:

> It would doubtless be nearer the facts to say that the asynergy . . . [in stuttering] consists in the failure of vocalization to be co-ordinated with articulation. This would point to the syllable rather than either the consonant or the vowel. (p. 221)

Van Riper's model emphasizes the contributions of motor pattern stability and motor learning in stuttering. It also indicates the importance of strategies used in monitoring longer speech units, such as phrases.

Adams' model of stuttering as a defect in airflow and vocalization clearly points out the interdependent relationship between those two processes. Phonatory irregularities are understood in terms of respiratory problems, and vice versa. Moreover, Adams leads us to suspect that breathing and voicing problems in stutterers are somehow more basic than articulatory problems, and that these may well be based, to a large extent, on aerodynamic laws. Indeed, as Baken (1975) pointed out in his overview of a recent conference on "Vocal Tract Dynamics and Disfluency," current views of stuttering involve a "retreat from the cortex" (p. 2) to brainstem or peripheral neuromotor processes.

Schwartz's model of stuttering as a learned extricatory response to a laryngeal abductor reflex has focused important attention on laryngeal behavior prior to speaking. Moreover, it leads us to suspect that voicing is the speech activity most likely to go awry in stuttering. The same can be said for the preliminary models of Freeman and Conture *et al.* which also view stuttering as a defect in laryngeal function. Hamre's language systems and processing model is compatible with many of the other models presented; that is, stuttering is best understood as a context-sensitive problem of speech formulation and production at the phonolgical level of language.

If one statement could summarize all of the models presented herein, it might be stated as follows. Stuttering is primarily a defect of syllable production due (1) to excessive tension and lack of coordination in the processes of respiration, phonation, and articulation, and (2) to breakdowns in normal phonological programming.

V. STUTTERING THERAPY APPROACHES INVOLVING LINGUISTIC AND MOTOR AWARENESS

Following is a sampling of current stuttering therapy approaches which **directly** involve teaching the stutterer to become aware of various linguistic and motor aspects of speaking. The review will be limited to those approaches which do not involve the addition of unusual stimulation, such as delayed auditory feedback, auditory masking, or rhythm during speech. It is true, however, that the results of such treatments often enhance linguistic or motor awareness of speech, either by design or by accident.

Descriptions of therapy approaches in this section will be brief. Consequently, they are not intended to provide sufficient detail for clinicians to carry out the therapy programs.

A. Proprioceptive Awareness (Van Riper)

Van Riper's well known approach to stuttering therapy involves four stages; identification, desensitization, modification, and stabilization (Van

Riper, 1973). Developed over many years predominantly for severe adult stutterers (Van Riper, 1958), Van Riper's goal is "fluent stuttering."

The aspect of his treatment singled out for consideration as a therapy approach involving linguistic and motor awareness is "proprioceptive awareness." Proprioceptive awareness is primarily involved in Van Riper's modification stage and, to a lesser extent, in the stabilization stage. In the sense intended here, proprioceptive awareness refers to the stutterer learning: (1) to become aware of the motoric aspects of stuttering, (2) to modify them, and (3) to replace them with more appropriate patterns.

Forty years ago, Van Riper described the stutterer's "preparatory set" to stutter, which consisted of "a pre-stimulus neuromuscular adjustment which selects, determines and controls the [stuttering] response" (Van Riper, 1937, p. 150). Much of his therapy can be viewed as a systematic means of teaching the stutterer to use correct preparatory sets.

After the stutterer is able to understand and describe his stuttering (identification) and is able to stutter openly without excessive fear (desensitization), he is taught to modify it. Through "cancellation," the stutterer is taught to modify his stuttering **after it occurs.** In cancellation, he learns to **feel** the excessive tension, abnormal postures, and inappropriate movements and then try the word again while concentrating on these motor features. Next, the stutterer learns to modify his stuttering **as it occurs** with the "pull-out." The pull-out involves changing the stuttering response in gradual approximations to the appropriate speech targets, then consciously and deliberately **pulling out** of the stuttering response to fluent speech. Finally, the "preparatory set" is taught in order to modify stuttering **before it occurs.** Here, the stutterer learns to identify subtle tactile and proprioceptive cues prior to stuttering and to modify them before attempting the feared word. The speech which results is deliberate, slightly slowed, and limited in stress and intonation variations. It is critical that the stutterer keep the "motor model" of what he intends to say in mind while utilizing a high degree of proprioceptive awareness during his ongoing speech as he uses the preparatory set.

During stabilization, the stutterer is taught consciously to shift his attention to fluency instead of stuttering. A large number of techniques are recommended, many of which involve linguistic and motor awareness. For example, Van Riper recommends a great deal of oral speaking practice, either reading or spontaneous speech. In these activities the stutterer is instructed to "smooth out" his speech, eliminating unusual pauses, and to achieve better phrasing patterns and prosody. He is taught to monitor his speech for fluency rather than to persist in vigilance only for stuttering.

B. Motor Planning (Frick)

Frick (1965) conducted a clinical investigation of the effects of a variety of "motor-planning" techniques in stuttering therapy. He compared motor-planning techniques with conventional therapy techniques in 12 matched pairs of stutterers. Frick tentatively concluded that the motor-planning procedures were superior to conventional procedures.[13]

The motor planning defect in stutterers was seen as a "deficit in auditory and/or kinesthetic imagery" (Frick, 1965, p. 21). Presumably, stutterers often cannot "hear beyond" or "feel beyond" initial stuttered phonemes.

The sequence of motor-planning techniques can be summarized as follows. First, various listening activities are introduced in which the stutterer is encouraged to improve his "images" of fluent and stuttered speech. Next, he is taught to utilize improved motor planning in his speech in several ways. One technique was Bluemel's (1957) "fluent-thinking" procedure in which the stutterer is taught to wait to speak until he can think of his utterance in "clear-cut, broadcastable words" (p. 91). Another procedure involves repeating a stuttered word over and over until fluent while focusing on the emerging motor plan. "Cancellation of entire phrases" is used to extend the length of the motor plan. Here, the stutterer pauses after a phrase in which a stuttering occurred to analyze his stuttering and the appropriate motor plan for that phrase. Then the phrase is repeated exactly as planned. Other techniques included placing exaggerated stress on all unaccented syllables, prewriting utterances prior to saying them, and motor planning entire phrases before uttering them.

Frick did not include Van Riper's preparatory set among his motor-planning techniques. Instead, rather surprisingly, he included it in the control group of conventional techniques which did **not** comprise motor planning. Perhaps Frick's rationale for this choice was that he believed that the motor plan for speech is generated in units of phrase length or longer.

C. Motor Speech Awareness (St. Louis)

The author conducted a study of the effects of motor speech awareness on stuttering in four adult stutterers who were run in a single-subject design (St. Louis, 1973; St. Louis & Martin, 1978). While the experimental procedure has not been utilized in pure form in clinical management of

---

[13] Frick's investigation had a number of problems in experimental design, data analysis, and conclusions. For a discussion of these problems, the reader is referred to St. Louis (1973).

stutterers, its focus on linguistic and motor awareness is germane to the present discussion.

Motor speech awareness, as operationally defined in the St. Louis study, involves the stutterer demonstrating awareness of certain motor features of word-initial phonemes before saying them. The stutterer is stopped at frequent, unpredictable intervals during spontaneous speech and required to make certain decisions about the first sound of the next word he will say. Specifically, he is obliged to make three binary choices on a response panel indicating whether the next sound is (1) voiced or unvoiced, (2) exploded (noncontinuant) or smooth (continuant), and (3) requires tongue tip contact or not.

Each stutterer was first run in a baserate condition until his percentage of words stuttered was operationally stable. Next, he was run in two identical control conditions which simply involved being stopped for 5-second intervals on a frequent but random schedule. The only difference between these two conditions was that the second was preceded by training to make the three binary choices on the response panel. Thus, the second control condition assessed the effects of motor speech awareness **training** on otherwise stable performance. The stutterer was then run in the motor speech awareness condition (described in the previous paragraph) and, finally, in an extinction condition.

Two of the four stutterers reduced their percentage of words stuttered in the motor speech awareness condition compared to the two control conditions. A third stutterer reduced his percentage of words stuttered after being trained to analyze "motor features" of word-initial sounds. The experimental procedures produced few systematic changes in stuttering for the fourth subject, except perhaps to limit the session-to-session variability of his stuttering.

With several modifications, the same procedure was used with eight stutterers uttering bisyllabic nonsense words, first in a control condition and then in a motor speech awareness condition (St. Louis & Martin, 1976). All but one subject in the second study reduced the mean duration of stuttering; however, a group reduction effect was present only for the four subjects who stressed the first syllable of the nonsense words.

As noted above, this procedure has not yet been adapted for clinical use with stutterers. It is likely, however, that future clinical modifications will involve aspects of speech production other than motor features. Several of the stutterers had difficulty learning the necessary feature choices, and accuracy of analyzing features did not appear to be important in whether or not subjects' stuttering was reduced in the motor speech awareness conditions.

D. Speech Target Shaping

At least three different clinicians have developed techniques and/or devices to teach stutterers to reliably achieve various fluency targets. Such approaches are based on the assumption that stuttering is best treated by teaching stutterers normally **fluent** speech targets. It is further assumed that as long as the stutterer can achieve such targets, stuttering cannot occur. This approach differs from the Van Riperian notion of "fluent stuttering" which implies that the stutterer must learn to intercept and change his stuttering. It also implies that the stutterer is capable of better fluency than that achieved in "controlled" stuttering.

1. Precision Fluency Shaping Program (Webster)

During the middle and late 1960s, Ronald Webster, an experimental psychologist, developed an empirically derived approach[14] for treating stutterers (Webster, 1974). Five different programs were developed, each new one building on the successes and failures of the last. The fifth program, termed a "**precision fluency shaping program**," is, in Webster's words, "a systematic means of purposefully modifying the characteristic movements and forces in the speech of stutterers" (p. 35). Since 1974, the program has undergone few additional refinements.

The program involves an intensive 3-week program at Hollins College in Roanoke, Virginia, of "speech reconstruction" for stutterers. From the results of 200 stutterers immediately after therapy, Webster reported that about 90% acquired normal fluency ($\leq 3\%$ disfluencies in oral reading) and that 89% perceived themselves to be within the range of normal on the Woolf (1967) *Perceptions of Stuttering Inventory* (PSI). Follow-up data obtained an average of 10 months later indicated that 75% maintained normal fluency and 72% maintained normal PSI ratings. In addition, responses of the stutterers to a questionnaire indicated that 95% felt that the precision fluency shaping program was worthwhile to them.

The program involves teaching small speech responses ('targets') defined in terms of duration, position, and velocity or force, within very small limits of tolerance. To enhance learning, the stutterer is signaled after every trial, usually by a light or short phrase, whether or not he is

[14] Although Webster (1974) describes his approach as empirically derived, he advanced "a multiple-feedback-loop servosystem model of stuttering" (p. 46). In essence, stuttering is hypothesized to result from "*an aberration of auditory feedback signals* that are normally employed in speech guidance" (p. 47). The main effect of such feedback difficulties is blockage of phonation. The reason this model was not included in the previous section is that it assumes that the focal problem in stuttering is sensory in nature rather than motor or linguistic.

"on-target." The targets include: prolonging the vowels of each syllable, making smooth transitions from one sound to the next, beginning each utterance with an adequate breath supply, and initiating phonation gently. Together these targets result in a fluent, but very slow, manner of speaking.

During training the client is given a model of a correct target and then asked to practice it in exaggerated form through a series of sounds arranged from easy to difficult (vowels, voiced continuant consonants, voiceless fricatives, and stop consonants). When he can generate the target reliably, he is taught to produce it in progressively less exaggerated forms until it falls within the range observed in normally fluent speech. The stutterer progresses through sounds, syllables, one-syllable words, two-syllable words, three- or more syllable words, short sentences, longer sentences, and conversation. Transfer to outside situations is programmed from the outset of the program.

The most unique aspect of the precision fluency shaping program is a "voice monitor." This device is a small "computer" which is programmed to accept or reject various amplitude-by-time slopes in the onset of voicing. To teach the "gentle onset" target, the slope is set at the most gradual level and the stutterer must maintain a gradual and steady increase in vocal intensity in order to be signaled by the monitor that he is "on target." Later, the slope tolerance is shifted to more normal voice onset characteristics. Finally, the stutterer is "weaned" from the "voice monitor" while keeping gentle voice onsets.

D. Schwartz and L. M. Webster (1977a, 1977b) reported on eight, then on 29, stutterers who had been treated with the precision fluency shaping program over a 3-month period rather than the 3-week period advocated by R. Webster. Their results were comparable to those of the 200 stutterers mentioned earlier, although not quite as impressive. Daly and Darnton (1976) assessed the immediate and long-term effects of the precision fluency shaping program used in conjunction with attitudinal therapy with nine adolescent male stutterers attending a 7-week summer camp. They found that stuttering was greatly reduced immediately after therapy but considerable relapse was observed 2 and 10 months later. The authors suggested that their finding of poor carryover might be attributed to the age of their stutterers, who were 12 years younger than the mean age reported by Webster (1976). They also mentioned that student clinicians who had not undergone the clinician's training program at Hollins College administered the therapy.[15]

---

[15] Webster is opposed to anyone other than his Hollins associates training clinicians to use the precision fluency shaping program. He is also opposed to any modifications in the program (Webster, 1976).

2. Easy Voice Onset (Agnello)

Agnello (1975) reported the construction of a device which is similar in function to the Hollins voice monitor. For the purpose of teaching easy voice onset, the device can be programmed to compare the slope of the amplitude growth of the voice of the stutterer to any reference value. Also, since intraoral air pressure was found to be sensitive to voice onset time, the device is also capable of using pressure as its input. At the time of Agnello's (1975) report, the easy-onset device was undergoing calibration for different syllabic patterns. Furthermore, a manual was in preparation for use of the device in the clinical management of stutterers.

3. Personalized Fluency Control Therapy (Cooper)

Recently E. B. Cooper (1976) developed a "personalized fluency control therapy" program designed to make desirable modifications in the stutterer's abnormal speaking symptoms as well as in his feelings and attitudes. Only the former will be discussed here.

Speech target shaping begins in Cooper's third and fourth stages of therapy ("cognition and behavior orientation" and "fluency control"). Cooper encourages the client (usually a school-aged child) to develop the "feeling of control" by learning to use "fluency initiating gestures" (FIGs) which are fluency targets. While the usefulness of specific FIGs varies from one stutterer to another, a list of "universal" FIGs is provided:

Slow Speech. Characterized by a reduction in the rate of speech typically involving the equalized prolongation of syllables.

Easy Onset. Characterized by the initiation of phonation with as little tension as possible.

Deep Breath. Characterized by a consciously controlled inhalation prior to the initiation of phonation and typically used in conjunction with the Easy Onset FIG.

Loudness Control. Characterized by a conscious and sustained increase or decrease in the volume of the client's speech.

Smooth Speech (Easy Contact). Characterized by light articulatory contacts with plosive and affricate sounds typically modified to resemble fricative sounds.

Syllable Stress. Characterized by conscious loudness and pitch variations. (E. B. Cooper, 1976, p. 98)

To date, no systematic data have been reported regarding the effectiveness of Cooper's personalized fluency control. Since the program is readily available in published form, it is very likely that such data will soon be forthcoming.

4. BRAT (Gronhovd)

BRAT stands for breathing, rate, airflow, and tension. These are the four primary targets in Gronhovd's (1977) "molecular approach" to shaping the fluent speech of stutterers. The BRAT approach, like Cooper's personalized fluency control therapy, does not rely exclusively on speech target shaping. BRAT activities are preceded by providing information about and identifying stuttering as well as by modifying stuttering symptoms. It is conducted concurrently with anxiety desensitization techniques and followed by transfer and maintenance programs. In essence, BRAT focuses on aspects of speech found to be deviant in the fluent speech of stutterers, such as respiratory patterns, pauses, rate, voice onset, intraoral air pressure, and tension (Gronhovd, 1975). It assumes that "fluency" or "fluent speech" are gross and nonspecific entities which must be further analyzed and shaped.

The BRAT approach proceeds as follows. First, the stutterer is taught deep muscle relaxation in a supine position. Next he is taught unvocalized, then vocalized, sighs. The next steps involve progressively counting up to four digits while maintaining: (1) smooth, moderately deep inhalations and smooth, easy exhalations; (2) a slow rate; (3) uninterrupted airflow; (4) no excessive tension; (5) a soft glottal attack with a breathy voice; and (6) subjective reports of easy, automatic production. Using the same or similar criteria, the stutterer then answers simple questions and speaks in short, then longer, monologues, still lying in the supine position. Propositional speech activities are next repeated in a semireclined position and subsequently in a sitting position. Speaking rate is increased from one to two syllables per second as the stutterer orally paraphrases silently read material and engages in conversation. Finally, rate, voice quality, intensity, intonation, rhythm, and phrasing are "normalized" to produce "an easy, relaxed, expressive, unmonotonous vocal quality and rate" (Gronhovd, 1977, p. 2).

Since the BRAT approach has only recently been advanced, no data are available regarding its effectiveness.

E. Airflow Therapy (Schwartz)

In a recent book, *Stuttering Solved*, M. F. Schwartz (1976) described in lay terms "a revolutionary new treatment" (p. i) termed "airflow therapy" with stutterers. He reported successful treatment rates of from 83 to 92%. With 185 adult stutterers, 89% were reported to be symptom free after 1 week of intensive therapy, and 83% were still successful after a 1-year follow-up period. During the follow-up period, the stutterer is expected to practice 1 hour each day and to tape record a sample of each practice period. Each week, the tape is sent to Schwartz for evaluation and comments. Schwartz's criteria for determining success are not provided in the book.

The airflow technique is based on the assumption that passive airflow is incompatible with the conditions which evoke laryngospasms, such as increased subglottal air pressure (Section IV,F). Thus, therapeutic procedures are focused on the period prior to speech.[16] The stutterer is taught to inhale, to relax, to begin to exhale passively, and, only when passive airflow is established, to begin to speak. Schwartz's motto to his stutterers is "passive flow, soft and slow." This implies that the airflow must not be forced, hurried, or assimilated into the next sound. Moreover, there should be no pause between the passive airflow and the onset of speaking. The stutterer is taught to slow, or prolong, the first syllable after each airflow.

According to Schwartz, about 12% of all stutterers experience frequent laryngospasms within sentences. These "severe" stutterers are taught to use a breathy voice throughout their utterances. Those who experience extremely high levels of psychological stress are referred to other appropriate professionals.

Schwartz reports that the airflow technique typically begins to become habitual for the stutterer after about 16 weeks of therapy. To facilitate this process, the stutterer is encouraged to establish a "key," or some **valid** cue associated with the airflow, on which he can concentrate. Typical "keys" are awareness of air flowing from the mouth, sensation of the chest walls dropping, or feelings of relaxation.

F. Aerodynamic and Phonatory Management (Adams)

Adams (1975a) outlined a clinical procedure centering on aerodynamic and phonatory management for three adult "laryngeal" stutterers. He stated that the therapy was effective. One subject reduced words stuttered in spontaneous speech from 9.7% prior to treatment to 1.9% at the end of direct therapy, and maintained his new fluency after therapy was terminated. Complete data were not reported for the other two stutterers.

Adams maintains that an aerodynamic analysis of stuttered speech can be made with a "good ear" and knowledge of the anatomic and physiological bases of respiration, phonation, and articulation. He also points out that aerodynamic therapy principles are not new and can be incorporated into other therapy plans.

The program described consists of three phases. First, the stutterer is taught to relax until he can maintain steady, effortless phonation. In the

---

[16] Since airflow therapy centers on the period prior to vocalization, Schwartz insists that it is **not** speech therapy.

second stage, he is taught to coordinate articulation with proper airflow and vocalization. To achieve this, the client is directed first to monitor very carefully the initiation of airflow and voicing. Once voicing has started, he is to begin to articulate at a slow rate. Later, unnatural phrasing and breathy voice quality are normalized with operant shaping procedures. Third, the stutterer works through a hierarchy of speech situations arranged from easiest to most difficult. After constructing a hierarchy, the subject is instructed to relax, imagine one of the situations, and then describe it aloud. If stuttering occurs, he is directed to be silent for a few seconds, to relax, and to think about starting again with "solid vocalization or airflow." Once he proceeds through the hierarchy via imagination, he repeats it with role playing in the clinic and then in real situations outside the clinic.

An interesting benefit of the aerodynamic techniques occurred in one stutterer who had the additional problem of speaking on residual air. He experienced a reduction in stuttering frequency in oral reading of more than 60% simply after being instructed to pause more frequently, exhale, then inhale in a quiet, relaxed fashion.

G. Prosodic Practice (Wingate)

Wingate (1976) describes a therapy program for stutterers which, in his view, follows logically from the model of stuttering as a defect in prosodic transition to stressed syllables. In this chapter, I have taken the liberty to term it "prosodic practice." Wingate states that the approach is effective but provides no treatment data.

According to Wingate (1976):

> The ultimate yet fundamental objective [of the approach] is to educate the stutterer regarding motor aspects of speech expression. In particular, he should come to appreciate the central importance of vocal modulation as the vehicle of fluency. (p. 330)

Therapeutic progress should be viewed as skill development in improving speech fluency rather than attempts to remove or reduce stuttering. In essence, the program involves a variety of overlapping techniques which "directly induce and support fluent speaking" (Wingate, 1976, p. 329).

The prosodic practice therapy program is carried out in two phases: instruction and implementation. The first phase of instruction begins by explaining the significance of vocalization in motor speech to the stutterer. Both reflexive and conscious control of the vocal folds is explained and demonstrated with visual aids such as diagrams or models. Next, vocal support of fluency is demonstrated by subjecting the stutterer to a variety of fluency enhancing techniques. In each technique, the underlying principle of vocal modulation is stressed as the responsible agent for fluency. The following is a list of techniques recommended: (1) singing: known songs and new words to known melodies; (2) speaking with an artificial larynx; (3) voicing chewing: a technique developed by Froeschels (1956), progressing from the chewing of oral noises to nonsense syllables to words and to sentences; (4) ventriloquism: another technique from Froeschels (1956), involving a manner of talking which emphasizes modulation of phonation and deemphasizes articulatory movements; (5) Speaking to rhythm: employing a variety of devices (e.g., desk metronome, ear-level miniature metronome, finger tapping) and speech rhythms; and (6) speaking in a foreign dialect.

The stutterer is next instructed in the relationship between speech melody, stress, and stuttering. Speech melody is illustrated by "sounding" or having the stutterer "hum" the melody of speech without using words. He is then shown the relationship between stuttering and linguistic stress. From tape recordings of his own stuttered speech, he is shown that stuttering is associated with stressed syllables and that stuttering does not occur "on" certain sounds but in "moving on" to stressed vowels. The notion of "ballistic" movements is introduced to indicate the proper kind of movements desired in speech. Ballistic movements are described by Wingate as smooth, easy, and continuous movements which are seen in activities such as well-executed dives and tennis serves.

The second phase of implementation involves any of the prior demonstration techniques which were particularly effective plus others to be introduced. Wingate suggests that three procedures are typically most useful: (1) intentional exaggeration of speech melody: speaking with a slight increase in vocal intensity with particular attention to "projecting" the voice and "swelling" into stressed vowels in order to "integrate" a speech utterance; (2) maintenance of a slow rate of speech; and (3) ventriloquism (described previously). Intentional exaggeration of speech melody is viewed as the "epitome" of all the therapy procedures. In addition to these three techniques and others tried earlier, Wingate (1976) also recommends reading poetry aloud and speaking with an assertive posture which involves "a 'leaning forward' psychologically, with an intent to 'speak out' " (p. 341). Finally, homework is encouraged which may involve additional practice in reading poetry aloud and "soliloquizing" with exaggerated speech melody.

H. Legato Therapy (Peins, Lee, & McGough)

B. S. Lee, McGough, and Peins (1973), McGough, Peins, and Lee (1971), Peins, Lee, and McGough (1970), and Peins, McGough, and Lee

(1972a, 1972b) developed an approach for treating the adult stutterer which may be called legato therapy. "Legato style," a term borrowed from music, means "smooth, flowing, and connected." The program is conducted with a tape recorder similar to one approach to foreign language teaching. Teaching material is recorded on tape and the stutterer is provided with gaps in which to record his response. Later he can listen to his own responses and compare them to those of the teacher. The stutterer practices 1 hour per day at home and proceeds through 12 lessons in 24 weeks.

Peins *et al.* (1972a) compared 12 stutterers using the tape recorded therapy method (legato therapy) with 12 receiving traditional therapy and 12 receiving no therapy. The two therapies produced statistically significant improvements over the no treatment control group but were not significantly different themselves. Nonetheless, the legato therapy group made quicker progress, required less of the clinician's time, effected improvement in mild, moderate, and severe stutterers, and provided the stutterers with the tools to proceed on their own.

In legato therapy, the stutterer is taught to begin voicing prior to speech and to maintain voicing throughout speech. In addition, the speech rate is slowed to a "deliberate pace." This style is reportedly used by radio announcers and others who must "respond with poise to extemporaneous questions" (B. S. Lee *et al.*, 1973, p. 188). The legato style is taught with single vowels and quickly progresses to "long, flowing phrases." The prespeech onset of voicing is exaggerated at first (at least 1/10 of a second) but later faded to a scarcely noticeable interval.

The program involves practice in imitating sentences, reading, describing pictures, extemporaneous speaking, talking on the telephone, and speaking to a group. In addition, it involves daily practice of legato style on difficult, feared words.

I. Muscle Biofeedback

Biofeedback can be defined as an amplified signal of some physiological function which the individual being recorded can use to become aware of, and to modify, that function. Since the function to be monitored is rendered more accessible to the individual's conscious awareness, he is typically better able to modify it than in the normal physiological state.

Properly speaking, the voice onset detectors described in the section on speech target shaping (Section V,D) can be considered biofeedback devices. Although they could have been included here, easy vocal onset is logically viewed as a fluency target.

Several studies have shown that stuttering frequency and severity can be reduced after stutterers are provided information regarding EMG muscle activity. Aten and Blanchard (1974) reported a preliminary investigation using EMG biofeedback with three stutterers and suggested that biofeedback procedures were an effective aid in reducing excessive muscular tension associated with stuttering.

Hanna, Wilfing, and McNeill (1975) reported reductions in both EMG activity and the percentage of syllables stuttered in oral reading in one severe adult stutterer when EMG activity was proportional to the frequency of an audio signal. The reductions in stuttering were most prominent when the subject heard true feedback from the laryngeal area, but even some reduction occurred when he was given false feedback.

Guitar (1975) reported reductions in stuttering in three severe adult stutterers when they monitored the EMG activity prior to speaking at selected laryngeal and facial muscle sites. One subject reduced his stuttering when he heard a tone proportional in frequency to EMG activity in the lip, another when he monitored laryngeal activity, and the third when he monitored either lip or laryngeal activity. None of the three showed sizable reductions in stuttering when biofeedback was provided from either chin or forehead. These three subjects were tested in oral reading. A fourth stutterer was trained to relax his chin muscles using EMG biofeedback in spontaneous conversation. With this procedure, stuttering was reduced to near zero. The subject later was able to apply the same muscle-relaxing techniques during telephone calls with similar positive effects on stuttering. These beneficial effects were reported to persist for 9 months after training.

Lanyon, Barrington, and Newman (1976) reported on eight severe stutterers who monitored visually presented EMG biofeedback from their masseter muscles. Two subjects were run in a pilot procedure and six in the experiment proper. After learning to reduce EMG activity in the masseter on command, words which were preceded by EMG-assisted relaxation were stuttered significantly less than matched words uttered without biofeedback in all six subjects. Subjects were able to reduce their stuttering in progressively more complex tasks using biofeedback procedures, and generalization of the positive effects of biofeedback to no feedback conditions was observed.

D. E. Cross (1977) found that four adult stutterers decreased their percentage of words stuttered when they heard frequency variant clicks which represented the level of EMG activity recorded at the larynx (true feedback). This result was dramatic because subjects were told **not** to attempt to modify the click rate or their degree of muscle tension. Stuttering also decreased when they received false biofeedback which increased regardless of the level of EMG activity. Little change was observed under a false decreasing biofeedback condition. The reports of the subjects after the study are particularly enlightening in understanding the effects of biofeedback. In the true feedback condition, subjects reported that the feedback made them more "aware" of their speech and helped them to "relax their speech." In the false increasing feedback condition, they again reported that the clicks caused them to focus their attention on their speech movements. In the false decreasing condition, they reported paying less attention to speech production.

Moore (1977) channeled white noise to three adult stutterers anytime EMG activity exceeded a criterion level during oral reading (and also spontaneous speech for one subject). Two subjects received biofeedback from the right masseter muscle, the third from the chin. In all three subjects, stutterings reduced under biofeedback conditions. For the most part, EMG levels varied with stuttering frequency, particularly in the initial sessions. Generalization to no feedback periods occurred both across and within sessions but, in one case, generalization was greatly enhanced when the stutterer was taken through a series of speech tasks of gradually increasing complexity.

Subjects developed a variety of strategies to keep the feedback noise off as evidenced by changes in their stutterings. Rapid, abrupt vocal onsets were replaced with gradual onsets, vocal intensity levels decreased, and pitch variability also decreased. These changes indicate that stutterers tended to reduce many of the "motoric and prosodic complexities" of speech during biofeedback.

Wilson (1977) utilized EMG biofeedback in 10 stutterers after a program of systematic desensitization. Biofeedback procedures occasioned further reductions in stutterings of from .5 to 5% in 9 of the 10 subjects. However, these reductions were not statistically significant.

The results of all of these studies, while not conclusive, suggest that monitoring of muscle activity has considerable positive potential in the treatment of stuttering. It is likely that detailed treatment programs utilizing EMG biofeedback will soon become available.

J. Stuttering Therapy Approaches: Summary

Stuttering therapy approaches which rely on linguistic and motor awareness can be compared in terms of the intended target of the stutterer's awareness. Table IV compares most of the approaches reviewed in this section according to various linguistic and motor targets of awareness. The degree of the stutterer's awareness or attention to each target is arbitrarily designated as 2 for *primary* (actually pointed out or trained), 1 for *secondary* (generally alluded to or a logical result of the primary

Table IV. Linguistic and Motor Targets of Awareness in Selected Stuttering Therapy Programs

Target of awareness	Proprioceptive awareness	Motor planning	Motor speech awareness	Precision fluency shaping program	BRAT	Airflow therapy	Aerodynamic and phonatory management	Prosodic practice	Legato therapy	Muscle biofeedback
Linguistic										
Distinctive features	0	0	2	1	0	0	0	0	0	0
Consonants	1	0	1	2	0	1	0	1	1	0
Vowels	1	0	1	2	2	1	0	2	1	0
Transitions and coarticulation	2	2	0	2	1	0	0	2	0	0
Syllabic stress	1	2	1	0	1	0	0	2	2	0
Words	0	1	0	1	1	1	1	1	1	0
Phrases and sentences	0	2	0	1	1	1	1	2	2	0
Motor										
Speech rate	1	0	0	2	2	2	2	2	2	0
General body tension	0	1	0	0	2	1	2	0	0	2
Inhalation and exhalation	0	0	0	2	2	2	2	1	0	0
Voice onset	1	0	1	2	2	2	2	2	2	0
Voice maintenance	1	0	2	1	2	0	2	2	2	0
Oral tension	2	1	0	1	2	1	2	2	0	2
Jaw placement	2	1	1	0	0	0	1	1	0	1
Tongue placement	2	1	2	0	0	0	1	1	0	1
Lip placement	2	1	1	0	0	0	1	1	0	1

focus), and 0 for *none* (no attention directed or suggested). Obviously, since the target and degree of awareness categories were quite arbitrarily chosen, no claim regarding the actual validity of these designations is intended. Its purpose is simply to provide the reader with a summary comparison of various approaches to stuttering therapy.

To the extent that Table IV is accurate, two interesting interpretations can be made. First, the inherent interrelationship between linguistic and motor aspects of speech production is clearly illustrated. It is practically impossible to direct the stutterer's attention to motor aspects of speaking without, by consequence, focusing his awareness of various linguistic aspects, and vice versa. The only exception is in the use of muscle biofeedback. Yet, even in the case of biofeedback, the stutterer probably does attend to selective linguistic aspects of speaking (Moore, 1977).

A second impression which emerges from Table IV is that certain linguistic and motor targets may be more fluency enhancing than others. Awareness of transitions or coarticulatory movements, syllabic stress, and speech rate seems to be more impressive than attention to distinctive features, consonants, vowels, words, or phrases and sentences. On the motor side, attention to aspects of breathing, voicing, and tension in the speech musculature appears to have greater salutary effects on fluency than awareness of general body tension or articulator placement.

VI. LINGUISTIC AND MOTOR ASPECTS OF STUTTERING: CURRENT STATUS AND FUTURE DIRECTIONS

A. General Summary

Research on linguistic determinants of the loci of stuttering can be summarized as follows. Stuttering is nearly always associated with the initial position of syllables, words, and sentences. This is true of children and adults in all kinds of speech tasks. In adults, the evidence indicates that stuttering is associated with long or multisyllabic words, stressed syllables, and consonant production. Other factors being equal, stuttering is also likely on words of high information load, infrequently occurring words, and content words, particularly in the oral reading of adult stutterers. Recent evidence suggests that stuttering is also influenced by contextual variables within phonetic and syllabic makeup of words. The linguistic determinants of the loci of stuttering in spontaneous speech, particularly in preschool children, are much less clear. It appears that beginning stutterers have the greatest difficulty with frequently occurring pronouns and conjunctions located at the beginning of sentences. Considerable recent evidence suggests also that language abilities of beginning stutterers are related to stuttering.

A comprehensive review of motor abilities of stutterers reveals that certain motor deficits are characteristic of stuttering. Nevertheless, it is premature to conclude that stuttering is caused by motor impairments. The weight of recent research suggests that stutterers have problems in coordinating the precise muscular adjustments necessary in initiating and maintaining normal phonation. These phonatory problems are, in turn, intimately related to abnormalities in breathing and consequent aerodynamic forces which affect laryngeal function. The convergence of findings on articulatory abilities in stutterers is less uniform. Some studies suggest that articulatory irregularities observed in stutterers are due, in part, to breakdowns in proper phonetic transition and coarticulatory patterns; others do not. Several studies suggest that the fluent speech of stutterers is abnormal, even if such abnormalities are not perceptible to the listener. In nonstuttered speech, stutterers appear to have slower vocal adjustments, more variable rates, and more short pauses than nonstutterers. The most questionable findings regarding motor abilities of stutterers are those derived from non-speech-related fine motor skills. Some studies have shown stutterers to be inferior to controls on fine motor tasks, and some have not.

Numerous models have been advanced to explain the linguistic and motor determinants of stuttering. While no model provides a completely satisfactory account of the linguistic and motor data, each has focused attention on important theoretical areas. A sufficient account must include consideration of contextual programming of phonetic, syllabic, and prosodic aspects of speech; interrelated irregularities in respiration, phonation, and articulation; and the differences between child and adult stutterers.

Therapy approaches which direct the stutterer's attention to various linguistic and motor aspects of speaking are currently very popular. This is not surprising because there is reason to speculate that linguistic and motor awareness is the common denominator underlying most successful approaches to treating stutterers. Regardless of how fluency is established, the stutterer must eventually learn to maintain his fluency without the aid of the clinician's suggestions or devices, and chances are good that he does so by learning to concentrate on what or how he is speaking. Nearly all of the therapies reviewed involve directing the stutterers attention to **both** linguistic and motor aspects of speaking. It seems that when the stutterer is directed to monitor a specific motor response, such as relaxing his jaw, he may achieve the desired result, i.e., jaw relaxation and fluent speech, in a variety of ways. He may relax his jaw as instructed, or he may concentrate on a slow speech rate, careful syllable production, or easy exhalation. In essence, we find from these therapy approaches that both linguistic and motor aspects of speaking are highly interrelated.

B. Future Directions

There is good reason to predict that research in the area of stuttering in the next several years will continue to focus heavily on linguistic and motor variables. Certainly if the recent interest continues in linguistic and motor-related approaches to stuttering therapy, the need for better explanations of their effectiveness, or lack thereof, will become increasingly apparent.

There are several directions which research can be expected to take. First, it is likely that stuttering will be considered carefully within existing models of speech production and new models to be developed. We might even predict that speech scientists will begin to use stutterers to study normal speech production in much the same way neurolinguists use aphasics to study language. Research in normal fluency and normal hesitation phenomena will undoubtedly increase also, with special attention to important qualitative differences between normal disfluency and stuttering. Through this research, we are likely to begin to answer such questions as: how the normal speaker monitors his speech for errors, the hierarchy of speech production units which are programmed, the structure of syllables, and the necessary programming prerequisites for coarticulation.

The beginning stutterer is likely to receive a great deal of research effort in the next few years. Differences between the loci of stutterings in beginning and experienced stutterers need to be documented. Furthermore, the relationships between stuttering and language development require extensive exploration.

As noted earlier, considerable evidence suggests that stutterers have difficulty coordinating the precise movements of breathing and voicing with those of articulating. We have already seen that aerodynamic forces can account for some of the problems observed in voice onset and maintenance in stutterers. Moreover, it appears that there are peripheral neural connections between the larynx and tongue as well as between the larynx and middle ear muscles (McCall, 1975). Therefore, it is possible that many of the respiratory, phonatory, and articulatory irregularities observed in stutterers are due to "peripheral mechanics" rather than cortical programming errors. Unquestionably, future research will investigate these possibilities.

One further question of critical importance is whether or not stuttering is primarily a result of defective laryngeal functioning. Since a number of recent writers have suggested, or declared, that this is so, it is important that the hypothesis be subjected to rigorous empirical testing.

In this chapter, I have attempted to review two large areas of research in stuttering, linguistic and motor determinants, and to show how they must be considered together. If my analysis is at least partly accurate, then perhaps these speculations about the future are not without justification.

Acknowledgments

The author wishes to acknowledge partial support for the preparation of this chapter from the West Virginia University Foundation, Incorporated, Morgantown, West Virginia. The invaluable assistance and support of Karen St. Louis is also acknowledged and deeply appreciated.

References

Adams, M. R. A physiologic and aerodynamic interpretation of fluent and stuttered speech. *Journal of Fluency Disorders,* 1974, *1*(1), 35–47.

Adams, M. R. Clinical interpretations and applications. In L. M. Webster & L. Furst (Eds.), *Vocal tract dynamics and dysfluency.* New York: Speech and Hearing Institute, 1975. Pp. 196–228. (a)

Adams, M. R. Vocal tract dynamics in fluency and stuttering: A review and interpretation of past research. In L. M. Webster & L. Furst (Eds.), *Vocal tract dynamics and dysfluency.* New York: Speech and Hearing Institute, 1975. Pp. 10–39. (b)

Adams, M. R., & Hayden, P. The ability of stutterers and nonstutterers to initiate and terminate phonation during production of an isolated vowel. *Journal of Speech and Hearing Research,* 1976, *19,* 290–296.

Adams, M. R., Lewis, J. I., & Besozzi, T. E. The effect of reduced reading rate on stuttering frequency. *Journal of Speech and Hearing Research,* 1973, *16,* 671–675.

Adams, M. R., & Moore, W. The effects of auditory masking on the anxiety level, frequency of dysfluency, and selected vocal characteristics of stutterers. *Journal of Speech and Hearing Research,* 1972, *15,* 572–578.

Adams, M. R., & Reis, R. The influence of the onset of phonation on the frequency of stuttering. *Journal of Speech and Hearing Research,* 1971, *14,* 639–644.

Adams, M. R., & Reis, R. Influence of the onset of phonation on the frequency of stuttering: A replication and reevaluation. *Journal of Speech and Hearing Research,* 1974, *17,* 752–754.

Adams, M. R., Riemenschneider, S., Metz, D., & Conture, E. Voice onset and articulatory constriction requirements in a speech segment and their relation to the amount of stuttering adaptation. *Journal of Fluency Disorders,* 1974, *1*(3), 24–31.

Adams, M. R., Runyan, C., & Mallard, A. R. Air flow characteristics of the speech of stutterers and nonstutterers. *Journal of Fluency Disorders,* 1975, *1*(2), 3–12.

Agnello, J. G. *Some acoustic and pause characteristics of nonfluencies in the speech of stutterers* (Tech. Rep., Grant No. 11067-01). Washington, D.C.: National Institute of Mental Health, 1966.

Agnello, J. G. Voice onset and voice termination features of stutterers. In L. M. Webster & L. Furst (Eds.), *Vocal tract dynamics and dysfluency.* New York: Speech and Hearing Institute, 1975. Pp. 40–70.

Agnello, J. G., & Buxton, M. A. *Effects of resonance and time on stutterers' and nonstutterers' speech under delayed auditory feedback* (HEW, Project No. 11067-01). Washington, D.C.: National Institute of Mental Health, 1966.

Agnello, J. G., & Goehl, H. Spectrographical patterns of disfluencies in the speech of stutterers. *Asha,* 1965, *7,* 315. (Abstract)

Agnello, J. G., & McGlone, R. E. Distinguishing features of /p/ and /b/. *Journal of the Acoustical Society of America,* 1970, *48,* 121. (Abstract)

Agnello, J. G., & Wingate, M. E. Air pressure and formants of stutterers and nonstutterers. *Asha,* 1971, *13,* 526. (Abstract)

Agnello, J. G., & Wingate, M. E. Some acoustic and physiological aspects of stuttered speech. *Asha,* 1972, *14,* 479. (Abstract)

Agnello, J. G., Wingate, M. E., & Moulin, L. Word availability, usage, and transitional features of stutterers and nonstutterers. *Asha,* 1970, *12,* 424. (Abstract)

Allen, G. D., Peters, R. N., & Williams, C. L. Spectrographic study of fluent and stuttered speech. *Asha,* 1975, *17,* 664. (Abstract)

Anderson, L. O. Stuttering and allied disorders—An experimental investigation of underlying factors. *Comparative Psychological Monographs,* 1923, No. 1, 1–78.

Aten, J. L., & Blanchard, S. EMG biofeedback in the treatment of stuttering. *Asha,* 1974, *16,* 555. (Abstract)

Baken, R. Overview of the conference. In L. M. Webster & L. Furst (Eds.), *Vocal tract dynamics and dysfluency.* New York: Speech and Hearing Institute, 1975. Pp. 1–9.

Baker, H. J., & Leland, B. *Detroit tests of learning aptitude.* Indianapolis: Bobbs-Merrill, 1967.

Bar, A., Singer, J., & Feldman, R. G. Subvocal muscle activity during stuttering and fluent speech: A comparison. *Journal of the South African Logopedic Society,* 1969, *19,* 9–14.

Bever, T. G., Fodor, J. A., & Weksel, W. Is linguistics empirical? *Psychological Review,* 1965, *72,* 467–482.

Bills, A. G. The relation of stuttering to mental fatigue. *Journal of Experimental Psychology,* 1934, *17,* 574–584.

Blackburn, B. Voluntary movements of the organs of speech in stutterers and nonstutterers. *Psychological Monographs,* 1931, *41,* 1–13.

Bloodstein, O. Studies in the psychology of stuttering: XIX. The relationship between oral reading rate and severity of stuttering. *Journal of Speech Disorders,* 1944, *9,* 161–173.

Bloodstein, O. Stuttering as an anticipatory struggle reaction. In J. Eisenson (Ed.), *Stuttering: A symposium.* New York: Harper, 1958. Pp. 3–69.

Bloodstein, O. *A handbook on stuttering.* Chicago: National Easter Seal Society for Crippled Children and Adults, 1969.

Bloodstein, O. Stuttering and normal nonfluency—A continuity hypothesis. *British Journal of Disorders of Communication,* 1970, *5,* 30–39.

Bloodstein, O. The anticipatory struggle hypothesis: Implications of research on the variability of stuttering. *Journal of Speech and Hearing Research,* 1972, *15,* 487–499.

Bloodstein, O. The rules of early stuttering. *Journal of Speech and Hearing Disorders,* 1974, *39,* 379–394.

Bloodstein, O. *A handbook on stuttering* (Rev. ed.). Chicago: National Easter Seal Society for Crippled Children and Adults, 1975. (a)

Bloodstein, O. Stuttering as tension and fragmentation. In J. Eisenson (Ed.), *Stuttering: A second symposium.* New York: Harper, 1975. (b)

Bloodstein, O., & Gantwerk, B. F. Grammatical function in relation to stuttering in young children. *Journal of Speech and Hearing Research,* 1967, *10,* 786–789.

Bluemel, C. S. *The riddle of stuttering.* Danville, Ill.: Interstate Printers & Publishers, 1957.

Boysen, A. E., & Cullinan, W. L. Object naming latency in stuttering and nonstuttering children. *Journal of Speech and Hearing Research,* 1971, *14,* 728–738.

Brookshire, B., & White, F. Language based intervention for early stuttering. *Asha,* 1977, *19,* 655. (Abstract)

Brown, S. F. The influence of grammatical function on the incidence of stuttering. *Journal of Speech Disorders,* 1937, *2,* 207–215.

Brown, S. F. A further study of stuttering in relation to various speech sounds. *Quarterly Journal of Speech,* 1938, *24,* 390–397. (a)

Brown, S. F. Stuttering with relation to word accent and word position. *Journal of Abnormal and Social Psychology,* 1938, *33,* 112–120. (b)

Brown, S. F. The loci of stuttering in the speech sequence. *Journal of Speech Disorders,* 1945, *10,* 181–192.

Brown, S. F., & Moren, A. The frequency of stuttering in relation to word length during oral reading. *Journal of Speech Disorders,* 1942, *7,* 153–159.

Bryngelson, B. A photophonographic analysis of the vocal disturbances in stuttering. *Psychological Monographs,* 1932, *43,* 1–30.

Bryngelson, B. A. A study of speech difficulties of thirteen stutterers. In W. Johnson & R. R. Leutenegger (Eds.), *Stuttering in children and adults.* Minneapolis: University of Minnesota Press, 1955. Pp. 393–395.

Chevrie-Müller, C. A study of laryngeal function in stutterers by the glottographic method. *Proceedings, VII Congrès de la Société Français de Medecine de la Voix et de la Parole, Paris,* 1963.

Chomsky, N. *Syntactic structures.* The Hague: Mouton, 1957.

Chomsky, N. *Aspects of the theory of syntax.* Cambridge, Mass.: MIT Press, 1965.

Conture, E. G., McCall, G. N., & Brewer, D. W. Laryngeal behavior during stuttering. *Journal of Speech and Hearing Research,* 1977, *20,* 661–668.

Conway, J. K., & Quarrington, B. Positional effects in the stuttering of contextually organized verbal material. *Journal of Abnormal and Social Psychology,* 1963, *67,* 299–303.

Cooper, E. B. *Personalized fluency control therapy: An integrated behavior and relationship therapy for stutterers.* Hingham, Mass.: Teaching Resources Corporation, 1976.

Cooper, M. H., & Allen, G. D. Timing control accuracy in normal speakers and stutterers. *Journal of Speech and Hearing Research,* 1977, *20,* 55–71.

Cross, D. E. Effects of false increasing, decreasing, and true electromyographic biofeedback on the frequency of stuttering. *Journal of Fluency Disorders,* 1977, *2,* 109–116.

Cross, H. M. The motor capacities of stutterers. *Archives of Speech,* 1936, *7,* 112–132.

da Costa, M. I. L. Os testes de Ozeretzky: Metodo, valor e resultados. *Crianca Portuguesa,* 1943, *2,* 193–228.

Daly, D., & Darnton, S. W. Intensive fluency shaping and attitudinal therapy with stutterers: A follow-up study. *Asha,* 1976, *18,* 682. (Abstract)

Danzger, M., & Halpern, H. Relation of stuttering to word abstraction, part of speech, word length, and word frequency. *Perceptual and Motor Skills,* 1973, *37,* 959–962.

Dunn, L. M. *Peabody picture vocabulary test.* Circle Pines, Minn.: American Guidance Service, 1965.

Egland, G. O. Repetitions and prolongations in the speech of stuttering and nonstuttering children. In W. Johnson & R. R. Leutenegger (Eds.), *Stuttering in children and adults.* Minneapolis: University of Minnesota Press, 1955. Pp. 181–188.

Fagan, L. B. Graphic stuttering. *Psychological Monographs,* 1932, *43,* 67–71.

Fairbanks, G. Some physical correlates of stuttering. *Quarterly Journal of Speech,* 1937, *23,* 67–69.

Fibiger, S. Stuttering explained as a physiological tremor. *STL-QPSR,* 1971, 1–23.

Finkelstein, P., & Weisberger, S. E. The motor proficiency of stutterers. *Journal of Speech and Hearing Disorders,* 1954, *19,* 52–58.

Fletcher, J. M. An experimental study of stuttering. *Journal of Applied Psychology,* 1914, *25,* 201–249.

Ford, S. C., & Luper, H. L. Aerodynamic, phonatory and labial EMG patterns during fluent and stuttered speech. *Asha,* 1975, *17,* 663. (Abstract)

Fossler, H. R. Disturbances in breathing during stuttering. *Psychological Monographs,* 1932, *43,* 218–275.

Fransella, F. *The effects of imposed rhythm and certain aspects of personality on the speech of stutterers.* Unpublished doctoral dissertation, University of London, 1965.

Freeman, F. J. Phonation and fluency. In L. M. Webster & L. Furst (Eds.), *Vocal tract dynamics and dysfluency.* New York: Speech and Hearing Institute, 1975. Pp. 229–266.

Freeman, F. J., & Ushijima, T. *Laryngeal activity accompanying the moment of stuttering: A preliminary report of EMG investigations.* Paper presented at the 87th meeting of the Acoustical Society of America, New York, April 1974.

Freeman, F. J., & Ushijima, T. Laryngeal activity accompanying the moment of stuttering: A preliminary report of EMG investigations. *Journal of Fluency Disorders,* 1975, *1*(2), 36–45. (a)

Freeman, F. J., & Ushijima, T. *The stuttering larynx: An EMG, fiberoptic study of laryngeal activity accompanying the moment of stuttering* (Status Report on Speech Research, SR-41). New Haven, Conn.: Haskins Laboratories, 1975. Pp. 217–228. (b)

Freeman, F. J., Ushijima, T., & Hirose, H. Reply to Schwartz's the core of the stuttering block. *Journal of Speech and Hearing Disorders,* 1975, *40,* 137–139.

Frick, J. V. *Evaluation of motor planning techniques for the treatment of stuttering* (No. 32-48-0720-5003). Washington, D.C.: Office of Education, 1965.

Froeschels, E. In E. F. Hahn (Ed.), *Stuttering: Significant theories and therapies* (2nd ed.). Stanford, Calif.: Stanford University Press, 1956. Pp. 41–47.

Fujimura, O. Acoustics of speech. In J. H. Gilbert (Ed.), *Speech and cortical functioning.* New York: Academic Press, 1972. Pp. 107–165.

Fujita, K. Pathophysiology of the larynx from the viewpoint of phonation. *Journal of the Japanese Society of Otorhinolaryngology,* 1966, *69,* 456.

Gautheron, B., Liorzou, A., Even, C., & Vallancien, B. The role of the larynx in stuttering. In Y. Lebrun & R. Hoops (Eds.), *Neurolinguistic approaches to stuttering.* The Hague: Mouton, 1973. Pp. 43–46.

Goldman-Eisler, F. *Psycholinguistics: Experiments in spontaneous speech.* New York: Academic Press, 1968.

Gronhovd, K. D. Fluency and the moment of stuttering: A closer look. *Asha,* 1975, *17,* 660. (Abstract)

Gronhovd, K. D. BRAT: Management of breathing, rate, airflow, and tension. *Asha,* 1977, *19,* 654. (Abstract)

Guitar, B. Reduction of stuttering frequency using analog electromyographic feedback. *Journal of Speech and Hearing Research,* 1975, *18,* 672–685.

Gutzmann, H. *Sprachheilkunde*. Berlin, 1912.

Hahn, E. F. A study of the relationship between stuttering occurrence and grammatical factors in oral reading. *Journal of Speech Disorders*, 1942, *7*, 329–335. (a)

Hahn, E. F. A study of the relationship between stuttering occurrence and phonetic factors in oral reading. *Journal of Speech Disorders*, 1942, *7*, 143–151. (b)

Halle, F. Ueber störungen der athmung bei stottern. *Monatsschrift für Sprachheilkunde*, 1900, *10*, 225–236.

Hamre, C. Stuttering: A language systems and processing model. *Asha*, 1976, *18*, 587. (Abstract)

Hanna, R., Wilfling, F., & McNeill, B. A biofeedback treatment for stuttering. *Journal of Speech and Hearing Disorders*, 1975, *40*, 270–273.

Hannah, E. P., & Gardner, J. G. A note on syntactic relationships in nonfluency. *Journal of Speech and Hearing Research*, 1968, *11*, 853–860.

Harvey-Fisher, C., & Brutten, G. J. Part-word repetitions in pre-school stutterers and nonstutterers. *Asha*, 1977, *19*, 652. (Abstract)

Hejna, R. F. *A study of the loci of stuttering in spontaneous speech*. Unpublished doctoral dissertation, Northwestern University, 1955.

Hejna, R. F. Stuttering frequency in relation to word frequency usage. *Asha*, 1963, *5*, 781. (Abstract)

Helmreich, H. G., & Bloodstein, O. The grammatical factor in childhood disfluency in relation to the continuity hypothesis. *Journal of Speech and Hearing Research*, 1973, *16*, 731–738.

Hill, H. E. *Perseveration in normal speakers and stutterers*. Unpublished master's thesis, Indiana University, 1942.

Hill, H. E. Stuttering. II: A review and integration of physiological data. *Journal of Speech Disorders*, 1944, *9*, 209–324.

Hoekstra, L. *A comparison of fundamental frequencies in the speech of stutterers and nonstutterers*. Unpublished master's thesis, Moorehead State University, 1975.

Hunsley, Y. L. Dysintegration in the speech musculature of stutterers during the production of a non-vocal temporal pattern. *Psychological Monographs*, 1937, *49*, 32–49.

Hunt, J. *Stammering and stuttering: Their nature and treatment*. New York: Hafner, 1967. (Originally published, 1861.)

Hutchinson, J. M. *The effect of oral sensory deprivation on stuttering behavior*. Unpublished doctoral dissertation, Purdue University, 1973.

Hutchinson, J. M. Aerodynamic patterns of stuttered speech. In L. M. Webster & L. Furst (Eds.), *Vocal tract dynamics and dysfluency*. New York: Speech and Hearing Institute, 1975, Pp. 71–123.

Hutchinson, J. M., & Navarre, B. M. The effect of metronome pacing on selected aerodynamic patterns of stuttered speech: Some preliminary observations and interpretations. *Journal of Fluency Disorders*, 1977, *2*, 189–204.

Hutchinson, J. M., & Watkin, K. L. A preliminary investigation of lip and jaw coarticulation in stutterers. *Asha*, 1974, *16*, 533. (Abstract)

Hutchinson, J. M., & Watkin, K. L. Jaw mechanics during release of the stuttering moment: Some initial observations and interpretations. *Journal of Communication Disorders*, 1976, *9*, 269–279.

Ingham, R. J., Martin, R. R., & Kuhl, P. Modification and control of rate of speaking by stutterers. *Journal of Speech and Hearing Research*, 1974, *17*, 489–496.

Johnson, W. Measurement of oral reading and speaking rate and disfluency of adult male and female stutterers and nonstutterers. *Journal of Speech and Hearing Disorders Monograph Supplement*, 1961, *7*, 1–20.

Johnson, W., & Brown, S. Stuttering in relation to various speech sounds. *Quarterly Journal of Speech*, 1935, *21*, 481–496.

Johnson, W., & Rosen, L. Studies in the psychology of stuttering: VII. Effect of certain changes in speech pattern upon frequency of stuttering. *Journal of Speech Disorders*, 1937, *2*, 105–109.

Kamiyama, G., Hirose, T., Ushijima, T., & Niimi, S. *Articulatory movements of the larynx during stuttering*. Tokyo: University of Tokyo, Faculty of Medicine, Research Institute of Logopedics and Phoniatrics, 1965. (Film)

Kasanin, H. R. I. The motor development of children suffering from stammering. *American Journal of Diseases of Children*, 1932, *44*, 1123–1125.

Kenyon, E. L. The etiology of stammering: The psychophysiologic facts which concern the production of speech sounds and of stammering. *Journal of Speech Disorders*, 1943, *8*, 337–348.

Kerr, S. H., & Cooper, E. B. Phonatory adjustment times in stutterers and nonstutterers. *Asha*, 1976, *18*, 664. (Abstract)

Kimura, D. Cerebral dominance and the perception of verbal stimuli. *Canadian Journal of Psychology*, 1961, *15*, 156–165.

Kirk, S. A., & McCarthy, J. J. The Illinois test of psycholinguistic abilities—An approach to differential diagnosis. *American Journal of Mental Deficiency*, 1961, *66*, 399–412.

Kirk, S. A., McCarthy, J. J., & Kirk, W. *The Illinois test of psycholinguistic abilities* (Rev. ed.). Urbana: University of Illinois Press, 1969.

Knabe, J. M., Nelson, L. A., & Williams, F. Some general characteristics of linguistic output: Stutterers versus nonstutterers. *Journal of Speech and Hearing Disorders*, 1966, *31*, 178–182.

Kopp, H. Psychosomatic study of fifty stuttering children. II. Oseretsky tests. *American Journal of Orthopsychiatry*, 1946, *16*, 114–119.

Kroll, R. M., & Hood, S. B. The influence of task presentation and information load on the adaptation effect in stutterers and normal speakers. *Journal of Communication Disorders*, 1976, *9*, 95–110.

Lanyon, R. I. Some characteristics of nonfluency in normal speakers and stutterers. *Journal of Abnormal Psychology*, 1968, *73*, 550–555.

Lanyon, R. I. Speech: Relation of nonfluency to information value. *Science*, 1969, *164*, 451–452.

Lanyon, R. I., Barrington, C. C., & Newman, C. Modification of stuttering through EMG biofeedback: A preliminary study. *Behavior Therapy*, 1976, *7*, 96–103.

Lashley, K. The problem of the serial order of behavior. In L. A. Jeffress (Ed.), *Cerebral mechanism in behavior*. New York: Wiley, 1951. Pp. 112–136.

Lee, B. S., McGough, W. E., & Peins, M. A new method for stutter therapy. *Folia Phoniatrica*, 1973, *25*, 186–195.

Lee, L. L. *Northwestern syntax screening test*. Evanston, Ill.: Northwestern University Press, 1971.

Lee, L. L. *Developmental sentence analysis*. Evanston, Ill.: Northwestern University Press, 1974.

Lisker, L., & Abramson, A. S. A cross language study of voicing in initial steps: Acoustical measurements. *Word*, 1964, *20*, 384–422.

Love, L. R. *Examination of silent intervals in the speech of stutterers and normal speakers*. Unpublished master's thesis, University of Texas, 1965.

Love, L. R., & Jeffress, L. A. Identification of brief pauses in the fluent speech of stutterers and nonstutterers. *Journal of Speech and Hearing Research*, 1971, *14*, 639–644.

MacKay, D. G. Forward and backward masking in motor systems. *Kybernetik*, 1969, *2*, 57–64.

MacKay, D. G. Context dependent stuttering. *Kybernetik*, 1970, *7*, 1–9. (a)

MacKay, D. G. Spoonerisms: The structure of errors in the serial order of speech. *Neuropsychologia*, 1970, *8*, 323–350. (b)

MacKay, D. G. The structure of words and syllables: Evidence from errors in speech. *Cognitive Psychology*, 1972, *3*, 210–227.

MacKay, D. G., & Soderberg, G. A. *Action at a distance in speech production: Context-dependent stuttering.* Unpublished manuscript, University of California, Los Angeles, 1970. (a)

MacKay, D. G., & Soderberg, G. A. *The context effect: Stuttering as a function of interactions between phonetic units.* Unpublished manuscript, University of California, Los Angeles, 1970. (b)

MacKay, D. G., & Soderberg, G. A. *Errors in patterns of finger movement rapidly produced by stutterers and nonstutterers.* Unpublished manuscript, University of California, Los Angeles, 1970. (c)

MacKay, D. G., & Soderberg, G. A. *The phonetic context effect and the structure of syllables.* Unpublished manuscript, 1970. (d)

MacKay, D. G., & Soderberg, G. A. *The syllabic form of stuttered segments.* Unpublished manuscript, 1970. (e)

Maclay, H., & Osgood, C. E. Hesitation phenomena in spontaneous English speech. *Word*, 1959, *15*, 19–44.

Mahl, G. F. Measures of two expressive aspects of a patient's speech in two psychotherapeutic interviews. In L. A. Gottschalk (Ed.), *Comparative psycholinguistic analysis of two psychotherapeutic interviews.* New York: International University Press, 1961. Pp. 91–114.

Mann, M. B. Nonfluencies in the oral reading of stutterers and nonstutterers of elementary school age. In W. Johnson & R. R. Leutenegger (Eds.), *Stuttering in children and adults.* Minneapolis: University of Minnesota Press, 1955. Pp. 189–196.

Manning, W. H., & Coufal, K. J. The frequency of disfluencies during phonatory transitions in stuttered and nonstuttered speech. *Journal of Communication Disorders*, 1976, *9*, 75–81.

Martin, R. R., & Ingham, R. Stuttering. In B. Lahey (Ed.), *The modification of language behavior.* Springfield, Ill.: Thomas, 1973. Pp. 91–129.

Massengill, R., Luper, H., Bryson, M., & Gertner, L. L. Severity of stuttering as rated by cinefluorography, tape recordings, and a comparison of these ratings with physiological observations. *Folia Phoniatrica*, 1967, *19*, 132–141.

McCall, G. N. Spasmodic dysphonia and the stuttering block: Commonalities or possible connections. In L. M. Webster & L. Furst (Eds.), *Vocal tract dynamics and dysfluency.* New York: Speech and Hearing Institute, 1975. Pp. 124–151.

McGough, W. E., Peins, M., & Lee, B. S. *A home-based tape recorder approach to rehabilitating the stutterer: Evaluation of an economic treatment* (No. 2932-5). Washington, D.C.: Social and Rehabilitation Service, 1971.

Metz, D. E., Conture, E. G., & Colton, R. H. Temporal relations between the respiratory and laryngeal systems prior to stuttered disfluencies. *Asha*, 1976, *18*, 664. (Abstract)

Miller, G. R., & Coleman, E. B. A set of thirty-six prose passages calibrated for complexity. *Journal of Verbal Learning and Verbal Behavior*, 1967, *6*, 851–854.

Montgomery, A. A., & Cooke, P. A. Perceptual and acoustic analysis of repetitions in stuttered speech. *Journal of Communication Disorders*, 1976, *9*, 317–330.

Moore, W. H., Jr. The effects of EMG feedback during verbal tasks on stuttering. *Asha*, 1977, *19*, 665. (Abstract)

Morávek, M., & Langová, J. Problems of the development of initial tonus in stuttering. *Folia Phoniatrica*, 1967, *19*, 109–116.

Morley, A. An analysis of associative and predisposing factors in the symptomatology of stuttering. *Psychological Monographs,* 1937, *49,* 50–107.

Mosier, K. V. *A study of the horizontal dysintegration of breathing during normal and abnormal speech for normal speakers and stutterers.* Unpublished master's thesis, Indiana University, 1944.

Murray, E. Disintegration of breathing and eye movements during silent reading and reasoning. *Psychological Monographs,* 1932, *43,* 218–275.

Murray, H. L., & Reed, C. G. Language abilities of preschool stuttering children. *Journal of Fluency Disorders,* 1977, *2,* 171–176.

Myers, F. L. Physiological correlates immediately prior to the speech of stutterers. *Asha,* 1977, *19,* 665. (Abstract)

Onufrak, J. A. *Stutterer's and nonstutterers location of clicks superimposed on sentences of various types.* Unpublished doctoral dissertation, State University of New York at Buffalo, 1973.

Oxtoby, E. T. Frequency of stuttering in relation to induced modifications following expectancy of stuttering. In W. Johnson & R. R. Leutenegger (Eds.), *Stuttering in children and adults.* Minneapolis: University of Minnesota Press, 1955. Pp. 218–225.

Peins, M., Lee, B. S., & McGough, W. E. A tape-recorded therapy method for stutterers: A case report. *Journal of Speech and Hearing Disorders,* 1970, *35,* 188–193.

Peins, M., McGough, W. E., & Lee, B. S. Evaluation of a tape-recorded method of stuttering therapy: Improvement in a speaking task. *Journal of Speech and Hearing Research,* 1972, *15,* 364–371. (a)

Peins, M., McGough, W. E., & Lee, B. S. Tape recorder therapy for the rehabilitation of the stuttering handicapped. *Language Speech & Hearing Services in Schools,* 1972, *3,* 30–35. (b)

Perkins, W., Rudas, J., Johnson, L., & Bell, J. Stuttering: Discoordination of phonation with articulation and respiration. *Journal of Speech and Hearing Research,* 1976, *19,* 509–522.

Platt, L. J., & Basili, A. Jaw tremor during stuttering block: An electromyographic study. *Journal of Communication Disorders,* 1973, *6,* 102–109.

Quarrington, B. Stuttering as a function of the information value and sentence position of words. *Journal of Abnormal Psychology,* 1965, *70,* 221–224.

Quarrington, B., Conway, J., & Siegel, N. An experimental study of some properties of stuttered words. *Journal of Speech and Hearing Research,* 1962, *5,* 387–394.

Reardon, J. M. Temporal characteristics of stutterers' and nonstutterers' voice initiation and termination. *Asha,* 1977, *19,* 668. (Abstract)

Rickenberg, H. E. Diadochokinesis in stutterers and nonstutterers. *Journal of the Medical Society of New Jersey,* 1956, *53,* 324–326.

Robbins, S. D. A plethysmographic study of shock and stammering. *American Journal of Physiology,* 1919, *48,* 285–330.

Ronson, I. Word frequency and stuttering: The relationship to sentence structure. *Journal of Speech and Hearing Research,* 1976, *19,* 813–819.

Ross, F. L. A comparative study of stutterers and nonstutterers on a psychomotor discrimination task. In W. Johnson & R. R. Leutenegger (Eds.), *Stuttering in children and adults.* Minneapolis: University of Minnesota Press, 1955. Pp. 361–366.

Rotter, J. B. A study of the motor integration of stutterers and nonstutterers. In W. Johnson & R. R. Leutenegger (Eds.), *Stuttering in children and adults.* Minneapolis: University of Minnesota Press, 1955. Pp. 367–376.

Schilling, A. Roentgen kymograms of the diaphragm of stutterers. *Folia Phoniatrica,* 1960, *12,* 145–153.

Schilling, A., & Krüger, W. Untersuchungen über die Motorik sprachgestörter kinder nach der motometrischen Skala von Oseretsky-Göllnitz unter Besonderer Berücksichtigung der Frühkindlichen Hirnschädigung. *HNO Wegweiser*, 1960, *8*, 205–209.

Schlesinger, I. M., Forte, M., Fried, B., & Melkman, R. Stuttering, information load, and response strength. *Journal of Speech and Hearing Disorders*, 1965, *30*, 32–36.

Schlesinger, I. M., Melkman, R., & Levy, R. Word length and frequency as determinants of stuttering. *Psychonomic Science*, 1966, *6*, 255–256.

Schmitt, L. S., & Cooper, E. B. Fundamental frequencies in the oral reading behavior of stuttering and nonstuttering male children. *Asha*, 1976, *18*, 593. (Abstract)

Schwartz, D., & Webster, L. M. A clinical adaptation of the Hollins precision fluency shaping program through de-intensification. *Journal of Fluency Disorders*, 1977, *2*, 3–10. (a)

Schwartz, D., & Webster, L. M. More on the efficacy of a protracted precision fluency shaping program. *Journal of Fluency Disorders*, 1977, *2*, 205–216. (b)

Schwartz, M. F. The core of the stuttering block. *Journal of Speech and Hearing Disorders*, 1974, *39*, 169–177.

Schwartz, M. F. Author's reply to Freeman, Ushijima, and Hirose. *Journal of Speech and Hearing Disorders*, 1975, *40*, 139–140. (a)

Schwartz, M. F. Author's response to Zimmermann and Allen, and Adams. *Journal of Speech and Hearing Disorders*, 1975, *40*, 136–137. (b)

Schwartz, M. F. *Stuttering solved*. Philadelphia: Lippincott, 1976.

Seth, G. An experimental study of the control of the mechanism of speech, and in particular that of respiration in stuttering subjects. *British Journal of Psychology*, 1934, *24*, 375–388.

Seth, G. Psychomotor control in stammering and normal subjects: An experimental study. *British Journal of Psychology*, 1958, *49*, 139–143.

Shaffer, G. Measures of jaw movement and phonation in nonstuttered and stuttered production of voiced and voiceless plosives. *Speech Monographs*, 1940, *7*, 85–92.

Shearer, W. M., & Williams, J. D. Self-recovery from stuttering. *Journal of Speech and Hearing Disorders*, 1965, *30*, 288–290.

Sheehan, J. G. Stuttering behavior: A phonetic analysis. *Journal of Communication Disorders*, 1974, *7*, 193–212.

Sheehan, J. G., & Voas, R. B. Tension patterns during stuttering in relation to conflict, anxiety-binding, and reinforcement. *Speech Monographs*, 1954, *21*, 272–279.

Shrum, W. F. *A study of the speaking behavior of stutterers and nonstutterers by means of multichannel electromyography*. Unpublished doctoral dissertation, University of Iowa, 1967.

Silverman, F. H., & Williams, D. E. Loci of disfluencies in the speech of stutterers. *Perceptual and Motor Skills*, 1967, *24*, 1085–1086.

Snyder, M. A. Stuttering and coordination: An investigation of the relationship between the stutterer's coordination and his speech difficulty. *Logos*, 1958, *1*, 36–44.

Soderberg, G. A. Phonetic influences upon stuttering. *Journal of Speech and Hearing Research*, 1962, *5*, 315–320.

Soderberg, G. A. The relations of stuttering to word length and word frequency. *Journal of Speech and Hearing Research*, 1966, *9*, 584–589.

Soderberg, G. A. Linguistic factors in stuttering. *Journal of Speech and Hearing Research*, 1967, *10*, 801–810.

Soderberg, G. A. Relations of word information and word length to stuttering disfluencies. *Journal of Communication Disorders*, 1971, *4*, 9–14.

Soderberg, G. A. The context effect: Stuttering as a function of interactions between phonetic features. *Asha*, 1972, *14*, 472. (Abstract)

Soderberg, G. A., & MacKay, D. G. The function relating stuttering to phoneme frequency and transition probability. *Journal of Verbal Learning and Verbal Behavior*, 1972, *11*, 83–91.

Spriestersbach, D. C. *An exploratory study of the motility of the peripheral oral structures in relation to defective and superior consonant articulation.* Unpublished master's thesis, University of Iowa, 1940.

Starkweather, C. W., Hirschman, P., & Tannenbaum, R. S. Latency of vocalization onset: Stutterers versus nonstutterers. *Journal of Speech and Hearing Research*, 1976, *19*, 481–492.

Steer, M. D. A qualitative study of breathing in young stutterers: A preliminary investigation. *Speech Monographs*, 1935, *2*, 152–156.

Steer, M. D. Symptomatologies of young stutterers. *Journal of Speech Disorders*, 1937, *2*, 3–13.

St. Louis, K. O. *The effects of motor speech awareness on stuttering.* Unpublished doctoral dissertation, University of Minnesota, 1973.

St. Louis, K. O., & Martin, R. R. The effects of motor speech awareness on stuttering. *Human Communication*, 1978, *3*, 159–169.

St. Louis, K. O., & Martin, R. R. Motor speech awareness in stutterers: Reorganization of distinctive features? *Asha*, 1976, *18*, 593. (Abstract)

Stocker, B. *The Stocker probe technique.* Tulsa: Modern Education Corporation, 1977.

Stocker, B., & Parker, E. The relationship between auditory recall and dysfluency in young stutterers. *Journal of Fluency Disorders*, 1977, *2*, 177–187.

Stromsta, C. A spectrographic study of dysfluencies labeled as stuttering by parents. *De Therapia Vocis et Loquellae*, 1965, *1*, 317–320.

Strother, C. R. A study of the extent of dyssynergia occurring during the stuttering spasm. *Psychological Monographs*, 1937, *43*, 108–127.

Strother, C. R., & Kriegman, L. S. Diadochokinesis in stutterers and nonstutterers. *Journal of Speech Disorders*, 1943, *8*, 323–335.

Strother, C. R., & Kriegman, L. S. Rhythmokinesis in stutterers and nonstutterers. *Journal of Speech Disorders*, 1944, *9*, 239–244.

Tatham, M. A. A. Implications on stuttering of a model of speech production. In Y. Lebrun & R. Hoops (Eds.), *Neurolinguistic approaches to stuttering.* The Hague: Mouton, 1973. Pp. 101–111.

Taylor, I. K. The properties of stuttered words. *Journal of Verbal Learning and Verbal Behavior*, 1966, *5*, 112–118. (a)

Taylor, I. K. What words are stuttered? *Psychological Bulletin*, 1966, *65*, 233–242. (b)

Taylor, I. K., & Taylor, M. M. Test of predictions from the conflict hypothesis of stuttering. *Journal of Abnormal Psychology*, 1967, *72*, 431–433.

Ten Cate, M. J. Ueber die untersuchung der athmungsbewegung bei sprachfehlern. *Monatsschrift für Sprachheilkunde*, 1902, *12*, 247–259.

Tornick, G. B., & Bloodstein, O. Stuttering and sentence length. *Journal of Speech and Hearing Research*, 1976, *19*, 651–654.

Travis, L. E. Studies in stuttering. I. Dysintegration of the breathing movements during stuttering. *Archives of Neurology and Psychiatry*, 1927, *18*, 673–690. (a)

Travis, L. E. Studies in stuttering. II. Photographic studies of the voice in stuttering. *Archives of Neurology and Psychiatry*, 1927, *18*, 998–1014. (b)

Travis, L. E. Dissociation of the homologous muscle function in stuttering. *Archives of Neurology and Psychiatry*, 1934, *31*, 127–133.

Trotter, W. D. Relationship between severity of stuttering and word conspicuousness. *Journal of Speech and Hearing Disorders*, 1956, *21*, 198–201.

Trumper, M. A. *Hemato-respiratory study of 101 consecutive cases of stammering.* Unpublished doctoral dissertation, University of Pennsylvania, 1928.

Van Riper, C. Study of the thoracic breathing of stutterers during expectancy and occurrence of stuttering spasm. *Journal of Speech Disorders,* 1936, *1,* 61–72.

Van Riper, C. The preparatory set in stuttering. *Journal of Speech Disorders,* 1937, *2,* 149–154.

Van Riper, C. Experiments in stuttering therapy. In J. Eisenson (Ed.), *Stuttering: A symposium.* New York: Harper, 1958. Pp. 275–390.

Van Riper, C. *The nature of stuttering.* Englewood Cliffs, N.J.: Prentice-Hall, 1971.

Van Riper, C. *The treatment of stuttering.* Englewood Cliffs, N.J.: Prentice-Hall, 1973.

Webster, R. L. A behavioral analysis of stuttering: Treatment and theory. In K. S. Calhoun, H. E. Adams, & K. M. Mitchell (Eds.), *Innovative treatment methods in psychopathology.* New York: Wiley, 1974. Pp. 17–61.

Webster, R. L. *An introduction to the precision fluency shaping program.* Paper presented at the New York State Speech and Hearing Convention, Liberty, New York, April 1976.

Welsh, J. J. *Stuttering tremor: An exploration of methodologies for recording and analysis.* Unpublished master's thesis, Western Michigan University, 1970.

Wendell, M. V. *A study of voice onset time and voice termination in stuttering and nonstuttering children.* Unpublished master's thesis, University of Cincinnati, 1973.

West, R., & Nusbaum, E. A motor test for dysphemia. *Quarterly Journal of Speech,* 1929, *15,* 469–479.

Westby, C. E. Language performance of stuttering and nonstuttering children. *Asha,* 1975, *17,* 613. (Abstract)

Westphal, G. An experimental study of certain motor abilities of stutterers. *Child Development,* 1933, *4,* 214–221.

Williams, A. M., & Marks, C. J. A comparative analysis of the ITPA and PPVT performance of young stutterers. *Journal of Speech and Hearing Research,* 1972, *15,* 323–329.

Williams, D. E. Masseter muscle action potentials in stuttered and nonstuttered speech. *Journal of Speech and Hearing Disorders,* 1955, *20,* 242–261.

Williams, D. E., Silverman, F. H., & Kools, J. A. Disfluency behavior of elementary-school stutterers and nonstutterers: Loci of instances of disfluency. *Journal of Speech and Hearing Research,* 1969, *12,* 308–318.

Wilson, J. R. Systematic desensitization combined with electromyography in the treatment of stuttering. *Asha,* 1977, *19,* 648. (Abstract)

Wingate, M. E. Stuttering and word length. *Journal of Speech and Hearing Research,* 1967, *10,* 146–152.

Wingate, M. E. Sound and pattern in "artificial" fluency. *Journal of Speech and Hearing Research,* 1969, *12,* 677–686. (a)

Wingate, M. E. Stuttering as phonetic transition defect. *Journal of Speech and Hearing Disorders,* 1969, *34,* 107–108. (b)

Wingate, M. E. Effect on stuttering of changes in audition. *Journal of Speech and Hearing Research,* 1970, *13,* 861–873.

Wingate, M. E. *The structural character of the most commonly occurring words.* Unpublished manuscript, 1973.

Wingate, M. E. *Stuttering theory and treatment.* New York: Irvington, 1976.

Wingate, M. E. The relationship of theory to therapy in stuttering. In R. W. Rieber (Ed.). *The problem of stuttering: Theory and therapy.* New York: American Elsevier, 1977. Pp. 37–44.

Woolf, G. The assessment of stuttering as struggle, avoidance, and expectancy. *British Journal of Communication Disorders*, 1967, *2*, 158–171.

Wulff, J. Lippen- Kiefer- Zungen-und handreaktronen auf riezdaibietungen nach unterschiedlichen zeitintervallen bei normalsprechenden und bei stotternden kindern im alter von etwa 14 jahren. *Vox*, 1935, *21*, 40–45.

Zaleski, T. Rhythmic skills in stuttering children. *De Therapia Vocis et Loquellae*, 1965, *1*, 371–373.

Zimmerman, I., Steiner, V., & Evatt, R. *Preschool language manual*. Columbus: Merrill, 1969.

Zimmermann, G., & Allen, E. L. Questions concerning Schwartz's "the core of the stuttering block." *Journal of Speech and Hearing Disorders*, 1975, *40*, 135–136.

Zinkin, N. I. *Mechanisms of speech*. The Hague: Mouton, 1968.

Zipf, G. K. *Human behavior and the principle of least effort*. Reading: Mass.: Addison-Wesley, 1949.

Anatomic Studies of the Perioral Motor System: Foundations for Studies in Speech Physiology

JESSE G. KENNEDY III and JAMES H. ABBS

Speech Motor Control Laboratories
Department of Communicative Disorders
University of Wisconsin
Madison, Wisconsin

SPEECH AND LANGUAGE: Advances in Basic Research and Practice, Vol. 1

The present series of studies was conducted because we felt
an acute need for more precise specification of the facial muscle structure
as a basis for our ongoing studies of the motor physiology of the perioral
muscle system. Following completion of this work, it appeared that our
observations would be of use to other speech physiologists and speech
pathologists who may have experienced similar frustrations in finding
detailed anatomic information regarding the facial musculature. Thus, in
large part, this work is directed to those who are conducting research on
the **speech function** of the orofacial system. However, in addition, we
hope that the line illustrations and quantitative descriptions of the perioral
muscles provided in this chapter will be of use to individuals working in
clinical settings, as well as to educators concerned with speech and
hearing sciences in which speech anatomy is considered an appropriate
background for either academic or professional degree programs.

I. A RATIONALE FOR ANATOMIC INVESTIGATION OF THE PERIORAL MUSCULATURE

One aspect of our current research program at the University of Wisconsin involves attempts to simulate the muscle forces and mechanical
properties which underlie movements of the lips and jaw for speech. In
the context of developing these models, due to the quantitative demands
of simulation, one quickly becomes aware of the need for concrete and
concise structural information with regard to these systems. The magnitude of this problem can be illustrated by referring to Fig. 1, which is a

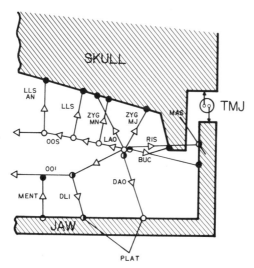

Figure 1. A schematic physiological model of three-dimensional lip movement. The nodes of this schematic representation describe a three-dimensional point of attachment for both active and passive tissues. (From Müller, 1975.) Node symbols: ●, muscle–bone attachment; ◓, muscle–passive tissue attachment; ◑, muscle to passive tissue **and** muscle; ○, muscle to muscle attachment. Branch symbols: ▷, muscle model (including passive components; ▶, passive connective tissue. Muscles: LLSAN, M. Levator Labii Superioris Alaeque Nasi; LLS, M. Levator Labii Superioris; ZYGMN, M. Zygomaticus Minor; ZYGMJ, M. Zygomaticus Major; LAO, M. Levator Anguli Oris; RIS, M. Risorius; MAS, M. Masseter; OOS, M. Orbicularis Oris Superior; OOI, M. Orbicularis Oris Inferior; MENT, M. Mentalis; DLI, M. Depressor Labii Inferior; DAO, M. Depressor Anguli Oris; BUCC, M. Buccinator; PLAT, M. Platysma.

simplified schematic representation of the muscular and connective tissue components of the upper and lower lip movement systems. This representation was devised to include all or most of the components that we thought **might** have a significant contribution in the generation of the three-dimensional movement of the lips. The connective nodes in this diagram represent the three-dimensional points of attachment (i.e., muscle origins and insertions) of the active and passive tissues that require initial consideration in the development of a simulation model. Symbolically, the variation in the nature of these nodes illustrates the range of dynamic linkage between active and passive components. The complexities imposed by the multiple, interacting components of this system clearly are nontrivial in terms of their mathematical simulation. In addition, based upon known properties of the various muscle and connective tissue elements represented here, it appears that these elements are inherently nonlinear. Thus, the complex system depicted in Fig. 1 represents a quantitative modeling problem of sizable proportions, not only in regard to numerical analysis but also in relation to experimental determination of the system coefficients. Fortunately, the complexity of this general model can be reduced without appreciable loss of its explanatory power by focusing on the special cases or unique actions of this system in the context of its behavior for speech movements. For example, based upon our observations of the labial system to date, it appears that the range of changes exhibited by the passive and active tissues for speech movements can be approximated in a much simpler form than that shown in Fig. 1. However, to accomplish this reduction on justifiable scientific grounds, one must have a reasonable understanding of the range and nature of tissue extensibility as well as a reasonable approximation of the geometry and gross dimensions of the muscle system.

Unfortunately, despite current research interest in the physiological mechanisms that underlie speech movements, we do not have descriptions of peripheral anatomy which provide this fundamental information. Traditionally, researchers interested in the physiology of speech have referred to three major sources for information regarding speech anatomy: anatomy texts, research literature, and limited samples of cadaveric material. While these sources of anatomic information are useful for teaching purposes, they have significant limitations for individuals attempting to conduct research on the functional aspects of speech production.

Anatomy texts frequently summarize findings from a limited number of cadavers. In working from these limited samples it is very difficult to specify the extent and nature of inter- and intraspecimen variability present in the peripheral speech structures. Many texts derive their information and/or graphic representations from other authors (Quiring & Warfel, 1965; J. H. Scott & Dixon, 1972) and thus perpetuate any inaccuracies, generalizations, or unrepresentative anatomic anomalies which may be present in the parent sources. The graphic format for presenting structural detail in anatomy texts is also of less than optimal value for speech researchers. Anatomic drawings have a tendency to present a general, unscaled, artistic view which has only abstract agreement with the specifics of reality (e.g., Bateman, 1977; Dickson & Maue, 1970; Diehl, 1968; Lightoller, 1925; Martone, 1962; Martone & Edwards, 1962). Likewise, photographs, because of the nature of the material being photographed and difficulties of photographic reproduction, seldom achieve optimum fidelity. In addition to the limitations of the graphic portrayal of anatomic material, anatomy textbooks typically present drawings or photographs of one, ideal specimen.

Research literature concerned with the anatomy of the head and neck (or speech) appears to be a somewhat better resource than anatomy texts as a basis for speech physiology research. However, upon review, one finds few articles which provide useful information to the speech physiologist. The articles which are available share many of the shortcomings of anatomy texts: poorly reproduced photographs, aesthetically oriented drawings, and little account of system variability. Indeed, occasionally a research article will apparently pay less attention to maintaining magnitude scale relationships than will anatomy texts (Leanderson, Persson, & Öhman, 1971). Photographs in research articles, due to the difficulties of multiple reproduction, seldom present any but the most salient structures with clarity. However, it should be noted that graphic illustrations in research articles often are employed for a purpose other than that of providing survey information; i.e., they are utilized to provide support for specific anatomic or functional hypotheses.

The best anatomic data are those gained through dissection. However, this source is not without limitations and is not, in many cases, a viable alternative to many speech physiologists. The work itself is quite time consuming and demands a relatively high degree of skill. In addition, the time involved in dissection often limits researchers, who do their own dissections, to one or two cadavers, resulting in observations based on limited populations. Perhaps the greatest difficulty of dissection involves the general unavailability of cadaveric materials and suitable facilities.

In short, there are no currently optimal materials to which a speech physiologist can refer concerning the structure of the component parts of the speech mechanism. One means of solving this problem is to acquire systematic information (from a relatively large number of cadavers) for each of the major subsystems of speech mechanisms. One such subsystem is composed of the muscles of facial expression. Due to the current focus on the physiology of the facial muscles in the production of speech (Abbs, 1973; Abbs, Folkins, & Sivarajan, 1976; Abbs & Gilbert, 1973; Cooker, 1974; Folkins, 1976; Folkins & Abbs, 1975; Folkins, Kennedy, & Loncarich, 1978; Gay & Hirose, 1973; Gay, Ushijima, Hirose, & Cooper, 1974; Isley & Basmajian, 1973; Kennedy, 1977; Leanderson et al., 1971; Muller, Abbs, Kennedy, & Larson, 1977; Sussman, MacNeilage, & Hanson, 1973; Vitti, Correa, Fortinguerra, Berzin, & Konig, 1972; Vitti, Fortinguerra, Correa, Konig, & Berzin, 1974), it appeared that detailed anatomic information on these muscles, for a representative sample of cadaveric specimens, would be particularly useful to speech researchers. The present investigations were an attempt to provide that information as a basis for our own research on the physiology of the speech system. In addition, those individuals attempting to treat speech disorders of a physiogenic origin, especially orofacial anomalies, might be assisted in their work if they had improved knowledge of normal orofacial anatomy. Specifically, the studies, conducted on 11 cadaveric specimens, included: (1) generation of reproducible line drawings from color photographs through application of a photographic transfer technique; (2) direct measures of perioral muscle topology, including selected muscle insertion angles, muscle lengths, muscle widths, and relative position information; (3) implantation of surrogate electrodes as a basis for validating the perioral electrode placement specifications currently advocated in speech studies of these muscles; and (4) a preliminary set of detailed recommendations for electrode placements in the perioral muscles utilizing information derived from the observations made in Sections I through III.

II. CHARACTERISTICS OF THE PERIORAL MUSCLES

The perioral musculature is typically classified as striated and, as such, shares many of the general characteristics of other striated muscle; i.e., the perioral muscles have cross-striations, are under direct nervous system control, and are capable of rapid changes in contractile state (Ruch, Patton, Woodbury, & Tower, 1966). However, from structural and neural control points of view, the perioral muscles exhibit some properties which distinguish them from most other striated muscle.

For example, the perioral muscles lack the fascial sheaths and tendonous attachments that are present in most other striated muscle. Moreover, while their origins are often found on the bony portions of the facial skeleton, their insertions are most frequently in soft tissue, i.e., other muscles or the dermal layer. Due to the absence of fascial tissue, the perioral muscles cannot be as conveniently classified into anatomic entities as other striated muscle. Moreover, fibers from allegedly separate peioral muscles frequently blend and interweave along the course of their contact. These ambiguities of classification are further exacerbated by the presence of yellow adipose tissue found between and within the fibers of various perioral muscles. These unique characteristics not only create difficulties for the structural specification of the perioral muscles, but make it very difficult to discern their functional properties as well.

From the standpoint of neural control, the facial muscles also present some anomalies in relation to other striated muscle. The perioral muscles are provided with a relatively dense supply of motor neurons per muscle fiber (estimated to be from 3:1 to 5:1 by Laurenson, 1968), implying a capability for very fine gradations of contraction. In contrast, however, the presence of typical muscle spindles in the perioral muscles (which typically implies a capability for fine control) is an issue of some controversy (Hosokawa, 1961). The innervation of the perioral muscles is also considerably more complicated than that of most other striated muscles. For example, while it appears that the major motor innervation to the facial musculature is through the seventh cranial nerve, reassessment of some earlier reports (Conley, 1964; Conley, Papper, & Kaplan, 1963; Martin & Helsper, 1957, 1960) as well as recent data (Abbs *et al.*, 1976; Baumel, 1974; Sutton, Larson, Lovell, & Lindeman, 1977) suggests that these muscles may receive some portion of their motor innervation from alleged sensory branches of the trigeminal nerve (the fifth cranial nerve). The specific sensory innervation to the receptors found in these muscles (or their vicinity) is also of some controversy. For example, it is not known whether these receptors receive their innervation through facial or trigeminal nerves. However, despite the ambiguity regarding the presence or absence of muscle spindles, a mechanical stretch stimulus applied to the lips produced a reflexive electromyographic response within a latency of 10–14 msec (Kugelberg, 1952; Larson, Folkins, McClean, & Müller, 1977; Netsell & Abbs, 1973). Some authors have suggested that, inasmuch as the perioral muscles insert into the facial skin, the dermal mechanoreceptors perform the same role as spindles for other striated musculature (Lindquist & Martensson, 1969). From the standpoint of reflexive actions, it has even been suggested that the entire perioral musculature may constitute a single functional entity, i.e., responding to mechanical stretch stimuli as a single striated muscle (Gandiglio & Fra, 1967).

A. Implications for the Development of Perioral Motor System Models

The idiomorphic characteristics of the peripheral perioral motor system pose some special problems for one attempting to understand this system based upon studies that have been conducted with other striated muscle systems. For example, if one is attempting to simulate the biomechanics of the perioral muscle system in the production of lip movements for speech, the models of muscle classically employed in the representation of other skeletal muscle must be substantially modified. Figure 2 is a schematic illustration of a basic model of striated muscle (Abbs & Eilenberg, 1976).

The special characteristics of the perioral musculature appear to require modification of this model in a number of ways. The lack of tendinous insertions by the perioral muscles appears to require the elimination or modification of K_s (the series elastic component). The prevalence of

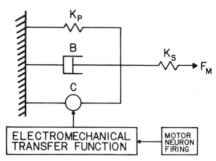

Figure 2. A schematic diagram representing the mechanical properties of isolated skeletal muscle and its neural input. K_p, K_s, and B are the parallel and series muscle elasticity and apparent viscosity, respectively, and C is the muscle contractile element. The muscle force, F_m, drives the speech articulator. (From Abbs & Eilenberg, 1976.)

muscle insertions into dermal tissue (because dermal tissue has elastic characteristics much different than those of tendon) requires changes in the coefficients of K_s as well as change in the vectorial orientation of K_s in relation to the muscle force. This modification would appear, in turn, to change the nature of the maximal elastic recoil, the recoil velocity (Wells, 1965), and the force–extension characteristics of the muscle (Aidley, 1971; Gottlieb & Agarwal, 1971). Some initial data on perioral muscle biomechanics are provided by Müller *et al.* (1977). The facial skin, which provides a common connective sheath for all of the facial muscles, further complicates an attempt to characterize the contributions of individual muscles to orofacial movement. That is, contraction force of one facial muscle is translated through this common connective dermal layer, thereby changing the angles of origin and insertion of other muscles. Furthermore, since many of the facial muscle forces are translated over bony surfaces, it is necessary to modify the uniaxial muscle model shown in Fig. 2 in order to take into account rotational force vectors in addition to translational force vectors.

These are but a few of the complications that make it difficult to characterize the perioral muscle system in terms of more conventional biomechanical muscle models and complicate the task of the speech physiologist attempting to understand the specific contributions of the individual muscles to speech production. In the context of these substantial difficulties, the present series of studies was an attempt to provide some basic structural information which might reduce the number of unknown variables that arise in attempts to simulate the peripheral physiology of the facial motor system and its actions during speech production.

B. Current Perspectives on Perioral Muscle Structure

As a basis for the studies that follow, and prior to presentation of the results of the present studies, it appears worthwhile to review current anatomic descriptions of the perioral musculature. Inasmuch as the present investigations were conducted to provide reference material for speech research, and the major speech contribution of the facial muscles is manifest in the movement of the lips, this section describes these muscles primarily in relation to their insertion into the labial structures.

1. The Sphincter Muscle of the Lips

The major muscle of the lips is the sphincter-like M. Orbicularis Oris (OO). It appears that M. OO can be divided into inferior and superior components functionally and/or anatomically (Diehl, 1968; Sicher, 1965). However, the criteria or information upon which this division is based are obscure. The superficial origin of M. OO is also in some dispute. Gardiner, Gray and O'Rahilly (1963) suggests that it has its deep origin in the deep fibers of M. Buccinator, with the surface fibers coming from M. Levator Anguli Oris and M. Depressor Anguli Oris. Other anatomists (Diehl, 1968; Shapiro, 1947; Woodburne, 1969; Zemlin, 1968) describe M. OO as being composed of fibers derived from all other perioral musculature, with the deep fibers derived mainly from M. Buccinator. This latter view appears to be most prevalent. It has been suggested that upon contraction, M. OO compresses, contracts, or protrudes the lips (Diehl, 1968; Quiring & Warfel, 1965; Shapiro, 1947). Some recent data, based upon direct electrical stimulation of M. OO inferior, provide more refined specification of this muscle's action (Folkins, 1976).

2. Muscles Inserting into the Upper Lip

The muscles which insert into the upper lip can be divided into two groups: (1) the superficial muscles, and (2) the deep muscles.

a. Superficial Muscles. The superficial muscles which insert into the upper lip include: M. Zygomaticus Minor, M. Levator Labii Superioris, M. Levator Labii Superioris Alaeque Nasi, and M. Zygomaticus Major.

M. Zygomaticus Minor, M. Levator Labii Superioris, and M. Levator Labii Superioris Alaeque Nasi have been referred to as the three heads of M. Quadratus Labii Superior. M. Zygomaticus Minor (ZMIN, zygomatic head of M. Quadratus Labii Superior, Caput Zygomaticum) apparently is the smallest and most variable of the three heads of this truncating muscle (M. Quadratus Labii Superior), and has been reported to be absent in 20% of the population (Sicher, 1965). The origin of M. ZMIN is designated as the exterior surface of the zygomatic bone beneath the lower border of the orbital portion of M. Orbicularis Oculi, while its insertion is the skin of the nasolabial furrow and upper lip (Quiring & Warfel, 1965). The apparent action of M. ZMIN is to raise the lateral protion of the upper lip and bow the nasolabial furrow. In terms of variation, M. ZMIN is reported to be occasionally: (1) fused with M. Zygomaticus Major, (2) doubled in size, and (3) originating from neighboring structures (Schaeffer, 1953).

M. Levator Labii Superioris (LLS, infraorbital head of M. Quadratus Labii Superior, Caput Infraorbital) has its origin at the lower margin of the eye orbit. M. LLS inserts into the lateral half of the upper lip and its action is to elevate and evert the upper lip (Zemlin, 1968).

M. Levator Labii Superioris Alaeque Nasi (LLSAN, angular head of M. Quadratus Labii Superior, Caput Angulare) originates at the frontal process and infraorbital margin of the maxilla and inserts both into the lateral cartilaginous framework of the nostril and M. OO. The action of M. LLSAN is to dilate the nostril and elevate the upper lip (Zemlin, 1968). The interspecimen variability of M. LLSAN is manifest in terms of its extent and the degree to which its fibers blend with surrounding muscles (Gray, 1959).

M. Zygomaticus Major (ZMAJ, M. Zygomaticus) is most often described as a long, ribbon-shaped muscle with an origin deep to M. Orbicularis Oculi and near the temporal suture of the zygomatic bone. M. ZMAJ is considered to be one of the best developed and most consistent of the supraoral muscles. It is divided at the angle of the mouth into deep and superficial portions by M. Levator Anguli Oris (Sicher, 1965). Due to its insertion in the skin and mucosa at the angle of the mouth, it is thought to provide forces that move the angle of the mouth superiorly and laterally (Schaeffer, 1953). The major variation observed and recorded for ZMAJ is that its origin may be located at either the temporal or massateric fascia (Schaeffer, 1953).

b. Deep Muscles. The only deep muscle inserting into the upper lip is M. Levator Anguli Oris (LAO, M. Caninus). While this muscle has been described by some as a superior counterpart of M. Depressor Anguli Oris (Zemlin, 1968), others suggest that it is an independent anatomic entity (Diehl, 1968). M. LAO has its origin in the canine fossa of the maxilla immediately below the infraorbital foramen where it is covered by M. ZMIN. The fibers of M. LAO insert at the angle of the mouth, mingling with the fibers of M. OO, M. Depressor Anguli Oris, and M. ZMAJ. The apparent action of M. LAO is to move the corner of the mouth superiorly and medially, thus apparently drawing the inferior portion of M. OO superiorly to aid in closing the mouth (Woodburne, 1969; Zemlin, 1968).

3. Muscles Inserting into the Lower Lip

a. Superficial Muscles. Those muscles with the greatest influence on the lower lip also can be classified as superficial and deep. The superficial muscle is the M. Depressor Anguli Oris (DAO, M. Triangularis) which is described as a broad, flat, and well-defined subcutaneous muscle originating on the oblique line of the mandible below the canine, bicuspid, and first molar teeth (Schaeffer, 1953). The insertion of M. DAO is the skin at the angle of the mouth and fibers of the inferior portion of M. OO. Its action appears to be to move the angle of the mouth inferiorly and, according to Schaeffer (1953), laterally. Other authors (Folkins, 1976; Sicher, 1965) consider the action of M. DAO to be a medial movement of the oral angle.

b. Deep Muscles. The deep muscles of the lower lip are M. Depressor Labii Inferior and M. Mentalis. M. Depressor Labii Inferior (DLI, M. Quadratus Labii Inferior) is a large, thin, rhomboid-shaped muscle that appears to be a part of M. Platysma (Schaeffer, 1953). The origin of M. DLI is the oblique line of the mandible between the symphysis and the mental foramen and it inserts with the integument of the lower lip. M. DLI is characterized as being interwoven with yellow fat throughout its length. The medial fibers decussate with the fibers of the opposite side (Woodburne, 1969). The apparent action of M. DLI is to draw the lower lip down and evert it, acting as an antagonist to M. Mentalis (Folkins, 1976; Schaeffer, 1953).

M. Mentalis (MENT, M. Levator Menti) is a muscle which varies greatly in size and generally is fused with M. Platysma (Schaeffer, 1953). While M. MENT has a deep origin, it has a superficial insertion. Its origin is the incisive fossa of the mandible from which point it runs anterior and inferior to insert in the integument of the chin (Palmer, 1972). It appears that the action of M. MENT is to draw the skin of the lip upward, and thus aid in protracting the lower lip and forcing it against the gum (Folkins, 1976; Hollinshead, 1961).

4. Muscles Inserting into the Angle of the Mouth

a. Superficial Muscles. The angle of the mouth is influenced on a superficial level by M. Risorius (RIS). This muscle varies from being quite prominent in some specimens to being totally absent in others, and in some specimens it was observed to blend with M. Platysma (Gray, 1959). M. RIS has its origin in the fascia over M. Masseter, superficial to M. Platysma. Insertion is reported to be the skin at the angle of the mouth (Quiring & Warfel, 1965). The action of M. RIS, the most variable muscle of the facial group, apparently is to move the angle of the mouth laterally (Palmer, 1972).

b. Deep Muscles. At the deep level the angle of the mouth is influenced by M. Buccinator (BUC), a narrow fibrous band which has been suggested to act as an antagonist to M. OO (Gardiner *et al.*, 1963). M. BUC has multiple origins, including: (1) the molar portion of the alveolar process of the maxilla, (2) the buccal crest of the mandible, and (3) the pterygomandibular raphe of the buccopharyngeal fascia. The insertion of M. Buccinator is also multiple. Its most cranial fibers go to the superior portion of M. OO, the second most cranial fibers go to the inferior portion of M. OO, the third most cranial fibers go to the superior portion of M. OO, and the most caudal fibers go to the inferior portion of M. OO (Schaeffer, 1953) (Fig. 3). The action of M. BUC, as suggested by Schaeffer (1953), is to draw the angle of the mouth laterally, to flatten the cheek and, by acting as an antagonist to M. OO, to tighten the lips. The major variation of M. BUC is that it is sometimes found to be divided into two distinct laminae.

C. Implications for the Study of Perioral Muscle Physiology

From this review it can be concluded that anatomy texts generally agree in their description of the perioral musculature. However, three significant omissions must be considered which, for the speech physiologist, limit the utility of these descriptions. First, the texts do not include any quantitative dimensional information from which we may derive a more accurate representation of the actual topology of the individual perioral muscles. This omission is significant for it deprives us of valuable information on muscle angle, length, and width from which, as a first approxi-

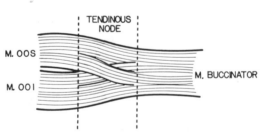

Figure 3. Schematic illustration of the deep insertion of M. Buccinator into M. Orbicularis Oris. (Adapted from Schaeffer, 1953.)

mation, the magnitude and direction of individual muscle force vectors may be inferred. Second, the juxtaposition of individual muscles in relation to other structures and muscles is not readily available. Presently this can be determined indirectly only by palpation of the underlying structures. Palpation, especially in regard to small or deep muscles, is greatly restricted in its utility by virtue of the relationship of the muscular structures to bony structures in general, as well as the varying amounts of subcutaneous fat and the volume of superficial musculature (Sicher, 1965). Without such information in a quantitative form, it is almost impossible to determine the influence which the contraction of one muscle has upon the action of other muscles. The third omission is the lack of information concerning the age, sex, or number of specimens from which the textual information has been gained. While this is primarily a methodological concern, it generates considerable questions concerning the range of variability which might be revealed by studies which employ large numbers of specimens.

III. CADAVERIC MATERIAL

The large number of specimens utilized in this study became available with the assistance of Dr. H. Kashiwa of the University of Washington's Department of Biological Structure. All of the cadavers utilized in the numerical and graphic analysis were caucasian. Age and sex records, along with cause of death information, are provided for all cadavers (except Specimens 9, 10, and 11) in Appendix A. Of those with records available, one was female (Specimen 1) and the remaining seven were male. The group had a terminal age ranging from 56 to 92 years, with an average of 74.25 years. The changes in tissue structure as a function of increasing age have been documented (Allen, 1967; Israel, 1973) and were considered to be negligible in terms of the measures and observations of this study. The cadavers had been embalmed in a buffered formalin solution which, as reported by both Mendelsohn (1940) and Polson, Brittain and Marshall (1953), produces minor tissue hardening and hence minimally restricted structure mobility. The cadaveric material was screened to eliminate any specimens with obviously atypical or distorted tissue. This screening eliminated specimens which had apparent age-related tissue distortions, i.e., extensive mandibular erosion or displacement in edentulous specimens. Specimens which appeared atypical because of trauma or facial surgery were also eliminated.

IV. QUALITATIVE DESCRIPTIONS: LINE TRACINGS OF PERIORAL MUSCLE TOPOLOGY (STUDY 1)

As noted previously, most graphic representations of the perioral muscles are either photographs (which present only the most salient features with clarity) or aesthetically oriented drawings (which bear far less than optimal resemblance to the actual muscle structure). Thus, in our experience, each time we have been faced with a specific question concerning facial muscle structure, it was necessary to inspect actual cadaveric material. However, even with cadaveric material available (which is not the case for all experimenters), it was frequently difficult, based upon one or two specimens, to acquire an appreciation of the variability between specimens or to develop generalizations that related to our *in vivo* experimentation. Therefore, one purpose of this first study was to provide, with as much detail and accuracy as possible, reproducible line illustrations that would serve as a qualitative resource for resolution of some of the issues that arise when one is studying the physiology of the perioral muscle system. The technique for generating accurate line drawings of facial muscle structures involved tracing muscle tissue boundaries from color slide transparencies.

A. Method

Color photographs of nine cadavers were taken before and after dissection (a single photograph for each side). As shown in Fig. 4, photographs were obtained with the camera mounted in a horizontal plane level with the inferior border of both nasal ala, at an angle of 45° lateral from the midline. The camera was a Nikkormat FTN full-frame 35-mm single-lens reflex utilizing a normal f1.4 lens fitted with a single element positive meniscus close-up lens. A shutter opening of f16 and a shutter speed of 1/60th of a second was used. To permit a small shutter opening (and thereby allowing a maximum depth of field), Kodak high-speed Ektachrome film (EHB 135-20), formulated for use with tungsten lamps, was used. This film has a nonpushed film speed of ASA 160 and generates photographs in the form of color slide transparencies. The lighting consisted of two General Electric ECA tungsten element photo flood lamps rated at 250 watts with a color temperature of 3200°K. The lights were placed 50 cm from the tissue surface and positioned 45° on each side of the camera in the same vertical plane.

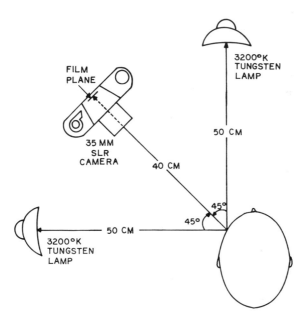

Figure 4. A schematic illustration of a superior view of the flood lamp and camera positions relative to the specimen as used to obtain the color slide transparencies.

B. Drawings

The black and white line drawings for this study were obtained by a photographic-transfer technique similar to that described by Tompsett (1970). The color slide transparencies obtained from the procedures described above were projected with a Keystone 990 slide projector (using a Keytar 4 inch, f3.5 lens) a distance of 93 cm onto white paper, resulting in a projected figure with dimensions of 20.5 by 30.5 cm. The line drawings were obtained by tracing the color projection, with ink, onto the white paper. These drawings were then reduced photographically by a factor of 50% and mounted on 21.6 by 28.0-cm paper for duplication.

C. Results and Discussion

The line drawings resulting from the photographic-transfer technique are presented in Figs. 5 through 13 for the nine cadavers dissected. As can be noted, these illustrations, in contrast to direct photographs or halftone drawings, have maximum contrast and clarity and are easily and inexpensively reproduced. Since the purpose of this first study was to provide a

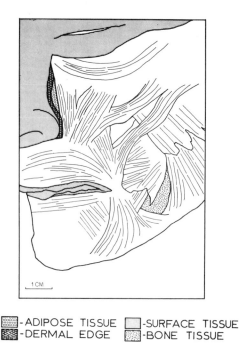

▦-ADIPOSE TISSUE ▢-SURFACE TISSUE
▨-DERMAL EDGE ▩-BONE TISSUE

Figure 5. The line drawing derived from the application of the photographic-transfer technique to Specimen 1.

series of reproducible drawings which would serve as a qualitative refer-ence source concerning the topology of the muscles, they do not, in themselves, provide explicit hypotheses concerning the topology of the facial muscles. However, even casual examination of these drawings raises a number of provocative issues concerning perioral muscle func-tion. Two of these issues, interspecimen variability and facial muscle asymmetry, are discussed in Sections IV,C,1 and IV,C,2.

1. Interspecimen Variability

It is apparent from the representations provided in Figs. 5 through 13 that a general characterization of this muscle system, applicable to a large component of the population, may be a difficult, if not impossible, task. This is particularly true in relation to those muscles which are superior and lateral to the oral opening. Admittedly, some of the specimens pre-sent a close approximation to classical representations of these muscles and their interrelations (e.g., Specimen 9). However, most are so very different from classical anatomy text presentations that they appear to require an entirely new interpretation of individual muscle function. For example, if the vector of muscle force provided by M. Zygomaticus Major

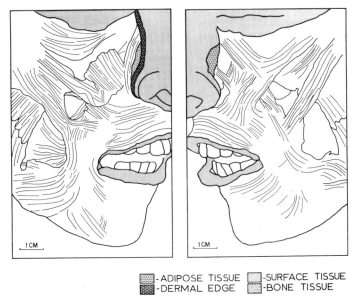

-ADIPOSE TISSUE ☐-SURFACE TISSUE
-DERMAL EDGE ☒-BONE TISSUE

Figure 6. The line drawing derived from the application of the photographic-transfer technique to Specimen 2.

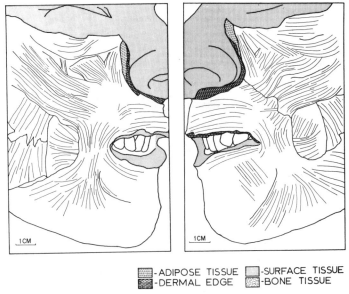

-ADIPOSE TISSUE ☐-SURFACE TISSUE
-DERMAL EDGE ☒-BONE TISSUE

Figure 7. The line drawing derived from the application of the photographic-transfer technique to Specimen 3.

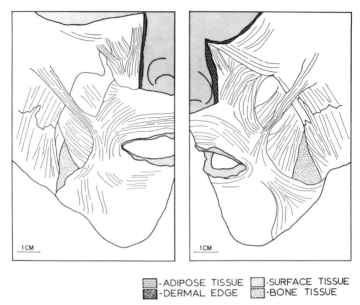

▓-ADIPOSE TISSUE ☐-SURFACE TISSUE
▓-DERMAL EDGE ▓-BONE TISSUE

Figure 8. The line drawing derived from the application of the photographic-transfer technique to Specimen 4.

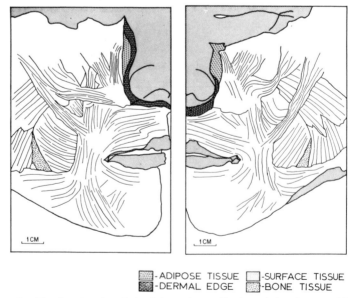

▓-ADIPOSE TISSUE ☐-SURFACE TISSUE
▓-DERMAL EDGE ▓-BONE TISSUE

Figure 9. The line drawing derived from the application of the photographic-transfer technique to Specimen 5.

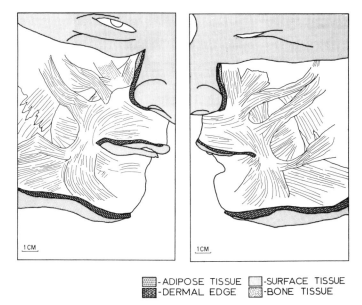

-ADIPOSE TISSUE -SURFACE TISSUE
-DERMAL EDGE -BONE TISSUE

Figure 10. The line drawing derived from the application of the photographic-transfer technique to Specimen 6.

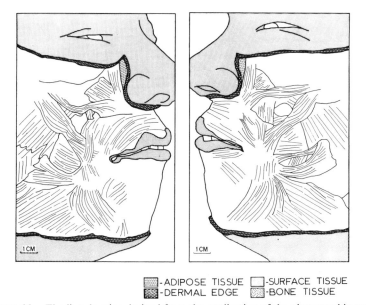

-ADIPOSE TISSUE -SURFACE TISSUE
-DERMAL EDGE -BONE TISSUE

Figure 11. The line drawing derived from the application of the photographic-transfer technique to Specimen 7.

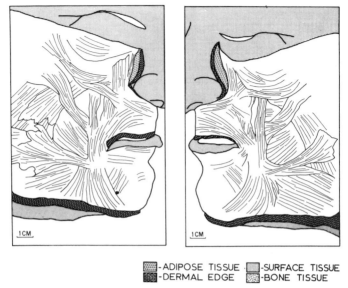

▨-ADIPOSE TISSUE ▨-SURFACE TISSUE
▨-DERMAL EDGE   ▨-BONE TISSUE

Figure 12. The line drawing derived from the application of the photographic-transfer technique to Specimen 8.

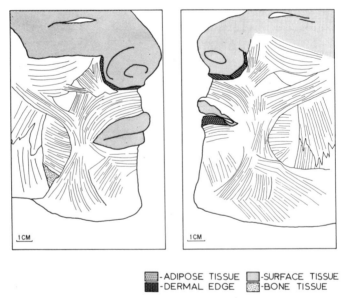

▨-ADIPOSE TISSUE ▨-SURFACE TISSUE
▨-DERMAL EDGE   ▨-BONE TISSUE

Figure 13. The line drawing derived from the application of the photographic-transfer technique to Specimen 9.

(ZMAJ) were characterized, this characterization would vary considerably from one specimen to another in the population sampled here. Similarly, the width of the insertion of the levator muscle group varies from extremely narrow (Specimens 7 and 9) to extremely wide (Specimen 3), resulting in a noticeable difference in the extent to which portions of the upper lip are directly elevated by these muscles. These variations point out the ambiguity which is likely to result in attempts to record and evaluate, *in vivo*, the muscle action potentials from these muscles. In addition, the difficulties of electrode placements in the perioral muscles, based solely upon superficial anatomic landmarks, become very apparent.

What also is obvious from these tracings is that a representation of the facial muscles, in a quantitative model which can be used to generalize to a large component of the population, may be somewhat difficult, at least to the extent that the model is incapable of being modified to incorporate idiosyncratic coefficients. Finally, the nature and degree of intersubject variability in these peripheral structures provide a profound indication of at least one reason why, when we observe the movements of these structures for speech production, we see such large magnitudes of intersubject variation in movement patterns. These intersubject variations, often referred to as anomalies, appear to be present in some form in all specimens. Indeed, these illustrations would suggest that variability is the rule rather than the exception and, moreover, that the term anomaly is, in itself, inappropriate in reference to these anatomic variations.

2. Intraspecimen Variability (Asymmetry)

Also quite discernible from these tracings is the bilateral asymmetry of the facial muscle system. As with interspecimen variability, asymmetry appears to be especially obvious in those muscles superior to the oral opening, as exemplified in Specimens 3, 4, and 6. However, some bilateral asymmetry is present also in the muscles lateral to, and inferior to, the oral opening. An example is the superior extension of the superior border of M. Platysma (PLAT) in Specimen 9. The observation of these subtle, and yet in some cases substantial, differences in facial symmetry would appear to provide at least partial explanation for some of the observed differences in muscle action potentials recorded from orofacial muscles that are bilaterally paired (C. H. Scott & Honet, 1972; Williams, 1955). Such observations also suggest that the development of biomechanical models of labial articulatory movement must have some facility to adjust to this asymmetry, at least where these models represent the system in three dimensions or attempt to characterize lateral–medial properties of labial movement.

V. QUANTITATIVE DESCRIPTIONS: DIRECT MEASURES OF PERIORAL MUSCLE TOPOLOGY (STUDY 2)

While the purpose of the previous study was to provide a resource for qualitative questions concerning perioral muscle topology, this second investigation focused upon quantification of selected anatomic features which we anticipated would be useful in attempt to characterize the actions of these muscles, both individually and in relation to one another. It must be noted, however, that while the specific physical features we chose to measure are extensive, they are by no means exhaustive. Indeed, as of this writing we are conducting additional analyses on some minor components of perioral muscle topology.

A. Method

The technique employed in this portion of the investigation involved direct bilateral measures of the perioral muscle topology from a major group of 11 specimens. The procedure involved: (1) measurement of surface facial landmarks prior to removal of the dermal layer (provided in Appendix B), (2) removal of the dermal layer and facial adipose tissue, taking considerable care not to disturb perioral muscles that inserted directly into the dermal layer, and (3) manual measurement of the features of facial structure, including: (a) the dimensions of each muscle individually as well as in relation to other anatomic landmarks, (b) the thickness of the dermal layer over select muscles for nine specimens, and (c) the thickness of the perioral adipose tissue layer of two specimens.

All measures were made using a transparent ruler graduate in metric units. Measures were not taken if a structure was missing or if precise borders had been distributed by removal of the dermal layer. A test–retest examination yielded a reliability estimate for linear measurement of 1.12 mm with a Pearson product–moment correlation of .99. A similar examination yielded a reliability measure for angular measurement in terms of a standard error of measurement of 2.71° with a Pearson product–Moment correlation of .99.

Measures were not taken regarding M. Depressor Labii Inferior, M. Mentalis, or M. Orbicularis Oris Inferior because of the indefinite nature of their borders. The data obtained were tabulated and statistically treated to yield mean values and variability in the form of standard deviations.

Due to the large number of anatomic measures (over 50), the definitions of those features employed in the measurement procedure itself are most efficiently discussed and presented with the data obtained therefrom. For correlative reference, the values obtained for all measures are provided in Appendix C.

B. Results and Discussion

As anticipated, the data obtained from this investigation do not, in themselves, provide explicit information concerning the functional role of the facial musculature during speech production. Such conclusions must come within the context of physiological studies. However, several issues, which appear to have implications for the manner in which physiologist might interpret these data, are apparent. For the purposes of clarity, presentation of the results of this study will be organized around these issues:

(1) Perioral musculature interspecimen variability and intraspecimen asymmetry.
(2) The magnitude and variability of the facial dermal layer.
(3) The extent of perioral muscle interweaving.
(4) The characteristics of perioral adipose tissue.
(5) Observed consistent traits of the perioral musculature.
(6) The presence of discrepancies between observations and text descriptions.

1. Perioral Musculature Interspecimen Variability and Intraspecimen Asymmetry

Based upon the extreme variability of facial expression and of superficial landmarks which characterize faces, one would expect the underlying muscle structure to have a corresponding degree of variability. Qualitatively, this variability was apparent from the line drawings obtained in the first study. In most instances the data collected in this second study documented and extended that expectation. Variability was manifest in the interspecimen mode (variation in the musculature between different specimens) and in the intraspecimen mode (asymmetry within a specimen).

a. M. Orbicularis Oris (Inferior and Superior Portions). Two anatomic features of M. OO were measured:

(A) The width of M. Orbicularis Oris Superior from its inferior border to its superior border, taken at the midline.
(B) The width of the oral opening, from the midline to the lateral oral angle.

Interspecimen variability. Figure 14 illustrates the features measured and provides the mean values and standard deviations of the measurements taken across all specimens. M. OO was found to be the most consistent muscle of the perioral system in terms of size, fiber development, and location. The superior portion was well defined in all specimens while the inferior portion had insertions from other muscles at all depths and locations throughout its course. Minimal intraspecimen variability was observed.

b. The Levator Group. Twelve anatomic features of the levator group were measured:

(C) The width of M. Levator Labii Superioris Alaeque Nasi from the lateral border to the lateral border of the nasal alae, taken 1 cm superior to the inferior border of both nasal alae.
(D) The width of M. Levator Labii Superioris at the widest point of its origin.
(E) The width of M. Zygomaticus Minor taken at the midpoint along its longitudinal axis.

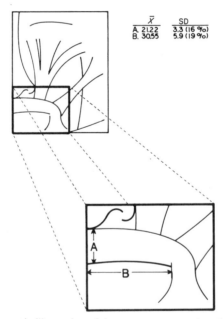

	$\bar{X}$	SD
A.	21.22	3.3 (16 %)
B.	30.55	5.9 (19 %)

Figure 14.   A schematic illustration of the measurements taken (in millimeters) and the measurement values derived from M. Orbicularis Oris. (A) The width of M. Orbicularis Oris Superior from its inferior border to its superior border, taken at the midline. (B) The width of the oral opening from the midline to the lateral oral angle.

(F) The width of the levator group from the lateral border of the nasal alae to the lateral border of the muscle group.

(G) The distance from the most lateral border of the levator group to the superior border of M. Zygomaticus Major, at their insertions.

(H) The length of M. Levator Labii Superioris from the widest part of the origin to the widest part of the insertion.

(I) The length of M. Zygomaticus Minor from the widest part of the origin to the widest part of the insertion.

(J) The angle of the course of the midline of M. Zygomaticus Minor with respect to a plane level with the inferior border of the nasal alae, measured at the midpoint of its longitudinal axis.

(K) The width of M. Zygomaticus Major taken at its midpoint.

(L) The width of M. Zygomaticus Major at the widest point of its insertion.

(M) The length of M. Zygomaticus Major from the widest part of the origin to the widest part of the insertion.

(N) The angle of the course of the midline of M. Zygomaticus Major with respect to a plane level with the inferior border of the nasal alae.

i. Interspecimen variability. The superficial levator group [M. Levator Labii Superioris Alaeque Nasi (LLSAN), M. Levator Labii Superioris (LLS), M. Zygomaticus Minor (ZMIN), and M. Zygomaticus Major (ZMAJ)] was found to be highly variable in muscle size and site of insertion. The average values and standard deviations of the measurements relating to the levator group are shown in Figs. 15 and 16. The greatest variation occurred in the distance between the lateral border of M. ZMIN and the medial border of M. ZMAJ (with a standard deviation of 55% of the mean measurement value), as can be seen in Specimen 3 (Fig. 7, with no separation) and Specimen 5 (Fig. 9, with 25 mm of separation). This observation generally agrees with the variability described by Schaeffer (1953). In Specimen 3 (Fig. 7), the levator group was totally fused, apparently supplying direct levating capability along the entire length of the superior portion of M. Orbicularis Oris. In 10 of the 17 views (one side of a specimen constituted a view), M. ZMIN and M. LLSAN coursed superficially to M. LLS, completely obscuring the latter muscle's insertion. The variability of M. LLSAN was seen mainly in its width and the amount of blending it had with the muscles immediately juxtaposed to it, which concurs with the observations of Gray (1959). M. ZMIN was the most variable muscle of the levator group in terms of: (1) the angle formed between the midline of the muscle and a plane level with the inferior border of the nasal alae (this being the single most variable

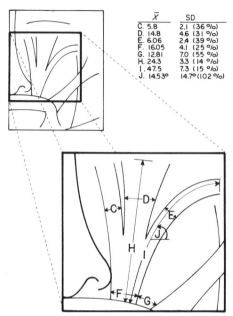

	$\bar{X}$	SD
C.	5.8	2.1 (36 %)
D.	14.8	4.6 (31 %)
E.	6.06	2.4 (39 %)
F.	16.05	4.1 (25 %)
G.	12.81	7.0 (55 %)
H.	24.3	3.3 (14 %)
I.	47.5	7.3 (15 %)
J.	14.53°	14.7° (102 %)

Figure 15. A schematic illustration of the measurements taken (in millimeters) and the measurement values derived from the levator group. (C) The width of M. Levator Labii Superioris Alaeque Nasi from the lateral border to the lateral border of the nasal alae, taken 1 cm superior to the inferior border of both nasal alae; (D) the width of M. Levator Labii Superioris at the widest point of its origin; (E) the width of M. Zygomaticus Minor taken at the midpoint along its longitudinal axis; (F) the width of the levator group from the lateral border of the nasal alae to the lateral border of the muscle group; (G) the distance from the most lateral border of the levator group to the superior border of M. Zygomaticus Major, at their insertions; (H) the length of M. Levator Labii Superioris from the widest part of the origin to the widest part of the insertion; (I) the length of M. Zygomaticus Minor from the widest part of the origin to the widest part of the insertion; (J) the angle of the course of the midline of M. Zygomaticus Minor with respect to a plane level with the inferior border of the nasal alae, measured at the midpoint of its longitudinal axis.

measure of those taken from this sytem, with a standard deviation equaling 102% of the average value), and (2) the location of its point of origin. M. ZMIN was often found to blend completely with M. Orbicularis Oculi (Specimen 8, Fig. 12) near its origin. M. ZMAJ was consistent in its size [with the exception of the width of its insertion (Fig. 16)], its origin, and the location of its insertion in relation to the insertion of M. ZMIN. M. ZMAJ of Specimens 5 (Fig. 9), 6 (Fig. 10, bilaterally), and 7 (Fig. 11, bilaterally) had inferior fiber bundles which, at the origin, coursed in a superior direction to become the superior fiber bundles at the insertion. Fiber bundles in the inferior position at the insertion often continued and

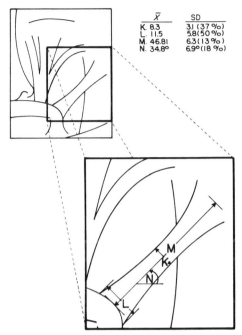

	$\bar{x}$	SD
K.	8.3	3.1 (37%)
L.	11.5	5.8(50%)
M.	46.81	6.3(13%)
N.	34.8°	6.9°(18%)

Figure 16. A schematic illustration of the measurements taken (in millimeters) and the measurement values derived from M. Zygomaticus Major. (K) The width of M. Zygomaticus Major taken at its midpoint; (L) the width of M. Zygomaticus Major at the widest point of its insertion; (M) the length of M. Zygomaticus Major from the widest part of the origin to the widest part of the insertion; (N) the angle of the course of the midline of M. Zygomaticus Major with respect to a plane level with the inferior border of the nasal alae.

coursed inferiorly to blend with M. Depressor Anguli Oris and M. Platysma.

ii. Intraspecimen variability. Specimen 2 (Fig. 6) showed the greatest intraspecimen variability in the levator muscle group. The right M. ZMAJ was a much larger muscle, both in terms of overall size and fiber bundle mass, than the left M. ZMAJ. The levator group was observed to be entirely fused on Specimen 3 (Fig. 7) and demonstrated an abrupt edge of insertion (on a superficial level) with left asymmetry. The levator group of Specimen 4 (Fig. 8) had an insertion which extended almost to the insertion of M. ZMAJ, which was not manifest on the right side of the specimen. Also on the left side of Specimen 4 (Fig. 8), M. LLS coursed superficially to M. LLSAN and M. ZMIN, while on the right it ran deep to these muscles. On the right view of Specimen 5 (Fig. 9), M. ZMIN and M. ZMAJ coursed parallel (in contact near their origin to a point near the midpoint of their length), while on the left the muscles were distinctly separated, from origin to insertion. The right M. ZMIN on Specimen 5 (Fig. 9) coursed in a relatively straight line from origin to insertion, while on the left it coursed first inferior, then medial and slightly superior to its insertion. As an additional asymmetrical feature, M. ZMIN on the right side of Specimen 6 (Fig. 10) twisted as it coursed from its origin to its insertion (i.e., the fiber bundles which were inferior at the origin were superior at the insertion), rather than the more common instance in which the fibers maintain their parallel attitude. The levator muscle group on the right side of Specimen 8 (Fig. 14) was more developed than on the left.

   c. M. Levator Anguli Oris.   Four anatomic features of M. Levator Anguli Oris (LAO) were measured:

   (O) The distance from lateral border of the nasal alae to the lateral muscle border, measured at the insertion.
   (P) The length of the muscle from the level of apposition of the lips to the farthest extent of the origin.
   (Q) The length from the insertion to the farthest extent of the origin.
   (R) The width at the midpoint between the origin and the insertion.

   i. Interspecimen variability.   The mean values and computed standard deviations for M. LAO are presented in Fig. 17. M. LAO was observed to have a distinct variation manifest in the presence or absence of muscle fiber bundles which coursed superficially to M. OOI and M. ZMAJ. This variation of M. LAO would appear to apply different muscle force vectors to the oral angle upon muscle contraction. In those instances with fiber bundles from M. LAO coursing superficially, perhaps a slight protrusion of the upper lip would occur upon muscle contraction. In the cases with large superficial fiber bundle courses (Specimen 2, Fig. 6; Specimen 7, Fig. 11; Specimen 8, Fig. 12), some of the bundles continued past the tendinous node to blend in with the anterior fibers of M. Depressor Anguli Oris (i.e., Specimen 2, Fig. 6, left view).

   ii. Intraspecimen variability. The major intraspecimen variability (asymmetry) of M. LAO was manifested in its course. On the left side of Specimen 2 (Fig. 6), M. LAO coursed superficially to M. ZMAJ and continued on to blend with fibers from M. Platysma. In contrast, on the right side of Specimen 2 (Fig. 6) M. LAO followed a course medial to M. ZMAJ. The right M. LAO of Specimen 5 (Fig. 9) was more prominent in both its muscle fiber bundle size and the definition of its borders than was the left. Specimen 8 (Fig. 12) had an M. LAO on the left which was extremely well developed and which coursed superficially to M. ZMAJ, then continued inferiorly to blend with M. Risorius, M. Platysma, and M.

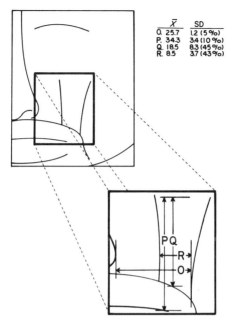

	$\bar{X}$	SD
O.	25.7	1.2 (5%)
P.	34.3	3.4 (10%)
Q.	18.5	8.3 (45%)
R.	8.5	3.7 (43%)

Figure 17. A schematic illustration of the measurements taken (in millimeters) and the measurement values derived from M. Levator Anguli Oris. (O) The distance from the lateral border of the nasal alae to the lateral muscle border, measured at the insertion; (P) the length of the muscle from the level of apposition of the lips to the farthest extent of the origin; (Q) the length from the insertion to the farthest extent of the origin; (R) the width at the midpoint between the origin and the insertion.

Depressor Anguli Oris, while on the right it appeared to blend mainly with M. Depressor Anguli Oris alone.

d. M. Depressor Anguli Oris. Five anatomic features relating to M. Depressor Anguli Oris (DAO) were measured:

(S) The width of the tendinous node, from the lateral angle of the mouth to the lateral border of the node.

(T) The width of the buccal fat pad area, from the lateral border of the tendinous node laterally to the anterior border of M. Masseter.

(U) The width of M. Depressor Anguli Oris 1 cm inferior to the level of the apposition of the lips.

(V) The angle of the anterior border of M. Depressor Anguli Oris with respect to a plane level with the inferior border of the nasal alae, measured 1 cm inferior to the level of the apposition of the lips.

(W) The angle of the posterior border of M. Depressor Anguli Oris with respect to a plane level with the inferior border of the nasal alae, measured 1 cm inferior to the level of the apposition of the lips.

i. Interspecimen variability. Figure 18 lists average values and standard deviations which resulted from measurements taken from M. DAO. M. DAO's major variation was manifest in the amount of fiber blending it shared with M. Platysma and M. Depressor Labii Inferior, and in the size of the angle created by its posterior border (which had a standard deviation equaling 39% of the mean value). In seven of the views M. DAO coursed inferior from the tendinous node and then anterior at its origin (Specimen 7, Fig. 11, left view; Specimen 8, Fig. 12, left view; Specimen 9, Fig. 13, left view). The remaining views had the canonically characteristic triangular shape. This variation would appear to have a major effect on the contribution of this muscle to movement of the angle

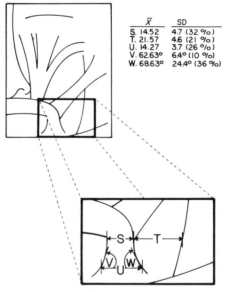

	$\bar{x}$	SD
S.	14.52	4.7 (32 %)
T.	21.57	4.6 (21 %)
U.	14.27	3.7 (26 %)
V.	62.63°	6.4° (10 %)
W.	68.63°	24.4° (36 %)

Figure 18. A schematic illustration of the measurements taken (in millimeters) and the measurement values derived from M. Depressor Anguli Oris. (S) The width of the tendinous node, from the lateral angle of the mouth to the lateral border of the node; (T) the width of the buccal fat pad area, from the lateral border of the tendinous node laterally to the anterior border of M. Masseter; (U) the width of M. Depressor Anguli Oris 1 cm inferior to the level of the apposition of the lips; (V) the angle of the anterior border of M. Depressor Anguli Oris with respect to a plane level with the inferior border of the nasal alae, measured 1 cm inferior to the level of the apposition of the lips; (W) the angle of the posterior border of M. Depressor Anguli Oris with respect to a plane level with the inferior border of the nasal alae, measured 1 cm inferior to the level of the apposition of the lips.

of the mouth. In those cases in which the muscle course was anterior immediately prior to the origin, the muscle action would appear to pull the angle of the mouth inferior and medial, while in those cases in which the classic triangular shape was observed, the action would appear to be to pull the mouth directly inferiorly. This variation of M. DAO may also account for the differing descriptions of M. DAO's action as supplied by Schaeffer (1953) and Sicher (1965).

ii. Intraspecimen variability. The largest amount of intraspecimen variability in M. DAO was manifest in its anterior and posterior angles (the angles formed by its border with M. Depressor Labii Inferior and M. Platysma, respectively). For example, Specimen 4 (Fig. 8) exhibited an M. DAO which was more prominent on the left than on the right. Specimen 5 (Fig. 9), in contrast, displayed a similar asymmetry of muscle development except that M. DAO was more prominent on the right. The right M. DAO of Specimen 6 (Fig. 10) coursed from its origin first posterior and slightly superior to a point approximately midway between the level of apposition of the lips and the anterior border of the chin, from which it then coursed directly superior to its insertion. The situation described for Specimen 6 (Fig. 10) was reversed for Specimen 8 (Fig. 12), with the right side demonstrating the triangular shape, while the left side M. DAO coursed first posterior, then directly superior to its insertion in the tendinous node.

e. M. Risorius. i. Interspecimen variability. M. Risorius (RIS) has been typically noted as being a highly variable and, in many cases, often absent muscle (Gray, 1959). In three of the dissections prominent M. RIS were found. In each case they were large muscles, often possessing two heads, which fanned out as they extended posterior from the tendinous node (Specimen 6, Fig. 10; Specimen 7, Fig. 11; Specimen 8, Fig. 12). Rather than inserting directly at the angle of the mouth [as is reported by Woodburne (1969) and Zemlin (1968)], the superior border was found to be even with the level of apposition of the lips or slightly inferior to that level. M. RIS was easily distinguishable from M. Platysma by virtue of its more superior position and course and its insertion in the fascia over M. Masseter. The attitude of M. RIS, as observed, was such that it would appear to provide a strong lateral force on the inferior portion of the angle of the mouth.

ii. Intraspecimen variability. The left side of Specimen 6 (Fig. 10) had a distinct M. RIS having a definite origin in the fascia over M. Masseter. The origin of M. RIS on the right side was not as definite, with fibers from M. Platysma blending with those of M. RIS at the origin, resulting in an abrupt angle at the point of origin. On the right side of Specimen 7 (Fig.

11), M. RIS demonstrated two distinct heads at its origin which blended as it coursed toward its insertion. On the left side of Specimen 7 (Fig. 11), M. RIS was joined at the origin and insertion, yet it was separated into two bellies between these points, the superior belly coursing directly anteriorly. The origin of M. RIS on the right side of Specimen 8 (Fig. 12) was broader than the origin on the left. The origin on the left side of Specimen 8 (Fig. 12), in addition to being narrower, was located slightly superior to that of the right. In each cadaver in which M. RIS was present, it was observed to be bilateral.

f. M. Orbicularis Oculi. Inter- and intraspecimen variability. A discussion of the inferior orbital portion of M. Orbicularis Oculi is included here because of its course, which often extended inferiorly to superficially overlap the levator muscle group. On Specimen 3 (Fig. 7) M. Orbicularis Oculi extended farther inferior on the left than on the right, extending almost to a level even with the inferior border of both nasal alae. M. Orbicularis Oculi on the left side of Specimen 4 (Fig. 8) extended to a level near that of the inferior border of the nasal alae.

g. M. Platysma. Inter- and intraspecimen variability. The major intraspecimen variability of M. Platysma (PLAT) was the degree to which it extended superiorly over M. Masseter. The course of M. PLAT on the left side of Specimen 3 (Fig. 7) arched from its insertion first inferiorly, then slightly superiorly, as it coursed posteriorly. The right side of M. PLAT on Specimen 3 (Fig. 7) coursed uniformly inferior and posterior from its insertion, along a course with a constant angle. M. PLAT was the major intraspecimen variable on Specimen 9 (Fig. 13). The superior fibers of the left side coursed superficially to M. DAO, extending directly posterior to a position over M. Masseter before it coursed inferiorly to its origin. M. PLAT appeared to be blended totally with the posterior border of M. DAO on the right side of Specimen 9 (Fig. 13), and it coursed directly inferior and posterior, where it crossed the mandible just anterior to the anterior border of M. Masseter.

h. M. Buccinator. i. Interspecimen variability. Physical measurements were not taken from M. Buccinator (BUC), but the fibers and fiber bundle direction of M. BUC were discernible following the removal of the buccal fat pad. The fiber bundle direction commonly was slightly inferior as the fibers coursed anteriorly to their insertion. A common variation in M. BUC was that the superior fibers coursed inferiorly while the inferior fibers coursed superiorly (Specimen 1, Fig. 5; Specimen 3, Fig. 7; Specimen 7, Fig. 11). This was seen as unique from the most commonly observed configuration in which the fibers were parallel as they coursed from origin to insertion.

ii. Intraspecimen variability. While measurements were not taken with regard to M. BUC, and its origin and insertion were not dissected out, one specimen did display intraspecimen variability. The left side of Specimen 3 (Fig. 7) demonstrated two branches: a superior branch coursing inferiorly at approximately 45° (in reference to a horizontal plane determined by the inferior border of the nasal alae), and an inferior branch coursing directly anteriorly toward its insertion. This diverse fiber bundle course was not manifest in the right side of the specimen.

Because of the extensive insertions of M. Depressor Labii Inferior and M. Mentalis, and because of the massive amounts of fiber interweaving (which, in turn, led to indistinct borders), measures were not taken from these muscles. A relatively clear muscle fiber bundle area of M. Depressor Labii Inferior was observed immediately medial to M. DAO and from 2.0 to 2.5 cm inferior to the angle of the mouth.

i. M. Masseter. Interspecimen variability. While M. Masseter is not usually considered to be a muscle of facial expression, observations were made regarding its interspecimen variability. The variability of M. Masseter was seen mainly in its fascial attachments. In seven of the views the fascial cover over M. Masseter extended inferiorly to a level more inferior than the level of the apposition of the lips (Specimen 2, Fig. 6; Specimen 5, Fig. 9; Specimen 9, Fig. 13). The striations of the masseteric fascia were frequently observed to course inferiorly and posteriorly at a distinctly different angle than the course of the muscle fiber bundles, which were either directed inferiorly or inferior and slightly anterior (Specimen 5, Fig. 9: Specimen 9, Fig. 13).

2. The Magnitude and Variability of the Facial Dermal Layer

As the dermal layer was removed, measurements were made regarding its dimensional variability. The measurements were made directly superficial to the midline of five muscles: M. Orbicularis Oris (both superior and inferior portions), M. Zygomaticus Major, M. Masseter, and M. Levator Labii Superioris. The results of these measurements are given in Fig. 19. The overall average dermal layer thickness was 2.26 mm, ranging from 1 to 4 mm, with a standard deviation of .77 mm. The thickest and most variable layer was found over the inferior portion of M. OO; perhaps this was influenced by the difficulty of dissection in this area caused by the extensive dermal muscle insertions. The inferior portion of M. OO was

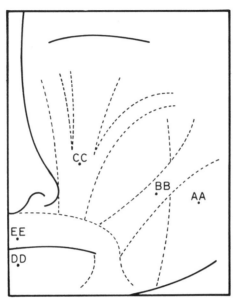

Figure 19. Schematic illustration of points at which dermal layer thickness measures were taken (in millimeters). Values represent $\bar{X}r$ (2.0 ± .53); ± SD: (AA) taken over the midline of M. Masseter (BB) taken over the midline of M. Zygomaticus Major (2.1 ± .63); (CC) taken over the midline of M. Levator Labii Superioris (1.8 ± .37); (DD) taken over the midline of M. Orbicularis Oris Inferior (2.7 ± 1.0); (EE) taken over the midline of M. Orbicularis Oris Superior (2.6 ± .72).

followed in dermal thickness (in descending order) by the superior portion of M. OO, M. ZMAJ, M. Masseter, and, with the thinnest and least variable dermal layer, over M. LLS.

3. The Extent of Perioral Muscle Interweaving

It was expected that extensive interweaving and blending of the muscle fiber bundles of all of the muscles of facial expression would be in evidence. This expectation was not upheld completely. The levator group and the muscles which act on the angle of the mouth were observed to be relatively free of blending and interweaving, with the exception of the area immediately juxtaposed to M. Orbicularis Oris (OO) and the tendinous node at the angle of the mouth. There was, however, consistent and extensive blending and interweaving of fibers in the area immediately inferior to the oral opening. This blending was accentuated by the insertion of M. DLI and M. MENT into the integument of the chin.

4. The Characteristics of Perioral Adipose Tissue

Extensive areas of fat were in evidence throughout the facial area, at times up to 21 mm thick (Specimen 10). The major fatty area was relatively consistent in its border. The superior border coincided with a line drawn from the medial angle of the eye immediately inferior to the prominence of the zygomatic bone, extending to the border of the mandible. The inferior border of this fatty area was a line drawn along the nasolabial furrow and extending to the inferior border of the mandible (Fig. 20). It would appear that any electrode placements in this area (i.e., the levator muscle group) would be greatly influenced by this fat pad and should be made with considerable attention to the insertion depth. The measurement values derived from the adipose layer are presented in Appendix C.

5. Observed Consistent Traits of the Perioral Musculature

While considerable variability exists in the perioral musculature, some consistent patterns were discernible. The superior portion of M. OO,

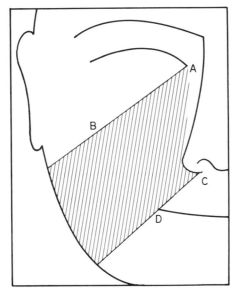

Figure 20. A schematic representation illustrating the boundaries of the facial fat pad in relation to: (A) the medial angle of the eye, (B) the inferior border of zygomatic prominence of the Maxilla, (C) the inferior border of the nasal alae, and (D) the lateral angle of the oral opening.

directly inferior to the nose, was relatively free of muscle fibers from other muscles. M. ZMAJ also was a clean muscle in terms of the absence of extraneous muscle fiber blending. The insertion of M. ZMAJ was consistently such that the inferior border of the muscle was superior to the angle of the mouth. The insertion of the levator muscle group, on a superficial level, demonstrated an abrupt edge, almost as if it were a flap over the superior portion of M. Orbicularis Oris, and its insertion was always observed to be immediately juxtaposed to the lateral border of the nasal ala at the level of the inferior border of the ala. The fascia over M. Masseter was consistent in that it usually extended inferiorly to a point level with, or just superior to, the angle of the mouth. M. LLSAN and M. ZMIN joined at their insertion to the upper lip to obscure superficially the insertion of M. LLS.

6. The Presence of Discrepancies between Observations and Text Descriptions

The observations of this study disclosed some items which differed slightly from their typical descriptions in anatomy texts. M. LAO and M. DAO, rather than appearing as two, distinctly separate structural entities, were seen basically as one unit; i.e., there was extensive sharing of their muscle fiber bundles. M. DAO, contrary to many textual descriptions, usually curved anteriorly just superior to the farthest extent of its origin. In contradiction to many texts, no superficial muscles were observed inserting directly lateral to the angle of the mouth; the insertions in this area were either superior or inferior to the angle of the mouth. M. LLS was usually observed on a deeper plane than M. LLSAN and M. ZMIN. The latter two muscles coursed in such a manner that they completely covered M. LLS at their point of insertion.

VI. EMPIRICAL VALIDATION OF ELECTRODE PLACEMENTS RECOMMENDED FOR THE PERIORAL MUSCLES (STUDY 3)

In the last 10 years a number of studies have been published which attempt to specify the function of the facial muscles during speech production through the use of electromyography (Basmajian, 1967). One of the significant limitations of these studies appears to be the validity of the electrode placements utilized to sample the perioral muscle activity. In many of these studies specification of electrode placement sites was not delineated, leaving some doubt as to the criteria which the authors may have employed to determine that they were indeed sampling from the muscle or muscles intended. In other cases in which placement descriptions were specified, the placement descriptions are often sufficiently ambiguous so as to make replication impossible. Because of these difficulties, the purpose of the present experiment was to attempt to verify the validity of electrode placement by simulating placement in the perioral muscles of our cadaveric specimens, utilizing the placements which have been described in the perioral physiology research literature.

Perhaps the most specific descriptions of perioral muscle electrode placements have been provided by Sussman *et al.* (1973) and Isley and Basmajian (1973). The descriptions given by these authors are provided in Table I. As can be noted, while these specifications are useful, they are ambiguous in terms of electrode placement specification.

A. Method

To evaluate the electrode placements suggested by Isley and Basmajian (1973) and Sussman *et al.* (1973), surrogate electrodes were placed in five specimens according to the specifications provided in Table I. The placements of Isley and Basmajian (1973) were used on the left side of the cadaver, while those of Sussman *et al.* (1973) were used on the right. The evaluation of these electrode placements was accomplished in five stages, as shown in Fig. 21: (1) a .635-mm-diameter chrome-plated brass wire bent in a configuration simulating a hooked wire electrode was inserted into the barrel of an 18-gauge hypodermic needle; (2) the needle was inserted as advocated by Isley and Basmajian (1973) or Sussman *et al.* (1973) (depending upon the side of the cadaver being utilized); (3) the hypodermic needle was then removed, leaving the surrogate electrode intact at the electrode position; (4) the surrogate electrode was then clipped off flush with the outer dermal layer; and (5) the actual position of the surrogate electrode with respect to the target muscle was ascertained during the process of dissection.

B. Results and Discussion

The electrode placement sites advocated by Isley and Basmajian (1973) generally were found to be inadequate. Regarding placements in M. Levator Labii Superioris Alaeque Nasi (LLSAN), M. Depressor Anguli Oris (DAO), and M. Mentalis (MENT), none of the surrogate electrodes was found to be in the target muscle. The placements suggested by Isley and Basmajian for M. Orbicularis Oris (OO), M. Levator Anguli Oris

Table I. Suggested Electromyographic Placements To Be Evaluated

Muscle sought	Isley & Basmajian (1973)	Sussman, MacNeilage, & Hanson (1973)
Orbicularis Oris	Inserted with a forward thrust through the mucosa, 2 cm to the right of the midline, at the level of the vermilion border	At the vermilion border, 1 cm lateral to the philtrum, at a slight angle, to a depth of 3 mm (downward angle for OOS, upward angle for OOI)
Zygomaticus Minor		
Levator Labii Superioris		The concavity that develops lateral to the nostril when snarling, in a direct upward direction to a depth of 1 cm
Levator Labii Superioris Alaeque Nasi	Inserted just left of the nose in the belly of the muscle	
Zygomaticus Major	Inserted into the middle of its belly through the skin of the left cheek	
Levator Anguli Oris	Inserted through the mucosa, 1/2 inch vertically upward opposite the gum of the right upper canine tooth, at an angle slightly forward	
Depressor Anguli Oris	Inserted through the skin on the left side, in the middle of the belly of the muscle	1/4 inch lateral to the lateral margin of the vermilion border 3/8 inch below the level of apposition of the lips, downward and inward at 30°, 7 mm deep
Depressor Labii Inferior	Inserted through the mucosa next to the root of the left lateral incisor, 2 cm from the midline	In the slight concavity which appears with the lip lowered in the region of the central fatty area of the tissue of the chin, downward and lateral 45°, to a depth of 7 mm
Mentalis	Inserted 1 cm to the right of the midline, 1.5 cm from the mandible	The superficial surface of the chin opposite the superior margin of the area in which tissue of the chin arises directly from the anterior surface of the mandible, downward and inward at 45°, 7 mm deep
Buccinator	Through the mucosa at the level of the corner of the mouth opposite the first molar tooth, thrust posteriorly to end opposite the second molar tooth	

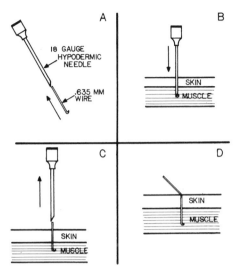

Figure 21. A schematic illustration of the technique employed to position the surrogate EMG electrodes: (A) a .635-mm-diameter wire is bent to simulate a hooked wire; (B) the needle is placed in the specified position; (C) the needle is removed, leaving the surrogate electrode intact; and (D) the surrogate electrode is clipped off flush with the dermal layer to facilitate removal of the skin.

(LAO), and M. Depressor Labii Inferior (DLI) were found to be appropriate. The placement for the inferior portion of M. OO was especially clear.

The electrode placements suggested by Sussman *et al.* (1973) also were unsuccessful in part. The placements for the muscles of the levator group (M. LLSAN, M. LLS, M. ZMIN, and M. ZMAJ), M. DLI, and M. MENT were unsuccessful. We did, however, have success in placing electrodes (using the specifications of Sussman *et al.*) in M. OO and M. DAO.

In the context of the lack of verification of electrode placements as suggested by these authors, it should be noted that the use of cadaveric material for this evaluation has some inherent limitations. For example, palpation of fixed tissue without some reference to active facial gestures is less than optimal and may hinder placement success. However, despite this limitation, it was found that many of the placement descriptions were too ambiguous for replication, especially Isley and Basmajian's placements for M. LLSAN, M. ZMAJ, M. DAO, and M. MENT.

C. Summary

While the surrogate electrode placements (as specified by previous authors) were discouraging in relation to the use of electromyography for observation of the perioral muscles, it would appear that the greatest difficulty is the paucity of specification concerning electrode placement criteria. That is, it would appear possible to develop adequate electrode placements for observation of the perioral muscles if authors involved in making such observations would critically evaluate and accurately specify those placement positions in a manner similar to that required for all aspects of scientific methodology. Certainly the specifications of Sussman *et al.* (1973) and Isley and Basmajian (1973) are a worthwhile exception to the general practice of not providing specifications. However, as an impetus to develop a standardized set of specifications for electrode placements in the perioral muscles, Section VII of this paper outlines electrode placements for the perioral muscles based upon the results of Studies 1 through 3.

VII. A SET OF PRELIMINARY SPECIFICATIONS FOR ELECTRODE PLACEMENTS IN THE PERIORAL MUSCLES

Based upon the graphic observations and the numerical measurements of the facial muscle topology in Studies 1 and 2, and the results of the surrogate electrode placement in Study 3, we have generated some initial specifications for placement of electrodes in selected perioral muscles. In the case of each muscle, we attempted to specify electrode placements which resulted in: (1) placement of the electrode in the center of the muscle (thereby providing some margin for error and minimizing the likelihood of a complete miss), and (2) the lowest possible probability of sampling from two interweaving muscles simultaneously. However, despite the considerable care that was taken in generating these placement specifications, it is likely that in some subjects, for some muscles, they will be inadequate. For that reason, we view these specifications as a basis for additional methodological experiments, both with cadaveric specimens and in the context of *in vivo* studies of the perioral system. Hopefully, as a result of these additional experiments, additional specifications can be developed which will better achieve the purpose of recording, without ambiguity, from the perioral muscles. It should be noted that the electrode placement specifications given incorporate absolute distances and angles derived from a population mainly composed of adult caucasian males.

Application to individuals who vary considerably in facial size from adult males will require the use of appropriate scale factors.

A. M. Orbicularis Oris (OO)

1. Placement Specification

Placement was lateral one-half the distance from the midline to the lateral border of the nasal alae, at an angle of 30° (downward for the superior portion, upward for the inferior portion), through the vermilion border, to a depth of 3.5 mm (Fig. 22).

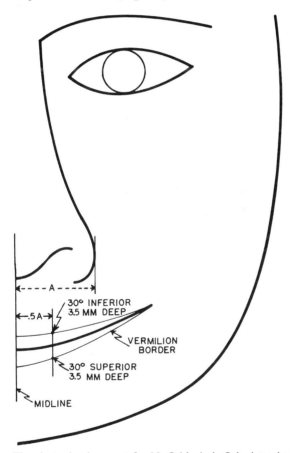

Figure 22. The electrode placement for M. Orbicularis Oris: lateral one-half the distance from the midline of the lateral border of the nasal alae, at an angle of 30° (downward for the superior portion, upward for the inferior portion), through the vermilion border, to a depth of 3 mm.

2. Placement Derivation

a. Horizontal and Vertical Positioning. In sagittal section, M. OO was often observed to present a teardrop profile (Fig. 23) which was widest at the level of the vermilion border. This observation led to the vertical positioning of the electrode at this area of the muscle. The horizontal positioning was based on the observation that no other muscles inserted in the area directly inferior to the nose. The placement of one-half the distance between the midline and the lateral border of the nasal alae positions the electrode in this area which is relatively clear of muscle insertions.

b. Insertion Angle. The teardrop profile of both the inferior and superior portions of M. OO was utilized in specifying the insertion angle of 30° (inferior for the superior portion, and superior for the inferior portion). The angle is designed to position the electrode in the widest portion of the teardrop and to direct the electrode away from the portion of the muscle in which other muscle insertions occur. Inserting the electrode in this angle also functions to increase the effective muscle thickness (since an insertion perpendicular to the muscle's longitudinal axis would have the least effective muscle thickness) and thereby increase the range of acceptable insertion depths.

c. Insertion Depth. Since no adipose tissue layer was found superficial to either the inferior or superior portions of M. OO (with the measured

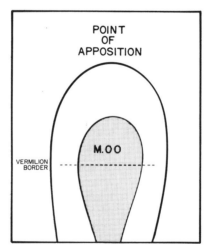

Figure 23. A schematic representation of a midsagittal view of the lip showing the teardrop shape of M. Orbicularis Oris.

average depth of the dermal layers of 2.7 and 2.6 mm, respectively), an insertion depth of 3.5 mm is advocated. It should be noted, however, that the dermal layer over the inferior portion was highly variable (with a standard deviation which equaled 38% of the mean measurement value) and may require, in some subjects, a deeper electrode insertion.

B. M. Levator Labii Superioris (LLS)

1. Placement Specification

Placement was 8 mm lateral to the lateral border of the nasal alae, superior 15 mm from the inferior border of the alae, superiorly at an angle of 30°, to a depth of 8 mm (Fig. 24).

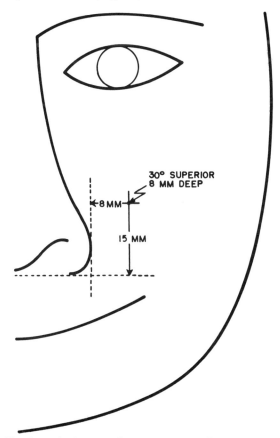

Figure 24. The electrode placement for M. Levator Labii Superioris: 8 mm lateral to the lateral border of the nasal alae, superior 15 mm from the interior border of the alae, superiorly at an angle of 30°, to a depth of 8 mm.

2. Placement Derivation

a. Horizontal and Vertical Positioning. M. LLS was observed to be superficially covered by M. Levator Labii Superioris Alaeque Nasi (LLSAN) and M. Zygomaticus Minor (ZMIN) at its insertion into the superior portion of M. OO (Fig. 25). This superficial covering extended 10 mm superiorly from the inferior border of the nasal alae, while the length of M. LLS, from the inferior border of the nasal alae to the farthest extent of the origin, averaged 24 mm. From these measurements and observations, a vertical position of 15 mm superior to the inferior border of the nasal alae was derived to situate the electrode placement superior to the overlap of M. LLSAN and M. ZMIN, yet inferior to its superior terminus.

M. LLS was observed to be the center head of the levator muscle group. This muscle's insertion had an average width of 16 mm when measured from the lateral border of the nasal alae. From this information, the horizontal component of the electrode insertion position of M. LLS was suggested to be 8 mm lateral to the lateral border of the nasal alae, thus centering the electrode in the muscle.

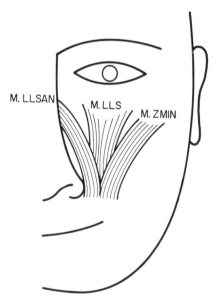

Figure 25. A schematic representation of the insertion of M. Levator Labii Superioris demonstrating the overlap of the insertion of M. Levator Labii Superioris by M. Levator Labii Superioris Alaeque Nasi and M. Zygomaticus Minor.

b. Insertion Angle. An angle of 30° superior was specified to decrease the possibility of inserting the electrode into either M. LLSAN or M. ZMIN. This insertion angle was also designed to avoid the inferior orbital portion of M. Orbicularis Oculi which was often observed to superficially cover the origin of M. LLS.

c. Insertion Depth. An average dermal thickness measure of 2 mm, coupled with an average adipose layer thickness of 5 mm, led to the suggestion of 8 mm as the electrode insertion depth to center the electrode in M. LLS.

C. M. Levator Labii Superioris Alaeque Nasi (LLSAN)

1. Placement Specification

Placement was 3 mm lateral to the lateral border of the nasal alae, superior 10 mm from the inferior border of the alae, superior at an angle of 30° and medial at an angle of 10°, to a depth of 8 mm (Fig. 26).

2. Placement Derivation

a. Horizontal and Vertical Positioning. A horizontal electrode insertion position of 3 mm lateral to the lateral border of the nasal alae was suggested for M. LLSAN, after considering the average muscle width of 5.8 mm when measured lateral to the lateral border of the nasal alae at a distance 10 mm superior to the inferior border of the nasal alae. The muscle width measurement displayed relatively high variability, however (with a standard deviation equaling 36% of the mean muscle measurement), which may, in some cases, require a horizontal position of 2 mm lateral to center the electrode in the muscle. The vertical insertion position of 10 mm was derived from observations of the superior and medial course of the muscle and because of the fact that the muscle width measurements of Study 2 were made at this level.

b. Insertion Angle. An insertion angle of 30° superior and 10° medial is suggested in order to position the electrode parallel to the superior and medial course of the muscle fiber bundles. This insertion angle also serves to avoid M. LLS which is situated on the lateral border of M. LLSAN.

c. Insertion Depth. An insertion depth of 8 mm is suggested in order to penetrate the fat pad of this region (which averaged 5 mm in thickness) and the dermal layer (which averaged 2 mm in thickness).

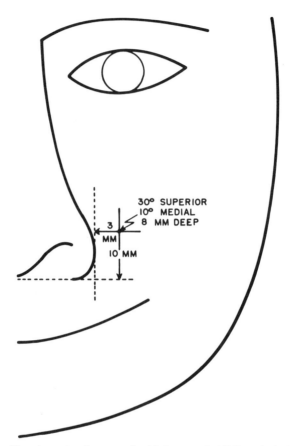

Figure 26. The electrode placement for M. Levator Labii Superioris Alaeque Nasi: 3 mm lateral to the lateral border of the nasal alae, superior 10 mm from the inferior border of the alae, superior at an angle of 30° and medial at an angle of 10°, to a depth of 8 mm.

D. M. Levator Anguli Oris (LAO)

1. Placement Specification

Placement was 20 mm lateral to the lateral border of the nasal ala, 20 mm superior to the level of the apposition of the lips, superiorly at an angle of 30°, to a depth of 8 mm (Fig. 27).

2. Placement Derivation

a. Horizontal and Vertical Positioning. M. LAO was consistently (with a standard deviation equaling only 5% of the average muscle measurement value) observed to have its lateral border averaging 25 mm

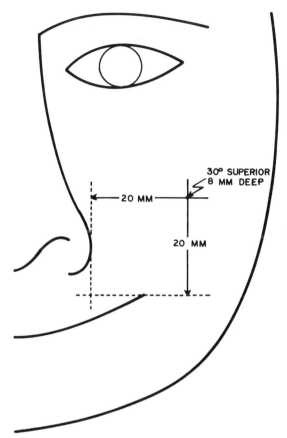

Figure 27.   The electrode placement for M. Levator Anguli Oris: 20 mm lateral to the lateral border of the nasal alae, 20 mm superior to the level of the apposition of the lips, superiorly at an angle of 30°, to a depth of 8 mm.

lateral to the lateral border of the nasal alae. The width of M. LAO at its insertion averaged 8 mm. From these observations, a horizontal position 20 mm lateral to the lateral border of the nasal alae was specified in order to remain medial to the lateral border of the muscle, yet within the muscle's border.

M. LAO averaged 18.5 mm in length when measured from the farthest extent of its origin to its insertion in the supeior portion of M. OO. The distance from the level of the apposition of the lips and the farthest extent of the origin of M. LAO averaged 34.3 mm. The vertical component of the electrode insertion position was specified from these observations at 20 mm superior to the level of the apposition of the lips to place the electrode in the center of the muscle, superior to its insertion into the upper lip, yet inferior to the farthest extent of its origin.

b. Insertion Angle. An angle of electrode insertion of 30° in a superior orientation was suggested to avoid the superior fibers of M. OO and M. Buccinator. The angle also served to increase the effective muscle thickness.

c. Insertion Depth. An insertion depth of 8 mm was suggested in consideration of the dermal thickness (which averaged 2 mm) and the thickness of the adipose layer in this region (which averaged 5 mm). It should be noted that an internal insertion (through the mucosa) would require less electrode penetration depth than the advocated external insertion (through the dermis), yet an internal electrode insertion poses two significant problems (both in regard to the electrode wires) which makes it less useful: (1) the wires could interfere with the labial movements and hence produce unwanted movement artifacts; and (2) the wires could be dislodged or broken by labial movements.

E. M. Depressor Anguli Oris (DAO)

1. Placement Specification

Placement was 7 mm medial to the inner angle of the mouth, inferior one-half the distance from the level of the apposition of the lips to the inferior border of the chin, to a depth of 4 mm (Fig. 28).

2. Placement Derivation

a. Horizontal and Vertical Positioning. M. DAO was frequently observed to course in an anterior direction just superior to its origin. This observation, along with the observation that M. Risorius inserted along its posterior border, led to a specification of the horizontal insertion position of 7 mm medial to the angle of the mouth, thus centering the electrode along the anterior border of the muscle.

The vertical component of the electrode insertion position was derived from the observation that the origin and insertion of M. DAO had extensive fiber blending with M. Platysma inferiorly and the tendinous node superiorly. The insertion position was suggested to be one-half the distance between these extreme points of the muscle to avoid this area of fiber blending.

b. Insertion Depth. No adipose layer was observed on a plane super-

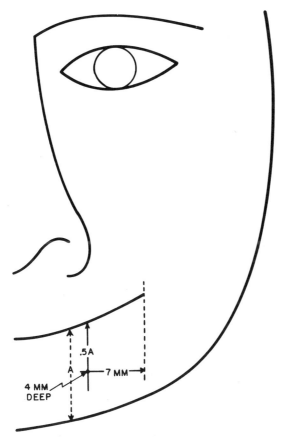

Figure 28. The electrode placement for M. Depressor Anguli Oris: 7 mm medial to the inner angle of the mouth, inferior one-half the distance from the level of the apposition of the lips to the inferior border of the chin, to a depth of 4 mm.

ficial to M. DAO. The dermal layer over M. DAO had an average thickness of 2 mm. From these observations an insertion depth of 4 mm was suggested in order to bypass the dermal layer and center the electrode in the muscle.

F. M. Depressor Labii Inferior (DLI)

1. Placement Specification

Placement was 15 mm medial to the inner angle of the mouth, inferior one-half the distance from the apposition of the lips to the inferior border of the chin, to a depth of 4 mm (Fig. 29).

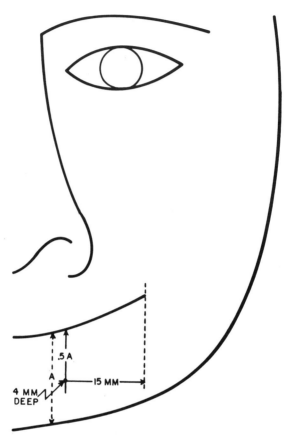

Figure 29. The electrode placement for M. Depressor Labii Inferior: 15 mm medial to the inner angle of the mouth, inferior one-half the distance from the apposition of the lips to the inferior border of the chin, to a depth of 4 mm.

2. Placement Derivation

a. Horizontal and Vertical Positioning. The horizontal electrode insertion position was suggested to be 15 mm medial to the angle of the mouth to avoid the anterior border of M. DAO. The vertical position of one-half the distance from the level of the apposition of the lips to the inferior border of the chin was set in order to avoid the fiber blending of the inferior portion of M. OO at M. DLI's insertion, and the fiber blending of M. Platysma at M. DLI's origin.

b. Insertion Depth. The insertion depth of 4 mm was derived from observations concerning the lack of an adipose layer in this area superficial to M. DLI, and by considering the dermal thickness which averaged 2 mm.

VIII. CONCLUSIONS

This chapter (1) provides descriptive information concerning the perioral musculature, (2) presents results from evaluations of electromyographic electrode placements utilizing cadaveric material, and (3) suggests preliminary specifications for electrode placements in the perioral muscles. Considering this, the many specific conclusions that might be drawn from this study depend largely upon the experimental intent and design of other investigators who might use this information. However, a number of conclusions are of general interest.

A. Conclusions from Studies 1 and 2

The descriptive material provided by Studies 1 and 2 takes the form of (1) graphic descriptions of the muscle systems of nine cadavers, and (2) measurements of muscle widths, lengths, and angular orientations taken from the muscle systems, along with considerations of the adipose thickness and dermal layer thickness in the perioral region from a major group of 11 specimens.

The system measurements quantitatively demonstrated that the perioral system has high degrees of intersubject variability. Regarding facial width measures, the width of the area between the borders of M. Zygomaticus Minor and M. Zygomaticus Major (ZMAJ) (Measure G, Fig. 15) was the most variable (with a standard deviation which equaled 55% of the mean measure value), while the width of the superior portion of M. Orbicularis Oris (OO) (Measure A, Fig. 14) was the least variable (with a standard deviation equaling only 16% of the mean measurement value). The oral opening length (Measure B, Fig. 14) was the most variable length observed, while the least variable length measure was taken from M. ZMAJ (Measure M, Fig. 16). Angular measures ranged in variability from a standard deviation equaling 102% of the mean value for the angle of the midline of M. ZMAJ to a standard deviation equaling 10% of the mean value for the angle of the anterior border of M. Depressor Anguli Oris (DAO). The thickness of the facial adipose layer was found to be quite variable (ranging from no adipose pad to an adipose pad 21 mm thick), yet it demonstrated consistency in its border locations. The dermal layer varied in thickness from 4 to 1 mm. The thickest and most variable layer was located over the inferior portion of M. OO, while the least variable

and thinnest dermal layer was observed over M. Levator Labii Superioris
(LLS). The descriptive information also led to a number of general observations which were apparently contradicted information contained in
some textual descriptions, particularly with respect to the interrelationship between M. Levator Anguli Oris (LAO) and M. Depressor Anguli
Oris (DAO), the shape of M. DAO, the presence of oral angle muscle
insertions, and the insertion of M. LLS.

B. Conclusions from Study 3

The evaluative technique described in Study 3 utilized surrogate electrodes to verify electromyographic electrode placement postions. The
surrogate electrodes were injected into cadaveric material and provided
placement position evaluation when dissection revealed the true electrode
position with respect to the target position. An application of this technique led to the conclusion that the electrode placement positions utilized
by Isley and Basmajian (1973) and Sussman *et al.* (1973) generally were
inaccurate when applied to the cadaveric specimens of this study.

A final utilization of the descriptive information derived in Studies 1 and
2 and the evaluation information provided in Study 3 led to the specification of new electrode placement positions for M. Levator Labii
Superioris, M. Levator Labii Superioris Alaeque Nasi, M. Levator Anguli
Oris, M. Orbicularis Oris (both superior and inferior portions), M. Depressor Anguli Oris, and M. Depressor Labii Inferior.

In summary, we should like to point out that the intent of this research
was not only to provide descriptive data on each of the isolated muscles of
the perioral region. A major secondary purpose was to emphasize the
complexity of perioral musculature in relation to its possible role in
speech. Clearly from these data it is apparent that the perioral region is a
unique muscular system in that its subcomponents are so intimately
interconnected that isolated muscle function can be described only with
extreme caution, if at all.

Figure B-1. A schematic illustration delineating the measures taken prior to dissection.
A_1, The width of the eye; B_1, length of the nose from the base of the nasal ala to the inner
angle of the eye; C_1, the width of the nose between the lateral borders of both nasal alae; D_1,
the width of the upper lip from the apposition of the lips to the base of the nose; E_1, the width
of the mouth from the inner angle, bilaterally; F_1, the width of the chin from the apposition of
the lips to the inferior border of the chin; G_1, the width of the face from the lateral border of
the nasal alae to the anterior and inferior most edge of the ear lobe.

APPENDIX A: SPECIMEN SPECIFICATIONS

Table A. Specimen Specifications

Specimen number	Age	Sex	Cause of death
1	75	F	Cardiopulmonary failure; metastatic CA; lungs, liver, cervic uterus
2	58	M	CA
3	64	M	Myocardial infarction
4	75	M	CA of the colon
5	88	M	Multiple myeloma
6	56	M	Acute myocardial infarction; coronary arterial thrombosis; probable atherosclerosis, coronary arteries
7	86	M	Unknown: possible CA, infections spondylitis thoracic spine
8	92	M	Pneumonia recurrent
9		Not available	
10		Not available	
11		Not available	

APPENDIX B: SURFACE LANDMARK MEASURES

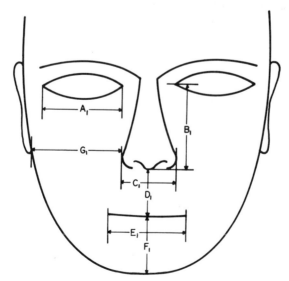

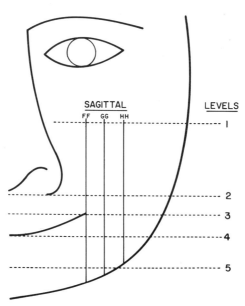

Figure B-2. Showing the positions at which adipose thickness measures were taken, each position indicated by the intersection of the solid vertical lines (labeled measures) and the dotted horizontal lines (labeled levels). (FF) From the medial surface of the dermal layer to the superficial surface of the underlying tissue lying along a line directed superior and inferior to the angle of the mouth; (GG) from the medial surface of the dermal layer of the superficial surface of M. Buccinator; (HH) from the medial surface of the dermal layer to the superficial surface of M. Masseter. Measurement levels: (1) midway between the angle of the eye and the border of the nasal alae; (2) at the inferior border of the nasal alae; (3) midway between the inferior border of the alae and the level of the apposition of the lips; (4) at the level of the apposition of the lips; (5) midway between the level of apposition of the lips and the inferior border of the chin.

APPENDIX C: Tabulated Results

Table C-I. Preliminary Measures A_1 through G_1 Taken before Dissections for Specimens 1 through 8[a]

Subject number	Measurements						
	A_1	B_1	C_1	D_1	E_1	F_1	G_1
1	30	40	37	24	48	33	111
2	42	45	35	24	55	46	124
3	35	39	40	22	60	45	122
4	32	46	40	23	43	50	107
5	36	42	43	28	55	43	125
6	40	44	47	20	60	42	125
7	50	42	43	26	60	60	142
8	40	42	46	22	55	50	135
N	8	8	8	8	8	8	8
$\bar{X}$	38.13	42.5	41.38	23.63	54.5	46.13	124.0
SD	5.93	2.24	3.90	2.34	5.77	7.27	10.67

[a] In millimeters.

Table C-II. Adipose Tissue Thickness Measures Taken over Points FF, GG, and HH, at Levels 1 through 5, for Specimens 10 and 11[a]

Section level	Measurement					
	FF		GG		HH	
	S 10	S 11	S 10	S 11	S 10	S 11
1	5	5	2	5	5	5
2	11	5	16	10	5	9
3	8		21		9	
4	5	4	11	13	0	0
5	7	5	9	2	2	0
N	5	4	5	4	5	4
$\bar{X}$	7.2	4.7	11.8	7.5	4.2	3.5
SD	2.23	.433	6.43	4.27	3.06	3.77

[a] In millimeters (see Fig. B-2).

Table C-III. Postdissection Measures[a]

Subject number	Length, width, and angular measures																						
	A	B	C	D	E	F	G	H	I	J	K	L	M	N	O	P	Q	R	S	T	U	V	W
1 R	20	27		22	4	6	13	26	43	2	6	7	47	25					6		12	65	75
L	17	32	2	20	8	11		22	55	30	5	6	43	45					6	22	14	70	65
2 R	19	40		20	11	16	7	25	42	20													
L	24	40		18	9	22	0	25	45	42			41	29					12	21			
3 R	22	25	6	15	10	20	0	32	47	10	11	20	42	32					17		24	50	40
L	22	32	6	10		17					12	20	47	28					16	20	17	55	30
4 R	19	18	3	12		13	20		60	49	16	5							13	21	10	60	90
L	18	22		11	5	11	19		62	10	5	3	67						12	25			
5 R	25	32	6	10	5	15	12				3	6	52	35					12	36	15	58	90
L	14	30	3	11	6	20	25			10	6	6	52	50					10	16	14	60	90
6 R	21	33	6	12	7	19	6	22	40	10	4	15	44	35	26	35	12	5	14	21			
L	22	26	10	22	6	18	9	30	50	10	10	15	45	25	25	37	16	10	13	16			
7 R	23	35	6	21	3	22	17	24	40	5	8	12	41	35	26	31	10	12	23	21			
L	23	35	8	15	4	16	20	25	40	5	8	12	45	41	24	35	13	14	19	21			
8 R	18	39	5	17	5	16	18	22	55	10	7	10	47	40	28	29	30	5	15	22	16	70	90
L	21	26	9	7	4	19	12	21	44	-10	7	10	40	37	25	39	30	5	18	21	13	70	90
9 R	28	30	4	11	4	13	17	20	42	15	8	14	50	35					19	19	10	68	70
L	26	28	7	13		15	10	23			7	23	46	30					22		12	63	25
N	18	18	15	18	15	16	16	13	14	15	16	16	16	15	6	6	6	6	17	14	11	11	11
$\bar{X}$	21	31	6	15	6	16	13	24	48	15	8	12	47	35	26	34	19	9	15	22	14	63	69
SD	3.3	5.9	2.1	4.6	2.4	4.1	7.0	3.3	7.3	15	3.1	5.8	6.3	6.9	1.2	3.4	8.3	3.7	4.7	4.6	3.7	6.6	24

[a] In millimeters or degrees. An unfilled section indicates that the measurement was omitted because of tissue removal or tissue border modification. Measures J, N, V, and W are calculated in degrees.

Table C-IV. Postdissection Measures[a]

Subject number		Muscle and dermal thickness[b]							
		X	Y	Z	AA	BB	CC	DD	EE
1	1 cm	3		1	1	1	2	3	2
	verm	3							
2	1 cm	0	2	3	2	2	1	1	2
	verm	4	2						
3	1 cm	4	9	4	2	3		2	2
	verm	4	7						
4	1 cm	2	2	1					
	verm	2	2						
5	1 cm	6	3	2	3	3	2	2	2
	verm	4	2						
6	1 cm	4	5	2	2	2	2	4	
	verm	4	3						
7	1 cm	5	3	3	2	2	2	4	3
	verm	6	3						
8	1 cm	3	7	3	2	2	2	3	3
	verm	1	5						
9	1 cm	6	8	2					
	verm		4						
N	1 cm	9	8	9	7	7	6	7	7
	verm	8	8						
$\bar{X}$	1 cm	3.7	4.9	2.3	2.0	2.1	2.1	2.7	2.6
	verm	3.5	3.5						
SD	1 cm	1.8	2.6	.92	.53	.63	.37	1.0	.72
	verm	1.4	1.6						

[a] In millimeters. An unfilled section indicates that the measurement was omitted because of tissue removal or tissue border modification.

[b] X and Y: thickness measures taken from M. Orbicularis Oris Inferior (measure X) and M. Orbicularis Oris Superior (measure Y); 1 cm = a measure taken 1 cm from the vermilion border; verm = a measure taken at the vermilion border. Z: the thickness of M. Zygomaticus Major measured at the longitudinal midpoint of the muscle. AA through EE: the thickness of the dermal layer taken over selected muscles (see Fig. 19).

Acknowledgments

The authors would like to express their gratitude to Dr. Herbert Kashiwa of the Department of Biological Structure of the University of Washington for his expert advice and direction, to Dr. Daniel Graney of the Department of Biological Structure of the University of Washington for his expert assistance, and to the University of Washington Dental School Class of 1976 for their ready assistance and tolerance. This research was supported in part by Research Program Projects NS-11780-02 and NS-13274.

References

Abbs, J. H. Some mechanical properties of lower lip movement during speech production. *Phonetica*, 1973, *23*, 65–75.

Abbs, J. H. & Eilenberg, G. R. Peripheral mechanisms of speech motor control. In N. J. Lass (Ed.), *Contemporary issues in experimental phonetics.* New York: Academic Press, 1976.

Abbs, J., Folkins, J., & Sivarajan, M. Motor impairment following blockade of the infraorbital nerve: Implications for the use of anesthetization techniques in speech research. *Journal of Speech and Hearing Research,* 1976, 19, 19–35.

Abbs, J. H., & Gilbert, B. N. A two dimensional strain gage transducer for the lips and the jaw: Design criteria and calibration data. *Journal of Speech and Hearing Research,* 1973, *16,* 248–256.

Abbs, J. H., & Netsell, R. An interpretation of jaw acceleration during speech as a muscle forcing function. *Journal of Speech and Hearing Research,* 1973, 16, 412–425.

Aidley, D. J. *The physiology of excitable cells.* London and New York: Cambridge University Press, 1971.

Allen, A. C. *The skin: A clinicopathological treatise.* New York: Grune & Stratton, 1967.

Basmajian, J. B. *Muscles alive: Their functions revealed by electromyography.* Baltimore: Williams & Wilkins, 1967.

Bateman, H. *A clinical approach to speech anatomy and physiology.* Springfield, Ill.: Thomas, 1977.

Baumel, J. J. Trigeminal-facial nerve communications: Their function in facial muscle innervation and reinnervation. *Archives of Otolaryngology,* 1974, *19,* 34–44.

Conley, J. J. Accessory neuromotor pathways to the face. *Transactions of the American Academy of Ophthalmology and Otolaryngology,* 1964, *68,* 1064–1067.

Conley, J., Papper, E., & Kaplan, N. Spontaneous return and facial nerve grafting: Trigeminal nerve significance. *Archives of Otolaryngology,* 1963, *77,* 643–649.

Cooker, H. S. *The kinetics of the lower lip and its control at maximum speech rates.* Paper presented at the annual convention of the American Speech and Hearing Association, Las Vegas, November 1974.

Dickson, D. R., & Maue, W. M. *Human vocal anatomy.* Springfield, Ill.: Thomas, 1970.

Diehl, C. F. *Introduction to the anatomy and physiology of the speech mechanism.* Springfield, Ill.: Thomas, 1968.

Folkins, J. W. *Multidimensional lower lip displacement resulting from activation of individual labial muscles: Development of a static model.* Unpublished doctoral dissertation, University of Washington, 1976.

Folkins, J. W., & Abbs, J. H. Lip and jaw motor control during speech: Responses to resistive loading of the jaw. *Journal of Speech and Hearing Research,* 1975, *18,* 207–220.

Folkins, J., Kennedy, III, J., & Loncarich, P. Standardization of lip muscle nomenclature. *Journal of Speech and Hearing Research,* 1978.

Gandiglio, G., & Fra, L. Further observations on facial reflexes. *Journal of Neurological Science,* 1967, *5,* 273–285.

Gardiner, E., Gray, D., & O'Rahilly, R. *Anatomy—A regional study of human structure.* Philadelphia: Saunders, 1963.

Gay, T., & Hirose, H. Effect of speaking rate on labial consonant production. *Phonetica,* 1973, *27,* 44–56.

Gay, T., Ushijima, T., Hirose, H., & Cooper, F. Effect of speaking rate on labial consonant articulation. *Journal of Phonetics,* 1974, *2,* 47–63.

Gottlieb, G. L., & Agarwal, G. C. Dynamic relationship between isometric muscle tension and the electromyogram in man. *Journal of Applied Physiology,* 1971, *30,* 345–351.

Gray, H. *Anatomy of the human body* (27th ed.). Philadelphia: Lea & Febiger, 1959.

Hollinshead, W. H. *Anatomy for surgeons* (Vol. 1): *The head and neck.* New York: Harper (Hoeber), 1961.

Hosokawa, H. Proprioceptive innervation of striated muscles in the territory of cranial nerves. *Texas Reports on Biology and Medicine*, 1961, *19*, 405–464.

Isley, C. L., & Basmajian, J. V. Electromyography of the human cheeks and lips. *Anatomical Record*, 1973, *176*, 145–148.

Israel, H. Age factor and the pattern of change of craniofacial structures. *American Journal of Physical Anthropology*, 1973, *39*, 11–128.

Kennedy III, J. G. *Conpensatory responses of the labial musculature to unanticipated disruption of articulation.* Unpublished doctoral dissertation, University of Washington, 1977.

Kugelberg, E. Facial reflexes. *Brain*, 1952, *75*, 385–396.

Larson, C. R., Folkins, J. W., McClean, M., & Müller, E. *Sensitivity of the human perioral reflex to parameters of mechanical stretch.* Unpublished manuscript, University of Washington, 1977.

Laurenson, R. D. *An introduction to clinical anatomy by dissection of the human body.* Philadelphia: Saunders, 1968.

Leanderson, R. *On the functional organization of facial muscles in speech.* Stockholm: Karolinska Sjukhuset, 1972.

Leanderson, R., Persson, A., & Öhman, S. Electromyographic studies of facial muscle activity in speech. *Acta Otolaryngologica*, 1971, *72*, 361–369.

Lightoller, G. H. S. Facial muscles: The modiolus and muscles surrounding the rima oris with some remarks about the panniculus adiposus. *Journal of Anatomy*, 1925, *60*, 1–85.

Lindquist, C., & Martensson, A. The possible role of exeroceptors in the control of facial muscles. *Acta Physiologica Scandinavica, Supplementum*, 1969, *330*, 116.

Martin, H., & Helsper, J. Spontaneous return of function following surgical section or excision of the seventh cranial nerve in the surgery of parotid tumors. *Annals of Surgery*, 1957, *146*, 715–727.

Martin H., & Helsper, J. Supplementary report on spontaneous return of function following surgical section or excision of the seventh cranial nerve in the surgery of parotid tumors. *Annals of Surgery*, 1960, *151*, 538–541.

Martone, A. L. Anatomy of facial expression and its prosthodontic significance. *Journal of Prosthetic Dentistry*, 1962, 1020–1042.

Martone, A. L., & Edwards, L. F. Anatomy of the mouth and related structures. *Journal of Prosthetic Dentistry*, 1962, *12*, 4–27.

Mendelsohn, S. *Embalming fluids.* New York: Chemical Publ. Co., 1940.

Müller, E. *Biomechanics of lip movement for speech production.* Unpublished manuscripts, University of Washington, Speech Physiology Laboratory, 1975.

Müller, E. M., Abbs, J. H., Kennedy III, J. G., & Larson, C. R. *Significance of biomechanical variables in lip movements for speech.* Paper presented at the annual convention of the American Speech and Hearing Association, Chicago, November 1977.

Netsell, R., & Abbs, J. H. *The usefulness of eye, lip, and jaw reflexes in the study of speech production.* Paper presented at the annual meeting of the American Association of Phonetic Sciences, Detroit, October 1973.

Palmer, J. M. *Anatomy for speech and hearing.* New York: Harper, 1972.

Polson, C. J., Brittain, R. P., & Marshall, T. K. *The disposal of the dead.* London: English Universities Press, 1953.

Quiring, D., & Warfel, J. *The head, neck, and trunk* (2nd ed.). Philadelphia: Lea & Febiger, 1965.

Ruch, T., Patton, H., Woodbury, J., & Towe, A. *Neurophusiology.* Philadelphia: Saunders, 1966.

Schaeffer, J. P. (Ed.). *Morris' human anatomy* (11th ed.). New York: McGraw-Hill (Blakiston), 1953.

Scott, C. H., & Honet, J. C. *An electromyographic investigation of bilaterally recorded action potentials from orbicularis oris muscles in stutterers and non-stutterers.* Paper presented at the American Congress of Rehabilitation Medicine, Denver, 1972.

Scott, J. H., & Dixon, A. D. *Anatomy for students of dentistry.* London: Churchill and Edinburgh: Livingstone, 1972.

Shapiro, H. H. *Applied anatomy of the head and neck: For students and practitioners of dentistry.* Philadelphia: Lippincott, 1947.

Sicher, H. *Oral anatomy.* St. Louis: Mosby, 1965.

Sussman, H. M., MacNeilage, P. F., & Hanson, R. J. Labial and mandibular movement dynamics during the production of bilabial stop consonants. *Journal of Speech and Hearing Research,* 1973, *16*, 397–420.

Sutton, D., Larson, C., Lovell, M., & Lindeman, R. Facial muscle innervation in Cebis (New World) and macaque (Old World) monkeys via a remus communicating with the trigeminal nerve. *Archives of Oral Biology,* 1977, *32*, 59–64.

Tompsett, D. H. *Anatomical techniques* (2nd ed.). Edinburgh: Livingstone, 1970.

Vitti, M., Correa, A. C. F., Fortinguerra, C. R. H., Berzin, F., & Konig, B. Electromyographic study of the musculus depressor anguli oris. *Electromyography,* 1972, *12*, 119–125.

Vitti, M., Fortinguerra, C. R. H., Correa, A. C. F., Konig, B. & Berzin, F. Electromyographic behavior of the levator labii superioris alaeque nasi. *Electromyography and Clinical Neurophysiology,* 1974, *14*, 37–43.

Wells, J. B. Comparison of mechanical properties between slow and fast mammalian muscles. *Journal of Physiology (London),* 1965, *178*, 252–296.

Williams, D. E. Masseter muscle action current potentials in stuttered and non-stuttered speech. *Journal of Speech and Hearing Disorders,* 1955, pp. 242–261.

Woodburne, R. T. *Essentials of human anatomy.* London and New York: Oxford University Press, 1969.

Zemlin, W. R. *Speech and hearing science: Anatomy and physiology.* Englewood Cliffs, N.J.: Prentice-Hall, 1968.

Acoustic Characteristics of Normal and Pathological Voices

STEVEN B. DAVIS

Signal Technology, Inc.
Santa Barbara, California

SPEECH AND LANGUAGE: Advances in Basic
Research and Practice, Vol. 1

In recent years, researchers in fields such as laryngology and speech pathology have become increasingly interested in the acoustic characteristics of normal and pathological voices (Davis, 1975, 1976a; Hiki, Imaizumi, Hirano, Matsushita, & Kakita, 1976; Murry, 1975). One reason for this trend is that acoustic methods have the potential to provide quantitative techniques for the clinical assessment of laryngeal function. The desire for an objective method for analysis of the pathological voice was expressed by the 1973 Conference on Early Detection of Laryngeal Pathology:

> The otologist and audiologist can employ standardized audiometric tests to evaluate hearing, the cardiologist has access to electrocardiograms to evaluate heart function, but the laryngologist and speech pathologist have no comparable aids that can be used in the clinical setting. (Moore, 1976, p. 276)

There are several methods currently used in laryngeal research and diagnosis, e.g., laryngoscopy, stroboscopy, thermography, electromyography, pneumotachography, glottography, and acoustic analysis. However, for routine clinical evaluation of laryngeal function (e.g., during a program of voice therapy), acoustic analysis appears to have an advantage over the other methods because of its nonintrusive nature and its potential for providing quantitative data with reasonable expenditures of analysis time.

In addition to its potential value in the clinical assessment of laryngeal function, a sensitive automatic acoustic technique could be used to screen individuals for early cases of laryngeal pathology. Moore (1973) has indicated that none of the other techniques is useful for screening and that these techniques are applied only if an individual specifically seeks aid. The development of portable instrumentation for acoustic analysis could lead to programs similar to audiometric testing in schools, industry, etc. Such instrumentation could provide substantial benefits in terms of overall health maintenance.

This chapter discusses methods for the acoustic analysis of voices affected by laryngeal pathology and procedures for determining acoustic parameters applicable to screening and to clinical assessment. These methods use digital computer techniques for voice analysis (developed originally to increase the efficiency of speech transmission systems) to extract acoustic measures of vocal function from the speech signal. A brief review provides information on some auditory and visual methods for diagnosing laryngeal pathology. Then the vocal fold movement is related to the acoustic output on which the acoustic methods are based, and the theoretical bases and results of several methods are compared, indicating the problems that require additional research. The chapter concludes with two appendixes, one formulating a theoretical basis for digital voice analysis and the other describing a FORTRAN program for extracting important acoustic parameters from the speech signal.

I. AUDITORY AND VISUAL METHODS

Historically, physicians have relied on two basic techniques in the diagnosis of pathological conditions of the larynx: (1) listening to the voice, and (2) viewing the larynx with a mirror or laryngoscope. Since laryngeal diseases are often accompanied by voice quality changes, simple listening tests sometimes give useful information. However, listening tests have been criticized for their subjectivity (i.e., even experienced laryngologists may offer different diagnoses for the same patient) and the related problem of the lack of quantitative standards.

Visual observations allow a physician to substantiate auditory evaluations. In indirect laryngoscopy, the larynx is viewed via a mirror inserted into the back of the mouth. The gross structure and movements of the vocal folds are observed; however, the amount of detail available by indirect laryngoscopy is limited because the field of view is small and the distance from the larynx is relatively long. Pathologies beneath the vocal folds frequently can be overlooked since only the superior surfaces of the larynx may be visualized from above. Also, the rapid vibratory motions of the vocal folds cannot be observed with indirect laryngoscopy. However, high-quality photographic records of the laryngeal image exposed by advanced laryngoscopes using fiberoptics have enhanced the clinical value of laryngoscopy (Gould, 1973; Sawashima & Hirose, 1968).

In direct laryngoscopy a viewing tube is inserted directly into the larynx. This technique is not used on a wide-scale basis because it is a medical procedure requiring anesthesia, it disturbs the positioning and function of the articulatory structures, and it is uncomfortable for the patient. Consequently, its application usually is confined to diagnosis and verification during the later stages of a laryngeal disease and to surgical situations (Koike, 1976).

Stroboscopic laryngoscopy combines a laryngeal mirror and a high-flash rate stroboscope to give either a stationary or slowly moving image of the vocal folds (Moore, 1938; Schönhärl, 1960; van den Berg, 1962). However, the image is a composite of many cycles of the vibration, and fine details of the individual periods cannot be observed.

The detailed movement of the vocal folds during individual periods can be seen, however, if a high-speed motion picture camera, a special light source, and a laryngeal mirror are used (Farnsworth, 1940; Koike & Takahashi, 1971). Compared to stroboscopic laryngoscopy, this high-speed technique captures all vibratory behavior in full detail. Studies based on high-speed motion pictures have demonstrated various vibratory patterns in patients with laryngeal pathology (Timcke, von Leden, & Moore, 1958, 1959; von Leden, Moore, & Timcke, 1960). In one study (Moore, 1968), high-speed motion pictures of pathological vocal folds were synchronized with acoustic recordings of the voice. Moore demonstrated complex and irregular vibratory patterns resulting in complicated changes in glottal width. He also noted the independence of each fold as a vibrator and suggested that this independence might be a cause of hoarseness. This observation was confirmed by Koike and Hirano (1973).

High-speed motion picture analysis is an important tool in basic voice and speech research, but there are several limitations for large-scale clinical applications. The most significant limitation is the time-consuming task of frame-by-frame data analysis. Even with the aid of digital computer programs designed to simplify the measurement process (Hayden & Koike, 1972; Hildebrand, 1976; Koike & Takahashi, 1971; Ramsey, 1964; Soron, 1967; Tanabe, Kitajima, Gould, & Lambiase, 1975), it is not an easy task to record the glottal widths or areas for a large number of frames. One preliminary study (Davis, 1976b) applied digital image processing to extract the glottal area information from successive picture frames automatically; however more research is needed before this method can become clinically useful. Nevertheless, the information obtained from high-speed motion pictures which are synchronized with the voice provides a basis for gaining a better understanding of the relationship between the acoustic signal and the physiological function of the larynx. Some of the parameters that can be measured from successive high-speed motion picture frames are the open quotient (OQ), which is the ratio of the open time of the glottis to the total time of one vibratory cycle, and the speed quotient (SQ), which is the ratio of the time of vocal fold abductory movement to the time of adductory movement. These parameters are important in assessing the vibratory behavior of the vocal folds (Hildebrand, 1976; Timcke *et al.*, 1958, 1959; von Leden *et al.*, 1960).

II. ACOUSTIC SYMPTOMS OF LARYNGEAL PATHOLOGY

Acoustic analysis of the voice is more objective than auditory methods for screening or voice therapy assessment (Koike, 1976). The validity of the acoustic approach, however, rests on the complex relationship between the physiological source function and the concomitant speech signal. A laryngeal pathology, such as tumors or paralysis, generally produces asymmetrical changes in the mass, elasticity, and tension of the vocal folds, leading to deviant vibration. In addition, weakness or paralysis of respiratory muscles may cause insufficient subglottal pressure, thus changing the aerodynamic forces acting on the vocal folds and hence their vibratory pattern. The subglottal airstream is modulated by this unbalanced vocal fold movement. Irregular air pulses emerge from the larynx, propagate through the pharynx and oral and nasal cavities, and radiate from the mouth and nose. The resultant acoustic signal is thus affected by a physiological disturbance in the larynx, and the acoustic signal may be used to measure the disturbance.

The primary acoustic symptoms of laryngeal pathology are a change in fundamental frequency, voice intensity, or voice quality. These symptoms are indicative of a multitude of organic diseases and functional disturbances (Moore, 1971; Zemlin, 1968), and the nature of these symptoms will vary for each patient and at each stage of pathological involvement.

A. Fundamental Frequency

The fundamental frequency of a voiced sound is a function of the mass, elasticity, compliance, and length of the vocal folds. It also depends to some extent on the subglottal pressure and the configuration (acoustic load) of the vocal tract. An assessment of whether a patient has adequate frequency regulation usually involves a judgment by a trained listener as to whether the fundamental frequency is too high or too low when compared to voices of persons of similar age, sex, and body size. If the fundamental frequency is judged to be too high, the voice may sound shrill or screechy. In functional disorders involving high fundamental frequency, the vocal folds tend to become abused at the point of maximum displacement. Vocal abuse may produce laryngitis, lead to the development of nodules, or worsen an existing pathology. Organic causes for high fundamental frequency include a laryngeal web, asymmetrical structures, or failure of a male larynx to develop to a normal size. A fundamental frequency which is judged to be too low may sound harsh, hoarse, husky, or rough. Low fundamental frequency stemming from functional vocal abuse may lead to contact ulcers, although the precise etiology of contact ulcers is unclear. Organic causes may include virilization, tumors, or other enlargements which increase the mass of the folds, or nerve paralysis which decreases the elasticity and compliance of one or both folds (Luchsinger & Arnold, 1965).

B. Vocal Intensity

Vocal intensity is a monotonically increasing function of the SQ and the air flow through the glottis; it is also a monotonically decreasing function of the OQ (Timcke *et al.*, 1958). Excessive vocal intensity usually is functional in origin. If it is also accompanied by high fundamental frequency, the voice may sound shrill or screechy, and if it is accompanied by low fundamental frequency, the voice may sound hoarse. When excessive vocal intensity is coupled with excessively high or low fundamental frequency, the severity of a pathology may increase. Weak voices generally have organic causes, and the etiology may be attributed to insufficient subglottal pressure caused by paralysis of the respiratory muscles or to poor vocal fold movement caused by muscle weakness or laryngeal paralysis (Luchsinger & Arnold, 1965).

C. Vocal Quality

A degradation in voice quality, generally categorized as hoarseness, is often the first, and sometimes the sole, symptom of laryngeal disease. This change, because of its initial presence, drew the early attention of several researchers (Arnold, 1955; Bowler, 1964; Frank, 1940; Jackson & Jackson, 1937; Palmer, 1959). However, these studies were perceptual, and they contained a multitude of concepts and terms. One review (Perkins, 1971) compared nine studies which assess quality defects and listed 27 terms used to describe those defects. Only hoarseness and nasality appear in all studies, and only 10 other terms appear in more than one study. Of these 10 terms, six are common to four studies: breathy, harsh, strident, denasal, husky, and metallic. Other terms are screechy, guttural, throaty, strained, shrill, and intense. There is a proliferation of descriptive terms but little agreement among researchers in describing voice quality.

This complexity of terminology led some researchers to attempt to identify the factors involved in listener judgments of pathological voice quality (Fritzell, Hammarberg, & Wedin, 1977; Isshiki, 1966; Isshiki, Okamura, Tanabe, & Morimoto, 1969; Takahashi & Koike, 1975). Using a technique based on the semantic differential (Osgood, Suci, & Tannenbaum, 1957), Isshiki (1966) suggested that the factors which operate in listener judgments are multidimensional, and he identified four major independent axes corresponding approximately to "roughness," "breathiness," "lack of power," and "normalcy." Using principal components analysis, Fritzell *et al.* (1977) identified five factors as "stable–

unstable,'' ''breathy–overtight,'' ''hypo–hyperkinetic,'' ''light–coarse,'' and ''head–chest register.''

In summary, vocal quality is a difficult parameter to assess and, unlike fundamental frequency or vocal intensity, no reliable physiological descriptions or measurements have been established. In general, vocal quality is determined on the basis of vocal fold vibration and vocal tract resonance (Luchsinger & Arnold, 1965). Furthermore, asymmetrical vibrations are a typical indication of a vocal quality defect. Such variations affect the fundamental frequency, SQ and OQ, and may be attributed to changes in the mass, elasticity, compliance, or length of one or both folds (von Leden *et al.*, 1960). Vocal phonatory defects range from aphonia and breathiness to hoarseness and rough hoarseness, and the organic causes include paralysis, weak muscles, extraneous masses, excessive mucus, and loss of tissue (Luchsinger & Arnold, 1965).

III. ACOUSTIC TECHNIQUES FOR VOICE ANALYSIS

Acoustic techniques for voice analysis are based on the source of the signal and the method of analysis. One source is **direct signals,** e.g., radiated sound pressure and throat contact signals. The other source is **indirect signals,** e.g., glottal or residue signals derived using inverse filtering techniques. For each of these sources, the signals may be analyzed in the **time domain** (e.g., to determine mean fundamental frequency or mean perturbation) or in the **frequency domain** (e.g., to determine long-term average spectral slope or energy distribution). The advantages and limitations of each signal source and analysis method are discussed in Sections IIIA,B,C,D,E.

A. Direct Signals

The radiated sound pressure waveform is the most readily available signal for acoustic analysis, but its usefulness for assessing laryngeal function is limited. The production of a steady vowel sound is controlled by the glottal source, which will be affected by laryngeal pathology, and the supraglottal structure, whose resonance characteristics will presumably be unaffected by laryngeal pathology. Therefore, acoustic measures of a laryngeal disorder from a sound pressure waveform are affected by a normal supraglottal structure. The effects of the supraglottal structure do not significantly hinder the detection or assessment of severe laryngeal disorders. However, at an early stage of pathology, or at a late stage of recovery, the supraglottal structure probably masks some of the important acoustic attributes of the pathology. A throat contact microphone is sometimes used to avoid supraglottal effects (Koike, 1969), but information from throat contact signals is limited because of the low-pass filtering action of intervening tissues and because the throat signal is sensitive to microphone placement.

B. Indirect Signals

A voiced sound such as a sustained vowel may be simply modeled as the sound pressure waveform resulting from the excitation by a periodic source (corresponding to the glottis) of an acoustic tube (corresponding to the vocal tract and lips). The technique of inverse filtering applied to the sound pressure waveform can remove the effects of the acoustic tube, and the resulting signal approximates the periodic source. If the supraglottal structure is relatively unaffected by laryngeal pathology, and the source of a voice change is the glottis, then this periodic source approximation contains sufficient information to analyze the acoustic effects of the pathology. Measures based on an inverse-filtered speech signal are not affected by the supraglottal structure and are potentially more informative than measures based on an unfiltered speech signal.

There are two inverse filtering methods used to obtain acoustic information about the glottal source. The first method is **glottal inverse filtering.** In this procedure, the inverse of the lip radiation and vocal tract spectral contributions is used to estimate the glottal volume velocity waveform as a function of time (Holmes, 1962; Lindqvist, 1965; Miller, 1959; Rothenberg, 1973; Takasugi & Suzuki, 1970). The theoretical starting point for glottal inverse filtering is the linear voiced speech production model (Fant, 1960; Flanagan, 1972). (See Appendix A for details.) Early glottal inverse filtering studies used analog techniques and usually eliminated only the first and second formants. Later studies employed digital computer techniques to process the speech signal in an interactive manner. The formant frequencies and bandwidths were estimated and used to adjust a glottal inverse filter until the expected waveform (roughly triangular in shape followed by a zero portion) appeared (Hiki *et al.*, 1976). However, the overall appearance of the resulting waveform generally did not satisfy intuitive concepts of vocal fold closure. The linear predictive technique of pitch-synchronous glottal inverse filtering produces acceptable waveforms without estimation of the formants, but the point of glottal closure for each pitch period must be located by visual inspection (Wong, Markel, & Gray, 1979).

Another method of glottal inverse filtering eliminates the vocal tract resonance by having a subject speak into a fairly long reflectionless tube (approximately 2.5 × 100 cm) (Sondhi, 1975). The resulting waveform is closely correlated with the glottal volume velocity waveform. However, this method is subjective since each speaker requires a different tube (matched to his vocal tract) for the best results.

Although some of these techniques have produced accurate estimates of the glottal signal, none is completely automated. Glottal inverse filtering can become a useful clinical tool only when the technique requires no user interaction.

The second indirect method for obtaining information about laryngeal activity is **residue inverse filtering.** This technique is based on a linear model of speech production (Atal & Hanauer, 1971; Davis, 1976a; Markel & Gray, 1976). (See Appendix A for details.) The residue inverse filter is the inverse of the estimated lip radiation, vocal tract, and glottal shaping spectral contributions to the speech signal. The result of filtering the speech signal with the residue inverse filter is the **residue signal.** This signal is an estimate of a periodic source function for an all-pole speech production model, and it exhibits strong peaks at the start of each pitch period and quasi-random noise between the pitch period peaks. Koike and Markel (1975), using the residue signal in a qualitative analysis of normal and pathological voices, indicated that for some intermediate and advanced cases of laryngeal pathology, the residue signal did not appear to convey more information about the vocal disorder than was already apparent in the speech signal. However, for some early cases, Koike and Markel claimed that the residue signal showed qualitative evidence of pathology even though the unfiltered speech signal showed no such evidence. Subsequently, Davis (1976a) substantiated these claims by developing quantitative measures based on the residue signal and verified the hypothesis that more acoustic information about a pathology is conveyed by the (indirect) residue signal than by the (direct) speech signal.

C. Comparison of Direct and Indirect Signals

Figure 1 depicts the sound pressure waveform (A), the glottal inverse-filtered signal (B), and the residue inverse-filtered signal (C) for a vowel segment. The inverse filter that produces the residue signal differs from the inverse filter that produces the glottal signal by the addition of several low-frequency poles (Appendix A). Thus the glottal signal is equivalent to a low-pass filtered version of the residue signal. In practice, the residue signal is considerably easier to obtain than the glottal signal since glottal inverse filtering has not been automated. As noted, the glottal inverse

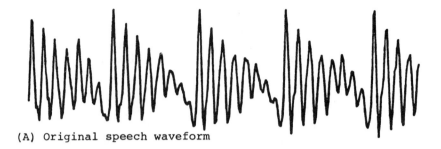

(A) Original speech waveform

(B) Glottal inverse filtered signal from speech waveform

(C) Residue inverse filtered signal from speech waveform

Figure 1. Comparison of speech, glottal, and residue signals for /a/. The glottal signal is closely correlated with the physiological glottal volume velocity waveform (Davis, 1976a).

filter coefficients must either be determined from the estimated formant frequencies and bandwidths (Hiki *et al.*, 1976) or the point of glottal closure must be marked for automatic evaluation of the formants (Wong *et al.*, 1979). In addition, any low-frequency phase distortion will prevent accurate approximation of the glottal signal (especially its closed interval), so the speech signal must be recorded on equipment having a good low-frequency phase response, even under 100 Hz (Holmes, 1975). A standard audio tape recorder has a poor low-frequency phase characteristic, and it is extremely difficult to estimate the glottal signal from a speech signal recorded on such equipment. An FM tape recorder avoids phase problems, but such tape recorders are generally not available in a clinic. In contrast, the residue inverse filter uses a phase-insensitive autocorrelation method to match the overall spectral envelope of the vocal tract, glottal shaping, and lip radiation (Appendix A). There is no need for visual inspection of formants, marking of pitch periods, or controlled recording conditions.

In a theoretical sense, the glottal signal has an important advantage over the residue signal, since the glottal signal is a good approximation to the glottal volume velocity waveform (Fig. 1), while the residue signal is not directly related to any physically observable signal. In a practical sense, however, the residue signal may be more easily obtained and, hence, has greater potential value than the glottal signal for the clinical assessment of pathological voices.

D. Time-Domain Acoustic Parameters

High-speed motion pictures of pathological vocal folds have revealed that there frequently are irregular vibratory patterns (von Leden *et al.*, 1960). Pitch period perturbation measures (Crystal & Jackson, 1970; Davis, 1976a; Hecker & Kreul, 1971; Hiki, Sugawara, & Oizumi, 1968; Kitajima, Tanabe, & Isshiki, 1975; Koike, 1967, 1973; Lieberman, 1961, 1963; Smith & Lieberman, 1964; Takahashi & Koike, 1975) and amplitude perturbation measures (Davis, 1976a; Koike, 1969; Takahashi & Koike, 1975) from acoustic signals are different between pathological and normal speakers. Two psychoacoustic studies (Wendahl, 1963, 1966) involved the synthesis of speech with pitch period and amplitude perturbations. The degree of perturbation in the sounds was closely correlated with subjective judgments of degree of roughness.

Measures based on pitch period and amplitude perturbations have been formulated in several different ways. The first of these measures is the pitch perturbation factor (Lieberman, 1961, 1963). This parameter is defined as the relative frequency of pitch period perturbations larger than .5 milliseconds occurring in a steady vowel sound. A pitch period perturbation is defined as the time difference between the durations of successive pitch periods in the speech signal. Lieberman showed that pathological voices generally have larger perturbation factors than normal voices with comparable fundamental frequencies, and that the perturbation factor is sensitive to the size and location of growths in the larynx.

A second perturbation measure is the relative average perturbation (Koike, 1973). This parameter differs from Lieberman's pitch perturbation factor in several respects. Koike observed that steady vowel sounds may normally exhibit slow and relatively smooth changes in pitch period; he measured rapid perturbations from a smoothed trend line. In addition, Koike suggested normalizing the pitch period perturbation measure by dividing it by the average pitch period. Finally, he suggested that the throat contact signal is a better indicator of laryngeal aperiodicity than the speech signal itself because the effects of the supraglottal structure on the speech sound are reduced. In consideration of these observations, Koike defined the relative average perturbation (RAP) as:

$$
\text{RAP} = \frac{\dfrac{1}{N-2} \displaystyle\sum_{i=2}^{N-1} \left| \dfrac{P(i-1) + P(i) + P(i+1)}{3} - P(i) \right|}{\dfrac{1}{N} \displaystyle\sum_{i=1}^{N} P(i)} \tag{1}
$$

where $P(i)$, $i = 1, 2, \ldots, N$, denotes the successive pitch periods. The numerator is the average perturbation measured for each pitch period smoothed by a three-point averaging window, and the denominator is the average pitch period. Koike concluded that the RAP of normal and pathological voices have different ranges, and that the RAP varies significantly between patients with neoplasms and patients with unilateral paralysis.

The basis for a third measure of perturbation is the quasi-periodic amplitude modulation observed in the steady vowel sounds of pathological speakers (Koike, 1969). Koike computed the serial correlation coefficients (correlograms) for the time series of amplitude values at each pitch period peak. He found that the correlograms of normal and pathological speakers are generally distinguishable from one another. The correlograms for speakers with laryngeal tumors usually show significant correlation peaks at lags between three and twelve fundamental periods, and those for speakers with laryngeal paralysis show no such peaks. Koike concluded that it might be possible to develop methods for differential evaluation of laryngeal pathologies based on information in the amplitude envelope of steady vowel sounds.

In a fourth approach, Kitajima *et al.* (1975) defined a fundamental frequency (F_0) perturbation measure as the average of 100 successive F_0 perturbations from an all-voiced phrase. An F_0 perturbation is the difference between a measured F_0 and a five-point weighted (in a least-squares sense) average centered around the measured value. A semitone scale (relative to 16.35 Hz or four octaves below middle C) was used since auditory perception of F_0 is approximately proportional to the logarithm of frequency. They found that normal female voices exhibit larger F_0 perturbation measures than normal male voices, which would be expected since the female F_0 is generally higher than the male. They also found that male voices affected by laryngeal cancer are distinguishable from normal male and female voices by using the F_0 perturbation measure.

Further advances in perturbation measures were made when Takahashi and Koike (1975) combined Koike's earlier results into two time-domain measures of the pathological voice based upon signals obtained from the throat contact microphone: the frequency perturbation quotient (FPQ) and the amplitude perturbation quotient (APQ). The FPQ is, by definition, analogous to the RAP, but the instantaneous F_0 (defined as the reciprocal of the pitch period) is substituted for the pitch period. The APQ is also, by definition, analogous to the RAP, but now peak amplitude values for each pitch period and an eleven-point, rather than a three-point, averaging window are used. Takahashi and Koike found that the APQ made a significant contribution in a principal components analysis of voice quality factors, and that although the FPQ was significantly correlated with the APQ, the FPQ did not make a significant contribution in the principal components analysis.

Davis (1976a) defined a pitch period perturbation quotient (PPQ) and an amplitude perturbation quotient (APQ) which were analogous to Koike's RAP and Takahashi and Koike's APQ, respectively. However, there were several differences in the acoustic definitions. Rather than using fixed three-point or eleven-point averaging windows, Davis, systematically investigating the benefit of changing the window size, found that five-point averaging windows for the PPQ and APQ produce the best perturbation measures for normal–pathological discrimination. He also found that perturbation measures based on the residue signal are better for discrimination than those based on the speech signal; however, he did not attempt any comparisons with the throat contact or glottal signals used by other researchers.

Davis also developed a completely automated procedure for extracting pitch period and amplitude sequences. Once the residue signal is obtained, the extraction procedure uses a peak-picking algorithm that finds the significant positive and negative excursions of the signal (Fig. 2). The APQs for the positive and negative amplitude sequences are calculated, and the smallest APQ is chosen. The PPQ is then found from the pitch period sequence corresponding to the smallest APQ.

Davis developed two additional time-domain acoustic measures of laryngeal pathology. One measure was based on the observation that the signal-to-noise ratio of the residue signal is a good cue for normal–pathological discrimination (Davis, 1976a; Koike & Markel, 1975). The

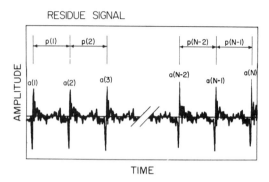

Figure 2. Extraction of pitch period and amplitude sequences from the residue signal (Davis, 1976a).

signal in this case is the sequence of spikes spaced at pitch period intervals, and the noise is the quasi-random energy between the spikes. Koike and Markel suggested that one measure of signal-to-noise ratio might be the average of the peak energy for each period divided by the noise energy in the last half of the period for successive pitch periods in a specified interval; however, they did not attempt any quantitative measurements.

For a residue signal from a normal speaker, the separation of signal from noise for each pitch period is straightforward, and a measure such as the one described by Koike and Markel would suffice. However, for a residue

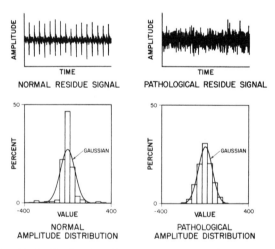

Figure 3. Amplitude distribution of normal and pathological residue signals. The decreased noise in the normal residue signal results in an amplitude distribution which is narrow and taller than the pathological amplitude distribution (Davis, 1976a).

signal from a pathological speaker, the pitch peak is not always distinct from the noise, and it would be very difficult to implement such a measure. The appearance of more noise in pathological cases and less noise in normal cases suggested to Davis that the amplitude distribution of the residue signal would be useful for a statistical measure of the signal-to-noise ratio. Figure 3 shows normal and pathological residue signals and the corresponding amplitude distributions. The distribution for the normal speaker is taller and narrower than the distribution for the pathological speaker.

The shape of these distributions may be quantified by a statistical measure called the coefficient of excess (EX) (Cramer, 1958). This coefficient is defined as the ratio of the fourth moment of a distribution to the square of the second moment of the distribution. The EX is zero for a Gaussian distribution. That is,

$$\text{EX} = \frac{E\{(x - \bar{x})^4\}}{E\{(x - \bar{x})^2\}^2} - 3 \tag{2}$$

where

$$E\{(x - \bar{x})^k\} = \frac{1}{N} \sum_{i=0}^{N-1} [x(i) - \bar{x}]^k \tag{3}$$

and

$$\bar{x} = \frac{1}{N} \sum_{i=0}^{N-1} x(i) \tag{4}$$

for a signal $x(i)$, $i = 0, 1, \ldots, N - 1$. The EX is positive if the distribution is taller and narrower than a Gaussian distribution and negative if the distribution is shorter and wider. Measurements from numerous speakers substantiate the correlation between the values of the EX and a judgment of the residue signal-to-noise ratio (Davis, 1976a).

The other time-domain acoustic parameter developed by Davis is based on the amount of voicing, or the strength of F_0, during a sustained vowel sound. The detection of F_0 is important in almost any analysis or synthesis study involving speech. In synthesis experiments, for example, the voiced–unvoiced decision is based on the presence or absence of F_0 and is used to determine whether impulses or noise should be utilized for the source excitation. One of the oldest digital methods for detecting F_0 is autocorrelation analysis (Markel, 1973). Figure 4 shows that a periodic signal (e.g., a vowel) exhibits a peak in the autocorrelation function of the residue signal at a duration corresponding to the period. The reciprocal of the period yields the fundamental frequency. Alternately, an aperiodic

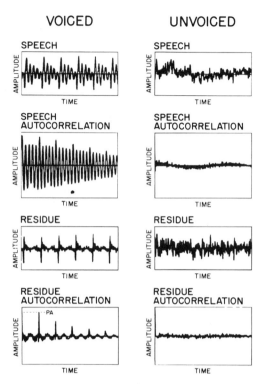

Figure 4. Comparison of voiced and unvoiced autocorrelation functions (Davis, 1976a). A pathological voiced sound may be like an unvoiced normal sound, and the PA will be low or nonexistent.

signal (e.g., an unvoiced fricative) shows no pitch period peak. It is evident from Fig. 4 that the residue signal is a better indicator of the autocorrelation peak than the speech signal. Davis (1976a) defined a time-domain acoustic parameter, called the pitch amplitude (PA), as the value of the pitch period peak in the residue signal autocorrelation function. The PA is high for vowels, small for voiced fricatives, and zero for unvoiced fricatives.

If a given sound is known to be voiced, then the PA becomes a measure of voicing. Voiced sounds from normal speakers have a clearly defined pitch period and a high PA. In these cases, there is strong periodicity in the glottal volume velocity and area waveforms, associated with symmetrical vocal fold movements. Alternatively, breathy voiced sounds from pathological speakers are acoustically analogous at the source level to unvoiced sounds from normal speakers. The PA is low or not measurable, the speech sounds have weak periodicity, and there is a significant increase in the amount of noise which is heard.

E. Frequency-Domain Acoustic Parameters

As an alternative to time-domain analysis, frequency-domain analysis provides a different set of acoustic features. A common instrument for frequency analysis of speech is the sound spectrograph, which analyzes the spectral energy distribution of a short speech segment (generally less than 3 seconds) by filtering the sound with a tracking bandpass filter. The output is a time-versus-frequency graph of the sound with spectral energy indicated by intensity. The formants and F_0 of a steady vowel are readily visualized in a spectrogram.

Several spectrographic studies have shown that there are differences between the spectra of pathological voices and those of normal voices (Gould, 1976; Nessel, 1960; Winckel, 1952, 1954; Yanagihara, 1967a, 1967b). The higher frequency harmonics of steady pathological vowels are attenuated in comparison with their normal counterparts. The loss of high-frequency harmonics may be caused by changes in the OQ or SQ. In particular, if there is no glottal closure (i.e., the OQ is equal to unity), the higher harmonics are sharply attenuated. Spectral noise components may originate in turbulent air flow resulting from incomplete glottal closure or irregular vocal fold vibration (Flanagan, 1958). These spectral noise components are distributed over the spectrum in varying degrees, and the extent of the distribution depends on the severity of the disease. The presence of spectral noise contributes to hoarseness, which is the first symptom of numerous pathologies. Some laryngologists use spectrograms to assess the degree of, and recovery from, vocal fold disorders (Gould, 1975; Rontal, 1975). The results of these studies of sound spectra indicate wide vocal variability, but they also illustrate the feasibility of using the acoustic spectrum to analyze laryngeal pathology.

In an attempt to quantify visual judgments of spectrograms, Hiki *et al.* (1976) measured the spectral slope of the glottal signal as a feature for acoustic analysis, but they did not present any quantitative results. However, other investigators, using a reflectionless tube (Fisher, Monsen, & Engebretson, 1975), indicate that a constant slope is not a particularly good approximation of the glottal spectral envelope even for normal speakers. Hence the glottal slope of pathological speakers may not be a good parameter for normal–pathological discrimination.

Using a filter bank and a digital computer, Frøkjær-Jensen and Prytz (1976) investigated changes in the long-term average spectrum (LTAS) in patients undergoing therapy for speech disorders such as recurrent nerve paralysis. The LTAS is determined by averaging the spectrum obtained from voiced 80-millisecond segments of a 45-second speech sample. They suggested that the ratio of the energy in the 1–5 kHz band to the energy in the 0–1 kHz band (or the decibel difference between the two energy bands) is a good spectral parameter of voice quality. As shown in Fig. 5, there is an increase in spectral energy above 1 kHz during therapy and histograms of the difference between the high- and low-energy bands (labeled α) indicate approximately a 4 dB increase. Frøkjær-Jensen and Prytz (1976), in analyzing the voices of more than 50 patients and several normal subjects, showed that a comparison between high- and low-energy bands may be used to assess vocal improvement.

Gauffin and Sundberg (1977) found some correlation between LTAS features and perceptual factors such as overtight–breathy and hyper–

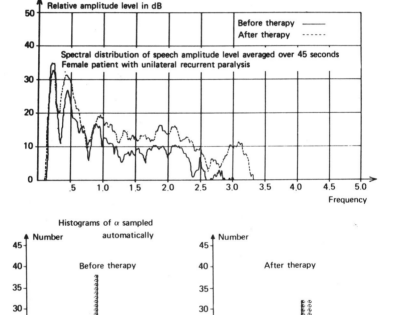

Figure 5. Comparison of long-term average spectra before and after voice therapy. There is a 3-dB increase in the energy above 1000 Hz relative to the energy below 1000 Hz after therapy. (From Frøkjær-Jensen & Prytz, 1976.)

hypokinetic obtained in a study by Fritzell *et al.* (1977). Their LTAS features were decibel energies in the 0–2, 2–5, and 5–8 kHz bands, and decibel energy differences among the bands. It is noteworthy that Gauffin and Sundberg's energy difference between the 2–5 and the 0–2 kHz bands is nearly identical to Frøkjær-Jensen and Prytz's energy difference, except that the former use 2 kHz as the energy boundary and the latter use 1 kHz. The idea of using long-term average spectral measures is a good approach to assessing voice quality and requires additional testing in future investigations.

Davis (1976a) measured normal and pathological spectral characteristics using the concepts of the spectral flatness of the residue inverse filter (SFF) and the spectral flatness of the residue signal (SFR) (Gray and Markel, 1974). Spectral flatness is defined as the ratio in decibels of the geometric mean of the spectrum to the arithmetic mean of the spectrum. Gray and Markel observed that the more noiselike a spectrum, the greater its spectral flatness, having a maximum value of 0 dB for a constant spectrum. Unvoiced sounds (e.g., fricatives), which are produced with an open glottis and a significant vocal tract constriction, have greater SFFs than voiced sounds (e.g., steady vowels). Since the spectrum of the residue signal is essentially flat, showing only the fine spectral behavior of F_0 and its harmonic components, unvoiced sounds will have lower SFRs than voiced sounds. This result is a consequence of the harmonic nature of normal voiced speech; there are large negative excursions of the residue signal spectrum for each harmonic. As the sound becomes more noiselike (i.e., pathological), the harmonic structure becomes less significant and the SFR increases.

Using a linear model of speech production (Appendix A), it can be shown that the SFF is the negative sum of the spectral flatnesses of the lip radiation, vocal tract, and glottal shaping spectra. If the vocal tract and lip radiation spectra are independent of laryngeal pathology, changes in the glottal shaping spectrum caused by pathology will be measured by the SFF. It can also be shown that the SFR may be determined by subtracting the SFR from the spectral flatness of the speech spectrum (Gray & Markel, 1974).

Yanagihara (1967a, 1967b) noted the presence of noise components in pathological speech which mask formant characteristics and F_0 harmonics. Davis (1976a) used this observation as a basis for choosing the SFF and the SFR as spectral measures for vocal assessment. He assumed that the SFF is a measure of the masking of formant frequency amplitudes and bandwidths by noise, and that the SFR is a measure of the masking of F_0 harmonic amplitudes by noise. Since the vocal tract is assumed to be fixed and independent of the source excitation for a steady vowel, these masking effects may be attributed to changes in the sound source harmonic amplitudes caused by variations in the OQ and the amount of source turbulence. The relationship between OQ and the harmonics of a periodic signal is evident from Fourier analysis; as the OQ increases, the amplitudes of the higher harmonics decrease. Physiologically, the OQ and the amount of turbulence are affected by any pathology interfering with the normal vibratory pattern of the vocal folds. Such effects may be caused by weak muscle action or by changes in the mass, elasticity, or compliance of the folds.

IV. VOICE PROFILES

Several of the previously mentioned studies relate acoustic features to listener judgments of voice quality. The results of these studies demonstrate that acoustic parameters, such as average pitch period perturbation, are significantly correlated with perceptual parameters, such as hoarseness. However, at least one basic question remains. Can acoustic parameters alone provide measures that are clinically useful for evaluating pathological conditions in the larynx? For early detection or therapeutic assessment of the pathological voice, it is important to use such parameters in an easily applied quantitative procedure. Davis (1975, 1976a) suggested that a profile of acoustic characteristics would be as useful to the laryngologist and speech pathologist as an audiogram is to the audiologist. Using features and signals obtained with residue inverse filtering, he developed a **Voice Profile** to display acoustic information about the voice and to serve as a record in a patient's medical history.

Davis (1978) examined the usefulness of the Voice Profile by comparing the visual and numerical information conveyed in the Voice Profiles of normal and pathological subjects (Davis, 1976a) with qualitative observations of the acoustic characteristics of the same subjects (Koike & Markel, 1975). Koike and Markel described representative residue signals selected from a data base of 10 normal and 10 pathological subjects and, although they indicated that the residue signal could be used to produce acoustic measures of laryngeal function, they did not make any measurements. Davis (1976a) actually made the acoustic measurements and demonstrated that the measures could effectively discriminate between normal and pathological speakers. The data base used by Koike and Markel (1975) and Davis (1976a) is summarized in Table I, and the acoustic features determined by Davis are listed in Table II. The Voice Profiles for two of the subjects, N1 and P2, are shown in Figs. 6 and 7, respectively. The Voice Profiles display six acoustic features (PPQ, APQ, EX, PA, SFF,

Table I. Description of Normal and Pathological Subjects by Age, Sex, Fundamental Frequency, and Diagnosis

Case	Age (years)	Sex	F_0	Diagnosis
N1	29	M	110	Normal
N2	27	M	92	Normal
N3	30	M	120	Normal
N4	33	M	138	Normal
N5	26	M	140	Normal
N6	24	M	106	Normal
N7	31	M	124	Normal
N8	27	M	130	Normal
N9	23	F	232	Normal
N10	36	F	180	Normal
P1	33	F	205	Vocal nodule
P2	16	M	175	Unilateral paralysis
P3	56	M	96	Hemilaryngectomized
P4	25	F	196	Vocal nodule
P5	39	F	231	Spastic dysphonia
P6	39	M	115	Vocal polyp
P7	77	M	164	Laryngeal papilloma
P8	28	F	189	Unilateral paralysis
P9	57	M	—	Glottic cancer
P10	64	M	—	Advanced laryngeal cancer

and SFR) and the signals required to compute the features. Appendix B includes a description and listing of a FORTRAN program to produce a Voice Profile. Sections IVA and B are based on Davis' (1978) comparisons between Koike and Markel's (1975) descriptions and Davis' (1976a) measurements.

A. Normal Voice Sample

Figure 6 shows the Voice Profile for subject N1. Koike and Markel observed that the speech and residue signals are very regular, with each signal indicating a relatively small amplitude perturbation. They noted that the amplitude perturbation for subject N1 is greater than for subject N7 (not shown), and Davis measured an APQ of 6.08% for subject N1 as compared to a measured APQ of 2.50% for subject N7. Koike and Markel commented that the residue signal has a high signal-to-noise ratio and near-constant periodicity. Davis found that the EX for this subject is 7.69 (the third highest value in the normal group), and the PPQ is 0.24% (the lowest value in both groups). Thus, Davis' acoustic measurements for this

Table II. Acoustic Features for Normal and Pathological Subjects[a]

Case	PPQ (%)	APQ (%)	PA	EX	SFF (dB)	SFR (dB)
N1	.24	6.08	.82	7.69	−11.3	−12.3
N2	.45	4.17	.65	8.30	−10.2	−7.6
N3	.47	5.42	.71	3.92	−12.4	−9.4
N4	.59	6.70	.72	2.24	−11.3	−8.7
N5	.34	11.63	.65	1.74	−13.6	−7.8
N6	.37	8.72	.64	5.23	−13.4	−9.4
N7	.46	2.50	.58	11.33	−12.2	−6.3
N8	.34	2.56	.67	7.54	−8.6	−10.4
N9	.51	4.59	.77	3.77	−11.2	−11.9
N10	5.01[b]	9.04	.77	.96	−11.1	−10.8
P1	2.61	9.07	.66	.63	−9.9	−10.5
P2	5.08	11.20	.72	1.90	−9.8	−9.3
P3	9.60	19.12	.25	2.05	−8.8	−4.3
P4	1.87	15.33	.60	.97	−6.6	−8.6
P5	.85	4.18	.71	7.27	−5.6	−6.5
P6	.60	11.68	.74	2.98	−8.7	−9.8
P7	3.29	10.98	.58	1.07	−13.0	−7.6
P8	13.25	14.71	.17	−.05	−7.4	−5.7
P9	10.68	16.00	.49	.28	−10.9	−7.4
P10	13.64	15.69	.26	.09	−5.3	−3.5

[a] The six principal features are the pitch period perturbation quotient (PPQ), amplitude perturbation quotient (APQ), pitch amplitude (PA), coefficient of excess (EX), spectral flatness of the inverse filter (SFF), and spectral flatness of the residue signal (SFR).
[b] Pitch period tracking errors.

normal subject correlate with Koike and Markel's qualitative descriptions.

B. Pathological Voice Sample

Figure 7 shows the Voice Profile for subject P2. Koike and Markel observed that this slightly hoarse subject represents a case of early laryngeal pathology which might not be detected by auditory perception alone but which might be detected with good acoustic measures of the residue signal. They indicated that the speech signal shows good periodicity and regularity among pitch periods, but the residue signal shows poor periodicity and a low signal-to-noise ratio. Davis found that the PPQ and APQ for subject P2 are higher than the corresponding measures for all but one of the normal subjects (N5), and the EX is lower than all but two of the normal subjects (N5 and N10), again substantiating Koike and Markel's

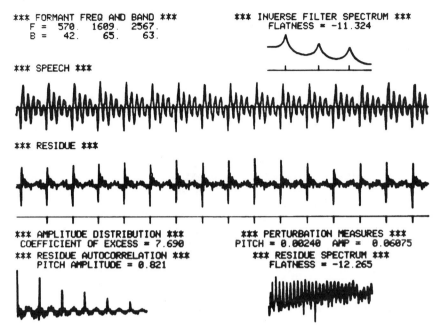

*** FORMANT FREQ AND BAND ***
 F = 570. 1609. 2567.
 B = 42. 65. 63.

*** INVERSE FILTER SPECTRUM ***
 FLATNESS = -11.324

*** SPEECH ***

*** RESIDUE ***

*** AMPLITUDE DISTRIBUTION ***
 COEFFICIENT OF EXCESS = 7.690
*** RESIDUE AUTOCORRELATION ***
 PITCH AMPLITUDE = 0.821

*** PERTURBATION MEASURES ***
 PITCH = 0.00240 AMP = 0.06075
*** RESIDUE SPECTRUM ***
 FLATNESS = -12.265

Figure 6. Voice Profile of subject N1 (Davis, 1976a). The waveforms and measures for this subject exemplify characteristics for a normal healthy voice.

observations. In addition, the observation that the pitch periods are visually similar to one another is confirmed by a high PA of .72, a value which is exceeded by only one other pathological subject (P6) and by only three of the normal subjects (N1, N9, and N10).

A comparison of the inverse filter spectra for subjects P2 and N1 shows noticeable differences (Figs. 6 and 7). For subject N1, the peaks and valleys of the spectrum are distinct, the bandwidths are small, and the SFF is a low value of −11.32 dB. For subject P2, the valleys between the formant peaks are more shallow, the bandwidths are larger, and the SFF is a higher value of −9.79 dB. These broadband differences would probably be observed in visual spectrogram analysis (Gould, 1975; Yanagihara, 1967a, 1967b).

A similar comparison applies between the residue spectra for subjects N1 and P2 (Figs. 6 and 7). The harmonic nature of the voice source is readily apparent for the normal subject, and the SFR is a low value of −12.27 dB. In contrast, the residue spectrum for subject P10 exhibits an aperiodic harmonic structure (and hence a more noisy appearance), and the SFR is a higher value of −9.35 dB. These source harmonic differences would also probably be observed in visual spectrogram analysis.

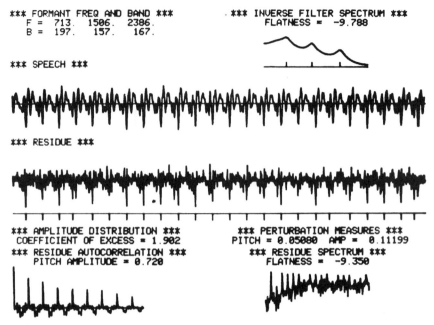

Figure 7. Voice Profile of subject P2 (Davis, 1976a). The subject had unilateral paralysis, and the pathology may have been undetected by auditory perception alone.

V. STATISTICAL ANALYSIS OF NORMAL AND PATHOLOGICAL DATA

In determining the advantages and limitations of the six acoustic features employed in his study, Davis (1976a) used the data from the 10 normal and 10 pathological subjects and from an additional 7 normal and 11 pathological subjects in a statistical analysis. The additional subjects had characteristics similar to the original subjects, and were included to increase the population size so that statistical results would be significant. The means, standard deviations, and correlations for the normal and pathological groups are listed in Tables III and IV, respectively.

A *t* test (Bruning and Kintz, 1968) shows that the normal and pathological means of the PPQ, APQ, and EX are significantly different at the 97.5% confidence level, the means of the PA and SFR are significantly different at the 95.0% level, and the means of the SFF are significantly different at the 90.0% level. Therefore, the PPQ, APQ, and EX are the best features for distinguishing between these normal and pathological groups. In addition, all of the differences between respective means have the correct sign; e.g., the mean normal PPQ is less than the mean patho-

Table III. Statistics for Pooled Normal Speakers (From Davis, 1976a)

	PPQ (%)	APQ (%)	PA	EX	SFR (dB)	SFF (dB)
Mean	.99	7.22	.725	5.17	−10.50	−11.849
SD	2.28	4.47	.105	4.29	2.50	1.84
Correlation		APQ	PA	EX	SFR	SFF
PPQ		.826[a]	−.115	−.258	.161	.039
APQ			−.100	−.409	.136	−.277
PA				−.015	−.812[a]	.164
EX					.262	.369
SFR						.018

[a] Significant at the 99.5% confidence level.

logical PPQ, and the mean normal EX is greater than the mean pathological EX. However, the difference between the normal and pathological means of the SFF is insignificant.

Using Pearson's *r* score (Bruning and Kintz, 1968), the correlation matrices show two important relationships. For normal and pathological speakers, the correlation between the PPQ and APQ is positive (+.826) and significant (at the 99.5% level). This correlation probably arises from the physical source of abnormal vocal fold vibrations (i.e., a change in the mechanical properties of the affected tissues), since this change will cause both pitch period and amplitude perturbations. Furthermore, for normal and pathological speakers, the correlation between the PA and SFR is negative (−.812) and significant (at the 99.5% level). This correlation may be explained as follows. A decrease in the PA indicates more noise and

Table IV. Statistics for Pooled Pathological Speakers (From Davis, 1976a)

	PPQ (%)	APQ (%)	PA	EX	SFR (dB)	SFF (dB)
Mean	4.54	11.99	.599	2.44	−9.11	−11.851
SD	4.93	6.90	.236	2.32	3.49	3.35
Correlation		APQ	PA	EX	SFR	SFF
PPQ		.625[a]	−.615[a]	−.564[a]	−.491	.064
APQ			−.687[b]	−.314	.607[a]	.070
PA				.240	−.869[b]	−.098
EX					−.011	.060
SFR						.137

[a] Significant at the 99.0% confidence level.
[b] Significant at the 99.5% confidence level.

less periodicity in the residue signal (analogous to the generation of unvoiced fricatives), which indicates more noise and less harmonic structure in the residue spectrum, and consequently an increase in the SFR.

In Fig. 8, the acoustic features for all subjects are cross-plotted by pairs together with two-sigma ellipses which are derived by a principal components analysis (Davis, 1976a). The axes of each ellipse intersect at the class means and represent orthogonal directions for the scatter of the data. The directions minimize the variance of the data within each normal or pathological class. The nonorthogonal appearance of the axes arises from the use of different scale factors for each axis. In the PPQ–APQ graph, logarithmic scaling is used since linear scaling does not adequately distinguish the normal and pathological classes. The use of logarithmic scaling is noteworthy because Kitajima *et al.* (1975) suggested that the use of a semitone scale (logarithmically based) is a better basis for quantifying the auditory perception of F_0 perturbation. As a minor point, the mean PPQ and the mean APQ in Fig. 8 are different from their respective values in Tables III and IV, since the mean of the logarithm of the values is computed for the principal components analysis rather than the logarithm of the mean of the values.

In Fig. 8, it is apparent that the normal and pathological classes are best distinguished by the perturbation quotients and least distinguished by the spectral flatness measures. However, even for the perturbation quotients, there are particular points (not indicated) which do not cluster in or near the correct group. Additionally, a normal speaker may have an abnormal value (outside a normal speaker ellipse) in one or possibly two dimensions, while measures in the remaining dimensions may be normal (inside a normal speaker ellipse). For this small number of subjects, it is unrealistic to expect all normal and pathological speakers to fall into tightly clustered groups. Larger populations grouped by age and sex might yield more representative clusters of normal and pathological data. Moreover, these results indicate the multidimensional nature of the acoustic detection problem, with some features contributing more information than others for different normal and pathological speakers.

VI. QUANTITATIVE ASSESSMENT OF VOICE THERAPY

The usefulness of acoustic features for the assessment of changes in voice quality can be determined by measuring changes in the features over time. In a pilot study, Davis (1977) analyzed acoustic features for a patient undergoing voice therapy following removal of a vocal polyp. A

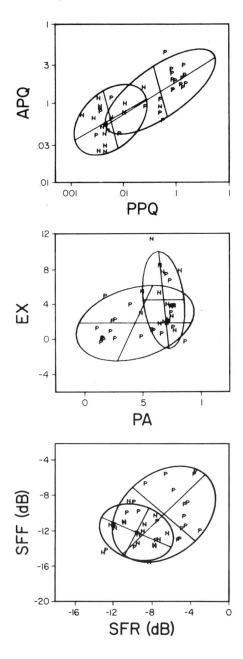

Figure 8. Scatter of normal and pathological features, showing two-sigma ellipses for each group (N = normal, P = pathological) (Davis, 1976a).

Table V. Acoustic Features for a Voice Therapy Patient

Date	PPQ (%)	APQ (%)	PA	EX	SFF (dB)	SFR (dB)
3/19/73	16.80	10.67	.86	−.30	−14.1	−12.7
6/16/73	4.85	15.51	.71	1.48	−12.4	−9.6
8/ 6/73	0.40	5.97	.79	6.20	−12.3	−13.0

trained listener subjectively observed that the voice quality continuously improved during the period of therapy. The data are summarized in Table V and compared with the distribution of the earlier data in Fig. 9.

The PPQ, APQ, and EX are the features in the *t* test which show the most significant separation between the normal and pathological mean values. These features also show the best improvement during therapy for

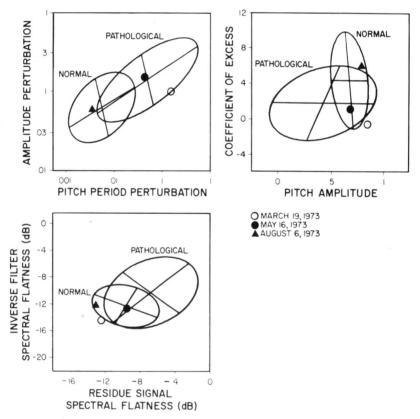

Figure 9. Comparison of features for a voice therapy subject with normal and pathological ellipses (Davis, 1977). The PPQ, APQ, and EX show the best improvement.

this patient. In comparison with the normal ellipses in Fig. 9, these parameter values shift from lying outside the normal range at the beginning of therapy to lying within the normal range after several months of therapy. Thus, the results indicate that changes in these features correlate with changes in voice quality for this patient.

None of the other features show changes that correlate with voice quality improvement. For the earliest session, although the voice quality is poor and the PPQ is high, the PA is **higher** than that of any normal or pathological subject listed in Table II. Visual observation of the speech signal reveals that there is a very high degree of regularity between adjacent pitch periods. The residue signal has a low EX and a very noisy appearance, but the high degree of pitch period regularity observed in the speech signal is maintained in the residue signal and leads to a high PA. Thus the PA may not be as good as the PPQ, APQ, or EX as a measure of improvement during therapy.

The SFF and SFR for this subject show no trends that can be correlated with the data used to derive the ellipses. The SFF decreases and the SFR fluctuates during therapy for this patient. Such trends suggest that these features may be inappropriate for quantifying observations from spectrograms, and perhaps modified or new features would reflect spectral changes more accurately.

Thus, the PA, SFF, and SFR show no consistent improvement during therapy, and their normal and pathological mean values show less significant separation. However, future testing is needed before rejecting them or reducing their weight in an overall assessment of voice quality.

VII. SUMMARY AND FUTURE INVESTIGATIONS

The results discussed in this chapter indicate the feasibility of using quantifiable acoustic features to distinguish between normal and pathological subjects. The acoustic features relating to laryngeal function provide more information when inverse filtering is used to remove the supraglottal structure from the speech signal. These features can be automatically computed from a digitized representation of the signal, and the results may be organized to form a Voice Profile.

However, the application of digital analysis techniques poses some difficulties. A linear model of speech production is used to derive the inverse-filtered signal, but the assumption of minimum glottal source–vocal tract interaction may be tenuous for some pathological conditions and requires further study. Nevertheless, the assumption of independence is reasonable for normal and mildly pathological subjects, and these subjects are the ones for whom acoustic analysis is potentially a valuable addition to existing medical procedures.

An additional problem is that different sustained vowel sounds will result in different perturbation values (Johnson, 1969). This effect is probably a consequence of the interaction between the glottal source and vocal tract and indicates the continuing need to study the complex relationships between the glottal sound source and the acoustic characteristics of the vocal tract. Since any single study uses the same vowel for all speakers, the effect of vowel type on the acoustic measures is probably uniformly distributed among the speakers and therefore is not a significant source of error. Further analysis is also required to determine how consistently acoustic features may be measured from independent samples of the same vowel from the same speaker. Additional statistics should be collected for both sexes and among different age groups.

Another goal is to analyze acoustic features in a clinic in an attempt to detect early cases of laryngeal pathology. Voice Profiles may be useful indicators of voice quality, especially during voice therapy, and it will be necessary for speech pathologists and physicians to evaluate their clinical usefulness. For efficient clinical implementation, tape-recorded voice samples may be sent from a clinic to a central computer facility, either indirectly via the mail system or directly via telephone lines. With the advent of hospital computers and remote terminals in outpatient clinics, an immediate acoustic evaluation of laryngeal pathology is a viable objective. Alternatively, voice samples could be analyzed with a microprocessor-based unit built especially for clinical use.

Further study should be directed to at least two problems: (1) the identification of additional features useful in acoustic evaluation of laryngeal pathology, and (2) the possibility of discriminating among types and degrees of pathology. Additional measures might involve the use of long-duration or short-duration voice samples and might include, for example: (a) formant frequencies, bandwidths, and amplitudes; (b) the amplitude of the first harmonic of F_0 in the residue signal autocorrelation; (c) the slope of the line through the peaks in the residue signal autocorrelation; and (d) the periodicity and peak amplitudes of the pitch period and amplitude correlograms. Some of these features have been suggested previously (Hiki *et al.*, 1976), but neither acoustic or physiological significance nor clinical analysis methods has been established yet for any of these additional features.

Finally, acoustic features should be compared with subjective voice quality ratings (Murry, 1975). Both real and synthesized pathological speech samples (with known acoustic deviations) could be examined. In addition, other parameters (e.g., the Euclidean distance between a given feature vector and an ideal feature vector having zero perturbation measures, unity pitch amplitude, etc.) might be analyzed as measures of voice quality.

It is evident that acoustic voice analysis using inverse filtering may be used for screening individuals for the early detection of laryngeal pathology or for assessing improvement during voice therapy. The fields of speech pathology and laryngology will benefit significantly from future continued research on the acoustic characteristics of normal and pathological voices.

APPENDIX A: LINEAR MODEL OF VOICED SPEECH PRODUCTION

Vowel sounds generally are used in studies of pathological speech because the vocal folds are vibrating during vowel phonation, and acoustic assessment of laryngeal function relates to adequacy of sustained vocal fold vibration. A linear model of speech production for nonnasalized voiced sounds (e.g., vowels) was proposed by Fant (1959, 1960), and the assumptions of this model were subsequently analyzed in detail (Flanagan, 1972). As shown in Fig. A1, this model is composed of three acoustic filters. The principal justifications for this model are based on acoustic tube theory, measurements of volume velocity and sound pressure waveforms, X-ray data, and results using electrical circuits to synthesize vowel sounds. One major assumption of the model is the separability of the filter segments during the generation of voiced speech. The model is rederived here using z-transform notation, principally for ease of solutions and computer implementation (Jury, 1964; Markel & Gray, 1976). (A z-transform represents a discrete signal as a Laplace transform represents a continuous signal.) A band-limited analog speech signal $s_a(t)$ is expressed in terms of a signal $s(n)$ sampled every T seconds as

$$s(n) = s_a(nT), \quad -\infty < n < \infty \tag{A1}$$

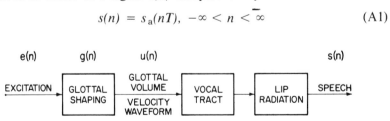

Figure A1. Linear voiced speech production model (Davis, 1976a).

and with a z-transform $S(z)$ given by

$$S(z) = \sum_{n=-\infty}^{\infty} s(n)z^{-n} \qquad (A2)$$

Any finite energy signal or filter impulse response may be expressed equivalently by its sampled representation or its z-transform. From Fig. A1, the glottal volume velocity waveform $u(n)$ is the output of the glottal shaping filter $G(z)$ when the input is the excitation $e(n)$. The glottal volume velocity waveform is a signal in the model which has a physiological correlate. The excitation and the glottal shaping filter are only models which are used to produce a representative glottal volume velocity waveform. The vocal tract filter $V(z)$ and the lip radiation filter $L(z)$ operate on the glottal volume velocity waveform $u(n)$ to produce the speech waveform $s(n)$.

A. Modeling the Excitation

The excitation $e(n)$ is modeled as a series of scaled unit impulses spaced at the pitch period for voiced sounds and is expressed as

$$e(n) = E_0 \sum_{j=0}^{\infty} \delta(n - jP), \, n = 0, 1, \ldots \qquad (A3)$$

where E_0 is a scale factor, $\delta(n)$ is the Kronecker delta function, and $\delta(n) = 1$ if $n = 0$ or $\delta(n) = 0$ if $n \neq 0$. The z-transform $E(z)$ of $e(n)$ is given by

$$E(z) = \frac{E_0}{1 - z^{-P}} \qquad (A4)$$

where P is the pitch period expressed in terms of an integral number of samples, and the fundamental frequency (F_0) is $1/PT$. The excitation $e_T(n)$ is shown in Fig. A2. The subscript T represents a truncated sequence with N points, thus $e_T(n) = e(n)$, $n = 0, 1, \ldots, N - 1$. The corresponding logarithmic spectrum is obtained by Hamming windowing the truncated excitation and evaluating $LM (E_T) = 10 \log |E_T(z)|^2$ on the unit circle $z = e^{j\theta}$, where $E_T(z)$ is the z-transform of the windowed sequence $e_T(n)$, $\theta = 2f/F_s$ is the normalized frequency, $F_s = 1/T$ is the sampling frequency, and f is the continuous frequency variable. The harmonics of F_0 are evident in Fig. A2. A Hamming window is used to reduce extraneous frequencies introduced into the spectrum when the temporal waveform is truncated (Blackman & Tukey, 1958).

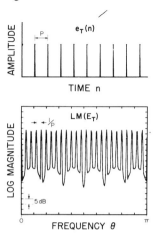

Figure A2. Model excitation signal and spectrum (Davis, 1976a).

B. Modeling the Glottal Shaping

The glottal shaping filter has been represented by several all-pole models (Flanagan, 1972) which are based on the physiologically observed waveform. One of the simplest models is the filter with unit impulse response given by

$$g(n) = G_0(n + 1)e^{-cnT}, \qquad n = 0, 1, \ldots \qquad (A5)$$

and z-transform $G(z)$ given by

$$G(z) = \frac{G_0}{(1 - e^{-cT}z^{-1})^2} \qquad (A6)$$

where G_0 is a scale factor and e^{-cT} is a pole (c is approximately $200\pi/$ second) in the unit circle in the z-plane. Using the scaled impulse train $e(n)$ as the input to the glottal shaping filter $G(z)$, the glottal volume velocity waveform $u(n)$ is modeled as the output of the filter and is represented by

$$u(n) = E_0 G_0 \sum_{j=0}^{\infty} (n + 1 - jP)e^{-c(n-jP)}, \, n = 0, 1, \ldots \qquad (A7)$$

and the temporal and spectral waveforms for the truncated windowed signal are illustrated in Fig. A3. The log magnitude spectrum of the model glottal volume velocity waveform is roughly comparable to the log magnitude spectrum of the glottal area and the glottal volume velocity waveforms derived from high-speed motion pictures of the glottis (Flanagan, 1958).

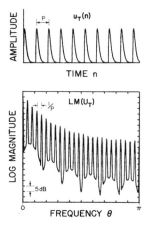

Figure A3.   Model glottal volume velocity signal and spectrum (Davis, 1976a).

C. Modeling the Vocal Tract

The vocal tract filter is used to model the acoustic resonance characteristics of the air spaces contained between the glottis and the lips. The
modeling has been well discussed in the literature (Chiba & Kajiyama,
1941; Fant, 1960; Kelly & Lochbaum, 1962) and is based on an acoustic
tube approximation to the vocal tract. This acoustic tube approximation is
composed of a specified number of sections, with each section having a
variable cross-sectional area. The z-transform $V(z)$ of the vocal tract filter
may be modeled by a small finite number K (generally three or four) of
narrow bandwidth complex poles whose center frequencies span the
range between zero and $1/2T$ Hz, but which are not near the endpoints of
the range. The z-transform is expressed as

$$V(z) = \prod_{i=1}^{K} \frac{1}{(1 - z^{-1}z_i)(1 - z^{-1}z_i^*)} \tag{A8}$$

or

$$V(z) = \prod_{i=1}^{K} \frac{1}{1 - e^{-\pi b_i T}\cos(2\pi f_i T)z^{-1} + e^{-2\pi b_i T}z^{-2}} \tag{A9}$$

A spectral resonance of center frequency f_i and two-sided bandwidth b_i is
defined by each complex pole pair (z_i, z_i^*), where $z_i = \exp[-\pi b_i T + j2\pi f_i T]$,
z_i^* is the complex conjugate of z_i, and T is the sampling period. These
resonances also are called formants. The formants in the model have

center frequencies generally less than 5000 Hz and bandwidths generally less than 150 Hz.

D. Modeling the Lip Radiation

The lip radiation filter represents the transformation from the volume velocity waveform at the lips to the sound pressure waveform. Its form results from assuming a situation analogous to a vibrating piston set in an infinite baffle. The transfer function is greatly simplified from Flanagan (1972) as the scaled derivative of the sound pressure waveform with respect to the lip volume velocity waveform, and hence the z-transform $L(z)$ is approximated by a difference function given as

$$L(z) = L_0(1 - \mu z^{-1}) \tag{A10}$$

where L_0 is a scale factor, and μ is a pole ranging from .95 to .98 in the z-plane.

The overall linear model of speech production for an acoustic sound pressure transform $S(z)$ is the product of the z-transforms of the lip radiation filter, the vocal tract filter, the glottal shaping filter, and the source excitation, and is given as

$$S(z) = L(z)V(z)G(z)E(z) \tag{A11}$$

or

$$S(z) = \frac{L_0 G_0 E_0[1 - \mu z^{-1}] \, [1 - e^{-cT}z^{-1}]^{-2}[1 - z^{-P}]^{-1}}{\prod_{i=1}^{K} 1 - e^{-\pi b_i T}\cos(2\pi f_i T)z^{-1} + e^{-2\pi b_i T}z^{-2}} \tag{A12}$$

Representative spectra for the various segments are shown in Fig. A4 along with a spectrum taken from a real sampled vowel segment.

E. Inverse Filtering of Speech: Solution of the Modeling Equations

The speech production model in Eq. (A12) is simplified for analysis by the following procedure. The numerator factor $[1-\mu z^{-1}]$ is assumed to cancel approximately one of the numerator factors $[1-e^{-cT}z^{-1}]^{-1}$, since cT is generally much less than unity. The remaining numerator factor $[1 - e^{-cT}z^{-1}]^{-1}$ is included in the denominator product factor. In practice, a few additional poles may be added arbitrarily to allow for general shaping of a model speech spectrum to a real speech spectrum and to account for some modeling errors, e.g., speech cannot be represented

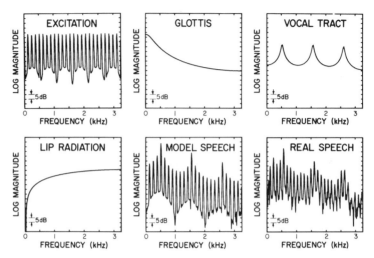

Figure A4. Representative spectra for the voiced speech model and real speech (Davis, 1976a).

simply as an all-pole model based on a periodic impulsive source and three independent acoustic filters. Markel (1971) illustrates the use of additional poles for better spectral matching. Finally, the powers of z are arranged in ascending order, and the constants are combined to produce the form

$$S(z) = \frac{\sigma}{\sum\limits_{i=0}^{M} a_i z^{-i}} E(z) \tag{A13}$$

where a_i is real, $a_0 = 1$, $M = 2K+m$ and usually $1 \leq m \leq 6$. Thus, voiced nonnasal speech production is modeled as the output of an all-pole filter which is excited by an impulse sequence.

The characteristics of the excitation are important in the study of pathological speech. The z-transform of the excitation is obtained from Eq. (A13) as

$$E(z) = \frac{1}{\sigma} \sum\limits_{i=0}^{M} a_i z^{-i} S(z) \tag{A14}$$

and the corresponding time sequence is

$$e(n) = \frac{1}{\sigma} \sum\limits_{i=0}^{M} a_i s(n - i), \quad -\infty < n < \infty \tag{A15}$$

If

$$A(z) = \sum_{i=0}^{M} a_i z^{-i} \qquad (A16)$$

then

$$E(z) = \frac{1}{\sigma} A(z)S(z) \qquad (A17)$$

and

$$LM(E_T) = LM(S_T) - LM(1/A) - 10 \log \sigma^2 \qquad (A18)$$

$A(z)$ is called the inverse filter of the speech spectrum because $A(z)S(z)$ approximates the desired excitation $E(z)$ to within the gain constant σ (Markel, 1971).

Inspection of Fig. A4 reveals that $LM(E_T)$ has a flat trend characteristic and that $LM(1/A)$ represents the smoothed spectral behavior of $LM(GVL)$. $LM(E_T)$ may be found by choosing σ and a fixed small number M of coefficients for $A(z)$ such that $LM(S_T) - LM(1/A) - 10 \log \sigma^2$ results in as flat a spectrum as possible or, alternately, $LM(\sigma/A)$ is matched to the envelope of the speech spectrum (Gray & Markel, 1974).

The inverse filter $A(z)$ is found by determining the σ and a_i which minimize the energy ξ in $LM(E_T)$ over all frequencies subject to the constraint $a_0 = 1$;

$$\xi = \int_{-\pi}^{\pi} |E_T(e^{j\theta})|^2 \frac{d\theta}{2\pi} \qquad (A19)$$

Substituting Eq. (A14) into Eq. (A19) with $z = e^{j\theta}$ and expanding and rearranging the factors gives

$$\xi = \frac{1}{\sigma^2} \sum_{i=0}^{M} \sum_{k=0}^{M} a_i a_k \int_{-\pi}^{\pi} |S_T(e^{j\theta})|^2 e^{j\theta(i-k)} \frac{d\theta}{2\pi} \qquad (A20)$$

The integral in Eq. (A20) is the inverse transform of the power spectrum of the speech signal and hence is one term in the time autocorrelation of the signal,

$$r(m) = \int_{-\pi}^{\pi} |S_T(e^{j\theta})|^2 e^{j\theta m} \frac{d\theta}{2\pi} = \sum_{n=-\infty}^{\infty} s_T(n)s_T(n-m) \qquad (A21)$$

where $s_T(n)$, $n = 0, 1, \ldots, N - 1$ is the truncated sampled speech signal, and the autocorrelation terms are calculated by assuming $s_T(n)$ to be zero outside the range $[0, N - 1]$. Therefore,

$$\xi = \frac{1}{\sigma^2} \sum_{i=0}^{M} \sum_{k=0}^{M} a_i a_k r(i - k) \qquad (A22)$$

The solution is obtained by setting $\partial \xi / \partial a_i = 0, i = 1, 2, \ldots, M$. The a_i are then found from the solution of

$$\sum_{i=1}^{M} a_i r(i - k) = -r(k), \qquad k = 1, 2, \ldots, M \qquad (A23)$$

and the solution is obtained iteratively using Levinson's method (Levinson, 1946; Markel & Gray, 1976). The choice of σ is often made to match the total energy in the speech signal spectrum to the total energy in the inverse filter spectrum (Markel and Gray, 1973), or σ may be set to unity if absolute signal energy is not a consideration.

The estimate of the (truncated) excitation signal in Eq. (A15) is found from the a_i and the (truncated) speech signal, and is called the **residue signal.** This form of inverse filtering is referred to as **residue inverse filtering.** In contrast, the estimate of the glottal volume velocity waveform by removing only the lip radiation and vocal tract characteristics is called the **glottal signal,** and the form of inverse filtering is referred to as **glottal inverse filtering.** One method of glottal inverse filtering would be to estimate K formant frequencies and bandwidths from the speech signal spectrum and to use Eq. (A9) to determine $2K$ coefficients for $V(z)$. Then the glottal inverse filter $A(z)$ is $V(z)L(z)$, where $L(z)$ is given by Eq. (A10). Finally, Eq. (A15) is used to find the glottal signal, which is represented by $e(n)$. Since the number of residue inverse filter coefficients M is generally greater than the number of glottal inverse filter coefficients $2K+1$, and the additional coefficients will represent the low-frequency poles of $G(z)$, the glottal signal is a low-pass filtered version of the residue signal.

It can be shown (Markel, 1972; Davis, 1976a) that the solution for the a_i is equivalent to the solution of a classic one-step optimal linear predictor using the criterion of least squares (Kolmogoroff, 1941; Levinson, 1946; Weiner, 1949). Thus, **linear prediction of speech** refers to a method of speech analysis based on an all-pole model of speech production (Atal & Hanauer, 1971; Makhoul, 1975; Makhoul & Wolf, 1972; Markel, 1972; Markel & Gray, 1976), and the residue signal is equivalent to the linear prediction error signal. The a_i are commonly referred to as inverse filter coefficients and, despite assumptions such as an all-pole model and glottal shaping–vocal tract–lip radiation separability, $LM(\sigma/A)$ is a good approximation to the smoothed log magnitude spectral behavior of voiced nonnasal sounds.

Typical normal speech and residue signals are shown in Fig. 6 for the sound /a/. A computer program for the generation of the residue signal is included in Appendix B. It is observed that the residue signal is impulselike in nature and indicates the pitch periods very well. There is no guarantee that inverse filtering of speech as formulated here will produce a residue signal similar in appearance to the model excitation. The generation of speech is a highly complex nonlinear pole-zero process, and the simple linear model is an all-pole approximation. Realistically, inverse filtering removes the important poles of the speech system and results in a complex residue signal. Typical complex-appearing residue signals are depicted in Figs. 6 and 7. Inverse filtering of speech based on an all-pole model of speech production produces a residue signal that is highly correlated with intuitive concepts of vocal fold vibration, but which is difficult to model precisely.

F. Practical Considerations

1. Segmentation

Isolated occurrences of the vowel /a/ frequently are used in the study of pathological speech. This phoneme for a normal adult male speaker is characterized approximately by formant frequencies of 700, 1100, and 2100 Hz (Peterson & Barney, 1952), which are easily eliminated by inverse filtering. The vowel /a/ has the highest average first formant frequency for the adult males in Peterson and Barney's data, and a high first formant frequency allows for easier discrimination between it and F_0. In the experiments conducted by Davis (1976a), at least 1 second of sustained sound was recorded and digitized, and a segment starting at 400 milliseconds past voice onset and extending approximately 300 milliseconds was used in the subsequent analysis. This time span was chosen to ensure a steady vowel sound free from transitions associated with voice onset and voice decay.

2. Windowing and Preemphasis

The choice of a sound segment for analysis is equivalent to multiplying the entire sound by a rectangular window, which has a value of unity for the segment of interest and a value of zero otherwise. This procedure, however, generally introduces extraneous high frequencies into the segment. Different windows may be used to reduce the extraneous high-frequency sidelobes introduced by rectangular windowing. One such window $h(n)$ is the Hamming window (Blackman & Tukey, 1958):

$$h(n) = .54 - .46 \cos\left(\frac{2\pi n}{N}\right), \qquad n = 0, 1, \ldots, N - 1 \qquad (A24)$$

where N is the number of samples in the window. Markel (1971) demonstrated that the Hamming window allowed for a better spectral match between the reciprocal of the inverse filter spectrum and the envelope of the speech spectrum than the rectangular window.

The spectrum of a steady vowel generally has a -6 dB/octave spectral slope. This fact is reflected in the modeling results of Eq. (A12). At frequencies past the poles and zeros, the glottal shaping spectrum has an approximate -12 dB/octave slope, the lip radiation spectrum has an approximate $+6$ dB/octave slope, and the vocal tract spectral peaks are approximately equal in amplitude. Consequently, the speech signal may be preemphasized prior to analysis to counteract the spectral slope and to obtain a closer match between the reciprocal of the inverse filter spectrum and the envelope of the speech spectrum. The z-transform of a simple preemphasis filter $P(z)$ is specified as

$$P(z) = 1 - P_0 z^{-1}, \qquad 0 \leq P_0 \leq 1 \qquad (A25)$$

and if the input is $x_T(n)$, then the output $s_T(n)$ is given by

$$s_T(n) = x_T(n) - P_0 x_T(n - 1), \qquad n = 0, 1, \ldots, N - 1 \qquad (A26)$$

where N is the number of samples in the segment and $x_T(-1)$ is the sample before $x_T(0)$.

Davis (1976a) systematically varied the amount of preemphasis and found that the best acoustic features for normal–pathological discrimination were obtained with no preemphasis.

3. Sampling Frequency and Window Length

The use of the digital computer requires that a signal be sampled and that the values for each sampling interval be stored. If the signal bandwidth is denoted by B, then the sampling frequency F_s is greater than $2B$ to avoid aliasing. The signal is filtered before sampling by a sharp cutoff analog filter at or slightly below $F_s/2$. For voiced sounds, Markel (1971) cited that a rule of thumb is to allow 700–800 Hz for each formant. Thus, smooth spectral matching of three or four formants would require a bandwidth of approximately 3.2 kHz or a sampling frequency slightly greater than 6.4 kHz. Davis (1976a) used a sampling frequency of 6.5 kHz and analog prefiltering of the signal at 3.2 kHz. This bandwidth would allow the use of telephone lines in future applications of voice data transmission from a clinic to a computer.

The duration of the speech segment analyzed is also an important consideration. For normal connected speech, formant transitions usually limit the practical window size to 20 milliseconds (130 data samples at a sampling frequency of 6.5 kHz), but for isolated vowel sounds, with no

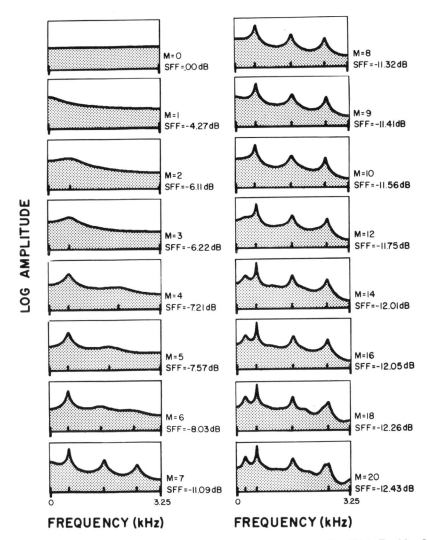

Figure A5.   Inverse filter spectra as a function of filter order (Davis, 1976a). For $M < 8$, the inverse filter does not eliminate enough supraglottal spectral components and for $M > 10$, the inverse filter eliminates fundamental frequency and harmonic spectral components.

formant transitions, larger windows may be used. Davis (1976a) systematically investigated the effects of the window size and found that 900 sample points (138 milliseconds at 6.5 kHz) produced the best acoustic measures for normal–pathological discrimination. For smaller window sizes, there were not enough pitch periods for an adequate perturbation measure, and for larger window sizes, formant variations in pathological steady sounds obscured the pitch period peaks.

4. Filter Order

A good choice for the filter order (number of inverse filter coefficients) is twice the number of formant frequencies plus a constant, whose value is generally between 1 and 6 to allow for overall spectral matching and to account for some modeling errors. The primary consideration, however, is the matching of the reciprocal of the inverse filter spectrum to the smooth behavior of the speech spectrum so that the fine harmonic characteristics of the residue spectrum remain after inverse filtering. Davis (1976a) investigated the effects of filter order and found that the best acoustic features for normal–pathological discrimination are obtained with eighth-, ninth-, and tenth-order inverse filters. The characteristics of the inverse filter as a function of filter order are depicted in Fig. A5. For filter orders less than seven, inverse filtering would not eliminate enough supraglottal structure, and the extraneous formant information would mask the acoustic attributes of a laryngeal pathology. For a filter order of seven, although all of the formants would be removed by inverse filtering, there are not enough inverse filter poles as yet to obtain a good residue signal. For filter orders greater than ten, inverse filtering would eliminate important spectral information representing F_0 and its harmonics.

APPENDIX B: COMPUTER PROGRAM FOR ACOUSTIC ANALYSIS

A FORTRAN program may be used to extract the acoustic features and to display the results in a Voice Profile. A block diagram of such a program is shown in Fig. B1, typical outputs are shown in Figs. 6 and 7, and the program listing is included at the end of this appendix.

The main program serves to link the major subroutines. These subroutines communicate via common areas, and, on a minicomputer, they may be overlaid since they are called sequentially. The subroutine RFINIT sets constants and prompts the user for the location of the speech data, which is then retrieved. The subroutine FILTER windows and preemphasizes the data and then computes the inverse filter coefficients and the spectral flatness measures (SFF and SFR). The subroutine RESON computes the vocal tract resonance frequencies and bandwidths and selects three formants from the resonances. The residue signal is then determined in subroutine RESIDU. One set of inverse filter coefficients are used for a continuous vowel segment up to 308 milliseconds (2000 sample points) in duration.

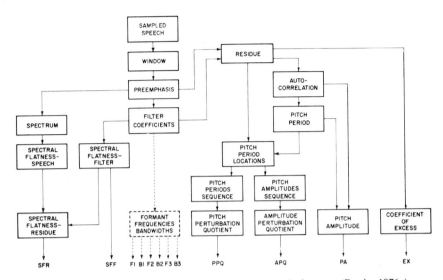

Figure B1. Block diagram for extraction of acoustic features (Davis, 1976a).

In contrast, one other technique of residue inverse filtering for a relatively long speech segment windows each 20-millisecond interval of speech, calculates a set of inverse filter coefficients, computes 10 milliseconds of the residue signal, then shifts the window ahead 10 milliseconds and repeats the procedure for the duration of the speech segment (Markel, Gray, & Wakita, 1973). The rationale for this sequential method is to ensure good spectrum matching (and hence formant tracking) for normal connected speech. For isolated steady vowels, this method is unnecessary and even undesirable because if the shift interval is not an integral number of pitch periods, there will be an energy ripple in the residue signal, leading to errors in calculating the APQ. Consequently, a single large analysis window is used.

The subroutine RFPLT1 then displays the first part of the results, including the SFF, formants, and speech and residue signals. Next, the subroutine PITCH finds the pitch period. For a normal steady vowel, the residue signal is nearly periodic, and the autocorrelation of the windowed residue signal exhibits peaks spaced at the pitch period (Fig. 6). A peak detector for the autocorrelation sequence (excluding the origin) is used to find a peak which is presumed to correspond to the PA, and then the distance from the origin gives the pitch period. In some pathological cases, this peak corresponds to a subharmonic of the fundamental frequency (F_0), and consequently, the pitch period is detected incorrectly. An algorithm is implemented to resolve the problem. The first four peaks (excluding the origin) are found, the peak nearest the origin is chosen as the pitch period peak, and the amplitude of the peak is chosen as the PA. For a few pathological cases, even this procedure fails to extract a reasonable pitch period.

Once the fundamental period is determined, subroutine PERTUR locates the pitch period peaks and the corresponding amplitudes. The algorithm used is discussed by Davis (1976a). The maximum positive value of the residue signal initially is assumed to be the location of one pitch period peak. A search is made for the previous positive peak in an interval centered at a point one pitch period (P points) removed from the first peak. The size of this interval is fixed at $2RP$ with $R = .30$. Once this point is located, the next previous pitch period peak is found, and the process is continued until the start of the sequence is reached. The location procedure is then repeated from the initial peak to the end of the sequence. Parabolic interpolation (Markel & Gray, 1976) is used on all peaks for greater accuracy in determining successive pitch period durations and pitch period amplitudes. The perturbation quotients (PPQ and APQ) are computed using a five-point averaging window. The entire procedure is then repeated for negative residue signal peaks, and the smaller APQ based on positive or negative peaks and the respective PPQ, pitch period sequence, and pitch amplitude sequence are retained.

For some pathological speakers, there is no observable pitch period or incorrect determination of the pitch period. In these cases, the algorithm yields large perturbation quotients since it is tracking quasi-periodic or incorrect pitch period peaks. In either case, these gross perturbation measures reflect an atypical pitch period and serve to indicate a strong acoustic cue for the presence of a pathology.

The EX is computed at the end of subroutine PERTUR using a factored form of Eq. (2). The subroutine RFPLT2 finally displays the second half of the results, including the PPQ, APQ, PA, EX, SFR, and the residue signal autocorrelation and spectrum.

The FORTRAN program in Fig. B2 provides a documented procedure for the acoustic analysis discussed. There are several system-dependent subroutines which are not included (e.g., graphics and disk file access) since these routines will vary with the type of computer employed.

Acknowledgments

The preparation of this chapter was supported by National Institutes of Health Grants NS 13309-01A1 to Speech Communications Research Laboratory, Inc. and NS 13870 to Haskins Laboratories, and by the Voice Foundation, New York.

```
C       PROGRAM   RF
C
C     PROGRAM TO EVALUATE FEATURES OF THE RESIDUE SIGNAL FOR
C     NORMAL-PATHOLOGICAL DISCRIMINATION OF SPEAKERS
C
C            AUTHORED BY STEVEN B. DAVIS
C
C     SPEECH COMMUNICATIONS RESEARCH LABORATORY, INC.
C                800A MIRAMONTE DRIVE
C                SANTA BARBARA, CA.  93109
C                   (805) 965-3011
C                    AUGUST 1976
C
      COMMON /RFCOM1/ RC(30),A(30),R(30),F(10),B(10)
      COMMON /RFCOM2/ N,M,PRE,IHAM,SF,PRNGE,LP,LA,NFFT,KBU
      COMMON /RFCOM3/ IX(3100),X(2048),FF(3),FB(3)
      COMMON /RFCOM4/ PPQ,APQ,PVA,EX,SFF,SFR,FU,PPER,NPP
      DIMENSION   Y(512)
      EQUIVALENCE    (IX(2077),Y)
C
C     THE PROGRAM IS SET UP FOR OVERLAID SEGMENTS
C
      CALL RFINIT         ! INITIALIZE AND READ SPEECH
      CALL FILTER         ! COMPUTE FILTER COEFFICIENTS
      CALL RESON          ! FIND FORMANT FREQ AND BAND
      CALL RESIDU         ! CALCULATE RESIDUE SIGNAL
      CALL RFPLT1         ! PLOT FIRST HALF OF RESULTS
      CALL PITCH          ! DETERMINE PITCH PERIOD
      CALL RESIDU         ! RECALCULATE RESIDUE SIGNAL
      CALL PERTUR         ! CALCULATE PERTURBATION QUO
      CALL RFPLT2         ! PLOT SECOND HALF OF RESULTS
C
      CALL EXIT
      END
C
C*********************************************************
C
      SUBROUTINE RFINIT
C
C     INITIALIZE VARIABLES FOR RF PROGRAM
C
C       AUTHORED BY STEVEN B. DAVIS - SCRL - AUGUST 1976
C
      COMMON /RFCOM1/ RC(30),A(30),R(30),F(10),B(10)
      COMMON /RFCOM2/ N,M,PRE,IHAM,SF,PRNGE,LP,LA,NFFT,KBU
      COMMON /RFCOM3/ IX(3100),X(2048),FF(3),FB(3)
      COMMON /RFCOM4/ PPQ,APQ,PVA,EX,SFF,SFR,FU,PPER,NPP
      DIMENSION   Y(512)
      EQUIVALENCE    (IX(2077),Y)
      DATA   ICHY/'Y '/
C
C     THE FOLLOWING VARIABLES ARE SYSTEM DEPENDENT CONSTANTS
C
      NDDPDB = 256     ! NUMBER OF DISPLAY POINTS PER DISK BLOCK
      NCWFH  = 64      ! NUMBER OF COMPUTER WORDS IN THE FILE HEADER
```

```
      KBU  =  5          ! LOGICAL UNIT NUMBER FOR INPUT/OUTPUT
C
C     READ THE INPUT VARIABLES
C
      WRITE(KBU,10)
10    FORMAT(' ENTER STARTING SAMPLE, NUMBER OF SAMPLES,',/
     1   ' FILE #, GROUP #, USER #, DISK #')
C
      READ(KBU,15) IS,N,NWD,IGRP,IUSR,IDK
15    FORMAT(6I6)
C
C     STORE ANALYSIS VARIABLES
C
      NFFT = MINU(N,1024)        ! NUMBER OF PTS FOR FFT
      M    = 8                   ! ORDER OF INVERSE FILTER
      PRE  = 0.                  ! PREEMPHASIS
      IHAM = ICHY                ! 'Y' OR 'N' FOR HAM WINDOW
      SF   = 6500.               ! SAMPLING FREQUENCY
      PRNGE = .30                ! FRACTIONAL PITCH RANGE
      LP   = 5                   ! LENGTH OF PPQ WINDOW
      LA   = 5                   ! LENGTH OF APQ WINDOW
C
C     GET THE SPEECH SAMPLES AND ENOUGH SAMPLES FOR FILTER
C     INITIALIZATION:  (IIB+M+1) CORRESPONDS TO X(1)
C
      NDPF = 1                   ! FRAME SIZE
      CALL FTOB(IS-M-1,N+M+1,NDPF)   ! CONVERT FIRST PT, # POINTS
     1   NCWFH,TP,ISDE,IIB,NDB,NDPDB) ! TO FIRST BLOCK, # BLOCKS
C
C     RWD IS A SYSTEM DEPENDENT ROUTINE FOR READING BLOCKS INTO IX
C     FROM A DISK FILE SPECIFIED BY FILE, GROUP, USER AND DISK.
C     ISDB = STARTING BLK, NDB = NUMBER OF BLKS
C
      CALL RWD(IX,ISDB,NDB,NWD,IGRP,    ! READ THE DISK FILE
     1   IUSR,IDK)
      CALL I2I(IX(IIB),IX,N+M+1,1.)     ! MOVE DATA TO START OF ARRAY
C
      RETURN
      END
C
C*********************************************************
C
      SUBROUTINE FILTER
C
C     FILTER COEFFICIENTS AND FLATNESS MEASURES FOR RF PROGRAM
C
C       AUTHORED BY STEVEN B. DAVIS - SCRL - AUGUST 1976
C
      COMMON /RFCOM1/ RC(30),A(30),R(30),F(10),B(10)
      COMMON /RFCOM2/ N,M,PRE,IHAM,SF,PRNGE,LP,LA,NFFT,KBU
      COMMON /RFCOM3/ IX(3100),X(2048),FF(3),FB(3)
      COMMON /RFCOM4/ PPQ,APQ,PVA,EX,SFF,SFR,FU,PPER,NPP
      DIMENSION   Y(512)
      EQUIVALENCE    (IX(2077),Y)
```

Figure B2. FORTRAN program.

```
      DIMENSION        AL(30),2(1024)
      EQUIVALENCE      (R,AL),(X(1025),Z)
C
C     PREMPHASIZE AND WINDOW THE DATA, FIND THE INVERSE FILTER
C     IX(1) - IX(M+1) CORRESPONDS TO PREVIOUS M+1 POINTS
C     IX(M+2) CORRESPONDS TO X(1)
C
      CALL I2R(IX(M+2),X,N,1.)         ! COPY SPEECH DATA
      XP = IX(M+1)                     ! PREVIOUS POINT
      CALL DWINDF(X,N,IHAM,PRE,XP)     ! DIF AND HAM WIND SPEECH
      CALL AUTO(N,X,M,A,AL,RC)         ! CALC INVERSE FILTER COEF
C
C     COMPUTE SPECTRAL FLATNESS OF INPUT DATA
C
      CALL I2R(IX(M+2),X,N,1.)         ! COPY SPEECH DATA
      CALL DWINDF(X,NFT,IHAM,PRE,XP)   ! DIF AND HAM WIND SPEECH
      CALL FFTMGR(X,X,2,NFFT,1U,XFSQU) ! FFT AND MAG SQ OF DATA
C
      SUM1 = 0.                        ! ZERO RUNNING SUM VARIABLE
      SUM2 = U.                        ! ZERO RUNNING SUM VARIABLE
      DO 1U J = 1,512                  ! START OF LOOP
      T = X(J)                         ! TEMPORARY STORAGE
      IF (T.GT.U.) SUM1=SUM1+ALOG(T)   ! SUM OF LOG OF DATA
   1U SUM2 = SUM2+T                    ! SUM OF DATA
C
      SFD = 10.*ALOG1U(EXP(SUM1/512.)
     1/(SUM2/512.))                    ! SPECTRAL FLATNESS OF DATA
      SFF = 1U.*ALOG1O(AL(M+1)/AL(1))  ! SPECTRAL FLATNESS OF FILTER
      SFR = SFD-SFF                    ! SPECTRAL FLATNESS OF RESIDUE
C
      RETURN
      END
C
************************************************
C
      SUBROUTINE RESON
C
C     RESONANCE FREQUENCIES AND BANDWIDTHS FOR RF PROGRAM
C
C     AUTHORED BY STEVEN B. DAVIS - SCRL - AUGUST 1976
C
      COMMON /RFCOM1/ RC(30),A(30),R(30),F(1U),B(1U)
      COMMON /RFCOM2/ N,M,PRE,IHAM,SF,PRNGE,LP,LA,NFFT,KBU
      COMMON /RFCOM3/ IX(31UU),X(2U48),FF(3),FB(3)
      COMMON /RFCOM4/ PPQ,APQ,PVA,EX,SFF,SFR,FU,PPER,NPP
      DIMENSION       Y(512)
      EQUIVALENCE     (IX(2U77),Y)
C
      DIMENSION FT(2U),BT(20),TMP1(2U),TMP2(20)
C
      NPEAK = 3                        ! SET NUMBER OF FORMANT PEAKS
      BAND = U.                        ! NO BANDWIDTH CONSTRAINT
      Q = 1.                           ! SET Q OF FORMANT PEAKS
      CALL A2FB(A,M,NPEAK,BAND,Q,SF,   ! FREQ AND BAND BY ROOT SOLVE
     1 FT,BT,NPK,TMP1,TMP2,U)
C
      IF (NPK.GE.3) GO TO 2U           ! 3 PEAKS FOUND
C
      CALL R2CR(FT(NPK+1),3-NPK,U.)    ! ZERO UNUSED LOCATIONS
      CALL R2CR(BT(NPK+1),3-NPK,U.)    ! ZERO UNUSED LOCATIONS
   2U CALL R2k(FT,FF,3,1.)             ! COPY TO OUTPUT ARRAY
      CALL R2R(BT,FB,3,1.)             ! COPY TO OUTPUT ARRAY
C
      RETURN
      END
************************************************
C
C     SUBROUTINE RESIDU
C
C     RESIDUE SIGNAL FOR RF PROGRAM
C
C     AUTHORED BY STEVEN B. DAVIS - SCRL - AUGUST 1976
C
      COMMON /RFCOM1/ RC(30),A(30),R(30),F(10),B(1U)
      COMMON /RFCOM2/ N,M,PRE,IHAM,SF,PRNGE,LP,LA,NFFT,KBU
      COMMON /RFCOM3/ IX(31UU),X(2U48),FF(3),FB(3)
      COMMON /RFCOM4/ PPQ,APQ,PVA,EX,SFF,SFR,FU,PPER,NPP
      DIMENSION       Y(512)
      EQUIVALENCE     (IX(2U77),Y)
C
      DATA ICHN       /'N '/
C
C     INITIALIZE FILTER WITH PAST [FILTERED] DATA POINTS
C     R(2)=X(-1)=IX(M+1),...,R(M+1)=X(-M)=IX(2)
C
      CALL I2R(IX(M+2),X,N,1.)         ! COPY SPEECH DATA
      XP = IX(M+1)                     ! FIRST PREVIOUS POINT
      CALL DWINDF(X,N,ICHN,PRE,XP)     ! DIFFERENCE AND WINDOW DATA
C
      IF (M.LE.0) GO TO 50             ! ANY FILTERING REQUIRED?
      IF (PRE.LT.U.) GO TO 20          ! LOW FREQUENCY PREEMPHASIS?
C
      T2 = IX(1)                       ! INIT FOR HF PREEMPHASIS
      DO 1U J = 2,M+1                  ! LOOP FOR HF PREEMPHASIS
      T1 = IX(J)                       ! SAVE CURRENT VALUE
   10 R(M+3-J) = T1-PRE*T2             ! CALC PREVIOUS VALUE
      T2 = T1                          ! SAVE PREVIOUS VALUE
      GO TO 40                         ! PREEMPHASIS DONE
C
   2U T2 = 0                           ! INIT FOR LF PREEMPHASIS
      DO 30 J = 2,M+1                  ! LOOP FOR LF PREEMPHASIS
      T1 = IX(J)                       ! SAVE CURRENT VALUE
      R(M+3-J) = -PRE*T2               ! CALC CURRENT VALUE
   30 T2 = T1                          ! SAVE PREVIOUS VALUE
   4U CALL DIRECT(X,N,R,1.,U,A,M,X)    ! FILTER SPEECH TO GET RESIDUE
C
   50 RETURN
      END
```

```fortran
      SUBROUTINE RFPLT1
C
C     PLOT FIRST HALF OF RESULTS FOR RF PROGRAM
C
C     AUTHORED BY STEVEN B. DAVIS - SCRL - AUGUST 1976
C
      COMMON /RFCOM1/ RC(30),A(30),R(30),F(10),B(10)
      COMMON /RFCOM2/ N,M,PRE,IHAM,SF,PRNGE,LP,LA,NFFT,KBU
      COMMON /RFCOM3/ IX(3100),X(2048),FF(3),FB(3)
      COMMON /RFCOM4/ PPQ,APQ,PVA,EX,SFF,SFR,F0,PPER,NPP
      DIMENSION       Y(512)
      EQUIVALENCE     (IX(2077),Y)
C
      DIMENSION       Z(256)
      EQUIVALENCE     (Y(257),Z)
C
C     ERASE IS A SYSTEM DEPENDENT ROUTINE FOR THE TEKTRONIX SCREEN.
C     FTPLOT IS A SYSTEM DEPENDENT ROUTINE FOR GRAPHICS ON THE
C     TEKTRONIX SCREEN. FIRST ARGUMENT FOR PEN MOVEMENT
C     (U IS MOVE WITH PEN UP, 1 IS MOVE WITH PEN DOWN),
C     SECOND ARGUMENT FOR X COORDINATE (U.LE.X.LE.1023.),
C     AND THIRD ARGUMENT FOR Y COORDINATE (U.LE.Y.LE.780),
C     ALPHA IS A SYSTEM DEPENDENT ROUTINE FOR ALPHANUMERIC MODE
C
      CALL ERASE                     ! ERASE THE SCREEN
C
C     PLOT INVERSE FILTER SPECTRUM
C
      CALL FTPLOT(0,0,750)           ! MOVE PEN TO (0,750)
      CALL ALPHA                     ! CHARACTER MODE
      WRITE(KBU,20)
20    FORMAT(39X,' *** INVERSE FILTER SPECTRUM ***')
      WRITE(KBU,30) SFF
30    FORMAT(39X,'        FLATNESS =',F8.3)
C
      CALL FFTMGR(A,Y,Z,M+1,9,XFSQ)  ! FFT MAG OF A-COEFF
      IDD = 0                        ! INITIALIZE FOR PLOT
      LO 40 I = 1,256                ! LOOP FOR SPECTRAL PLOTTING
      IBB = -ALOG10(Y(I))*16.        ! CALC SCALED INTEGER VALUE
      CALL FTPLOT(IDD,625+I,650+IBB) ! DRAW A LINE TO NEXT PT
      IDD = 1                        ! TURN PEN ON
C
C     PLOT FORMANT FREQUENCIES AND BANDWIDTHS
C
      CALL FTPLOT(0,0,750)           ! MOVE PEN TO (0,750)
      CALL ALPHA                     ! CHARACTER MODE
      WRITE(KBU,50)
50    FORMAT(' *** FORMANT FREQ AND BAND ***')
      WRITE(KBU,60) FF(1),FF(2),FF(3)
      WRITE(KBU,70) FB(1),FB(2),FB(3)
60    FORMAT('   F  = ',F6.0,2F7.0)
70    FORMAT('   B  = ',F6.U,2F7.0)
C
      DELTHZ = SF/2./256.            ! CALC HZ/SCREEN PT
      CALL FTPLOT(U,625+ 1,610)      ! MOVE PEN TO (626,610)
      CALL FTPLOT(1,625+256,610)     ! DRAW A LINE TO (781,610)
C
      DO 8U J = 1,3
      IAA = FF(J)/DELTHZ+.5          ! LOOP TO PLOT FREQ LOC
      CALL FTPLOT(0,625+IAA,610)     ! CALC SCALED FREQ POSITION
      CALL FTPLOT(1,625+IAA,620)     ! MOVE PEN TO FREQUENCY LOC
80                                   ! DRAW A SHORT LINE AT THE LOC
C
C     PLOT DATA
C
      CALL FTPLOT(0,0,630)           ! MOVE PEN TO (0,630)
      CALL ALPHA                     ! CHARACTER MODE
      WRITE(KBU,90)
90    FORMAT(' *** SPEECH ***')
C
      IDD = U                        ! INITIALIZE FOR PLOTTING
      XSCL = 1024./N                 ! X-AXIS SCALE FACTOR
      CALL PPIC(IX,1,N,LOC)          ! FIND PEAK OF SPEECH DATA
      YSCL = 60./IX(LOC)             ! Y-AXIS SCALE FACTOR
      IF (YSCL.LT.0.) YSCL = -YSCL   ! USE POSITIVE SCALE FACTOR
C
      DO 100 J = 1,N
      IAA = (J-1)*XSCL               ! CALC SCALED X COORDINATE
      IBB = IX(M+1+J)*YSCL           ! CALC SCALED Y COORDINATE
      CALL FTPLOT(IDD,IAA,IBB+525)   ! DRAW A LINE TO NEXT PT
      IDD = 1                        ! TURN PEN ON
100   CALL FTPLOT(0,0,525)           ! MOVE PEN TO (0,525)
      CALL FTPLOT(1,1023,525)        ! DRAW A LINE ON THE SCREEN
C
C     PLOT RESIDUE
C
      CALL FTPLOT(0,0,450)           ! MOVE PEN TO (0,450)
      CALL ALPHA                     ! CHARACTER MODE
      WRITE(KBU,110)
110   FORMAT(' *** RESIDUE ***')
C
      IDD = 0                        ! INITIALIZE FOR PLOT
      CALL PPIC(X,1,N,LOC)           ! FIND PEAK OF RESIDUE DATA
      YSCL = 60./X(LOC)              ! CALC Y-AXIS SCALE FACTOR
      IF (YSCL.LT.0.) YSCL = -YSCL   ! USE POSITIVE SCALE FACTOR
C
      DO 120 J = 1,N
      IAA = (J-1)*XSCL               ! CALC SCALED X COORDINATE
      IBB = X(J)*YSCL                ! CALC SCALED Y COORDINATE
      CALL FTPLOT(IDD,IAA,IBB+345)   ! DRAW A LINE TO NEXT PT
      IDD = 1                        ! TURN PEN ON
120   CALL FTPLOT(0,0,345)           ! MOVE PEN TO (0,345)
      CALL FTPLOT(1,1023,345)        ! DRAW A LINE ON THE SCREEN
      CALL ALPHA                     ! CHARACTER MODE
C
      RETURN
      END
```

```fortran
      SUBROUTINE PITCH
C
C     PITCH PERIOD AND PITCH LOCATIONS FOR RF PROGRAM
C
C     AUTHORED BY STEVEN B. DAVIS - SCRL - AUGUST 1976
C
      COMMON /RFCOM1/ RC(30),A(30),R(30),F(10),B(10)
      COMMON /RFCOM2/ N,M,PRE,IHAM,SF,PRNGE,LP,LA,NFFT,KBU
      COMMON /RFCOM3/ IX(3100),X(2048),FF(3),FB(3)
      COMMON /RFCOM4/ PPQ,APQ,PVA,EX,SFF,SFR,FU,PPER,NPP
      DIMENSION       Y(512)
      EQUIVALENCE     (IX(2077),Y)
C
      DIMENSION       IPPT(20),PAT(20)
      DATA            LPER,SFL,SFH/4,2u.,4uu./
C
C     FIND FUNDAMENTAL PITCH AND PITCH CORRELATION
C     COMPUTE FLOATING POINT AUTOCORRELATION OF RESIDUE SIGNAL
C
      ILOW = SF/SFH                    ! LOW END FOR PITCH PERIOD
      IHGH = SF/SFL                    ! HIGH END FOR PITCH PERIOD
      IF (IHGH.GT.N) IHGH = N          ! REDUCE HIGH END IF NECESSARY
C
      CALL DWINDF(X,N,IHAM,U,.U.)      ! HAM WIND RESIDUE SIGNAL
      CALL RACOR(IHGH,N,X,Y,SCM)       ! AUTOCORR OF RESIDUE SIGNAL
C
      DO 10 I = 1,LPER                 ! FIND LPER PEAKS FROM ORIGIN
      CALL PPPICF(Y,ILOW,IHGH,LOC)     ! FIND HIGHEST PEAK IN RANGE
      IPPT(I) = LOC                    ! SAVE THE LOCATION
      PAT(I) = Y(LOC)                  ! SAVE THE VALUE
10    Y(LOC) = U.                      ! ZERO THE SAVED LOCATION
C
      IP = IPPT(1)                     ! SET PITCH TO HIGHEST PEAK
      DO 20 I = 2,LPER                 ! LOOP ON NEXT 3 PEAKS
      IPX = IPPT(I)                    ! RETRIEVE THE PEAK
      IF (IPX.LT.IP-3) IP = IPX        ! RESET PITCH PER IF NECESSARY
C
      DO 30 I = 1,LPER                 ! LOOP ON THE SAVED PEAKS
      LOC = IPPT(I)                    ! RETRIEVE THE LOCATION
30    Y(LOC) = PAT(I)                  ! RESET THE PEAK VALUE
C
      CALL PARAB(Y(IP-1),Y(IP),        ! PARABOLIC INTERPOLATION
     1  Y(IP+1),PVA,PINCR)
C
      PPER = IP+PINCR                  ! ADD OFFSET TO PITCH PERIOD
      F0 = SF/PPER                     ! CALC FUNDAMENTAL FREQUENCY
C
      RETURN
      END
```

```fortran
      SUBROUTINE PERTUR
C
C     PITCH PERIOD LOCATIONS AND PERTURBATION QUOTIENTS FOR RF PGM
C
C     AUTHORED BY STEVEN B. DAVIS - SCRL - AUGUST 1976
C
      COMMON /RFCOM1/ RC(30),A(30),R(30),F(10),B(10)
      COMMON /RFCOM2/ N,M,PRE,IHAM,SF,PRNGE,LP,LA,NFFT,KBU
      COMMON /RFCOM3/ IX(3100),X(2048),FF(3),FB(3)
      COMMON /RFCOM4/ PPQ,APQ,PVA,EX,SFF,SFR,FU,PPER,NPP
      DIMENSION       Y(512)
      EQUIVALENCE     (IX(2077),Y)
C
      DIMENSION       IPL(100,2),PTLOC(100),PTAMP(100),
     1                APQQ(2),PPQQ(2),NNPP(2),XMOM(4)
      EQUIVALENCE     (IX,IPL),(IX(2u1),PTLOC),(IX(4u1),PTAMP)
C
C     GET PEAK LOCATIONS AND VALUES (WITH PARABOLIC INTERPOLATION)
C     COMPUTE PITCH BY SUCCESSIVE DIFFERENCES OF PERIODS
C     IPL CONTAINS THE PITCH LOCATIONS
C     USE POSITIVE AND NEGATIVE PEAKS AND CHOOSE THE SMALLEST APQ
C
      DO 40 K = 1,2
      CALL PLOCF(X,N,PPER,PRNGE,       ! LOOP FOR POS AND NEG PEAKS
     1  IPL(1,K),NNPP(K))              ! FIND PEAK LOCATIONS
      PTOLD = 0.                       ! PREVIOUS PEAK LOCATION
C
      DO 30 J = 1,NNPP(K)              ! INTERPOLATE PEAKS
      L = IPL(J,K)                     ! RETRIEVE LOCATION
      IF (L.GT.1.AND.L.LT.N) GO TO 1u  ! TEST FOR IN RANGE
      PTINC = 0.                       ! NO INTERPOLATION AT ENDPTS
      PTAMP(J) = X(L)                  ! USE ORIGINAL VALUE
      GO TO 20                         ! SKIP INTERPOLATION
10    CALL PARAB(X(L-1),X(L),X(L+1),   ! PARABOLIC INTERPOLATION
     1  PTAMP(J),PTINC)
20    PTNEW = L+PTINC                  ! INTERPOLATED NEW LOCATION
      PTLOC(J) = PTNEW-PTOLD           ! STORE INTERPOLATED PERIOD
30    PTOLD = PTNEW                    ! RESET PREVIOUS VALUE
C
C     COMPUTE PERTURBATION COEFFICIENTS
C
      CALL PTBQUO(PTLOC(2),NNPP(K)-1,  ! PITCH PERIOD PERTURB QUO
     1  LP,PPQQ(K))
      CALL PTBQUO(PTAMP,NNPP(K),       ! AMPLITUDE PERTURB QUO
     1  LA,APQQ(K))
40    CALL R2R(X,X,N,-1.)              ! NEGATE RESIDUE SIGNAL
C
      K = 1                            ! DEFAULT TO POSITIVE PEAKS
      IF (APQQ(2).LE.APQQ(1)) K = 2    ! USE NEG PEAKS IF SMALLER APQ
      APQ = APQQ(K)                    ! SET APQ
      PPQ = PPQQ(K)                    ! SET PPQ
      NPP = NNPP(K)                    ! SET NNP
      IF (K.EQ.2) CALL I2I(IPL(1,K),   ! SET PITCH PERIOD LOCATIONS
     1  IPL(1,1),NPP,1.)
```

```
C
C      FIND MOMENTS AND COMPUTE COEFFICIENT OF EXCESS
C
      CALL MOMENT(N,X,4,XMOM)        ! FIND 4 MOMENTS OF RESIDUE
      RM1 = XMOM(1)                  ! SAVE FIRST MOMENT
      RM2 = XMOM(2)                  ! SAVE SECOND MOMENT
      RM3 = XMOM(3)                  ! SAVE THIRD MOMENT
      RM4 = XMOM(4)                  ! SAVE FOURTH MOMENT
      VAR = RM2-RM1*RM1              ! COMPUTE VARIANCE
      VAR2 = VAR*VAR                 ! SQUARE OF VARIANCE
      EX = 0.                        ! DEFAULT COEFF OF EXCESS
      IF (VAR.LE.0.) GO TO 50        ! DO NOT DIVIDE BY ZERO
      EX = (RM1*(RM1*(RM1*(-3.*RM1)  ! CALC COEFF OF EXCESS
     1 +6.*RM2)-4.*RM3)+RM4)/VAR2-3.
C
50    RETURN
      END
C**********************************************************
      SUBROUTINE RFPLT2
C
C     PLOT SECOND HALF OF THE RESULTS FOR RF PROGRAM
C
C     AUTHORED BY STEVEN B. DAVIS - SCRL - AUGUST 1976
C
      COMMON /RFCOM1/ RC(30),A(30),R(30),F(10),B(10)
      COMMON /RFCOM2/ N,M,PRE,IHAM,SF,PRNGE,LP,LA,NFFT,KBU
      COMMON /RFCOM3/ IX(3100),X(2048),FF(3),FB(3)
      COMMON /RFCOM4/ PPQ,APQ,PVA,EX,SFF,FU,PPER,NPP
      DIMENSION Y(512)
      EQUIVALENCE (IX(2077),Y)
C
      DIMENSION Z(1024)
      EQUIVALENCE (X(1025),Z)
      DATA SFL/20./
C
C     PLOT RESIDUE AUTOCORRELATION
C
      CALL FTPLOT(0,0,195)           ! MOVE PEN TO (0,195)
      CALL ALPHA                     ! CHARACTER MODE
      WRITE(KBU,10)
10    FORMAT(' *** RESIDUE AUTOCORRELATION ***')
      WRITE(KBU,20) PVA
20    FORMAT('      PITCH AMPLITUDE =',F6.3)
      IHGH = SF/SFL                  ! HIGH NUMBER OF AUTOCORR PTS
      IF (IHGH.GT.N) IHGH = N        ! USE MINIMUM OF IHGH AND N
      IDD = 0                        ! INITIALIZE FOR PLOT
C
      DO 30 J = 1,IHGH               ! LOOP ON NO. OF AUTOCORR PTS
      IBB = Y(J)*100.                ! CALC SCALED Y COORDINATE
      CALL FTPLOT(IDD,J-1,IBB+45)    ! DRAW A LINE TO (J-1,IBB+45)
      IDD = 1                        ! PUT PEN DOWN
      CALL FTPLOT(0,0,45)            ! MOVE PEN TO (0,45)
30    CALL FTPLOT(1,IHGH,45)         ! DRAW A LINE ON THE SCREEN
```

```
C
C      WRITE COEFFICIENT OF EXCESS
C
      CALL FTPLOT(0,0,245)           ! MOVE PEN TO (0,245)
      CALL ALPHA                     ! CHARACTER MODE
      WRITE(KBU,40)
40    FORMAT(' *** AMPLITUDE DISTRIBUTION ***')
      WRITE(KBU,50) EX
50    FORMAT(' COEFFICIENT OF EXCESS =',F6.3)
C
C      WRITE PERTURBATION QUOTIENTS
C
      CALL FTPLOT(0,0,245)           ! MOVE PEN TO (0,245)
      CALL ALPHA                     ! CHARACTER MODE
      WRITE(KBU,60)
60    FORMAT(39X,' *** PERTURBATION MEASURES ***')
      WRITE(KBU,70) PPQ,APQ
70    FORMAT(39X,' PITCH =',F8.5,' AMP =',F8.5)
C
C      PLOT PITCH LOCATIONS
C
      XSCL = 1024./N                 ! CALC X-AXIS SCALE FACTOR
      DO 80 I = 1,NPP                ! PLOT PITCH PERIOD LOCATIONS
      IAA = (IX(I)-1)*XSCL           ! CALC SCALED X COORDINATE
      CALL FTPLOT(0,IAA,255)         ! MOVE PEN TO (IAA,255)
      CALL FTPLOT(1,IAA,270)         ! DRAW A LINE TO (IAA,270)
      CALL FTPLOT(0,0,270)           ! MOVE PEN TO (0,270)
80    CALL FTPLOT(1,1023,270)        ! DRAW A LINE ON THE SCREEN
C
C      CALCULATE MAGNITUDE OF RESIDUE SPECTRUM
C
      CALL FTPLOT(0,0,195)           ! MOVE PEN TO (0,195)
      CALL ALPHA                     ! CHARACTER MODE
      WRITE(KBU,90)
90    FORMAT(39X,' *** RESIDUE SPECTRUM ***')
      WRITE(KBU,100) SFR
100   FORMAT(39X,'      FLATNESS =',F8.3)
C
      CALL DWIND(X,NFFT,IHAM,0.,0.)  ! HAMMING WINDOW RESIDUE
      CALL FFTMGR(X,X,2,NFFT,10,XFSQ)! FFT MAG OF RESIDUE
C
      IDD = 0                        ! INITIALIZE FOR PLOT
      DO 110 I = 1,256               ! PLOT RESIDUE SPECTRUM PTS
      IBB = ALOG10(X(I+I-1))*16.     ! CALC SCALED Y COORDINATE
      CALL FTPLOT(IDD,625+I,IBB)     ! DRAW A LINE TO (625+I,IBB)
110   IDD = 1                        ! PUT PEN DOWN
      CALL FTPLOT(0,0,25)            ! MOVE PEN TO (0,25)
      CALL ALPHA                     ! CHARACTER MODE
C
      RETURN
      END
```

```fortran
      SUBROUTINE A2FB(A,M,NPEAKS,BAND,Q,SF,F,B,NP,ROOTR,ROOTI,IDEV)
C
C     FREQUENCIES AND BANDWIDTHS FROM INVERSE FILTER POLYNOMIAL
C
C     AUTHORED BY STEVEN B. DAVIS - SCRL - JANUARY 1976
C
C     DESCRIPTION OF ARGUMENTS
C
C     A       POLYNOMIAL OF "A" COEFFICIENTS WITH A(1) = 1.
C     M       ORDER OF THE POLYNOMIAL
C     NPEAK   NUMBER OF PEAKS TO SEARCH FOR
C     BAND    MAXIMUM BANDWIDTH TO SEARCH FOR
C     Q       MINIMUM CUTOFF FOR PEAKING ( F(I)/B(I) MUST BE > Q )
C     SF      SAMPLING FREQUENCY
C     F       VECTOR OF FORMANT FREQUENCIES IN HZ (DIM > M+1)
C     B       VECTOR OF FORMANT BANDWIDTHS IN HZ (DIM > M+1)
C     NP      NUMBER OF FORMANTS FOUND
C     ROOTR   REAL WORKING ARRAY
C     ROOTI   IMAG WORKING ARRAY
C     IDEV    DEVICE FOR PRINTING INTERMEDIATE RESULTS (IF > 0)
C
C     NOTE:   IF NPEAK > 0, BAND IS IGNORED
C     NOTE:   IF NPEAK = 0, ALL PEAKS WITH B(I) < BAND WILL BE USED
C     NOTE:   A "Q"TEST: IS PERFORMED IF Q > 0
C     NOTE:   NP < 0 CORRESPONDS TO THE FOLLOWING ERROR CONDITIONS
C     NOTE:     NP = -1        ORDER OF POLYNOMIAL < 1
C     NOTE:     NP = -2        ORDER OF POLYNOMIAL > 36
C     NOTE:     NP = -3        UNABLE TO DETERMINE ROOT
C     NOTE:     NP = -4        HIGH ORDER COEFFICIENT IS ZERO
C
      DIMENSION A(1),F(1),B(1),ROOTR(1),ROOTI(1)
      DATA PI/3.14159265/,ROOTR(1),ROOTI(1)
      DATA CFREQ,CBAND/'FREQ','BAND'/
C
      NPEAK = NPEAKS
      NP = 0
      IF (M.LE.0) GO TO 140
C
C     INVERT ORDER OF COEFFICIENTS AND SOLVE FOR ROOTS
C
      CALL R2KR(A,F,M+1,1.)
      CALL POLRT(F,B,M,ROOTR,ROOTI,IER)
      IF (IER.EQ.0) GO TO 10
      NP = -IER
      GO TO 140
C
C     COMPUTE FREQUENCIES AND BANDWIDTHS FROM ROOTS
C
   10 DO 20 I = 1,M
      RTR = ROOTR(I)
      RTI = ROOTI(I)
      F(I) = 0.
      IF (RTI.EQ.0..AND.RTR.EQ.0.) GO TO 20
      RAD = SQRT(RTR*RTR+RTI*RTI)
      IF (RTI.LT.0.) RTI = -RTI
      ANGLE = PI/2.
      IF (RTR.NE.0.) ANGLE = ATAN(RTI/RTR)
      IF (RTR.LT.0.) ANGLE = PI+ANGLE
      F(I) = SF*ANGLE*0.5/PI
      B(I) = -SF*ALOG(RAD)/PI
   20 CONTINUE
C
C     PRINT INTERMEDIATE RESULTS
C
      IF (IDEV.LE.0) GO TO 50
      MM = MIN0(M,8)
      WRITE(IDEV,30) CFREQ,(F(I),I=1,MM)
      IF (M.GT.8) WRITE(IDEV,40) (F(I),I=9,M)
      WRITE(IDEV,30) CBAND,(B(I),I=1,MM)
      IF (M.GT.8) WRITE(IDEV,40) (B(I),I=9,M)
   30 FORMAT(T4,A4,8F8.0)
   40 FORMAT(T6,8F8.0)
C
C     FIRST ORDER THE RESULTS BY INCREASING BANDWIDTH, THEN
C     ORDER THE ACCEPTABLE BANDWIDTHS BY INCREASING FREQUENCY
C
   50 CALL ORDERF(M,B,F,NP,ROOTR,ROOTI)
      IF (NP.LE.0) GO TO 140
      NPEAK = MIN0(NPEAK,NP)
      IF (NPEAK.GT.0) GO TO 100
      LPEAK = 0
   60 DO 70 JJ = 1,NP
      IF (B(JJ).GT.BAND) GO TO 80
   70 NPEAK = NP
      GO TO 90
   80 NPEAK = JJ-1
   90 IF (NPEAK.GT.0) GO TO 100
      NP = 0
      GO TO 140
  100 CALL ORDERF(NPEAK,F,B,NP,ROOTR,ROOTI)
      IF (NP.LE.0.OR.Q.LE.0.) GO TO 140
C
C     TEST THAT ALL F(I),B(I) SATISFY THE Q RESTRAINT
C
      K = 1
  110 IF (B(K).LE.0.) GO TO 120
      QT = F(K)/B(K)
      IF (QT.LE.Q) GO TO 120
      IF (K.EQ.NP) GO TO 140
      K = K+1
      GO TO 110
  120 NP = NP-1
      IF (NP.LE.0) GO TO 140
      DO 130 L = K,NP
      F(L) = B(L+1)
      B(L) = B(L-1)
  130 GO TO 110
  140 RETURN
      END
```

```
      SUBROUTINE AUTO(N,X,M,A,ALPHA,RC)
C
C     CALCULATE INVERSE FILTER COEFFICIENTS USING LEVINSON'S METHOD.
C     SEE MARKEL AND GRAY (1976, PG. 219) FOR DESCRIPTION.
C
C     AUTHORED BY JOHN D. MARKEL - SCRL - JANUARY 1976
C
C     DESCRIPTION OF ARGUMENTS
C
C     N        NUMBER OF POINTS
C     X        VECTOR OF SAMPLED SPEECH POINTS
C     M        ORDER OF INVERSE FILTER
C     A        VECTOR OF INVERSE FILTER COEFFICIENTS
C     ALPHA    VECTOR OF ENERGY TERMS FOR EACH ITERATION
C     RC       VECTOR OF REFLECTION COEFFICIENTS
C
      DIMENSION X(1),A(1),RC(1),ALPHA(1),R(51)
C
      DO 10 K = 1,M+1
      R(K) = 0.
      DO 10 NP = 1,N-K+1
10    R(K) = R(K)+X(NP)*X(NP+K-1)
      ALPHA(1) = R(1)
      IF (M.EQ.0) GO TO 60
      RC(1) = -R(2)/R(1)
      A(2) = RC(1)
      ALPHA(2) = R(1)+R(2)*RC(1)
      IF (M.EQ.1) GO TO 60
      DO 40 MINC = 2,M
      S = 0.
      DO 20 IP = 1,MINC
20    S = S+R(MINC-IP+2)*A(IP)
      RC(MINC) = -S/ALPHA(MINC)
      MH = MINC/2+1
      DO 30 IP = 2,MH
      IB = MINC-IP+2
      AT = A(IP)+RC(MINC)*A(IB)
      A(IB) = A(IB)+RC(MINC)*A(IP)
30    A(IP) = AT
      A(MINC+1) = RC(MINC)
      ALPHA(MINC+1) = ALPHA(MINC)-ALPHA(MINC)*RC(MINC)*RC(MINC)
      IF (ALPHA(MINC)) 50,50,40
40    CONTINUE
50    M = MINC-1
60    RETURN
      END
```

```
      SUBROUTINE DIRECT(X,N,D,A,M,P,L,Y)
C
C     DIRECT FORM FILTER IMPLEMENTATION
C
C     AUTHORED BY JOHN D. MARKEL - SCRL - JANUARY 1976
C
C     DESCRIPTION OF ARGUMENTS
C
C     X        VECTOR OF INPUT SAMPLES
C     N        NUMBER OF INPUT SAMPLES
C     D        VECTOR FOR FILTER DELAYS (INIT WITH PREVIOUS SAMPLES)
C     A        VECTOR OF DENOMINATOR TERMS (ASSUMES A(1) = 1.)
C     M        ORDER OF DENOMINATOR (M+1 DENOMINATOR TERMS)
C     P        VECTOR OF NUMERATOR TERMS
C     L        ORDER OF NUMERATOR (L+1 NUMERATOR TERMS)
C     Y        VECTOR OF OUTPUT SAMPLES
C
      DIMENSION X(1),A(1),P(1),D(1),Y(1)
C
      MAX = L
      IF (M.GT.L) MAX = M
      DO 60 I = 1,N
      DD = X(I)
C
C     TEST FOR ALL ZERO FILTER (M = 0)
C
      IF (M.EQ.0) GO TO 20
      DO 10 J = 2,M+1
10    DD = DD-D(J)*A(J)
20    D(1) = DD
      YY = DD*P(1)
C
C     TEST FOR ALL POLE FILTER (L = 0)
C
      IF (L.EQ.0) GO TO 40
      DO 30 J = 2,L+1
30    YY = YY+D(J)*P(J)
40    Y(I) = YY
C
C     UPDATE DELAY BUFFER
C
      DO 50 J = MAX+1,2,-1
50    D(J) = D(J-1)
60    CONTINUE
      RETURN
      END
```

```
      SUBROUTINE DWINDF(Y,N,IHAM,PRE,XPRE)
C
C     PREEMPHASIS AND WINDOWING OF A SIGNAL
C
C     AUTHORED BY STEVEN B. DAVIS - SCRL - AUGUST 1976
C
C     DESCRIPTION OF ARGUMENTS
C
C     Y      ARRAY CONTAINING THE SIGNAL TO BE USED
C     N      NUMBER OF POINTS
C     IHAM   ALPHABETIC 'Y' OR 'N ' TO CONTROL WINDOW USE
C     PRE    PREEMPHASIS FACTOR (-1.LE.PRE.LE.1)
C     XPRE   PREVIOUS SIGNAL POINT FOR PROPER PREEMPHASIS
C
C     IF PRE>0, HIGH FREQUENCY PREEMPHASIS IS USED
C     IF PRE<0, LOW FREQUENCY PREEMPHASIS IS USED
C     IF IHAM = 'Y ', A HAMMING WINDOW IS USED
C     IF IHAM = 'N ', NO WINDOW IS USED
C
      DIMENSION Y(1)
      DATA PI/3.14159265/
      DATA ICHY/'Y '/
C
      HAM(I) = .54-.46*COS((I-1)*PDN)    ! HAMMING WINDOW FUNCTION
C
      IF (IHAM.NE.ICHY) GO TO 50         ! TEST FOR HAMMING WINDOW
      PDN = 2*PI/N                       ! CONSTANT 2 PI/N FOR HAM
C
C     HIGH FREQUENCY PREEMPHASIS AND HAMMING WINDOW
C
      IF (PRE.LT.0.) GO TO 30            ! TEST FOR LOW FREQ PRE
      B = XPRE                           ! RETRIEVE PREVIOUS INPUT PT
      DO 20 I = 1,N                      ! LOOP FOR EACH PT
      A = Y(I)                           ! RETRIEVE CURRENT INPUT PT
      Y(I) = (A-PRE*B)*HAM(I)            ! CALCULATE OUTPUT PT
      B = A                              ! SAVE PREVIOUS INPUT PT
   20 GO TO 100                          ! END OF ROUTINE
C
C     LOW FREQUENCY PREEMPHASIS AND HAMMING WINDOW
C
   30 B = 0.                             ! RETRIEVE PREVIOUS OUTPUT PT
      DO 40 I = 1,N                      ! LOOP FOR EACH PT
      A = Y(I)-PRE*B                     ! CALC UNWINDOWED OUTPUT PT
      Y(I) = A*HAM(I)                    ! SAVE WINDOWED OUTPUT PT
      B = A                              ! SAVE UNWINDOWED OUTPUT PT
   40 GO TO 100                          ! END OF ROUTINE
C
C     HIGH FREQUENCY PREEMPHASIS AND NO WINDOWING
C
   50 IF (PRE.LT.0.) GO TO 80            ! TEST FOR LOW FREQ PRE
      B = XPRE                           ! RETRIEVE PREVIOUS INPUT PT
      DO 70 I = 1,N                      ! LOOP FOR EACH PT
      A = Y(I)                           ! RETRIEVE CURRENT INPUT PT
      Y(I) = A-PRE*B                     ! CALCULATE OUTPUT PT
   70 B = A                              ! SAVE PREVIOUS INPUT PT
      GO TO 100                          ! END OF ROUTINE
C
C     LOW FREQUENCY PREEMPHASIS AND NO WINDOWING
C
   80 B = 0.                             ! RETRIEVE PREVIOUS OUTPUT PT
      DO 90 I = 1,N                      ! LOOP FOR EACH PT
      A = Y(I)-PRE*B                     ! CALCULATE OUTPUT PT
      Y(I) = A                           ! SAVE OUTPUT PT
   90 B = A                              ! SAVE OUTPUT PT
  100 RETURN
      END
C
***********************************************************
C
      SUBROUTINE FFFT(X,Y,M,L)
C
C     FAST FOURIER TRANSFORM WITH PRUNING
C
C     AUTHORED BY JOHN D. MARKEL - SCRL - JANUARY 1975
C
C     DESCRIPTION OF ARGUMENTS
C
C     X      VECTOR OF REAL DATA POINTS
C     Y      VECTOR OF IMAGINARY DATA POINTS
C     M      ORDER OF FFT
C     L      ORDER OF PRUNED DATA (N < 2**L)
C
      DIMENSION X(1),Y(1)
      DATA PI/3.14159265/
C
      N = 2**M
      L2 = 2**L
      DO 40 LO = 1,M
      LMX = 2**(M-LO)
      LMM = LMX
      LIX = 2*LMX
      SCL = 2*PI/LIX
      IF (L.LT.M-LO) LMM = L2
      DO 40 LM = 1,LMM
   30 ARG = (LM-1)*SCL
      C = COS(ARG)
      S = SIN(ARG)
      DO 40 LI = LIX,N,LIX
      J1 = LI-LIX+LM
      J2 = J1+LMX
      T1 = X(J1)-X(J2)
      T2 = Y(J1)-Y(J2)
      X(J1) = X(J1)+X(J2)
      X(J2) = C*T1+S*T2
      Y(J1) = Y(J1)+Y(J2)
   40 Y(J2) = C*T2-S*T1
      RETURN
      END
```

```
      SUBROUTINE FFTMGR(A,Y,X,N,NBITS1,XFSQ)
C
C     CALCULATE MAGNITUDE SQUARED OF FOURIER SPECTRUM
C
C     AUTHORED BY CRAIG S. LEEDS - SCRL - JANUARY 1975
C
C     DESCRIPTION OF ARGUMENTS
C
C     A      VECTOR OF INPUT SAMPLES
C     X      VECTOR OF REAL SPECTRUM POINTS ON OUTPUT
C     Y      VECTOR OF MAGNITUDE SPECTRUM POINTS ON OUTPUT
C     N      NUMBER OF POINTS
C     NBITS1 ORDER OF FFT
C     XFSQ   MAGNITUDE OF FOLDING FREQUENCY SPECTRUM POINT
C
      DIMENSION X(1),Y(1),A(1)
C
      NBITS = NBITS1-1
      NT = 2**NBITS
      L = 1.442695*ALOG(N-1.E-5)
C
      CALL SHUFR(X,Y,NBITS,A,XF,N)
      CALL FFFT(X,Y,NBITS,L)
      CALL RBT(X,Y,NBITS)
      CALL USCRM(X,Y,NBITS)
C
C     MAGNITUDE SPECTRUM IN Y ARRAY AND REAL PART IN X ARRAY
C
      CALL MAGSQ(Y,X,NT)
      XFSQ = XF*XF
      RETURN
      END

************************************************************

      SUBROUTINE FTOB(ISTF,NFR,NDPF,NCWFH,TPTS,ISDB,IIB,NDB,NDPDB)
C
C     CONVERT "STARTING FRAME" AND "NUMBER OF FRAMES"
C     TO "STARTING DISK BLOCK", "NUMBER OF DISK BLOCKS",
C
C     AUTHORED BY LARRY L. PFEIFER - SCRL - JANUARY 1975
C
C     DESCRIPTION OF ARGUMENTS
C
C     ISTF   STARTING FRAME
C     NFR    NUMBER OF FRAMES
C     NDPF   NUMBER DATA POINTS PER FRAME
C     NCWFH  NUMBER COMPUTER WORDS IN FILE HEADER
C     TPTS   NUMBER OF TOTAL POINTS
C     ISDB   STARTING DISK BLOCK
C     IIB    STARTING INDEX IN THE FIRST BLOCK
C     NDB    NUMBER OF DISK BLOCKS
C     NDPDB  NUMBER DATA POINTS IN DISK BLOCK
C
      STPT = (FLOAT(ISTF-1))*(FLOAT(NDPF))+1.+NCWFH
      ISDB = (STPT-1.)/FLOAT(NDPDB)
      IIB  = STPT-(FLOAT(ISDB)*FLOAT(NDPDB))
      TPTS = FLOAT(NFR)*FLOAT(NDPF)
      NLIB = NDPDB-IIB+1
      TLEFT = TPTS-NLIB
      IF (TLEFT.GT.0.) GO TO 10
      NDB = 1
      GO TO 20
   10 NDB = (TLEFT-1.)/FLOAT(NDPDB)+2.
   20 RETURN
      END

************************************************************

      SUBROUTINE I2CI(IX,N,ISCL)
C
C     SET AN INTEGER ARRAY TO A CONSTANT VALUE
C
C     AUTHORED BY STEVEN B. DAVIS - SCRL - AUGUST 1976
C
C     DESCRIPTION OF ARGUMENTS
C
C     IX     VECTOR OF DATA
C     N      NUMBER OF POINTS
C     ISCL   DESIRED CONSTANT VALUE
C
      DIMENSION IX(1)
C
      DO 10 I = 1,N
   10 IX(I) = ISCL
      RETURN
      END

************************************************************

      SUBROUTINE I2I(IX,IY,N,SCL)
C
C     TRANSFER AN INTEGER ARRAY TO AN INTEGER ARRAY
C
C     AUTHORED BY CRAIG S. LEEDS - SCRL - JANUARY 1975
C
C     DESCRIPTION OF ARGUMENTS
C
C     IX     ARRAY FOR INPUT
C     IY     ARRAY FOR OUTPUT
C     N      NUMBER OF POINTS
C     SCL    SCALE FACTOR
C
      DIMENSION IX(1),IY(1)
C
      DO 10 J = 1,N
   10 IY(J) = IX(J)*SCL
      RETURN
      END
```

```
      SUBROUTINE I2R(IX,Y,N,SCL)
C
C     TRANSFER AN INTEGER ARRAY TO A REAL ARRAY
C
C     AUTHORED BY CRAIG S. LEEDS - SCRL - JANUARY 1975
C
C     DESCRIPTION OF ARGUMENTS
C
C     IX      ARRAY FOR INPUT
C     Y       ARRAY FOR OUTPUT
C     N       NUMBER OF POINTS
C     SCL     SCALE FACTOR
C
      DIMENSION IX(1),Y(1)
C
      DO 10 J = 1,N
   10 Y(J) = IX(J)*SCL
      RETURN
      END
***************************************************
      SUBROUTINE I2RI(IX,IY,N,SCL)
C
C     COPY AN INTEGER ARRAY TO AN INTEGER ARRAY IN REVERSED ORDER
C     WRITTEN SO THAT AN ARRAY MAY BE REVERSED IN PLACE
C
C     AUTHORED BY STEVEN B. DAVIS - SCRL - AUGUST 1976
C
C     DESCRIPTION OF ARGUMENTS
C
C     IX      ARRAY FOR INPUT
C     IY      ARRAY FOR OUTPUT
C     N       NUMBER OF POINTS
C     SCL     SCALE FACTOR
C
      DIMENSION IX(1),IY(1)
C
      NP1 = N+1
      NPD2 = NP1/2
      DO 10 I = 1,NPD2
      ISAV = IX(I)
      IY(I) = IX(NP1-I)*SCL
   10 IY(NP1-I) = ISAV*SCL
      RETURN
      END
```

```
      SUBROUTINE MAGSQ(X,Y,N)
C
C     COMPUTE MAGNITUDE SQUARED OF TWO ARRAYS
C
C     AUTHORED BY CRAIG S. LEEDS - SCRL - JANUARY 1975
C
C     DESCRIPTION OF ARGUMENTS
C
C     X       FIRST ARRAY FOR INPUT AND MAGNITUDE ARRAY FOR OUTPUT
C     Y       SECOND ARRAY FOR INPUT
C     N       NUMBER OF POINTS
C
      DIMENSION X(1),Y(1)
C
      DO 10 J = 1,N
   10 X(J) = X(J)*X(J)+Y(J)*Y(J)
      RETURN
      END
***************************************************************
      SUBROUTINE MOMENT(N,X,M,XM)
C
C     COMPUTE THE MOMENTS OF A SERIES
C
C     AUTHORED BY STEVEN B. DAVIS - SCRL - AUGUST 1976
C
C     DESCRIPTION OF ARGUMENTS
C
C     N       NUMBER OF POINTS IN THE SERIES
C     X       INPUT SERIES
C     M       NUMBER OF MOMENTS TO COMPUTE
C     XM      OUTPUT MOMENTS
C
      DIMENSION X(1),XM(1)
C
      RPTS = 1./N
      CALL R2CR(XM,M,0.)
      DO 20 I = 1,N
      S = 1.
      T = X(I)
      DO 20 J = 1,M
      S = S*T
   20 XM(J) = XM(J)+S
      CALL R2R(XM,XM,M,RPTS)
      RETURN
      END
```

```
C     SUBROUTINE ORDERF(M,X,Y,MX,A,B)
C
C     ORDER THE POINTS IN AN ARRAY BY INCREASING VALUE
C     AND MATCH ANOTHER ARRAY ACCORDINGLY
C     ELIMINATE NONPOSITIVE AND DUPLICATE ENTRIES
C
C     AUTHORED BY CRAIG S. LEEDS - SCRL - JANUARY 1975
C
C     DESCRIPTION OF ARGUMENTS
C
C     M       NUMBER OF INPUT POINTS
C     X       ARRAY TO BE ORDERED
C     Y       CORRESPONDING ARRAY TO BE MATCHED
C     MX      NUMBER OF OUTPUT POINTS
C     A       ARRAY BUFFER
C     B       ARRAY BUFFER
C
      DIMENSION X(1),Y(1),A(1),B(1)
C
      CALL R2CR(A,M,0.)
      CALL R2CR(B,M,0.)
C
C     ORDER THE COMPRESSED ARRAY
C
      MX = M
      SMIN = 1.E-37
      YP = 0.
      DO 80 JX = 1,MX
      TMIN = 1.E-37
      JLOC = 0
      YPP = 1.E+37
      DO 60 JY = 1,MX
      IF (Y(JY)) 60,60,10
10    IF (X(JY)-SMIN) 60,30,20
20    IF (X(JY)-TMIN) 50,40,60
30    IF (Y(JY)-YP) 60,60,40
40    IF (Y(JY)-YPP) 50,60,60
50    YPP = Y(JY)
      TMIN = X(JY)
      JLOC = JY
60    CONTINUE
C
C     TEST FOR DUPLICATES IN ARRAY
C
      IF (JLOC.GT.0) GO TO 70
      MX = JX-1
      GO TO 90
C
C     MOVE INTO NEW ARRAY
C
70    A(JX) = X(JLOC)
      YP = Y(JLOC)
      B(JX) = YP
80    SMIN = TMIN
```

```
C     MOVE TEMPORARY ARRAY INTO OUTPUT ARRAY
C
90    IF (MX.LE.0) GO TO 100
      CALL R2R(A,X,MX,1.)
      CALL R2R(B,Y,MX,1.)
      RETURN
100   END
C
C     *********************************************
C
      SUBROUTINE PARAB(YM,YO,YP,YMAX,XMAX)
C
C     PARABOLIC INTERPOLATION
C
C     AUTHORED BY STEVEN B. DAVIS - SCRL - AUGUST 1976
C
C     DESCRIPTION OF ARGUMENTS
C
C     YM      Y(-1) - PREVIOUS DISCRETE POINT
C     YO      Y(0)  - PEAK DISCRETE POINT
C     YP      Y(-1) - NEXT DISCRETE POINT
C     YMAX    INTERPOLATED MAXIMUM VALUE
C     XMAX    RELATIVE POSITION OF YMAX  (-1.LE.XMAX.LE.1)
C
      XMAX = 0.
      YMAX = YO
      A = (YP+YM)/2.-YO                 ! SEE MARKEL AND GRAY
      B = (YP-YM)/2.                    ! [1976, PG. 167] FOR A
      IF (A.EQ.0.) GO TO 10            ! DESCRIPTION OF THE ALGORITHM
      XMAX = -B/(2.*A)                 ! FOR PARABOLIC INTERPOLATION
      YMAX = YO+(B/2.)*XMAX
10    RETURN
      END
C
C     *********************************************
C
      SUBROUTINE PLOCF(Y,N,PPER,PRNGE,IPL,NP)
C
C     LOCATION OF POSITIVE DATA PEAKS GIVEN THE PERIOD
C
C     AUTHORED BY STEVEN B. DAVIS - SCRL - AUGUST 1976
C
C     DESCRIPTION OF ARGUMENTS
C
C     Y       DATA ARRAY
C     N       NUMBER OF DATA POINTS
C     PPER    PEAK PERIOD
C     PRNGE   ALLOWABLE SEARCH RANGE FOR SUCCESSIVE PEAKS
C     IPL     PEAK LOCATION ARRAY
C     NP      NUMBER OF PEAKS FOUND
C
      DIMENSION Y(1),IPL(1)
C
C     FIND MAX VALUE AND ASSUME IT IS A PEAK LOCATION
```

```
C     CALL PPP1CF(Y,1,N,MAX)           ! FIND MAX VALUE IN THE DATA
      IPL(1) = MAX                     ! SAVE AS THE FIRST LOCATION
C
C     SET RANGE ON SEARCH AREA FOR NEXT PEAK
C
      MLOW = (1.-PRNGE)*PPER           ! LOW END OF SEARCH RANGE
      MHGH = (1.+PRNGE)*PPER           ! HIGH END OF SEARCH RANGE
C
C     SEARCH FOR PEAKS FROM MAX TO BEGINNING OF DATA
C
      NP = 1                           ! INITIALIZE NUMBER OF PEAKS
      INDX = MAX                       ! INITIALIZE CURRENT LOCATION
10    INDX1 = INDX-MHGH                ! SET NEXT LOW END
      INDX2 = INDX-MLOW                ! SET NEXT HIGH END
      IF (INDX1.LE.1) GO TO 20         ! TEST FOR START OF ARRAY
      CALL PPP1CF(Y,INDX1,INDX2,INDX)  ! FIND PEAK VALUE
      NP = NP+1                        ! INCREMENT NUMBER OF PEAKS
      IPL(NP) = INDX                   ! SAVE PEAK LOCATION
      GO TO 10                         ! LOOK FOR NEXT PEAK
C
C     REORDER PEAK LOCATIONS IN ASCENDING ORDER
C
20    CALL I2RI(IPL,IPL,NP,1)          ! REVERSE ORDER OF IPL ARRAY
C
C     SEARCH FROM MAX TO END OF DATA
C
      INDX = MAX                       ! RETRIEVE STARTING POINT
30    INDX1 = INDX+MLOW                ! SET NEW LOW END
      INDX2 = INDX+MHGH                ! SET NEW HIGH END
      IF (INDX2.GE.N) GO TO 40         ! TEST FOR END OF ARRAY
      CALL PPP1CF(Y,INDX1,INDX2,INDX)  ! FIND PEAK VALUE
      NP = NP+1                        ! INCREMENT NUMBER OF PEAKS
      IPL(NP) = INDX                   ! SAVE PEAK LOCATION
      GO TO 30                         ! LOOK FOR NEXT PEAK
40    RETURN
      END
C
C *************************************************************
C
      SUBROUTINE POLRT(XCOF,COF,M,ROOTR,ROOTI,IER)
C
C     REAL AND COMPLEX ROOTS OF A REAL POLYNOMIAL (FROM IBM SSP)
C
C     DESCRIPTION OF ARGUMENTS
C     XCOF   ARRAY OF M+1 COEFFICIENTS OF THE POLYNOMIAL
C     COF    WORKING ARRAY OF LENGTH M+1
C     M      ORDER OF POLYNOMIAL
C     ROOTR  OUTPUT ARRAY OF LENGTH M OF REAL PARTS OF THE ROOTS
C     ROOTI  OUTPUT ARRAY OF LENGTH M OF IMAG PARTS OF THE ROOTS
C     IER    ERROR FLAG  = U IF NO ERROR
C                        = 1 IF M < 1
C                        = 2 IF M > 36
C                        = 3 IF UNABLE TO DETERMINE ROOT
C                        = 4 IF HIGH ORDER COEFFICIENT IS ZERO
```

```
      DIMENSION XCOF(1),COF(1),ROOTR(1),ROOTI(1)
      DATA XINIT,YINIT/-.09,-.03/
C
      IFIT = 0
      N = M
      IER = 0
      IF (XCOF(N+1)) 10,25,10
10    IF (N) 15,15,32
C
C     SET ERROR CODE TO 1
C
15    IER = 1
      GO TO 200
C
C     SET ERROR CODE TO 4
C
25    IER = 4
      GO TO 200
C
C     SET ERROR CODE TO 2
C
30    IER = 2
      GO TO 200
C
32    IF (N-36) 35,35,30
35    NX = N
      NXX = N+1
      N2 = 1
      KJ1 = N+1
      DO 40 L = 1,KJ1
      MT = KJ1-L+1
40    COF(MT) = XCOF(L)
C
C     SET INITIAL VALUES (DIFFERENT FROM ORIGINAL ROUTINE)
C
45    XO = XINIT
      YO = YINIT
C
C     ZERO INITIAL VALUE COUNTER
C
      IN = 0
50    X = XO
C
C     INCREMENT INITIAL VALUES AND COUNTER
C
      XO = -10.0*YO
      YO = -10.0*X
      X = XO
      Y = YO
      IN = IN+1
      GO TO 59
55    IFIT = 1
      XPR = X
      YPR = Y
```

```
C     EVALUATE POLYNOMIAL AND DERIVATIVES
59    ICT = 0
60    UX = 0.0
      UY = 0.0
      V = 0.0
      YT = 0.0
      XT = 1.0
      U = COF(N+1)
      IF (U) 65,130,65
      L = N-I+1
65    TEMP = COF(L)
      XT2 = X*XT-Y*YT
      YT2 = X*YT+Y*XT
      U = U+TEMP*XT2
      V = V+TEMP*YT2
      FI = I
      UX = UX+FI*XT*TEMP
      UY = UY-FI*YT*TEMP
      XT = XT2
      YT = YT2
70    SUMSQ = UX*UX+UY*UY
      IF (SUMSQ) 75,110,75
75    DX = (V*UY-U*UX)/SUMSQ
      X = X+DX
      DY = -(U*UY+V*UX)/SUMSQ
      Y = Y+DY
78    IF (ABS(DY)+ABS(DX)-1.E-5) 100,80,80
C
C     STEP ITERATION COUNTER
C
80    ICT = ICT+1
      IF (ICT-500) 60,85,85
85    IF (IFIT) 100,90,100
90    IF (IN-5) 50,95,95
C
C     SET ERROR CODE TO 3
C
95    IER = 3
      GO TO 200
C
100   DO 105 L = 1,NXX
      MT = KJ-L+1
      TEMP = XCOF(MT)
      XCOF(MT) = COF(L)
105   COF(L) = TEMP
      ITEMP = N
      N = NX
      NX = ITEMP
110   IF (IFIT) 120,55,120
115   IF (IFIT) 115,50,115
      X = XPR
      Y = YPR
120   IFIT = 0
142   IF (ABS(Y/X)-1.E-4) 135,125,125
125   ALPHA = X+X
      SUMSQ = X*X+Y*Y
      N = N-2
      GO TO 140
130   X = 0.0
      NX = NX-1
      NXX = NXX-1
135   Y = 0.0
      SUMSQ = 0.0
      ALPHA = X
      N = N-1
140   COF(2) = COF(2)+ALPHA*COF(1)
145   DO 150 L = 2,N
150   COF(L+1) = COF(L+1)+ALPHA*COF(L)-SUMSQ*COF(L-1)
155   ROOTI(N2) = Y
      ROOTR(N2) = X
      N2 = N2+1
160   IF (SUMSQ) 160,165,160
      Y = -Y
      SUMSQ = 0.0
      GO TO 155
165   IF (N) 200,200,45
200   RETURN
      END
C*****************************************************************
      SUBROUTINE PPIC(IX,JMI,JMA,JLOC)
C
C     FIND THE MAXIMUM ABSOLUTE AMPLITUDE IN AN INTEGER ARRAY
C
C     AUTHORED BY CRAIG S. LEEDS - SCRL - JANUARY 1975
C
C     DESCRIPTION OF ARGUMENTS
C
C     IX    INPUT ARRAY
C     JMI   STARTING SEARCH LOCATION
C     JMA   ENDING SEARCH LOCATION
C     JLOC  LOCATION OF MAXIMUM ABSOLUTE VALUE
C
      DIMENSION IX(1)
C
      MAXA = 0
      JLOC = JMI
      DO 10 J = JMI,JMA
      IF (IABS(IX(J)).LE.MAXA) GO TO 10
      MAXA = IABS(IX(J))
      JLOC = J
10    CONTINUE
      RETURN
      END
```

```
      SUBROUTINE PPICF(X,JMI,JMA,JLOC)

C     FIND THE MAXIMUM ABSOLUTE AMPLITUDE IN A REAL ARRAY

C     AUTHORED BY CRAIG S. LEEDS - SCRL - JANUARY 1975

C     DESCRIPTION OF ARGUMENTS

C        X      INPUT ARRAY
C        JMI    STARTING SEARCH LOCATION
C        JMA    ENDING SEARCH LOCATION
C        JLOC   LOCATION OF MAXIMUM ABSOLUTE VALUE

      DIMENSION X(1)

C
      XMAXA = 0.
      JLOC = JMI
      DO 10 J = JMI,JMA
      IF (ABS(X(J)).LE.XMAXA) GO TO 10
      XMAXA = ABS(X(J))
      JLOC = J
   10 CONTINUE
      RETURN
      END
************************************************

      SUBROUTINE PPPICF(X,JMI,JMA,JLOC)

C     FIND THE MAXIMUM POSITIVE AMPLITUDE IN A REAL ARRAY

C     AUTHORED BY CRAIG S. LEEDS - SCRL - JANUARY 1975

C     DESCRIPTION OF ARGUMENTS

C        X      INPUT ARRAY
C        JMI    STARTING SEARCH LOCATION
C        JMA    ENDING SEARCH LOCATION
C        JLOC   LOCATION OF MAXIMUM POSITIVE VALUE

      DIMENSION X(1)

C
      XMAXP = -1.E+35
      JLOC = JMI
      DO 10 J = JMI,JMA
      IF (X(J).LE.XMAXP) GO TO 10
      XMAXP = X(J)
      JLOC = J
   10 CONTINUE
      RETURN
      END
```

```
      SUBROUTINE PTBQUO(D,N,K,Q)

C     PERTURBATION QUOTIENT

C     AUTHORED BY STEVEN B. DAVIS - SCRL - AUGUST 1976

C     DESCRIPTION OF ARGUMENTS

C        D      INPUT VECTOR OF DATA POINTS
C        N      NUMBER OF DATA POINTS
C        K      LENGTH OF MOVING AVERAGE
C        Q      OUTPUT QUOTIENT

      DIMENSION D(1)

C
      XNUM = 0.                          ! INITIALIZE NUMERATOR
      XDEN = 0.                          ! INITIALIZE DENOMINATOR
      Q = 0.                             ! INITIALIZE QUOTIENT
      M = K/2                            ! CENTER OF MOVING AVERAGE
      IF (K-M-M-1.NE.0) GO TO 40         ! K MUST BE ODD
      NK = N-K+1                         ! NUMBER OF DATA POINTS TO USE

C     COMPUTE NUMERATOR
C
      DO 20 I = 1,NK                     ! LOOP FOR NUMBER OF POINTS
      YNUM = 0.                          ! INITIALIZE MOVING AVERAGE
      DO 10 J = 1,K                      ! LOOP FOR PTS IN MOV AVERAGE
   10 YNUM = YNUM+D(I+J-1)               ! SUM POINTS IN MOVING AVERAGE
   20 XNUM = XNUM+ABS(YNUM/K-D(I+M))     ! SUM OF PERTUR FROM MOV AVR
      XNUM = XNUM/NK                     ! AVERAGE PERTURBATION

C     COMPUTE DENOMINATOR
C
      DO 30 I = 1,N                      ! LOOP FOR ALL DATA POINTS
      XDEN = XDEN+D(I)                   ! SUM OF DATA
   30 XDEN = XDEN/N                      ! AVERAGE OF ALL DATA

C     COMPUTE QUOTIENT
C
   40 Q = XNUM/XDEN                      ! NORMALIZED PERTURBATION
      RETURN
      END
**********************************************************

      SUBROUTINE R2CR(X,N,SCL)

C     SET A REAL ARRAY TO A CONSTANT VALUE

C     AUTHORED BY STEVEN B. DAVIS - SCRL - AUGUST 1976

C     DESCRIPTION OF ARGUMENTS

C        X      VECTOR OF DATA
C        N      NUMBER OF POINTS
```

```
C     SCL    DESIRED CONSTANT VALUE
C
      DIMENSION X(1)
C
      DO 10 I = 1,N
   10 X(I) = SCL
      RETURN
      END
C*****************************************************
      SUBROUTINE R2R(X,Y,N,SCL)
C
C  TRANSFER A REAL ARRAY TO A REAL ARRAY
C
C  AUTHORED BY CRAIG S. LEEDS - SCRL - JANUARY 1975
C
C  DESCRIPTION OF ARGUMENTS
C
C     X      ARRAY FOR INPUT
C     Y      ARRAY FOR OUTPUT
C     N      NUMBER OF POINTS
C     SCL    SCALE FACTOR
C
      DIMENSION X(1),Y(1)
C
      DO 10 J = 1,N
   10 Y(J) = X(J)*SCL
      RETURN
      END
C*****************************************************
      SUBROUTINE R2RR(X,Y,N,SCL)
C
C  COPY A REAL ARRAY TO A REAL ARRAY IN REVERSED ORDER
C
C  AUTHORED BY STEVEN B. DAVIS - SCRL - AUGUST 1976
C
C  DESCRIPTION OF ARGUMENTS
C
C     X      ARRAY FOR INPUT
C     Y      ARRAY FOR OUTPUT
C     N      NUMBER OF POINTS
C     SCL    SCALE FACTOR
C
      DIMENSION X(1),Y(1)
C
      NP1 = N+1
      DO 10 I = 1,NP1/2
      SAV = X(I)
      Y(I) = X(NP1-I)*SCL
   10 Y(NP1-I) = SAV*SCL
      RETURN
      END


      SUBROUTINE RACOR(M,N,Y,R,SCL)
C
C  CALCULATE NORMALIZED AUTOCORRELATION COEFFICIENTS
C
C  AUTHORED BY STEVEN B. DAVIS - SCRL - AUGUST 1976
C
C  DESCRIPTION OF ARGUMENTS
C
C     M      DESIRED NUMBER OF AUTOCORRELATION COEFFICIENTS
C     N      NUMBER OF INPUT POINTS
C     Y      INPUT ARRAY OF DATA
C     R      OUTPUT ARRAY OF AUTOCORRELATION COEFFICIENTS
C     SCL    SCALE FACTOR FOR UNNORMALIZING
C
      DIMENSION Y(1),R(1)
C
      DO 20 I = 1,M
      SS = 0.
      DO 10 J = 1,N-I+1
   10 SS = SS+Y(J)*Y(J+I-1)
   20 R(I) = SS
      SCL = R(1)
      RSCL = 1./SCL
      CALL R2R(R,R,M,RSCL)
      RETURN
      END
C*****************************************************
      SUBROUTINE RBT(X,Y,M)
C
C  BIT REVERSAL OF FFT POINTS
C
C  AUTHORED BY JOHN D. MARKEL - SCRL - JANUARY 1975
C
C  DESCRIPTION OF ARGUMENTS
C
C     X      REAL FFT POINTS
C     Y      IMAG FFT POINTS
C     M      ORDER OF FFT
C
      DIMENSION X(1),Y(1),L(9)
C
      DO 20 J = 1,9
      L(J) = 1
   20 IF (J.LE.M) L(J) = 2**(M+1-J)
      JN = 1
      DO 50 J9 = 1,L(9)
      DO 50 J8 = J9,L(8),L(9)
      DO 50 J7 = J8,L(7),L(8)
      DO 50 J6 = J7,L(6),L(7)
      DO 50 J5 = J6,L(5),L(6)
      DO 50 J4 = J5,L(4),L(5)
      DO 50 J3 = J4,L(3),L(4)
      DO 50 J2 = J3,L(2),L(3)
```

```
      SUBROUTINE USCRM(X,Y,M)
C
C     UNSCRAMBLE FOURIER TRANSFORM OF REAL DATA
C
C     AUTHORED BY JOHN D. MARKEL - SCRL - JANUARY 1975
C
C     DESCRIPTION OF ARGUMENTS
C
C     X       ARRAY OF REAL TRANSFORM POINTS
C     Y       ARRAY OF IMAG TRANSFORM POINTS
C     M       ORDER OF TRANSFORM
C
      DIMENSION X(1),Y(1)
      DATA PI/3.14159265/
C
      I = 2**M
      LO2 = I/2
      SA = PI/I
      X(1) = X(1)+Y(1)
      Y(1) = 0
      LLL = LO2+1
      Y(LLL) = -Y(LLL)
      DO 10 K = 2,LO2
      J = I-K+2
      ANG = SA*(K-1)
      C = COS(ANG)
      S = SIN(ANG)
      AA = X(K)+X(J)
      BB = Y(K)-Y(J)
      CC = X(K)-X(J)
      DD = Y(K)+Y(J)
      XR = C*DD-S*CC
      XI = S*DD+C*CC
      X(K) = (AA+XR)*.5
      Y(K) = (BB-XI)*.5
      X(J) = (AA-XR)*.5
   10 Y(J) = (-BB-XI)*.5
      RETURN
      END
```

```
      DO 50 J1 = J2,L(1),L(2)
      IF (JN.GT.J1) GO TO 50
      R = X(JN)
      X(JN) = X(J1)
      X(J1) = R
      FI = Y(JN)
      Y(JN) = Y(J1)
      Y(J1) = FI
      JN = JN+1
   50 RETURN
      END
C
C*******************************************************
C
      SUBROUTINE SHUFR(X,Y,M,A,XF,NPTS)
C
C     SHUFFLE A REAL ARRAY INTO ODD AND EVEN PARTS FOR EFFICIENT FFT
C
C     AUTHORED BY CRAIG S. LEEDS - SCRL - JANUARY 1975
C
C     DESCRIPTION OF ARGUMENTS
C
C     X       OUTPUT REAL ARRAY (LENGTH 2**M)
C     Y       OUTPUT IMAGINARY ARRAY (LENGTH 2**M)
C     M       ORDER OF TRANSFORM
C     A       INPUT FLOATING POINT ARRAY (LENGTH NPTS)
C     XF      OUTPUT RUNNING TOTAL X-Y
C     NPTS    NUMBER OF REAL DATA POINTS  (MAX = 2**(M+1))
C
      DIMENSION X(1),Y(1),A(1)
C
      XF = 0.
      I = 0
      J = 0
   10 I = I+1
      J = J+1
      X(I) = A(J)
      XF = XF+X(I)
      IF (J.GE.NPTS) GO TO 20
      J = J+1
      Y(I) = A(J)
      XF = XF-Y(I)
      IF (J.LT.NPTS) GO TO 10
C
C     ZERO-FILL THE REST OF THE OUTPUT ARRAYS
C
   20 IF (MOD(NPTS,2).EQ.1) Y(NPTS/2+1) = 0.
      M2 = 2**M
      IF (I.GE.M2) GO TO 40
   30 I = I+1
      X(I) = 0.
      Y(I) = 0.
      GO TO 30
   40 RETURN
      END
```

References

Arnold, G. Vocal rehabilitation of paralytic dysphonia: II. Acoustic analysis of vocal function. *Archives of Otolaryngology*, 1955, *62*, 593–601.

Atal, B. S., & Hanauer, S. L. Speech analysis and synthesis by linear prediction of the speech wave. *Journal of the Acoustical Society of America*, 1971, *50*, 637–655.

Blackman, R. B., & Tukey, J. W. *The measurement of power spectra*. New York: Dover, 1958.

Bowler, N. W. A fundamental frequency analysis of harsh vocal quality. *Speech Monographs*, 1964, *31*, 128–134.

Bruning, J. L., & Kintz, B. L. *Computational handbook of statistics*. Glenview, Ill.: Scott, Foresman, 1968.

Chiba, T., & Kajiyama, M. *The vowel, its nature and structure*. Tokyo: Tokyo Kaiseikan, 1941.

Cramer, H. *Mathematical methods of statistics*. Princeton, N.J.: Princeton University Press, 1958.

Crystal, T. H., & Jackson, C. L. Extracting and processing vocal pitch for laryngeal disorder detection. *Journal of the Acoustical Society of America*, 1970, *48*, 118. (Abstract)

Davis, S. B. Preliminary results using inverse filtering of speech for automatic evaluation of laryngeal pathology. *Journal of the Acoustical Society of America*, 1975, *58*, S111. (Abstract)

Davis, S. B. *Computer evaluation of laryngeal pathology based on inverse filtering of speech*. Unpublished doctoral dissertation, University of California, Santa Barbara, 1976. (Also SCRL Monograph No. 13. Santa Barbara, Calif.: Speech Communications Research Laboratory, 1976.) (a)

Davis, S. B. Determination of glottal area based on digital image processing of high-speed motion pictures of the vocal folds. *Journal of the Acoustical Society of America*, 1976, *60*, S65. (Abstract) (b)

Davis, S. B. *Acoustic analysis of voice pathology*. Paper presented at the annual convention of the American Speech and Hearing Association, Chicago, November 1977.

Davis, S. B. *Acoustic measures of laryngeal pathology using inverse filtered speech*. Unpublished manuscript, Haskins Laboratories, 1978.

Fant, C. G. M. Acoustic analysis and synthesis of speech with applications to Swedish. *Ericsson Technics*, 1959, *15*, 3–108.

Fant, C. G. M. *Acoustic theory of speech production*. The Hague: Mouton, 1960.

Farnsworth, D. W. High speed motion pictures of human vocal cords. *Bell Laboratories Record*, 1940, *18*, 203–208.

Fisher, W. M., Monsen, R. B., & Engebretson, A. M. Variations in the normal male glottal wave. *Journal of the Acoustical Society of America*, 1975, *58*, S41. (Abstract)

Flanagan, J. L. Some properties of the glottal sound source. *Journal of Speech and Hearing Research*, 1958, *1*, 99–116.

Flanagan, J. L *Speech analysis, synthesis, and perception*. Berlin and New York: Springer-Verlag, 1972.

Frank, D. I. Hoarseness—A new classification and a brief report of four interesting cases. *Laryngoscope*, 1940, *50*, 472–478.

Fritzell, B., Hammarberg, B., & Wedin, L. *Clinical applications of acoustic voice analysis, Part I* (Quarterly Progress and Status Report, No. 2–3). Stockholm: Royal Institute of Technology, Speech Transmission Laboratory, 1977. Pp. 31–38.

Frøkjær-Jensen, B., & Prytz, S. Registration of voice quality. *Bruel and Kjær Technical Review*, 1976, No. 3, 3–17.

Gauffin, J., & Sundberg, J. *Clinical applications of acoustic voice analysis, Part II* (Quarterly Progress and Status Report, No. 2–3). Stockholm: Royal Institute of Technology, Speech Transmission Laboratory, 1977. Pp. 39–43.

Gould, W. J. The Gould laryngoscope. *Transactions of the American Academy of Ophthalmology and Otolaryngology*, 1973, *77*, 139–141.

Gould, W. J. Quantitative assessment of voice function in microlaryngology. *Folia Phoniatrica*, 1975, *27*, 157–165.

Gould, W. J. Personal communication, 1976.

Gray, A. H., Jr., & Markel, J. D. A spectral flatness measure for studying the autocorrelation method of linear prediction of speech analysis. *IEEE Transactions on Acoustics, Speech, and Signal Processing*, 1974, *ASSP-22*, 207–217.

Hayden, E., & Koike, Y. A data processing scheme for frame by frame film analysis. *Folia Phoniatrica*, 1972, *24*, 169–186.

Hecker, M. H. L., & Kreul, E. J. Descriptions of the speech of patients with cancer of the vocal folds. Part 1: Measures of fundamental frequency. *Journal of the Acoustical Society of America*, 1971, *49*, 1275–1282.

Hiki, S., Imaizumi, S., Hirano, M., Matsushita, H., & Kakita, Y. Acoustical analysis for voice disorders. *Conference Record, IEEE International Conference on Acoustics, Speech, and Signal Processing*, 1976, pp. 613–616.

Hiki, S., Sugawara, K., & Oizumi, J. On the rapid fluctuation of voiced pitch. *Reports of the Research Institute of Electrical Communication, Tohoku University*, 1968, *19*, 237–239.

Hildebrand, B. *Vibratory patterns of the human vocal folds during variations in frequency and intensity.* Unpublished doctoral dissertation, University of Florida, 1976.

Holmes, J. N. An investigation of the volume velocity waveform at the larynx during speech by means of an inverse filter. *Proceedings of the Speech Communication Seminar, Speech Transmission Laboratory, Royal Institute of Technology, Stockholm*, 1962, B-4.

Holmes, J. N. Low frequency phase distortion of speech recordings. *Journal of the Acoustical Society of America*, 1975, *58*, 747–749.

Isshiki, N. A method of classified description of hoarse voice (in Japanese). *Japanese Journal of Logopedics and Phoniatrics*, 1966, *7*, 15–21.

Isshiki, N., Okamura, H., Tanabe, M., & Morimoto, M. Differential diagnosis of hoarseness. *Folia Phoniatrica*, 1969, *21*, 9–19.

Jackson, C., & Jackson, C. L. *The larynx and its diseases.* Philadelphia: Saunders, 1937.

Johnson, K. W. *The effect of selected vowels on laryngeal jitter.* Unpublished master's thesis, University of Kansas, 1969.

Jury, E. I. *Theory and application of the Z-transform method.* New York: Wiley, 1964.

Kelly, J. L., & Lochbaum, C. Speech synthesis, *Proceedings of the 4th International Congress on Acoustics, Copenhagen*, 1962, G42.

Kitajima, K., Tanabe, M., & Isshiki, N. Pitch perturbation in normal and pathologic voice. *Studia Phonologica*, 1975, *IX*, 25–32.

Koike, Y. Application of some acoustic measures for the evaluation of laryngeal dysfunction. *Journal of the Acoustical Society of America*, 1967, *42*, 1209. (Abstract)

Koike, Y. Vowel amplitude modulations in patients with laryngeal diseases. *Journal of the Acoustical Society of America*, 1969, *45*, 839–844.

Koike, Y. Application of some acoustic measures for the evaluation of laryngeal dysfunction. *Studia Phonologica*, 1973, *7*, 17–23.

Koike, Y. Personal communication, 1976.

Koike, Y., & Hirano, M. Glottal area time function and subglottal pressure variation. *Journal of the Acoustical Society of America*, 1973, *54*, 1618–1627.

Koike, Y., & Markel, J. D. Application of inverse filtering for detecting laryngeal pathology. *Annals of Otology, Rhinology, & Laryngology*, 1975, *84*, 117–124.

Koike, Y., & Takahashi, H. Glottal parameters and some acoustic measures in patients with laryngeal pathology. *Studia Phonologica*, 1971, *7*, 45–50.

Kolmogoroff, A. N. Interpolation und Extrapolation von stationaren zufalligen Folgen. *Bulletin de l'Academie des Sciences de U.S.S.R., Serie des Mathematiques*, 1941, *5*, 3–14.

Levinson, N. The Wiener RMS (Root Mean Square) error criterion in filter design and prediction. *Journal of Mathematical Physics*, 1946, *25*, 261–278.

Lieberman, P. Perturbations in vocal pitch. *Journal of the Acoustical Society of America*, 1961, *33*, 597–603.

Lieberman, P. Some acoustic measures of the fundamental periodicity of normal and pathologic larynges. *Journal of the Acoustical Society of America*, 1963, *35*, 344–353.

Lindqvist, J. Studies of the voice source by means of inverse filtering technique. *Proceedings of the 5th International Congress on Acoustics, Liege*, 1965, A35.

Luchsinger, R., & Arnold, G. E. *Voice-speech-language, clinical communicology: Its physiology and pathology*. Belmont, Calif.: Wadsworth, 1965.

Makhoul, J. I. Spectral linear prediction: Properties and applications. *IEEE Transactions on Acoustics, Speech, and Signal Processing*, 1975, *ASSP-23*, 283–296.

Makhoul, J. I., & Wolf, J. J. *Linear prediction and the spectral analysis of speech* (BBN Rep. No. 2304). Cambridge, Mass.: Bolt, Beranek, & Newman, 1972.

Markel, J. D. *Formant trajectory estimation from a linear least-squares inverse filter formulation* (SCRL Monograph No. 7). Santa Barbara, Calif.: Speech Communications Research Laboratory, 1971.

Markel, J. D. Digital inverse filtering—A new tool for formant trajectory estimation. *IEEE Transactions on Audio and Electroacoustics*, 1972, *AU-20*, 129–137.

Markel, J. D. Application of a digital inverse filter for automatic formant and F_0 analysis. *IEEE Transactions on Audio and Electroacoustics*, 1973, *AU-21*, 154–160.

Markel, J. D., & Gray, A. H., Jr. On autocorrelation equations as applied to speech analysis. *IEEE Transactions on Audio and Electroacoustics*. 1973, *AU-20*, 69–79.

Markel, J. D., & Gray, A. H., Jr. *Linear prediction of speech*. Berlin and New York: Springer-Verlag, 1976.

Markel, J. D., Gray, A. H., Jr., & Wakita, H. *Linear prediction of speech-theory and practice* (SCRL Monograph No. 10). Santa Barbara, Calif.: Speech Communications Research Laboratory, 1973.

Miller, R. L. Nature of the vocal cord wave. *Journal of the Acoustical Society of America*, 1959, *31*, 667–677.

Moore, G. P. Motion picture studies of the vocal folds and vocal attack. *Journal of Speech and Hearing Disorders*, 1938, *3*, 235–238.

Moore, G. P. Otolaryngology and speech pathology. *Laryngoscope*, 1968, *78*, 1500–1507.

Moore, G. P. Voice disorders organically based. In L. E. Travis (Ed.), *Handbook of speech pathology and audiology*. New York: Appleton, 1971. Pp. 535–569.

Moore, G. P. *Terminal Report for a Conference on Early Detection of Laryngeal Pathology*. Gainesville: University of Florida, Department of Speech, Communication Sciences Laboratory, 1973.

Murry, T. Some acoustic features of hoarseness. *Journal of the Acoustical Society of America*, 1975, *58*, S111. (Abstract)

Nessel, E. Über das Tonfrequenzspectrum der pathologisch veränderten Stimme. *Acta Oto-Laryngologica, Supplementum,* 1960, No. 157.

Osgood, C. E., Suci, G. J., & Tannenbaum, P. H. *The measurement of meaning.* Urbana: University of Illinois Press, 1957.

Palmer, J. M. Hoarseness in laryngeal pathology, a review of the literature. *Laryngoscope,* 1959, *61,* 500–516.

Perkins, W. H. Vocal function: A behavioral analysis. In L. E. Travis (Ed.), *Handbook of speech pathology and audiology.* New York: Appleton, 1971. Pp. 481–503.

Peterson, G. E., & Barney, H. L. Control methods used in a study of vowels. *Journal of the Acoustical Society of America,* 1952, *24,* 175–184.

Ramsey, J. L. *Logical techniques for glottal source measurements* (Instrumentation Papers No. 48, Data Sciences Laboratory Project 5628). L. G. Hanscom Field, Mass.: Air Force Cambridge Research Laboratories, 1964.

Rontal, E. "Picturing" vocal cord therapy results. *Journal of the American Medical Association,* 1975, *233,* 1149–1150.

Rothenberg, M. A new inverse filtering technique for deriving the glottal air flow waveform during voicing. *Journal of the Acoustical Society of America,* 1973, *53,* 1632–1645.

Sawashima, M., & Hirose, H. New laryngoscopic technique by use of fibre optics. *Journal of the Acoustical Society of America,* 1968, *43,* 168–169.

Schönhärl, E. *Die Stroboskopie in der praktischen Laryngologie.* Stuttgart: Thieme, 1960.

Smith, W., & Lieberman, P. *Studies in pathologic speech production* (Final Report, AFCRL-64-379). L. G. Hanscom Field, Mass.: Air Force Cambridge Research Laboratories, 1964.

Sondhi, M. M. Measurement of the glottal waveform. *Journal of the Acoustical Society of America,* 1975, *57,* 228–232.

Soron, H. I. High-speed photography in speech research. *Journal of Speech and Hearing Research,* 1967, *10,* 768–776.

Takahashi, H., & Koike, Y. Some perceptual dimensions and acoustical correlates of pathologic voices. *Acta Oto-Laryngologica, Supplementum,* 1975, No. 338, 1–24.

Takasugi, T., & Suzuki, J. Consideration of voice source in Analysis by Synthesis Technique. *Journal of the Radio Research Laboratory,* 1970, *17,* 153–168.

Tanabe, M., Kitajima, K., Gould, W. J., & Lambiase, A. Analysis of high speed motion pictures of the vocal folds. *Folia Phoniatrica,* 1975, *27,* 77–87.

Timcke, R., von Leden, H., & Moore, P. Laryngeal vibrations: Measurements of the glottic wave. Part I. The normal vibratory cycle. *Archives of Otolaryngology,* 1958, *68,* 1–19.

Timcke, R., von Leden, H., & Moore, P. Laryngeal vibrations: Measurements of the glottic wave. Part II. Physiologic variations. *Archives of Otolaryngology,* 1959, *69,* 438–444.

van den Berg, J. Modern research in experimental phoniatrics. *Folia Phoniatrica,* 1962, *14,* 81–149.

von Leden, H., Moore, P., & Timcke, R. Laryngeal vibrations: Measurements of the glottic wave. Part III. The pathologic larynx. *Archives of Otolaryngology,* 1960, *71,* 16–35.

Weiner, N. *Extrapolation, interpolation and smoothing of stationary time series.* Cambridge, Mass.: MIT Press, 1949.

Wendahl, R. W. Laryngeal analog synthesis of harsh voice quality. *Folia Phoniatrica,* 1963, *15,* 241–250.

Wendahl, R. W. Laryngeal analog synthesis of jitter and shimmer, auditory parameters of harshness. *Folia Phoniatrica,* 1966, *18,* 98–108.

Winckel, F. Electroakustische Untersuchungen an der menschlichen Stimme. *Folia Phoniatrica,* 1952, *4,* 93–113.

Winckel, F. Physikalische Kriterien für objektive Stimmbeurteilung. *Folia Phoniatrica,* 1954, *5,* 232–252.

Wong, D. W., Markel, J. D., & Gray, A. H., Jr. Least squares glottal inverse filtering from the acoustic speech waveform. *IEEE Transactions on Acoustics, Speech, and Signal Processing,* 1979, *ASSP-27.*

Yanagihara, N. Hoarseness: Investigation of the physiological mechanisms. *Annals of Otology, Rhinology, & Laryngology* 1967, *76,* 472–489. (a)

Yanagihara, N. Significance of harmonic changes and noise components in hoarseness. *Journal of Speech and Hearing Research,* 1967, *10,* 531–541. (b)

Zemlin, W. R. *Speech and hearing science: Anatomy and physiology.* Englewood Cliffs, N.J.: Prentice-Hall, 1968.

Synergy: Toward a Model of Language

CAROL A. PRUTTING and JUDY B. ELLIOTT

Department of Speech
University of California
Santa Barbara, California

Six thousand years ago the Babylonians conceived of the universe as an oyster with water underneath and overhead. The Earth was a hollow mountain, placed in the oyster's center, floating on water; the oyster's shell formed a solid dome around the Earth. The upper waters seeped down through the dome as rain, while the lower waters rose through the floor to become fountains and springs. The sun, moon, and stars progressed in a slow dance across the dome of the oyster, entering through doors in the east and vanishing through doors in the west. Similarly, the Egyptians conceived of the universe as a more rectangularly shaped oyster or box; the Earth was its floor, while the sky was a cow whose feet rested on the four corners of the Earth. Placed around the inner walls of the box, on an elevated gallery, a river flowed on which the sun and moon gods sailed their barques. These barques entered and exited through various stage doors. Planets sailed their own boats along the canals on the inner walls of the box to create the Milky Way. The Babylonians and Egyptians, as well as other great early civilizations, employed mythology to explain astronomical phenomena. For example, according to Egyptian myth, toward the fifteenth of every month, the moon god was attacked by a ferocious sow and devoured. Sometimes the sow swallowed the god whole, causing a lunar eclipse. The Babylonians, the Egyptians, and other

SPEECH AND LANGUAGE: Advances in Basic Research and Practice, Vol. 1

early civilizations discovered, however, that in spite of the turbulent behaviors of the private lives of the various gods, their positions and their movements were always reliable and predictable.

At the same time, Chaldean priests were observing the stars and making maps and timetables of their positions and movements. These timetables were developed into calendars which were used to regulate organized activity, from the growing of crops to religious ceremonies. Their observations and calculations of star positions and movements were so precise that their computation of the length of the year deviated less than .001% from modern calculations. In this respect, theirs was an exact science; their observations were verifiable and enabled them to make precise predictions of astronomical events. In making their predictions, Chaldean priests followed a pattern that was to be adopted by the scientific community over the next six thousand years. The pattern they employed consisted of using observations and verifiable quantitative measures of one aspect of a phenomenon to account for, and substantiate, the function of a whole system. Specifically, Chaldean priests employed their reliable quantitative measures derived from the positions and movements of the planets and stars in an explanatory fashion to substantiate their mythological theories. It is interesting to note that since that time many other workable theories have been proposed and widely accepted, only to be replaced or refined by new theoretical orientations, investigative methods, and quantitative measures.

Two distinct strategies exist which may act as constraints and therefore obscure discovery processes in scientific inquiry. The first strategy centers around how man conceptualizes, categorizes, or segments observed phenomena; that is, how man divides phenomena into component parts. The second obscuring strategy, which is an outgrowth of the first, centers around the use of quantified representations of observed phenomena, reflecting the operations of a defined category or component, to substantiate or explain the function of a total system. These constraints and their interaction are clearly illustrated by the example of the Chaldean priests. Their conceptualization of astronomical phenomena exemplifies obscuring strategies based on conceptualization or segmentation of natural phenomena; that is, reliable quantitative measures were derived from both the positions and the movements of stars. The segmentation or conceptualization, however, was based on mythological criteria. The second obscuring strategy is exemplified by the use of data based on the positions and movements of the stars and planets to account for, or explain, both the structural and functional aspects of the mythologically based universe. Galileo observed that the processes which blind man to discovery operate not only in the minds of the ignorant and superstitious but in the minds of all great thinkers. The work of Galileo, Aristotle, Ptolemy, and Kepler exhibited these constraints, as does the work of modern thinkers and scientists in all disciplines concerned with inquiry and discovery. Numerous difficulties, both internal and external to man's investigative abilities, have resulted in a scientific history that is characterized by constant upheavals in thinking followed by revision and refinement of both the questions investigated as well as the methodologies employed in investigations.

Investigations in the behavioral sciences, specifically in human language behavior, have evolved in a context similar to other scientific disciplines; as a result, there has been a series of significant changes in how language has been conceptualized and subsequent revisions and refinements in investigative tactics.

Traditionally, most philosophical or scientific investigations of the language process followed an approach whereby observed phenomena were segmented according to the criteria of a specific theoretical approach; questions were then formulated, and experimental procedures were devised for the purpose of describing and/or accounting for portions of the process. Examples of this strategy date back to the fifth century B.C. when notions of innateness and environment as variables responsible for shaping language were investigated. Researchers employing the approach of dividing natural phenomena into component parts make, possibly inadvertently, two assumptions: first, that this segmentation is not arbitrary but reflects natural divisions of the system; and second, that the sum of the quantitative measures of this segmentation reflects the operations of the total system. Scientists have primarily examined component parts of a system independently, placing minor emphasis on the phenomena as they exist and operate within a total system. It can be argued that the measurements of component parts reflect, in a quantified manner, some descriptive aspects of artificially or externally defined or segmented phenomena. However, these measurements do not necessarily reflect how the component parts relate to one another within the system or how the total system operates. Therefore, it may be necessary to reexamine findings based on theoretical approaches employing systematic assumptions.

I. HISTORICAL APPROACHES TO THE STUDY OF LANGUAGE

A concise historical summary of major theoretical orientations and investigative strategies into human language behavior clearly illustrates some of the constraints imposed by the assumptions stated above. Traditionally, language has been segmented and investigated in parts or components, with the areas of pragmatics, semantics, syntax, and phonology examined individually.

Although the major theoretical orientations employed in the exploration of language over the last 50 years do not follow a patterned developmental sequence, when examined chronologically two consistent investigative trends become apparent. The first is related to examination of the areas of pragmatics, semantics, syntax, and phonology as individual or independent components. The second relates to a cyclic process whereby new data, from a variety of related disciplines, changed or modified how language was conceptualized and therefore changed how language, as a natural phenomenon, was segmented into components and investigated. To examine the process of changes that has occurred in the investigation of language, some major theories that have led to current conceptualizations of pragmatics, semantics, syntax, and phonology will be reviewed.

John Watson, in the early 1920s, reshaped the investigation of human behavior by shifting the emphasis from introspection to behaviorism. This orientation gave new impetus to psychological experimentation by providing criteria for the study of behavior based on the notions of objectivity and direct observation. To the behaviorist, therefore, only data obtained by objective observable tests were considered valid. The implications of this theoretical framework had a 2-fold impact upon the effectiveness of research in the behavioral sciences. First, it helped establish psychology and the study of human behavior as a scientific discipline by requiring observable criteria for psychological explanation and, second, it acted as a constraint on behavioral research by requiring that only observable physical phenomena be employed as objects of scientific inquiry. Therefore, all phenomena had to be both observable and quantifiable as a precondition to scientific investigation. This behavioral orientation had profound effects on the investigation of language in the 1920s, 1930s, and 1940s. During this time investigators employed objective-quantified procedures to describe and account for language. Linguistic behavior was characterized by segmenting observable behaviors into categories or component parts and assigned numerical representations such as percentages of occurrence and age correlates. Those adhering to this orientation assumed that semantics, syntax, and phonology were independent components of language and could be studied individually.

Shannon and Weaver (1949) introduced information theory which was a refinement of the earlier left-to-right probabilistic models. Information theory dealt with concepts related to physical characteristics of electronic communication and employed the notions of probability, entropy (or uncertainty), and redundancy. The basic unit of measurement was considered the *bit* (taken from 'binary digit') and was defined as the amount of information needed to specify one of two classes of equally probable events. Information theory, although based on notions of probability, went several steps further than the earlier left-to-right models by attempting to specify some of the contingencies or relationships that existed among words in a sentence. Information theory, however, did not clearly define the semantic, syntactic, or phonological relations among words in a string.

Learning theory approaches to the study of language evolved through the development of two different, but related, theoretical orientations: mediational and nonmediational learning paradigms. Skinner (1957) presented a theory of verbal behavior based on Hull's earlier work. His theory included a basic S–R system with a stimulus (antecedent or input) and a response (behavior or output). He argued from a behavioral standpoint that the shortcomings of prior attempts to create adequate theories of verbal learning were a consequence of trying to describe the internal processing of language states. Skinner suggested that methodological difficulties arose; that is, findings were confounded by investigating nonobservable or subjective data. He argued for a theoretical framework which accommodated only an interaction of observable stimulus and response relationships. Verbal behaviors were thought of as operants regarding basic functional forms of response. Some verbal operants were thought to function directly as a consequence of the need state of the organism (**mands**) or operants in close association or conditioned by reinforcers (**tacts**).

Osgood (1957) also drew upon Hull's previous theoretical framework in developing a mediational theory. He maintained that language consisted of three classes of phenomena: symbolic processes, perceptual integration, and motor skill integration and suggested that language processing was an integration of perceptual and motor processes and, as such, an S–R model was unable to characterize this process. In an attempt to explain this, Osgood developed a three-level model which included an associative or mediational level. His model refined the conceptualization of language by reconsidering variables (specifically mediation or processing) as central to the complete characterization of language. However, since his theory did not refine the variable associated with the linguistic code itself, Osgood's model operated under the assumption that language could be segmented for the purposes of investigation.

Wittgenstein (1953) and Austin (1962), reflecting an analytical and philosophical approach, had a profound impact on the conceptualization of the semantic aspect of language. Prior to their writings, meaning was assumed to be at the word, phrase, object, or entity level. Both Wittgen-stein and Austin argued that semantics should go beyond the considera-tion of the word or entity level to include how the word functioned. Although not explicitly stated, this theory suggested that basic semantic operations and basic pragmatic operations may be related.

Jakobson, Fant, and Halle (1963) proposed a distinctive feature theory which provided the basis for, or was an underlying aspect of, lexical and morphological units as represented by 12 binary-opposing units. This theory was a refinement of Jakobson's earlier distinctive feature theory. The revised version attempted to relate sounds by means of a broad classification of articulatory, perceptual, and physiological fea-tures. Again, although not implicitly stated, this theory attempted to specify the relationships among variables within the phonological compo-nent as well as between the phonological and semantic components of language.

In the late 1950s and early 1960s primary emphasis was placed upon the development of linguistic models for the purpose of describing as well as explaining the generation of language. Chomsky (1957, 1965) proposed a theory of language which was syntactically based. He suggested that a finite set of rules is capable of generating an infinite number of acceptable sentences as well as appropriate phonological representations. Although Chomsky's earlier model (1957) did not adequately deal with semantic and phonological components of language, his 1965 model did attempt to reflect the intradynamics of these components. Similarly, Fillmore (1968) developed a rule-based case grammar which characterized the linguistic code primarily in terms of semantic relations.

Summarizing, historical perspectives in the study of language have exhibited two major trends: first, constant changes and refinements in theoretical orientations have directly influenced how linguistic behavior has been conceptualized and, therefore, segmented; and, second, mod-ifications and refinements in conceptualization have resulted in data that, hopefully, mirror the linguistic code more accurately and, therefore, move closer to adequate explanations.

Primary emphasis has thus been placed on explaining parts and/or components of language as opposed to specifying the degree or type of relationship which may exist among parts of a system. As suggested by Koestler (1959), it is sometimes necessary to reexamine evidence, look for new applications or correlations, or join together concepts not usually seen in juxtaposition. One purpose of this chapter is to introduce the notion of synergy, the consideration of whole systems unpredicted by the parts taken separately, as a theoretical framework from which language can be investigated. This framework should permit an integrated analysis of the language system rather than an analysis of component parts. A second purpose is to provide evidence for the relevance of synergistic considerations in the development of a model of language.

II. SYNERGY OF LANGUAGE: A RATIONALE

Traditional approaches to the investigation of language have typically generated types of questions and devised experimental procedures characterizing language in a unidimensional, categorical, or taxonomic fashion. Specifically, language has been segmented into the component parts of pragmatics, semantics, syntax, and phonology, and the functioning of these independent components has then been investigated apart from the context of the language system. All of the theoretical orientations that have been reviewed above are based, in part, on the assumption that language could be segmented into component parts and that the summation of these components reflects the operation of the total system. This chapter questions that assumption and proposes an alternate theoretical orientation based on Fuller's (1975) synergistic model. This section provides a rationale for the use of a synergistic orientation in the development of a model of language.

Watts (1963, p. 212) stated, "It becomes suddenly clear that things are joined together by the boundaries we ordinarily take to separate them." This statement was made in the context of how man, both past and present, operates under perceptual constraints and, as a consequence, perceives and investigates natural phenomena in a linear and singular manner. This manner of thought processing is clearly exemplified in the well-known Gestalt experiment regarding figure–ground relationships. The image in Fig. 1 is commonly recognized as either a chalice or kissing faces; due to linear, singular thought processes, which operate as constraints on perceptual processes, these images are perceived as mutually exclusive. Because of constraints on human perception strategies, one attends to only one aspect of this relationship (the figure or the ground). It has been argued that it is not possible to entertain the images simultaneously as they exist. Watts argues that natural phenomena do not exist in a polarized fashion, but that Western thinking emphasizes categorization and segmentation and, therefore, engineers polarization in human perceptual and conceptual processes.

As proposed by Koestler, scientific inquiry may be facilitated through the use of new or different theoretical orientations which provide for a reorganization or reorientation of how we perceive and/or conceptualize natural phenomena. He argues that reorganization or reorientation pro-

Figure 1. An image of either kissing faces or a chalice, depending upon whether one attends to one term of a relationship (the figure) or the other (the ground). (From Watts, 1963.)

vides the basis for a new or different conceptual template which allows the generation of creative hypotheses as well as creative investigative strategies.

Traditional theoretical orientations often dictate the segmentation of a natural phenomenon into its component parts for the purpose of investigation. Based on the arguments presented by Watts, it appears that these strategies may be due, in part, to man's perceptual constraints. Therefore, new strategies must be developed that address the problems resulting from these constraints and alternative approaches should be implemented incorporating the following criteria: first, segmentation or categorization should reflect natural divisions within the system; and second, if divisions exist, the type and degree of relationships between components should be specified. An orientation meeting these criteria has been suggested by Fuller (1975).

Fuller stated that investigation of natural phenomena leading to the prediction of the behavior of natural phenomena takes place by investigating whole systems, that is, by perceiving and investigating synergistic systems. He defines synergy as "the behavior of whole systems unpredicted by the behavior of their parts taken separately" (p. 3). Restated, the behavior of any components or subsystems is not equal to, that is, does not predict, the behavior of whole systems. As evidence for this notion of synergy, he employs as a demonstration Four triangles Out of Two. He states that triangles cannot be structured into planes; they are either positive or negative helixes. To demonstrate his point, Fuller breaks the triangles open to add them together, the triangles becoming a flat spiral open at the recycling point (see Fig. 2).

By conventional arithmetic, one triangle plus one triangle equals two triangles. But in association as left helix and right helix, they form a six-edged tetrahedron of four triangular faces. Thus, two triangles may be combined in such a manner that they create a tetrahedron, a figure which

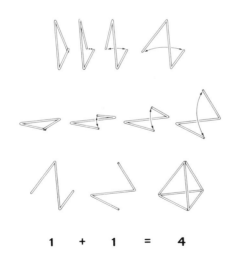

1   +   1   =   4

Figure 2.   Two triangles may be combined in such a manner as to create the tetrahedron, a figure which is volumetrically embraced by four triangles. Therefore, one plus one appears to equal four. (From Fuller, 1975.)

is composed of four triangles. Therefore, one plus one now equals four. Fuller pointed out that this is the way atoms behave. For example, chemists have found that when they separated atoms or molecules out of compounds, the separate parts never explained the associated behavior of the compounds; that is, when part of a system is abstracted from that system, there seemed to be lost energies. The theoretical orientation of scientific investigations, including both physical and behavioral sciences, has tended to employ the traditional investigative strategy of polarization and categorization of the phenomena being scrutinized, at times basing macroscopic inferences regarding a system on microscopic aspects of the phenomenon or system. Traditional theoretical orientations in the behavioral sciences (specifically those disciplines investigating human language behavior) appear, in some instances, to operate under these investigative constraints.

The notion of synergy as defined and illustrated by Fuller clearly has implications for any scientific investigation designed to explore physical or behavioral phenomena. As an outgrowth of Koestler's notion that reexamination of natural phenomena often provides new insights and of Fuller's notion, based on evidence from natural phenomena, that parts within a system operate in a synergistic fashion, an alternative theoretical orientation to the investigation of human language behavior can be developed. However, first it is necessary to provide evidence that language operates within a synergistic framework and to identify some of the critical implications generated by a synergistic model in the study of language.

III. EVIDENCE FOR SYNERGISTIC RELATIONSHIPS

Evidence for synergistic relationships in the linguistic system is presented here in two sections, both of which deal specifically with relational aspects among pragmatics, semantics, syntax, and phonology. Section III,A is divided into three parts: section III,A,1 focuses primarily on linguistic arguments supporting a relational syntactic–semantic process; section III,A,2 illustrates semantic and pragmatic aspects of a selected syntactic structure; and section III,A,3 examines a universal, multifactor pragmatic–semantic–syntactic definition of the notion of subject. Section III,B is a reexamination and reinterpretation of derived synergistic data from both descriptive and experimental investigations of pragmatic (III,B,1), semantic (III,B,2), phonological (III,B,3), and syntactic (III,B,4) aspects of the linguistic system. Both the linguistic arguments and the reexamination of derived data are organized under their traditional investigative areas of pragmatics, semantics, syntax, and phonology. This division is for organizational purposes only; inclusion of a descriptive or experimental investigation under one of these headings reflects the major focus of investigation for a given study.

A. Linguistic Data

1. An Argument for a Relational Syntactic–Semantic Process

Linguists are concerned with the logical–systematic structure of language. Traditionally, they have examined this structure at pragmatic, semantic, syntactic, and phonological levels. Historically, they have investigated the phrase and sentence structures of language as being an inventory of phonemes, word types, and parts of speech. They have also examined various processes underlying how words may combine to form acceptable phrases and sentences of a language. Until recently, linguistic investigations have been based on a framework in which words have been classified into parts of speech or into taxonomic categories such as nouns, verbs, adjectives, etc. These categories have provided, in part, a basis for linguistic research whose major purpose was to describe and explain language. Currently, however, the developing trend in linguistic thought is to question the premise that syntactic structure may be examined and described as an individual or isolated entity. Specifically, it is hypothesized that syntactic and semantic considerations are not mutually exclusive but relational. Furthermore, there is evidence that the subparts of the syntactic component, the traditional taxonomic syntactic classifications, may not reflect natural divisions of the system. The present section provides evidence supporting a syntactic–semantic relational process and is based on a reexamination of the taxonomic categories of verbs, nouns, and adjectives in terms of relational syntactic and semantic processes.

Verbs have traditionally been semantically defined as words that represent or reflect an action. For example;

I. *Jon jumped*

However, if we add the following examples to the list,

II. *Jon slept*
III. *Jon appreciated the favor*
IV. *Jon had a bad night*

it is clear that the verbs in III and IV do not reflect an action, yet native English speakers know these words are verbs. The traditional semantic definition of a verb as an action appears to be limited; sometimes verbs reflect a variety of semantic interpretations such as causation (e.g., *push*) or state (e.g., *dried*). Therefore, descriptions of verbs which are semantically based are inadequate because it is not feasible to specify all of the potential semantic possibilities that may represent a class of words called verbs.

An alternative definitional approach to the traditional semantic categorization centers around the principle of distributional analysis. This type of analysis provides descriptions of how a word may be distributed in a sentence, that is, where it may and may not occur. The principle of distributional analysis as it relates to redefining taxonomic classifications is illustrated below.

> V. *Jon* *jumped*
> (noun) (verb)
> VI. ∅ *jumped*
> VII. *Jon* ∅

In VI, although the noun is deleted, meaning, though limited, is maintained. However, when the verb is deleted from the construction, as in VII, meaning is not maintained, even in a limited sense. As shown in the above example, it appears that verbs serve a central notion in the construction of a sentence and, as shown in the example below, in English the verb always takes a tense inflection.

> VIII. *Jon* *jumping up and down looked ridiculous*
> IX. *jumped*
> X. *jumps*

Nouns also can be described in terms of distributional analysis. For example, in English, a noun can always be preceded by an article, *a, the, this, that*, or by modifiers such as adjectives.

A distributional analysis may be employed to investigate the traditional divisions of the syntactic component, the parts of speech categories. It should be noted that distribution refers to a statistical notion; that is, while distributional principles operate much of the time, they do not operate all of the time. A distributional analytic approach, however, provides more flexibility and information and is more accurate than semantically defined classifications. The set of examples in this section utilizes a distributional analysis to provide evidence for a relational syntactic–semantic process.

Lists 1 and 2 contain words that represent the traditionally semantically defined syntactic categories of adjectives and verbs.

1. Adjective		2. Verb	
tall	*noisy*	*hear*	*listen*
thin	*careful*	*know*	*learn*

In order to indicate the similarities and differences among the adjectives and verbs (their distributional characteristics), they are embedded in three different types of sentence constructions: (1) imperative command, (2) progressive tense, and (3) Do sentences.

Imperative command

1. *listen to the music*
2. *hear the music*
3. *be careful*
4. *be tall*

These examples illustrate that the distributional characteristics of verbs and adjectives in imperative constructions do not reflect their traditional categorical definitions. Although *listen* and *hear* are both classified as verbs and *careful* and *tall* are both classified as adjectives, they do not operate in the same manner; that is, some verbs and adjectives may occur in imperative commands while others may not.

Similarly, the distributional feature of these adjectives and verbs may also be illustrated in the progressive tense:

		learning	
		listening	
1. *I am*		*knowing*	*to the music*
		hearing	

		careful
		noisy
2. *I am being*		*fat*
		tall

Similar distributional dynamics and resulting word inclusion constraints are also evident in Do sentence construction:

		listen	
		learn	
1. *What I did was*		*know*	*to music*
		hear	

                                              careful
                                              noisy
      2. *What I did was to be*   *tall*
                                              thin

Adjectives and verbs in Do sentence constructions operate differently
than in other types of construction. Specifically, there is no distinction
between adjective and verb; instead, their operation takes on a stative
verb and active verb type of status.

Stative Verbs	Active Verbs
tall	*careful*
thin	*noisy*
hear	*listen*
know	*learn*

   In summary, the employment of a distributional analysis to reexamine
semantically defined syntactic categories of parts of speech illustrates
some of the limitations of traditional divisions. Results of these distributional analyses provide evidence which indicates that traditional parts of
speech (verbs and adjectives) do not appear to reflect natural divisions in
the language system. Specifically, the operational characteristics of both
verbs and adjectives are not clear cut; they may each function differently
across syntactic constructions. The variation in their operational characteristics is due, at least, to both syntactic and semantic relational constraints.

2. Semantic and Pragmatic Aspects of Syntactic
Structures

   Relativization. This section reexamines a traditionally defined syntactic
structure from a synergistic framework. Relativization was selected because the complexity of its internal processes as well as its universal
features provides clear evidence of semantic and pragmatic relational
processes operating in a parallel, relational manner to syntactic processes. To express the relational processes operating within the traditionally defined syntactic structure of relativization, several prerequisite
notions must be outlined: (1) the distributional characteristics of noun
phrases (NPs); (2) the distributional characteristics and functions of adjectives to NPs; and (3) the distribution of adjectives and NPs across universal language typologies. Once these processes are clear, it is possible to
examine both semantic and pragmatic operations occurring within the
relativization process. An NP is a constituent that behaves like a noun;

that is, it is a group of words that operates as a unit and functions in an identical fashion and has the same distributional characteristics as a noun. Adjectives function to modify nouns. Specifically, they add an attribute or some information which modifies a noun or noun phrase. There are universal features, based on language typology or word order, that dictate adjectival placement in relationship to noun phrases.

There are six basic word orders that, on a statistical basis, universally represent all natural languages having sentences constructed from two NPs and one verb:

Subject	Verb	Object	(S–V–O)
Verb	Subject	Object	(V–S–O)
Subject	Object	Verb	(S–O–V)
Object	Verb	Subject	(O–V–S)
Object	Subject	Verb	(O–S–V)
Verb	Object	Subject	(V–O–S)

The first three linear orders represent the predominant word order arrangement for the vast majority of languages; these are all subject-preceding-object types of languages. The latter three object-preceding-subject arrangements are rare or nonexistent as predominant word orders. All languages have more than one word order, but the object-before-subject relationship occurs only rarely and does not represent a predominant word order. The syntactic–semantic relations among words can provide a basis for looking at language and making universal predictions about language. One of the predictions that has been documented relates to the relative placement of adjectives and nouns. The following represents a universal adjective–noun word order according to Li (1976):

1. In SVO languages, adjectives or modifiers precede nouns.
2. In VSO languages, nouns precede adjectives or modifiers.
3. In SOV languages, adjectives or modifiers precede nouns.

Therefore, typology of language type based on linear arrangement of subject–verb–object determines the relative word ordering or placement of adjectives or modifiers in relation to NPs. Traditionally, this is viewed as a syntactic relationship.

Modifiers, like adjectives, function to provide additional attributes or information about the noun or noun phrase they modify. Relative clauses operate in a fashion parallel to modifiers; that is, they modify the head noun of a noun phrase in the same manner as adjectives modify nouns. Therefore, the relativization process serves to add information about the head noun that it modifies.

By definition, a relative clause is a sentence within a sentence. For example, *the boy whom I like is sick* is comprised of the following sentences:

I. *The boy is sick*
II. *I like the boy*

Relativization involves several processes: the embedding of one sentence into another, the use of a relative pronoun to represent the deleted coreferential NP, and the fronting of the relative pronoun to the beginning of the clause. As a result of these processes, the relative construction serves to modify the head noun of the sentence and provides new and/or additional information about the head noun. To illustrate these processes, examine the following steps of relativization:

The boy who I like is sick.

The sentence, *the boy is sick,* has embedded within it the sentence *I like the boy.* The NP in the former sentence is the head noun of the construction in that it controls subject verb agreement, and the NP in the latter sentence (specifically, the relative pronoun that represents the deleted NP) modifies the head noun of the construction. At this point in the process the sentence reads as follows:

III. *The boy I like the boy is sick*
$\quad$ NP$_1$ $\qquad\qquad$ NP$_2$

Because NP$_1$ [the head noun (HN)] and NP$_2$ are coreferential and identical, NP$_2$ may be deleted, which results in the following:

IV. *The boy I like is sick*

The deleted NP$_2$ is replaced by a relative pronoun and that pronoun is then fronted to complete the process:

V. *The boy I like who is sick*
VI. *The boy who I like is sick*

This relative clause may be characterized by the following paradigm in which WH represents *who*:

$$\left[\left({NP \atop \text{Head Noun}} \right) NP + \left| \left({WH + S \atop \text{clause}} \right) S \right| NP \right]$$

$$\left[{HN \atop (\textit{The boy})} NP + \left({\text{Relative clause} \atop \textit{who I like}} \right) S \right] NP$$

In this instance, the head noun is being modified by the relative clause or functions in the embedded sentence. In SVO and SOV constructions, the above paradigm represents the form that a relative clause takes. In SOV languages, however, the relative clause takes the following form:

$$\left[\begin{pmatrix} S + WH \\ clause \end{pmatrix} S + \begin{pmatrix} N \\ Head\ Noun \end{pmatrix} NP\right] NP$$

$$\quad\quad\text{Modifier} \quad\quad\quad\quad\quad \text{Modified}$$

Although a relative clause modifies a head noun in the same way an adjective modifies a noun, one would expect the modifier–noun relationship to parallel the universal ordering of modifier noun. However, when relativization occurs, this positional relationship is violated. For example, I (below) represents the universal modifier–noun relation, whereas II represents the modifier–noun relation in relative constructions.

I. *The old*   *man*
(modifier)   (modified)

II. *The boy who I like is sick*
(modified)   (modifier)

As stated, relativization serves as a focusing mechanism (which is a pragmatic function) and adds information or attributes through the process of modification (which is a pragmatic–semantic function). Based on the data provided, it appears that the word order or syntax, as reflected in NP and modifier relationships, changes as a function of semantic and pragmatic considerations. Therefore, the traditionally defined syntactic construction of relativization appears to be characterized by a syntactic–pragmatic–semantic process.

3. A Multifactor Pragmatic, Semantic, Syntactic Definition of Subject

Recently, the development of universal grammars and the incorporation of universal generalizations, such as accessibility hierarchy (Keenan & Comrie, 1972), the functional succession principle (Perlmutter & Postal, 1974), and the advancement continuity principle (Johnson, 1974; Keenan, 1975; Trithart, 1975), have established the need for a universalist redefinition of the notion of subject. Keenan argues that the above-stated generalizations determine constraints on both the form and the substance of human languages, and, if these generalizations are to be verified and their universality determined, it is necessary to be able to identify subjects, direct objects, etc. in a principled way across languages. Keenan (1976) abstracted from a diverse set of cases a set of properties which is characteristic of subject NPs, and, in order to establish criteria for the multifactor concept of subject (that is, attempt to specify some combination of characteristic properties which are both necessary and sufficient to pick out the subject of a sentence in any language), he devised a framework to specify these properties. He pointed out that subjects across languages are not characterized by properties which are universally valid; that is, they function differently across languages. He therefore wanted to phrase a universal definition of subject which would allow for differential means of marking subject NPs. In order to derive a set of characteristic properties of a subject, Keenan proposed a universal means of distinguishing a privileged subset of sentences in any given language. A privileged subset is a means of describing the variation of basic sentences across languages through the use of specified common denominators. He called these sentences semantically basic (b-sentences) and their subjects basic subjects (b-subjects).

A basic sentence for any language (L) is defined by two criteria:

1. A syntactic structure X is semantically more basic than a syntactic structure Y if, and only if, the meaning of Y depends on that of X. That is, to understand the meaning of Y it is necessary to understand the meaning of X.
2. A sentence in L is a basic sentence (in L) if, and only if, no (other) complete sentence in L is more basic than it.

Keenan also listed some general principles of basic sentences, such as basic sentences have the greatest privilege of occurrence, and they are easiest to embed, nominalize, and internally reorder, to derive question form, and to topicalize and pronominalize. Based on semantically basic sentences, Keenan provided some universally valid criteria, a set of characteristic properties for identifying subjects of b-sentences in any language. These properties may be pragmatic, semantic, and/or syntactic. He further specified that an NP in a b-sentence (any L) is a subject of that S-sentence to the extent that it has this set of characteristic properties. Therefore, NPs which are more subject like have a fuller complement of subject properties; subject is defined, then, not by a single dimension but rather by a cluster concept of properties that may be pragmatic, semantic, or syntactic in nature. Sections III,A,3,a,b, and c partially list these pragmatic, semantic, and syntactic cluster characteristics.

a. Pragmatic Cluster Characteristics. One pragmatic property of b-subjects is that the reference of a b-subject must be determinable by the addressee at the moment of utterance. It cannot be made to depend on the reference of other NPs which follow it. Keenan notes that b-subjects are normally the topic of the b-sentence, identifying what the speaker is talking about. The object to which b-subjects refer is usually known to both speaker and addressee and is therefore old information. Both of these examples provide evidence for pragmatic functions relating to the notion of subject as well as pragmatic properties or cluster characteristics illustrating relational aspects of the notion of subject.

   b. Semantic Cluster Characteristics. Keenan states that the semantic role (agent, object, etc.) of the referent of the b-subject is predictable from the form of the main verb (Li and Thompson, 1976); that is, verbs play a central role in sentence construction, determining both the number and types of NPs that may occur within a given sentence construction. Verbs function to dictate or to act as constraints upon the type of semantic roles an NP may occupy. Also, b-subjects will occasionally express the agent of the action if there is one. These two characteristics of b-subjects provide evidence that subject NPs (traditionally a syntactic notion) display semantic properties and are determined by, and are therefore predictable from, the verb in a sentence construction. These examples also provide evidence for syntactic–semantic relational operations among subjects, verbs, and objects.

   c. Syntactic Cluster Characteristics. Concerning syntactic properties or characteristics of b-subjects, Keenan stated that the b-subject is the NP immediately dominated by the root node S. This is the type of definition given in *Aspects* (Chomsky, 1965) and may represent a necessary condition of b-subjecthood. Keenan provided some rare counterexamples and suggested that this arrangement may be a necessary, but not sufficient, characteristic of b-subjecthood. He also noted that b-subjects, in general, can control reflexive pronouns. In some languages, control of reflexives within clauses is largely restricted to b-subjects. B-subjects are also among the possible controllers of coreferential deletions and pronominalizations. These syntactic characteristic properties illustrate some of the syntactic operations which comprise part of the multifactor complement of characteristics that define the notion of subject.

   Keenan described a number of characteristic properties or complement of characteristics of b-subjects; several examples of pragmatic, semantic, and syntactic properties were presented for the purpose of illustrating what Keenan refers to as the multifactor or cluster concept that defines the universalist notion of subject. This multifactor approach to the definition of subject supports the synergistic contention regarding the relational, systemic dynamics of the linguistic code. These examples also illustrate that this multifactor synergistic approach can be employed in a universal definition of subject.

B. Derived Data

In this section the data used to support a synergistic model are presented in two parts. First, for each study cited, explicit descriptive or experimental findings are stated. Second, all explicit descriptive and experimental findings are reexamined through a synergistic paradigm to obtain and specify implicit or derived synergistic relational processes. To discuss these derived relational or synergistic findings, the studies are organized in terms of their original explicit investigative purposes and findings (e.g., pragmatics, semantics, phonology, and syntax) and then discussed in terms of their synergistic dynamics.

1. Pragmatics

Halliday (1975) found that at approximately 24 months of age, a child could mark new and old information through the use of different syntactic structures, such as declarative sentence constructions. If the child wanted to code new information, an interrogative form was employed. Synergistic implications derived from this investigation include a cooccurring or functional relationship between pragmatics, coding old and new information, and syntax, the use of different syntactic structures to code known and unknown information. Further, phonological stress is part of the interrogative form and phonological modifications (i.e., rising pitch) serve to reinforce syntactic and pragmatic relations. Bates (1976) also provides data for the use of differential syntax to mark old and new information in early childhood.

Oller (1975) hypothesized that the child's use of various phonological rules was governed, in part, by pragmatic factors. He speculated that the child's phonological rules varied because phonological productions are the output of a process which operates under, and therefore responds to, various pragmatic factors. At an early age, the child's phonological system is not complete; nevertheless, vocalizations must be capable of communicating intentions. Therefore, Oller suggests that in communication, the child develops a strategy in which sounds that are not produced adequately are replaced by sounds that differ by relatively small amounts. He suggested that the child substitutes the perceptually closest element in the inventory of acceptable or preferred elements, and not the easiest. The implication is that the substitution of very different elements for nonpreferred elements would interfere with communication. This explanation suggests that pragmatic aspects of language interact with and form a reciprocal type of relationship with phonological variables. Oller speculates that this relationship may account for the systematic nature of the child's phonological substitutions.

Code switching also illustrates the relational aspects among pragmatic and phonological functions. Gleason (1973) reported that children varied their speaking styles depending on whether they directed their communication toward adults, peers, or infants. Code styles varied on pragmatic, syntactic, semantic, and phonological levels, depending upon the age of the listener and the communicative context. It was also observed that the ability to code switch evolves through developmental processes before it reflects adult capabilities. Data derived from this investigation were used to view the relational aspects of pragmatics, semantics, syntax, and phonology in a developmental manner. A study by Shatz and Gelman (1973) also provides evidence for the child's use of stylistic variations when communicating with younger children. They reported, for example, that 4-year olds used shorter sentences and avoided complex structures such as subordinate, coordinate, and predicate complement construction when addressing younger children in specific conversational settings. These stylistic variations were reflected in syntactic variations and operated as a function of communicative setting and age of addressee.

The notion of givenness, or old information, the knowledge the speaker assumes is known by the listener at the time of utterance, was discussed by Chafe (1976). He found that, in English, old information or givenness is expressed by lower and weaker pitch and is subject to both pronominalization as well as the use of generic expressions. Similarly, in Japanese, old and new information is marked overtly with sentence particles: *wa* for old information, *ga* for new information. Again, this illustrates the relational aspects among pragmatic, phonological, and syntactic processes. The studies cited in this section investigated explicit pragmatic functions. However, when these functions were reexamined within a synergistic framework, derived evidence illustrated the semantic, syntactic, and phonological relational operations.

2. Semantics

Bowerman (1973) observed that children understand basic grammatical relationships through an increasing comprehension of the way semantic relationships are specifically dealt with in their language. Based upon this, she suggested that children learn the various positions of words or syntactic rules as a result of understanding basic semantic relationships. Syntax, therefore, is viewed as a device for coding semantic relations.

Rodgon (1976) provided evidence that children at the single word stage exhibited the relational use of single words. He suggested that the child can generate the same word in various contexts and thereby convey different meaning in the same way that the child can produce different words in similar contexts and thereby convey similar meaning. Again, derived data or the implicit synergistic findings provide evidence for relational operations among pragmatic, semantic, and syntactical processes.

3. Phonology

Greenberg (1966) provided the following examples illustrating the relations between phonological and syntactic aspects of the linguistic system: (1) the use of the marked category of final rising pitch for the expression of interrogation; and (2) the use of the marked category in phonology for the expression of a marked category in grammar. He provides the example of the use of the marked feature of glottalization in Amerind languages to express the marked grammatical category of diminutive and the use of phonemes of pitch having progressively lower allophones. The latter then occur within the syntactic frame.

Brown (1973) illustrated phonologic and syntactic relations with examples in which children developing syntax acquire the uncontractible copula form and the uncontrollable auxiliary form prior to the acquisition of the corresponding contractible forms. He speculated that the development of these forms is related to the complexity of the phonological rules necessary to express these notions. The production of the uncontractible form requires less complex phonological rules than does the production of the contracted form and, as a result, the uncontractible form appears earlier in the acquisition process. In addition to illustrating syntactic and phonological relations, this information provides evidence indicating that relational aspects of language are developmental in nature.

Halliday (1975), in his description of early pragmatic language functions, found that the child he observed employed consistent sound sequences to communicate different pragmatic functions. He characterized these early pragmatic utterances as sounding like words but not consisting of the same sound sequences found in adult phonological productions. Halliday observed six early pragmatic functions and each function was communicated by different phonological sequences. The sound sequences produced by the child for each of these functions were used in a consistent fashion. One of the earliest pragmatic functions to be identified was regulation. Halliday referred to this function as the "do as I tell you function." As proposed by Halliday, this function served to initiate an action by someone in the environment for the purpose of carrying out a specific act. He also noted that, in addition to employing sound sequences to communicate a pragmatic function, the child systematically used stress to mark the degree, intensity, or pragmatic function of his utterance. For example, when producing the phonological sequence which was used to communicate a regulatory function, the child employed stress to mark intensity or urgency. This illustrates the relational dynamics among the phonological, semantic, and pragmatic aspects of the language system at the preverbal stage. Specifically, the addition of phonological information (stress) underlies or marks new semantic information in the communication of the regulatory function.

Bloom (1973) also reports the use of stress to mark semantic differences at the one-word stage. These examples demonstrate the child's use of differential stress to convey various semantic states. Ervin-Tripp (1964) showed that differential stress patterns change semantic functions. For example, in the two-word combination, *Christy room,* differential semantic functions result from placing stress on *Christy* or *room*; that is, the utterance can be represented as possession if the stressed component is *Christy,* whereas the locative function is communicated when the stressed component is *room.* This provides clear evidence for the relational aspects among semantics, phonology, and syntax. In addition to the use of phonological stress to mark the semantic function of possession, possession is marked at a later stage by the addition of a syntactic modulation, the possessive morpheme ['s].

Adults also use stress to mark syntactic information. Schane (1973) provided examples of the use of differential stress to mark nouns or verbs. If the word *survey* is to function as a noun, the first syllable is stressed, whereas the second syllable is stressed if the word is to function as a verb. Adults also use stress to mark contrastiveness; that is, they stress certain lexical items for the purpose of focusing attention. The use of intonation as a focusing device is illustrated by the following.

$$Jon\ brought\ the\ record.$$
$$NP_1 \qquad\qquad NP_2$$

The listener's attention focuses on the noun that is stressed (NP_1 or NP_2). The marking of contrastiveness functions as a mechanism for focusing on specific parts within the semantic function of an utterance.

Gleason (1973), studying adult stylistic variations across communicative settings, has noted that there are pitch variations resulting from pragmatic considerations. She stated, "mother uses a normal voice when speaking to her husband, a high pitch to her four year old, a slightly raised pitch to her eight year old, and squeaked to her baby" (p. 161). Her description illustrates the relational aspects of pragmatics (taking into account the listener) and phonology (pitch variations).

Hetzron (1972) has shown that some syntactic rules are applied only after certain phonological information has been made available. He cites examples in English, German, and Greek, in which there is a tendency to place phonetically longer elements after shorter ones for adjective placement. This process is sometimes referred to as the law of increasing members. Thus, the sentence, *she is a shy and thoughtful person* is the preferred word order, as opposed to *she is a thoughtful and shy person*. Bolinger (1962), in an experimental study on adjective ordering, found that subjects preferred phonologically shorter sequences to precede phonologically longer sequences. Based on these findings, word order is conditional, in part, on a phonological consideration: specifically, the number of phonological syllables. Although the rule is actually stylistic and optional, it is the consistent preference of native speakers of English, German, and Greek.

4. Syntax

Schane (1973) points out that in English, compounds and phrases have different stress contours. For compounds composed of two words, the primary stress is placed on the first word, while the second word has a weaker or secondary stress. Conversely, the primary stress for phrases is on the second word, while weaker or secondary stress is placed on the first word.

Compound Nouns		Noun Phrases	
1 2		2 1	
blackbird	('a certain spe-	*black bird*	('any bird which
1 2	cies of bird')	2 1	is black')
bird's-nest	('a type of	*bird's nest*	('a nest belong-
	nest')		ing to a bird')

These examples provide evidence for relational operations between syntax and phonology.

5. Summary

For the purpose of identifying synergistic relations among pragmatic, semantic, syntactic, and phonological operations, the following types of data were examined:

1. Semantic–syntactic unity.
2. Semantic–pragmatic aspects of a syntactic structure.
3. Pragmatic–semantic–syntactic definition of the notion subject.
4. Experimentally and descriptively derived data illustrating pragmatic, semantic, syntactic, and phonological relational operations.

Evidence from all of these areas indicates that relational operations exist among the pragmatic, semantic, syntactic, and phonological processes and that these traditionally defined areas may not reflect natural divisions of the linguistic system.

IV. DISCUSSION AND IMPLICATIONS

Based on the evidence that the linguistic system operates in a synergistic manner, there are two broad areas of implications. The first area relates to implications based on new linguistic notions reflected in synergistic operations; the second relates more broadly to implications for the future investigation of the linguistic system.

Evidence reflecting synergistic operations and new notions regarding the linguistic system can be employed to begin to characterize the linguistic code. Some relevant notions that have surfaced in this paper are: (1) the notion of cluster concept or complement of characteristics to reflect the degree or extent of operation of a specific process within the system; (2) notions underlying subject–object relationships; and, (3) a synergistic notion of complexity.

Examples illustrating distributional variations for both adjectives and nouns reflect the limitations of absolute classification of parts of the syntactic system. As shown, these items function in a differential manner, depending upon other syntactic and semantic variables. For example, in certain contexts, adjectives can be adjective-like, while in other contexts they operate in a more verb-like fashion. Keenan (1976) proposed the notion of multifactor or complement of characteristic properties. This, although intended to define the universal subject notion, has implications for characterizing other aspects of the linguistic system. The premise underlying a multidimensional definition of subject is that it reflects the various processes or operations that combine in order to express different communicative functions or intentions. In the case of defining subject, the fuller the complement of properties, the more subject like the NP. The notion of complement of properties may have utility for other definitional or descriptive functions as well.

Perhaps the notion of complement of characteristics can be used as a measure to reflect pragmatic, semantic, syntactic, and phonological processes as well as to characterize other aspects of the system, such as adjectives and verbs. That is, the notion may help to begin characterizing various operations by providing a means of specifying extent or degree of pragmatic and/or semantic and/or syntactic and/or phonological involvement in various linguistic operations. Instead of talking about a syntactical relativization process, the specific relational processes that combine to generate this structure can be specified.

Another set of important implications relates to notions underlying subject–object relationships. As presented in Section III,A,2, there are six typologies which reflect the basic linear subject–verb–object word order of natural languages; on a statistical basis, the three subject-preceding-object orders reflect the predominant linear word orders. In his multifactor definition of subject, Keenan pointed out that the b-subject must be determinable by the addressee at the moment of utterance; it cannot be made to depend upon the reference of other NPs (object NPs) which follow it. The b-subject, as described, usually identifies what the speaker is talking about and is usually known to both the speaker and listener as old information. It is important to note that the subject-before-object relationship and, therefore, the coding of known information is maintained in the interval reordering that takes place in the relativization process. Further, if two NPs in a sentence are to be stipulated as being the same in reference, it will be either the nonsubject which gets marked (perhaps deleted) or the rightmost NP. Thus, in English, we cannot say *He-self admires Jon* for *Jon admires himself,* because in the first sentence the reference of the subject cannot be determined independently of the following NP. These facts may indicate, or may result from, human conceptual constraints; that is, a subject's referent must first be established and be known, as well as having a clear referent for the listener to process the communicative unit. It appears that syntactic processes operate in a manner to preserve the subject-before-object relationship.

A third set of implications centers around the notion of complexity. Historically, the notion of linguistic complexity has been of interest to both linguists and psychologists. Although a number of explanations have been proposed regarding the nature of linguistic complexity, to date none has gained wide acceptance. The derived data presented in this paper provided evidence for relational functions among pragmatic, semantic, syntactic, and phonological processes. Aside from the relational aspects among the four levels, at least two other processes appear to be operating. First, a function or intention can be, and usually is, marked by more than one operation. For example, the expression of interrogation is marked, at least, by syntactic information (i.e., wh word) and by phonological information (i.e., final rising pitch). The second process that is operating relates back to the notion of complement of characteristic properties. Specifically, pragmatic, semantic, syntactic, and phonological aspects of the linguistic code operate in a relational manner and, at times, some of these aspects may exist to a greater degree, or control the operation of the other aspects of the system. This type of relational principle was illustrated by Keenan's universal definition of subject, where the definitional aspects of subject were related to both the function and content of the utterance.

These data may have some direct implications in terms of offering an explanation for the notion of linguistic complexity. The fact that the function and intention of an utterance can be marked in more than one way, and that pragmatic, semantic, syntactic, and phonological processes may vary in their degree or extent of operation, may be the underlying principles which govern or give rise to linguistic complexity.

A second broad area of implication relates to the implementation of synergistic notion in the development of a language model. As pointed out by Koestler (1959), "old hunches are then confirmed by new application of the evidence or by unexpected correlations between sources" (p. 11). In working toward a model of language there are several major issues that must be addressed. First, it will be necessary to describe or specify the notion of degree or extent of relational operations of the various processes within the system. The identification of these relational operations will require a methodology that permits the specification or identification of the degree, extent, or state of relatedness of each of the four processes. It will also be necessary to describe when these processes exist in a peaceful state of coexistence rather than in an intrarelated fashion. At this point it should be noted that there has been no mention of the number of processes or components involved in the system. As the evidence has indicated, the traditional definitions of pragmatics, semantics, syntax, and phonology may not, at least on a one-to-one basis, necessarily reflect natural divisions of the language system. Therefore, a question that arises is: What is or are the units of analysis which reflect the synergistic operations?

To investigate any natural phenomena for the purpose of making predictions, it is necessary to obtain measures which directly and accurately reflect the units or operations within the system. In order to explain the language system, criteria for investigation must be established. Traditionally we have characterized units or components. At this point in time it is appropriate to focus on identification of the synergistic operations which reflect the language system as well as to specify the degree or extent of a complement of characteristics for these operations.

Acknowledgments

The idea of the application of a synergistic model to the study of language behavior was originally presented to the senior author by her advisor, Professor Thomas H. Shriner, while a student at the University of Illinois. The senior author is grateful to Professor Shriner for modeling creativity, sharing his respect for asking questions, and especially his gentle and not-so-gentle support. Impetus, direction, confrontation, growth: integral parts of the process of understanding and expression. The second author expresses her appreciation to Professor D. D. Kluppel Vetter.

References

Austin, J. L. *How to do things with words.* Cambridge, Mass.: Harvard University Press, 1962.

Bates, E. *Language and context: The acquisition of pragmatics.* New York: Academic Press, 1976.

Bloom, L. *One word at a time.* The Hague: Mouton, 1973.

Bolinger, D. L. Binomials and pitch accent. *Lingua,* 1962, *11,* 34–44.

Bowerman, M. *Early syntactic development: A crosslinguistic study with special reference to Finnish.* London and New York: Cambridge University Press, 1973.

Brown, R. *A first language.* Cambridge, Mass.: Harvard University Press, 1973.

Chafe, W. L. Givenness, contrastiveness, definiteness, subjects, topics, and point of view. In C. N. Li (Ed.), *Subject and topic.* New York: Academic Press, 1976. Pp. 25–55.

Chomsky, N. *Syntactic structures.* The Hague: Mouton, 1957.

Chomsky, N. *Aspects of the theory of syntax.* Cambridge, Mass.: MIT Press, 1965.

Ervin-Tripp, S. N. Imitation and structural change in children's language. In E. H. Lenneberg (Ed.), *New directions in the study of language.* Cambridge, Mass.: MIT Press, 1964. Pp. 163–189.

Fillmore, C. J. The case for case. In E. Bach & R. T. Harms (Eds.), *Universals in linguistic theory.* New York: Holt, 1968. Pp. 1–87.

Fuller, R. B. *Synergetics.* New York: Macmillan, 1975.

Gleason, J. B. Code-switching in children's language. In T. E. Moore (Ed.), *Cognitive development and the acquisition of language.* New York: Academic Press, 1973. Pp. 159–167.

Greenberg, J. H. Language universals. In T. A. Sebeok (Ed.), *Current trends in linguistics.* The Hague: Mouton, 1966. Pp. 61–112.

Greenfield, P. M., & Smith, J. H. *The structure of communication in early language development.* New York: Academic Press, 1976.
Academic Press, 1976.

Halliday, M. A. K. *Learning how to mean: Explorations in the development of language.* London: Arnold, 1975.

Hetzron, R. Phonology in syntax. *Journal of Linguistics,* 1972, *8,* 251–265.

Jakobson, R., Fant, C. G. M., & Halle, M. *Preliminaries to speech analysis.* Cambridge, Mass.: MIT Press, 1963.

Johnson, D. *Prepaper on relational constraints on grammar.* Yorktown Heights, N.Y.: IBM, T. J. Watson Research Center, Mathematical Sciences Department, 1974.

Keenan, E. L. *The logical diversity of natural languages.* Paper presented at the Conference on the Origins and Evolution of Language and Speech, New York Academy of Sciences, New York. October, 1975.

Keenan, E. L. Toward a universal definition of subject. In C. N. Li (Ed.), *Subject and topic.* New York: Academic Press, 1976. Pp. 305–333.

Keenan, E. L., & Comrie, B. *Noun phrase accessibility and universal grammar.* Paper presented at the 47th annual meeting of the Linguistic Society of America, Atlanta, December, 1972.

Koestler, A. *The sleep walkers.* New York: Grosset, 1959.

Lashley, K. S. The problem of serial order in behavior. In L. A. Jeffress (Ed.), *Cerebral mechanisms in behavior.* New York: Wiley, 1951. Pp. 112–136.

Li, C. N. *Material derived from lectures in Syntax 110A, B.* Santa Barbara: University of California at Santa Barbara. Department of Linguistics, 1976.

Li, C. N., & Thompson, S. A. Subject and topic: A new typology of language. In C. N. Li (Ed.), *Subject and topic.* New York: Academic Press, 1976. Pp. 457–489.

Lyons, J. *Introduction to theoretical linguistics.* London and New York: Cambridge University Press, 1968.

Oller, D. K. *Why are phonological production rules so varied?* Paper presented at the American Speech and Hearing Association Convention, Washington, D.C., November 1975.

Osgood, C. E. A behavioristic analysis of perception and language as a cognitive phenomena. In *Contemporary approaches to cognition*. Cambridge. Mass.: Harvard University Press, 1957.

Perlmutter, D., & Postal, P. *Linguistic Institute Lectures*. Amherst: University of Massachusetts, 1974.

Rodgon, M. *Single-word usage, cognitive development, and the beginnings of combinatorial speech*. Cambridge, Mass.: Cambridge University Press, 1976.

Schane, S. A. *Generative phonology*. Englewood Cliffs, N.J.: Prentice-Hall, 1973.

Shannon, C. E., & Weaver, W. *The mathematical theory of communication*. Urbana: University of Illinois Press, 1949.

Shatz, M., & Gelman, R. The development of communication skills: Modification in the speech of young children as a function of listener. *Monographs of the Society for Research in Child Development*, 1973, *38*.

Skinner, B. F. *Verbal behavior*. New York: Appleton, 1957.

Trithart, L. Relational grammar and Chichewa subjectivization rules. Paper presented to the 11th Chicago Linguistic Society Meeting. Chicago, April, 1975.

Watson, J. B. *The ways of behaviorism*. New York: Harper, 1925.

Watts, A. W. *The two hands of God: Myths of polarity*. New York: Macmillan, 1963.

Wittgenstein, L. *Philosophical investigations*. Oxford: Blackwell, 1953.

Subject Index